The Infinite City

The Infinite City

Utopian Dreams on the Streets of London

Niall Kishtainy

WILLIAM
COLLINS

William Collins
An imprint of HarperCollins*Publishers*
1 London Bridge Street
London SE1 9GF

WilliamCollinsBooks.com

HarperCollins*Publishers*
Macken House
39/40 Mayor Street Upper
Dublin 1
D01 C9W8, Ireland

First published in Great Britain in 2023 by William Collins

1

Copyright © Niall Kishtainy 2023

Niall Kishtainy asserts the moral right to be identified as the author of this work in accordance with the Copyright, Designs and Patents Act 1988

A catalogue record for this book is available from the British Library

ISBN 978-0-00-832585-5 (hardback)
ISBN 978-0-00-832586-2 (trade paperback)

HarperCollins has used all efforts to credit the authors of the works used herein, and if any work has been wrongly credited, please contact us and we will provide the correct credit in future editions.

All rights reserved. No part of this publication may be reproduced, stored in a retrieval system, or transmitted, in any form or by any means, electronic, mechanical, photocopying, recording or otherwise, without the prior permission of the publishers.

This book is sold subject to the condition that it shall not, by way of trade or otherwise, be lent, re-sold, hired out or otherwise circulated without the publisher's prior consent in any form of binding or cover other than that in which it is published and without a similar condition including this condition being imposed on the subsequent purchaser.

Typeset in Bembo Std by Palimpsest Book Production Ltd, Falkirk, Stirlingshire

Printed and Bound in the UK using 100% Renewable Electricity
at CPI Group (UK) Ltd

This book is produced from independently certified FSC™ paper to ensure responsible forest management.

For more information visit: www.harpercollins.co.uk/green

Contents

Map	vi
1. What a Wondrous World Would This Abstract London Be!	1
2. A Truly Golden Handbook	17
3. London, Look to Thy Freedom	55
4. Full Bellies, Fools!	85
5. The Hive of Dreams	125
6. The Garden in the City	155
7. Town Hall Utopias	193
8. Beneath the Tarmac	223
9. The Golden Thread	253
Endnotes	285
References	315
List of illustrations	327
Acknowledgements	331
Index	333

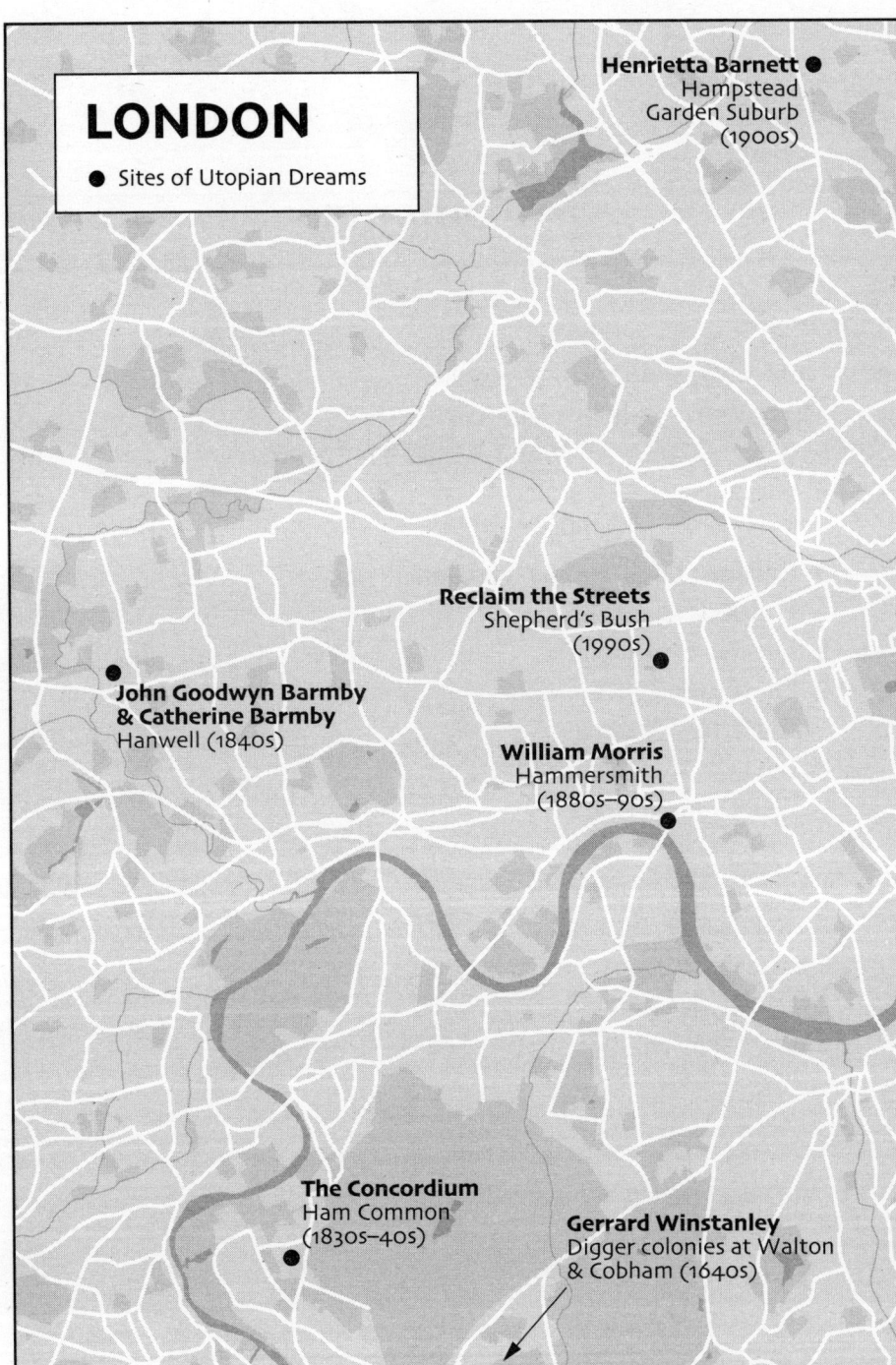

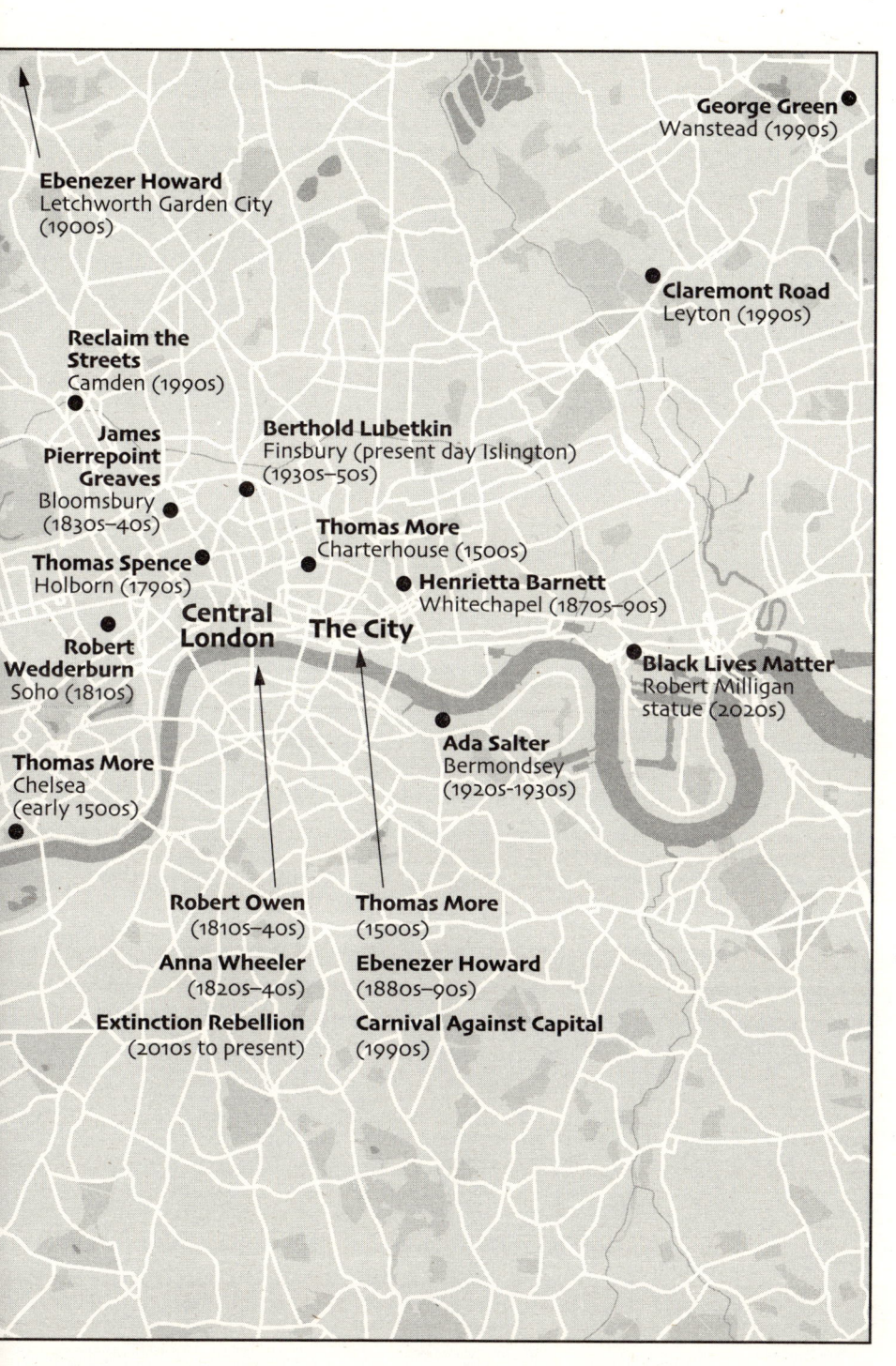

Chapter One

What a Wondrous World Would This Abstract London Be!

On an autumn day in 1852, the journalist and social investigator Henry Mayhew took to the skies above London to try to make sense of his vast city. 'Ah, balloon!' the crowd gasped in wonder as Mayhew and his companions rose into the sky from Vauxhall Gardens in the red- and yellow-striped Royal Nassau. He looked down from the basket and saw a multitude of faces gazing up at him. Despite his fear of heights, Mayhew had joined the flight to satisfy his craving to contemplate from above the whole expanse of London, the city in which there is 'more virtue and more iniquity, more wealth and more want huddled together on one vast heap than in any other part of the earth'. The passengers threw scraps of paper over the side which fluttered down towards the streets, giving a sense of the speed of the balloon's ascent. Soon the houses looked like wooden toys, streets like ruts in the ground and the Thames like a winding metallic snake. Little puffs of steam rose up from trains travelling into the city.

After a few minutes, the earth far below seemed to Mayhew like an endless series of scenes being drawn along under the balloon on a moving screen, the city a specimen that could be coolly examined from a distance: a sequence of palaces, workhouses, prisons, chimneys, steeples, docks, parks, courts and alleys. For a few fleeting moments, Mayhew was able to escape the whirlpool of London, to see it as a whole and to consider what it all might mean.

Watercolour of Charles Green's Royal Vauxhall ('Nassau')

By the eighteenth century, Londoners had become conscious of living in a special kind of place that had a different kind of society from that of the countryside and smaller towns. London had grown from an enclosed medieval city to become a sprawling imperial metropolis, the first 'world' city. Mayhew's investigations helped shape the image of London that followed. He had spent long days exploring the most obscure of the city's districts, interviewed watercress sellers, bone-grubbers and mudlarks, and sought out the haunts of beggars and thieves. He set out his discoveries in reports and newspaper articles, and in 1851 published his massive *London Labour and the London Poor*, full of vivid accounts of the street life of the Victorian city, which influenced

Charles Dickens's depictions of London's working-class people and districts.

Mayhew thought that all Londoners had the desire to experience the city's hidden depths, to feel exhilarated at the whirling life all around them, but then to somehow find a way of seeing it as a whole, to combine the pieces 'like the coloured fragments of the kaleidoscope, into one harmonious and varied scene'. He followed this impulse to all the smells and sounds of the most obscure streets of the city, and then on that autumn afternoon up into the sky. His detailed reports of poverty and suffering had shocked middle-class Londoners, who rarely strayed beyond the respectable thoroughfares. Soaring high above the metropolis, Mayhew was a kind of everyman of London, a symbol of its popular conscience. He was no radical thinker or utopian, but his determination to observe the city with an unflinching eye could provoke dissatisfaction with things as they are, and thus be the seedbed for imagining what a new city might look like.

One source of unease about London was the fact that its ever-increasing size and complexity made it that much harder to comprehend. Even from up in the air Mayhew found it impossible to tell where the city ended, and he grew weary trying to follow the progress of the buildings, which stretched far into the horizon where chimney smoke made the metropolis seem to blend into the sky. London had become a world, no longer just a city, wrote Mayhew. He wondered whether some of the moons and asteroids wheeling about in space might not be much bigger than the Great Metropolis. He imagined planet earth bursting as a result of some eruption and shattering into fragments, one of them London, severed from the rest but big enough to be a planet on its own spinning around the sun; Hampstead and Sydenham would be the north and south poles, the central axis of Oxford Street and Holborn the scorching equator, and when it was day in Kensington it would be night in Mile End. 'What a wondrous World, too, would this same abstract London be!' he declared.

But if London was a world, then it was also a place of mystery that could bewilder as well as amaze – and evoke fear of the threats to morality that might lie within its hazy boundaries. In the nineteenth century, writers began to apply to the city the Romantics' notion of the sublime, qualities that evoke awe and terror, which had originally been used to describe imposing natural phenomena like thunder and mountains. William Wordsworth likened London's 'huge fermenting mass of human-kind' to a 'black storm', and a German visitor wrote of the 'stream of faces of living men' rushing through its 'stone forest of houses'. Observers could now only stand in terrified astonishment at the monster city, the sublime sense emerging especially through evocations of London as an endless labyrinth of twisted alleys and wretched slums. In Dickens's *Bleak House*, the place of deepest obscurity is found at the entrance to the City of London at Temple Bar and the adjacent courts, the fog and mud there emblems of the impenetrability of the city and its laws, powers that cannot be reckoned with, except, perhaps, by the dark forces at the centre of the maze.

This image of London acts as a foil for the city's utopian dreamers, who, through their theories of society and schemes for social betterment, attempted to make the city legible: to shine an illuminating beam on the origins of its defects and to picture the means for eliminating them. But such yearnings do not have to be expressed through the scathing social critiques and ambitious programmes of avowed utopians: they can glimmer, too, in the minds of practical, matter-of-fact Londoners such as Mayhew as they encounter the capital in their daily lives.

A few years before his ascent, Mayhew had visited the notorious slum of Jacob's Island in Bermondsey on the south side of the Thames – and what he saw there fed the flicker of a social dream. On the island he discovered a hellish enclave of wooden hovels built over channels of water full of rotting animal carcasses, and into which a leather works discharged its blood-red waste. Mayhew observed a woman throw a bucket of excrement into the water at the same time as a child in the next room drew up a can for drinking. The people of the slum made a precarious living on the docks, earning money for a few days and then nothing for weeks. They slept in rooms that overhung the ditches, breathing in noxious fumes that bubbled up from the water below. They had pale skin and glassy eyes, and when Mayhew visited, many of them lay dead from the cholera that was then ravaging London's slums.

A woman living on the island told Mayhew that they had to drink the filthy water because their landlord would do nothing about the water supply – nor about the missing tiles which let the rain pour in – and Mayhew noticed a sign announcing the sale of 'this valuable estate'. This seemed to Mayhew to be the great social evil: the freedom enjoyed by mercenary landlords to exploit their tenants. He contrasted the riverine hell with how it had been in days gone by. The island used to be surrounded by a running stream fed by water from the hills at Sydenham and Nunhead to the south. Flour mills stood on the banks and on summer evenings people would sit in the shade of trees and drink ale together. It was a place of repose and harmony, an idyll on the margins of the city, but the old summer houses had long since been replaced by hovels and heaps of muck, the stream turned into a fetid ditch.

Here we have a hint of one ingredient of an incipient utopianism: the myth of a lost Arcadia that holds up an unflattering mirror to the world of today and can turn the mind towards a critique of the present. In his account of the island, Mayhew briefly reaches towards the beginnings of a solution: that the poor need to be freed from the control of the landlords. Even in Mayhew's plain, practical reporting, then, are the seeds of utopian longing. In the twentieth century the Marxist philosopher Ernst Bloch would call these 'traces', filaments of 'anticipatory consciousness', premonitions of the 'not yet'. They appear not only in the imaginings of committed utopians, but also become spread through culture as collective yearnings continually bubble to the surface of social reality. On departing Jacob's Island, Mayhew noticed that in front of some of the cholera-ridden houses people had pulled up a few paving stones and planted flowers – perfumed stocks

– in the earth below, splashes of colour and scent in the grim surroundings: small acts of hope germinating in the everyday life of the slum.

The contemporary London writer Iain Sinclair has written that the only way to survive the squalor and degradation of the city is to enter into the 'fog of otherness' – which Mayhew had attempted to do by plunging into the world of the slums – or to cultivate the kind of visionary faculty possessed by the London poet William Blake. Blake did not need to look at his city from the air to make it understandable to himself, because in his imagination London was already a symbol. London was Babylon, a place of corruption and spiritual confinement, but could also be imagined as Jerusalem, one of spiritual regeneration and of new human possibilities. 'The fields from Islington to Marybone . . . Were builded over with pillars of gold,' he wrote, and London shines 'in Jerusalem's pleasant sight'. In the lyric popularly known as 'Jerusalem', Blake recreated the Golden Age myth of a serene green land located in England, turning it into a utopian dream in which he affirmed that a collective human struggle will go on 'Till we have built Jerusalem'. In Blake's cosmic imagination there was no conflict between the myriad faces of the London streets and London as a totality. Eternity shone through every alley and clod of mud, and a transcendent golden string could lead you through the crooked lanes to Heaven's gate.

The idea of London as a symbolic city of sin and of redemption is entrancing to social prophets, but utopians who wish to connect a visionary instinct with a more practical refashioning of the city have also to harness prosaic ways of understanding and imagining. Often these come in the form of the sorts of schemes pursued by urban reformers and city planners. Wren's never-realised plan for the rebuilding of London after the Great Fire of 1666 in the form of wide avenues radiating out of a series of piazzas is a famous example. In the nineteenth century, elegant boulevards such as John Nash's Regent Street sliced through

London, fashioning ordered spaces within the chaotic metropolis. Slums such as Jacob's Island were demolished and railway lines laid. But utopias do more than simply propose a more rational use of urban space. They attempt to create new social geometries that do away with the irrationality and injustices symbolised by the crooked mazes of the old city.

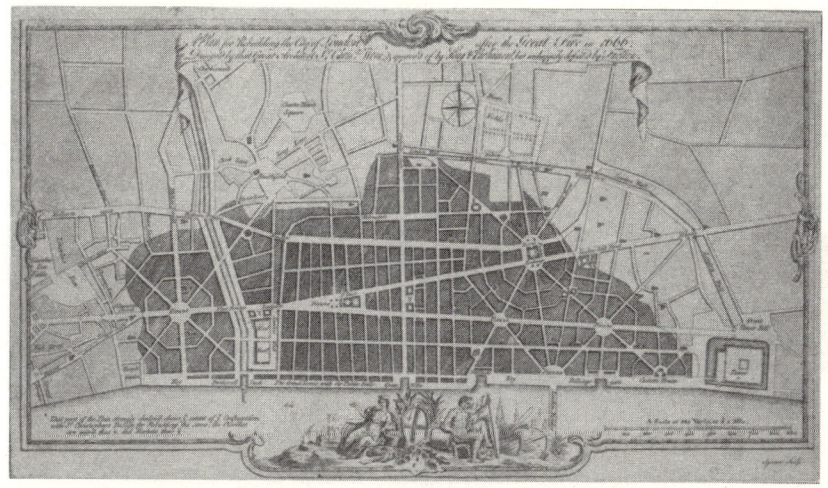

Christopher Wren, 'A Plan for the Rebuilding the City of London after the Great Fire in 1666'

Cities, and the utopias that are intended to remake them, are therefore mental as well as physical constructs. They are characterised as much by their culture and values as by their buildings and bridges, and utopian dreams are not only of elegant houses and gleaming streets but of a transfigured human spirit. A vast city such as London, with its layers of history and plurality of experiences, is both palimpsest and kaleidoscope, and can never be completely pinned down. Its inhabitants have to imagine what it is out of their own impressions and the stories that they inherit. If people can conjure a vision of what the city is, they can imagine what it could be. In this way, the city exists not just through acts of building but through feats of the imagination that are distilled into symbolic forms as myths, images and stories. It is a space of being and becoming, and the bridge between the two is the locus of social dreaming. Utopia finds its place, therefore, in the heart of the metropolis.

But according to those who disparage utopia, this would be an oppressive rather than a liberating force within the city. In the twentieth century, utopians were accused of advocating methods of social engineering that would lead to totalitarianism, or of peddling useless fantasies. 'Utopian' became a term of insult, but the charges are unjustified. Rather than being rigid blueprints that smother human diversity, many utopian ideas allow for change and experimentation, and refrain from setting out social plans in exact inches and feet. Neither do they aim to obliterate everything to create a perfect society inhabited by perfect people. And far from conjuring fantastical worlds, utopians have imagined societies that give form to people's social desires, whether for equality, human connection or environmental regeneration. The apparent impracticality of utopian ideas is the source of their special logic and power. Existing beyond actuality and calling out to our deepest yearnings, they pull us towards new social possibilities, previously only dimly imagined; they urge us: 'Be realistic: demand the impossible'.

This book traces an imaginative lineage that connects through time a selection of London's utopian visionaries, from Thomas More in the sixteenth century, who invented the word utopia, to the activists of the twentieth and twenty-first centuries who, through protest, find new means of animating collective social dreams. Their stories create a layer in the palimpsest of London, a means of threading together a plot for the city from its various symbolic and visionary fragments. Alongside dominant depictions of London – as an infernal maze, as a centre of wealth, power and empire, and as a maelstrom of protest and disorder – is another narrative of it as a place of utopian possibility and experiment. Narratives matter because they define our sense of possibility in the present. In particular, without stories that aid social dreaming, society becomes rigid and confined, just as life at the individual level does if deep yearnings are not given space to breathe. Although we may seem to live in anti-utopian times, utopian dreaming is essential to a vibrant society that is truly conscious of its own desires; without it we fall back on ideas dictated by the powerful about how we should live. London is often thought of as a white-hot turbo of capitalism — but what else exists within its complex mosaic that could provide ingredients for an alternative to this dominant image?

It was once said that utopians traced the outlines of the first cities. London itself could be an emblem of utopian longing, and yet it is a fortress of power and money that so many utopians have yearned to tear down or to escape from. London over the centuries has stirred up these contradictory desires like no other city. It yields to and resists our social imaginations and today, with its spirit of openness and innovation alongside ever-rising concentrations of wealth and power, it remains a grand untapped arena for bold utopian experimentation.

If they could send him a message, the utopians in our story would tell Mayhew — tell us — to fly above the vast city on the edge of cosmic dust, to go high enough for it to begin to look like an abstraction, a symbol, to stand for all cities, to be in some sense the original city, and then, looking down through the clouds, to try to sense the outlines of a new kind of city. But we cannot stay in that balloon forever. New worlds have to be made down in the noisy, smoky streets and in the taverns and halls. A visionary would tell Mayhew to bring the heavenly light that he saw shining on the clouds into London's crowded lanes — or, like Blake, to see it in the shimmer on the surface of a muddy puddle, to perceive the heavenly and the everyday as one and to set them in unified motion.

Utopia is a picture of social desire. Through the description of an imaginary good place, it criticises the existing social order and provides a plan for a new kind of society. Traditional utopias do this by means of storytelling, the archetypal form being that of the traveller's tale. A mariner is shipwrecked on a strange island, encounters a perfect society and returns to tell the story. But utopians have also taken their readers on travels into the past and the future, and far into space. Seeing is believing and, perhaps more importantly, feeling; it is stories, with their sensory and psychological qualities, that move people's hearts and minds – and propel them into action. Travellers returning from an island, a new planet or a different century tell in the first place not of justice, rights and law but of wondrous gardens and rivers, handsome dwellings and a serene, contented people. They let their audiences see from the inside what it would be like to live in Atlantis or the City of the Sun. They show us how ethical principles might play out in the life of an imagined society: in the organisation of politics, in the education of children and in the arrangement of work and leisure.

Utopias draw on age-old images of the ideal society. All peoples have had myths of the Golden Age and of past paradises in which innocent humans lived in harmony with nature and each other. In the eighth century BC, the Greek poet Hesiod traced the decline of humanity since the end of a lost Golden Age in which people lived free from toil and suffering. Centuries later, the Roman poet Virgil in his *Eclogues* conjured up a sunlit Arcadia of poetry and song, and imagined the return of the Golden Age. With Christianity came millenarianism, prophecies of cataclysm and upheaval followed by the second coming of Christ and the appearance of a perfect celestial city. In the Middle Ages, the story of the Land of Cockaigne – a place where rivers flowed with wine, churches were made of puddings and tasty larks flew into people's open mouths – was a 'poor man's heaven' of sensual excess, a caricature of the utopian dream of material abundance.

Although utopias have been influenced by these recurring images, they are distinct from them in imagining good societies constructed with human intervention and based on institutions that regulate social and economic life in new ways. And while they always harness imagination and yearning for change, they can take forms other than literary ones of pure storytelling. Some utopians imagine new societies through theories, blueprints and manifestos. Some create their own communities, which attempt to enact utopia in the present or to prefigure a future utopian society. All of these approaches are found in the utopias of London, often combined within single utopian movements.

Some London utopians seek to create a new city from inside the shell of the old. Others retreat to the edges or even outside of the city, trying to escape from the suffocating effects of the power and money at its heart, and creating prototypes of utopia just beyond its reach. Our story will on occasion make brief forays beyond the boundaries of London, always to be pulled back in. London's borders are constantly shifting outwards, and as they moved westwards from the original mercantile and religious heartland of the old city, new utopian spaces and possibilities emerged.

Thomas More, the London visionary with whom this story begins, did not attempt to build a utopian movement or to actively proselytise for his utopia. In his time, the composition of utopias was a purely literary activity, not yet made practical and urgent by being connected to the philosophy of progress which emerged later during the Enlightenment. Most of the figures in our story did want to remake London, though, and made attempts to do so. Thomas More nevertheless provides an important starting point and framework, and his ideas have been the fountainhead for many later utopias. His subtle, elusive text also raised a set of dilemmas that have run through the utopian project ever since.

One of those has to do with the relationship between utopia and politics. A central question in More's *Utopia*, published in 1516, is whether and how utopians should get involved with the compromised world of politics and diplomacy. For some social visionaries, the adoption of utopian schemes goes hand in hand with a rejection of mainstream society including its politics, often through a retreat into experimental communities removed from the unredeemable social order. In the nineteenth century, many of London's utopian prophets stayed aloof from the epochal struggles over the reform of Parliament and the expansion of the franchise that animated so many radicals of the time. Utopians of this ilk believed that attempts to reform but leave in place a fundamentally corrupt system were futile and would not create a just new world. And many utopians have set their faces against the revolution and class struggle promoted by political radicals.

Social visions, although imagined, can be conventional in scope, projecting future societies that are not markedly different from those of the present. Even if denied by their advocates, at the heart of established political creeds such as liberalism and conservatism lie implicit utopias: visions of idealised societies based on the free market, democracy or traditional family values. Daniel Defoe's 1719 novel, *Robinson Crusoe*, for example, has been viewed by some as a utopia of the self-made bourgeois individual who builds a new society with his own ingenuity, a vision far from the communal one that is most often associated with utopianism. Quite a few of the London utopians that appear in this book did imagine alternatives to capitalism and might be classified as leftwing, but utopianism does not always entail radical politics or a complete overturning of the status quo.

Conversely, one must be cautious in labelling radical causes as utopian, particularly if 'utopian' has the connotation of a far-off dream, or, worse, if it is used as a term of disparagement for demands that are judged to be naively grandiose or hopelessly optimistic. Radicals have fought for women's right to be safe from violence and for people of colour to be treated with respect by state institutions, but the satisfaction of such demands does not require visionary social dreaming and therefore their deferral to some unspecified time when a new world replaces the current imperfect one. Our stories of utopia shadow the histories of politics and radicalism, sometimes touching them, sometimes veering away.

Any attempt to trace over time the contours of a single idea or social concept, such as capitalism, radicalism or utopianism, brings with it the hazard of anachronism, of erroneously assuming the existence of particular social arrangements in the past or elements of our modern world view in the minds of earlier people. London's politics and society have changed so much over the centuries that there is a danger in considering its problems to be timeless and in drawing unbroken lines between visionary impulses in diverse eras. What, for example, does Thomas More, a great Catholic whose heart ached after the medieval world, have in common with the visionaries of Victorian London who lived through the Industrial Revolution? Later utopians often appeal to earlier ones and use them as a stimulus for their own visions. One nineteenth-century London utopian named his commune and his son after Thomas More. More and his visionary descendant lived in different Londons and had different world views, yet when a utopian cites an earlier one as inspiration, an imaginative connection is made across time that can powerfully influence how collective desires are articulated in the present.

In the eighteenth century, Samuel Johnson hailed London as a 'heaven upon earth' for people of ideas and curiosity. The attraction of the biggest market in the world was felt by the poor and middling people, and by aristocrats, who were enticed by the city's fashions and the potential for social advancement found there. In his seminal 1776 work of political economy, *The Wealth of Nations*, the philosopher and economist Adam Smith argued that the existence of specialised occupations was limited by the size of the market and could only develop in an advanced form in large cities. Cities could contain economic and cultural niches to serve all kinds of people, however unusual. But this 'division of labour' had a dark side: a narrowing of human experience and a fragmentation of life into separate spheres that could lead to alienation and social atomisation.

In the early twentieth century, one of the founders of the modern field of urban studies, the American sociologist Robert Park, wrote that the creation of the city had been humans' most successful way of moulding the world to their desires. To Park, the city was a social laboratory where the mixing of so many kinds of people could open up new human possibilities. It was a place that held the promise of freedom while generating forces that could circumscribe that freedom: 'if the city is the world which man created, it is the world in which he is henceforth condemned to live,' he wrote.

The tension between the city as a place of opportunity and one of limitation is a trigger for utopian dreaming, which is rooted in a critique of the present so fervent that it leads to an estrangement from what is and a search for new possibilities for what could be. While poets and novelists have attempted to capture the mysteries and strange obscurities of London, its utopians have built on specific complaints about the city, and not just those of radicals and social visionaries. Despite changing conditions over the centuries, many of the criticisms have been made again and again. Long before Mayhew surveyed London from above, people were worrying about the effect of its great size on the rest of the nation. Early in the seventeenth century, James I remarked that 'with time, *England* will onely be *London*, and the whole country be left waste', and similar anxieties about the dominance of the city have continued up to the present. A related complaint has been that governance of a sprawling London is weak and haphazard, overseen by a jumble of overlapping authorities, the city impervious to proper planning, its alleys branching and its edges spreading without rhyme or reason.

Then there is the seemingly relentless power of money to coldly reshape the social make-up of the city, a phenomenon that has been given the name gentrification in recent times but which goes back centuries. Again and again, newcomers have been warned that London is full of dangers ready to snare the naive or unwary; that it is a brutal place into which people can be swallowed up and forgotten. Early in the twentieth century, the German sociologist Georg Simmel argued that cities' social anonymity brings a state of personal freedom and creative possibility, but comes at the cost of loneliness and disorientation. 'London has never acted as England's heart but often as England's intellect and always as her moneybag,' he wrote.

To many visionaries, the problem of London was rooted more deeply in its underlying systems of power. In his 1794 poem 'London', Blake condemned the interlocking set of social and political institutions that held sway over a morally diseased city and that in the shadow of the French Revolution were seen by radicals as the tools of tyranny. In a few lines Blake indicted state and Church, the empire, the system of property ownership and the hypocrisies of marriage and the family. In Blake's London, blood runs down palace walls, chimney sweeps' cries ring through the streets, harlots curse. On the faces of passing people the poet sees 'Marks of weakness, marks of woe'. He wanders through 'charter'd' streets and by the 'charter'd Thames', the very topography of London a reflection of money and law, powers which keep people down, not ensure their prosperity and their rights. Londoners' suffering was above all a psychological imprisonment – the result of 'mind-forg'd manacles' – in which the oppressive dogmas that ruled the city had become so thoroughly absorbed that human freedom could no longer be imagined.

By Mayhew's time, long-standing anxieties about London had become part of its image: the foggy Dickensian city both romanticised and condemned, full of starving street urchins and displaying riches amid its poverty. That picture still haunts discussions of the injustices of the city – today expressed in the language of 'social exclusion' and the 'underclass' – even if modern London seems more presentable and orderly than it did in Mayhew's century. Because of its dominance, London crystallises anxieties about the nation at large and the operation of the capitalist system more broadly; through the specifics of a place, these stories of London's visionaries therefore illuminate different ways of facing up to and reimagining systems of power whose ubiquity often allows them to carry on almost unnoticed.

London's utopians, past and present, love and loathe their city.

One of them, the visionary town planner of the nineteenth and early twentieth centuries, Ebenezer Howard, once rode a bus through London and felt delighted to the point of ecstasy at the bustle and disorder all around him. On another day he walked in the alleys of a poor district and was struck by the wretched conditions in which people lived. Howard then made the utopian leap: imagining a city built according to a just moral and physical topography. He perceived in the endless maze of hovels not the sublime – the action of some eternal power before which people were small and impotent – but the effects of a bad economic system that humans themselves had created. Like the other figures in this story, he perceived that all of what he saw was temporary and could be swept away in favour of a better order if only people dared to imagine. Some of these visionaries tried to make their hopes real, and changed London in the process. Through their stories London appears as a city of dreams, a place both to celebrate and to rebel against, where anything might be possible. These are the people who made that leap and gave voice to the city of their most fervent imaginings.

Chapter Two

A Truly Golden Handbook

According to the ancients, the city contains two cities, the sacred and the profane. Can the people of the worldly city ever reach its holy twin? Today we might ask: can we hope for the creation of utopia in a world of suffering and discord? At the beginning of the sixteenth century, in the heart of London's winding lanes, a young scholar and lawyer stands in front of an august audience and in fine Latin explores these questions, locating them in the ancient division between the heavenly and the earthly.

Thomas More and his audience have gathered close to the Guildhall, London's seat of power and a symbol of its riches, at the church of St Lawrence Jewry. More is delivering a lecture on *The City of God*, the great patristic work written during the last years of the Western Roman Empire by St Augustine, who is revered by More as 'a zealous enemy of lies'. In it Augustine condemns the corruption and avarice of Rome, where the rich get richer and abuse the poor. Its central motif is the two cities: the divine and the profane. More deftly explicates Augustine's vast text to the admiration of his listeners, many of whom have an interest in the new style of humanist learning of which More is fast becoming a celebrated exponent.

The City of God was a response to the sacking of Rome in 410, the shocking fall of the eternal city, keeper of Europe's classical inheritance, engulfed by barbarous forces just as it had become Christian. In his book Augustine weighed in against those who blamed Rome's fall on its abandonment of the pagan gods. Like all earthly cities, he argued, Rome was not inherently good or bad. The earthly city could be imagined as containing two symbolic cities: one a realm of faith and purity, the other of unbelief and corruption. The two realms – the idealised Jerusalem and Babylon – are intermingled on earth, to be separated through Christ's judgment at the end of time. Until then, inhabitants of the earthly city can find true happiness only by turning to the heavenly city through directing their love to God above all.

There is no surviving text of More's lectures. It is said, however, that his interpretation of *The City of God* was full of historical as well as spiritual meaning. Most likely, he was moving towards ideas that a few years later would inspire the most famous and unorthodox of his works, in which he takes us to the city of Amaurot on the island of Utopia – a kind of reordered London emptied of its complacent pomp and showiness and so brought to a state of reason and virtue.

More's feat in tackling *The City of God* came to the attention of the great scholar of the northern Renaissance, the Dutch humanist Desiderius Erasmus, who became close friends with him. Some years later, Erasmus would note his friend's clear and cheerful speech, sometimes livened 'with a little air of raillery'. More was a man of frugal habits, only wearing silk or gold when public duties required him to and preferring to drink water, though occasionally allowing himself the pleasure of a simple dish of eggs. He developed a reputation of being free from avarice and acted with perfect integrity, wrote Erasmus, qualities which made him sought after as a lawyer and as a public official in the years following his lectures. More's addresses at the church of St Lawrence were delivered in front of London's leading lawyers, clergy and scholars, and Erasmus wrote that these venerable figures were not 'ashamed to take a lesson in divinity from a young layman, and not at all sorry to have done so'.

More steps out of the church and plunges into the city, and marks of the profane city and the holy city mingle all around him. A forest of church spires rises over London and the sound of bells rings through the alleys below, while the names of nearby streets – Ironmonger Lane, Goldsmiths Row – attest to the worldly economy that hurries on around St Lawrence's. Leading up from the market street of Cheapside to the south is St Lawrence Lane, where the Blossom's Inn for travellers displays its sign depicting the saint bordered in flowers. More proceeds westwards, perhaps on his way back to his law offices beyond the city walls. Just north of his birthplace, Milk Street, which is lined with the large houses of wealthy merchants and city officers, he passes a well. To the west of the well is Love Lane, a haunt of those seeking to satisfy their sexual lusts. Continuing onwards, he sees beggars, rich people, holy folk and madmen. He sees butchers, fishmongers, confectioners and fowlers, all of them serving the appetites of a sinful world. Despite the abundance of holy buildings pointing upwards to eternity, London's dark and closely packed streets make him feel shut in, and 'prevent one from seeing the heavens'.

In More's time, London was at the start of the fast expansion that would eventually turn it into the world's largest city and still felt like a compact medieval city. Even so, there was already a tradition of imagining it as a disorientating place, ready to defeat the unwary. A fourteenth-century poet wrote of a penniless visitor who was thwarted at every turn by rapacious lawyers and merchants, suffering the theft of his hood in the throng at Westminster only later to see it for sale on Cornhill, before retreating to the fields of Kent. Still earlier, a monk-chronicler warned of the multitude of parasites at work in the city – actors, jesters, flatterers, pederasts, quacks, extortioners, night-wanderers, beggars and buffoons – a collection of earthy London types of a kind that over the centuries would become a staple of literature depicting the seamy underbelly of the city.

To More, London was a perfidious but mesmerising place where the favoured few failed to realise just how temporary their good fortune really was. London's worthies may preside over the streets and halls of the city, but they are as captive as the swindlers locked in the stocks by the fish and meat stalls. They buy and sell, brawl and chide and take to dice and cards. They pipe and revel, sing and dance and think themselves at liberty. But the city is a prison, says More, its inhabitants ensnared in the desire for earthly achievement and acquisition that can never be satisfied. They chase after fleeting pleasures and are dazzled by silver and gold, fame and flattery. Full of worry about their worldly goods, they become misers heaping up their coins or waste their money on gluttony and display. If the city had a reasonable soul, one like Plato's full of wit and understanding, says More, the ground would laugh scornfully at great men when they boast of owning land and grand houses.

And so, lamented More a few years after he delivered his lectures, as soon as one stepped into the city one was lured by false love on one side and attacked by quarrels and legal wrangles on the other. 'What is there in the city to incite to virtue?' he asked; 'when one wishes to live well, by a thousand devices and seductions the life of a city drags one down', and hence London's heavenly city stays hidden in the cycles of distraction and pride which give energy to the labours of its streets.

More's lectures at St Lawrence's were the culmination of an elite education that had prepared him for the life of a scholar and royal official; the contrast between these roles would later be dramatised at a moral level in *Utopia*. From the age of twelve, More had been inducted into the world of politics and power, having become a page in the household of John Morton, the Lord Chancellor and Archbishop of Canterbury and one of the most important men in England, who years later would be depicted in *Utopia* as a curious-minded and shrewd man who knew how to use his influence wisely. More's appointment, arranged by his well-connected lawyer father, took him across the river to Lambeth Palace and was a mark of the privilege and patronage enjoyed by the boy. Among his various tasks, More served at feasts in the great hall during which he would have witnessed the etiquette and pomp on display at the gatherings of noble guests. At Christmas revels More was sometimes invited to take part in theatrical performances; he would step into the action and improvise his part with a cleverness that drew the admiration of the spectators. Morton would often say to his visitors: 'This child here waiting at the table, whosoever shall live to see it, will prove a marvelous man.'

One can well imagine that More soon became valued not just for his intelligence, but for gaining a mastery of the manners needed when serving powerful men. One manual of etiquette of the time advised young people working in a great household to be both cheerful and deferential, and when spoken to 'look . . . with a steady eye, and give good ear to their words', qualities not just of a useful page boy but of the valued royal counsellor that More would grow up to be. This early training, as well as smoothing his ascent, would bring alive to him the question of how far to compromise one's beliefs when serving power, and this was to become one of the central debates in *Utopia*.

By the time he began conceiving his work – it would be published in 1516, when he had reached his late thirties – More had entered public life and become known in Europe's intellectual circles. He had qualified as a barrister, become a Member of Parliament and gained the friendship of Erasmus, ten years his senior. For his talents More had also come to the attention of Henry VIII, the man who would become the agent of his worldly fortune, carrying him to fame and honour, and in later years to disgrace. The trigger for the composition of *Utopia* arose out of a change of scene from the confining alleys of London when Henry sent More abroad on a special diplomatic mission.

In May 1515 More joined a delegation to Bruges that was charged with renegotiating a commercial treaty between England and Flanders. The talks concerned the valuable trade in wool and cloth, which was endangered by disputes about taxes and ports, and More had a reputation as a shrewd lawyer and commercial negotiator. After an initial round of talks there was a break in proceedings. More took the opportunity of visiting Antwerp, where he stayed with Peter Giles, the Flemish humanist, city official and friend of Erasmus. More described Giles as a well-read and trustworthy man whose company eased the long separation from home and family. With the talks on hold, More found himself with sudden leisure at hand. Placed in a kind of temporary exile during which he was mixing with some of Europe's leading humanists and administrators and staying in its most advanced cities – a colleague of his described Antwerp as 'one of the flowers of the world' – More began to compose his highly unorthodox work *Utopia*, which he would complete in London. It was a narrative of intertwined travellers' tales rooted in true places and events with More as one of its main characters.

At the start of *Utopia*, More is depicted in Antwerp, where he has just heard Mass, as he would have done in reality when staying in the city. He steps out of the church and immediately spots Giles standing in the street talking to an unusual-looking stranger. It is at this point that the fictional More – in the story named Morus – peels apart from the real one; More steps into the character and takes on a role. Over the centuries More's readers have puzzled over what his fictional doppelgänger represents – utopian or sceptic, moraliser or mischievous satirist – and how close Morus's beliefs as revealed in the subsequent story were to the real More's.

The man that Morus sees talking to Giles is advanced in years, sunburnt and wears a long beard and a cloak. Morus thinks that he must be a ship's captain. Giles sees Morus and comes over to him, telling him of the newcomer that 'there's no man living today who can give you such an account of unknown people and lands, a topic that I know you are always keen to hear about'.

Giles says that the man, Raphael Hythloday, is a voyager who discovers new lands and new intellectual territories, a latter-day Plato. He is 'far from incompetent in Latin and is especially well versed in Greek', and he believes that Greek is the key to true philosophy. He renounced his inheritance and joined the ship of

Amerigo Vespucci. On Vespucci's final voyage, Raphael asked to be left behind and travelled through many lands, finally reaching Ceylon and then Calicut, where he found a ship that took him back to his native land of Portugal. He cares more for travel than for his final resting place, says Giles; 'he who has no grave is covered by the sky,' he is fond of saying.

Morus and Raphael greet each other and go back to Morus's lodgings, where they rest on a turf-covered bench in the garden. There Raphael tells him more of his history. After he took leave of Vespucci's ship he gradually befriended the local people and their prince, who helped him to explore further. Raphael and his men crossed scorching deserts, harsh lands full of fierce beasts and wild men, and then reached gentler climes and well-organised cities that engaged in trading across the oceans using many different kinds of boats.

Raphael, Morus and Peter conversing in a garden, woodcut by Ambrosius Holbein in Thomas More, *Utopia*, 1518 edition

Giles and Morus question Raphael more closely about what he discovered on his journey – not the monsters that he might have come across because these are found everywhere – but the sagacious and informed citizens who are such a rarity. In the course of his tale, Raphael mentions a people he encountered whose society Europeans might learn from. His two listeners beg Raphael to tell them more about these virtuous people. Raphael sits silently for a moment, then begins the tale.

Utopia is an island in the shape of a crescent moon, Raphael tells them, 200 miles across at its widest extent and encircling a large bay that is sheltered from the winds by the land. The island was created by King Utopus, who dug a channel to form it. Reaching it is difficult because there are treacherous rocks under the surface of the water along all the routes into the bay. The only way for outsiders to find a way in is to have a Utopian pilot to guide them.

Raphael and his friends managed to reach the bay and then the capital, Amaurot, a city designed for the public good. Amaurot lies on a gentle hill running down to the River Anyder and is surrounded by a wall and a moat. As in London, the city's river ebbs and flows with the tide, merges with the sea after sixty miles and is spanned by a stone bridge; a pleasant stream rises on the hill and flows through the city into the main river. The Utopians – a cheerful, easy-going and intelligent people – rise early and dress in undyed woollen cloaks worn over hard-wearing garments of leather and skin. Before starting work many of them attend public lectures held before dawn on a variety of topics. The working day is not particularly onerous. They work at agriculture or crafts such as linen-making or carpentry for six hours, with lunch and a siesta in the middle. After work the Utopians read and study, though some prefer to perfect their craft skills. The Utopians use reason to guide themselves to the pursuit of wholesome pleasures, not false, harmful delights like gambling or senseless luxury. They love the pleasures of the mind that arise from the pursuit of truth as well as those of the body that come from healthy living.

Utopia is the quintessential communal society, based on a community of goods and a city of disciplined citizens united in their high purposes. When a household is in need of supplies, one of its members goes to the market and takes what they need. No payment is made because there is plenty to go round and no one would dream of taking more than they require. They are not driven to grab at goods by extreme want or by the desire to show off possessions. City spaces, too, are communal and not governed by money. Behind the houses are shared gardens full of vines and flowers, and the doors have no locks so that anyone can enter – they 'yield to the touch of the hand and close of themselves'. Every ten years the houses are reallocated by lot.

At mealtimes a trumpet call summons the Utopians to their dining halls. Meals open with a reading on a moral theme which the elders use to stimulate discussion among the youngsters; young and old are mixed at the tables so that elders can encourage good manners in the young and discourage useless chatter. In the evenings there is music, and spices are burned and perfumes sprinkled around the hall, for the Utopians believe that 'no kind of pleasure is forbidden, provided that no harm comes from it'. After supper the people converse in their gardens or make music. Sometimes they play games. One is a sort of mathematical combat in which different numbers battle it out. Another is a contest between the vices and the virtues, the vices attacking the virtues or cunningly undermining them and the virtues defending themselves against the attacks.

The absence of a money economy is symbolised most strikingly by the negligible value placed on gold and silver. Raphael was amazed to see it himself and was hesitant to tell of it, 'for fear that you won't believe me'. The Utopians have so little respect for gold that they use it to make their chamber pots, preferring to eat from simple earthenware dishes. Any precious stones that they find lying around they give to their children to play with; when they get older the children throw them away. What the Utopians find especially perverse is that in so many societies gold is valued more than the people who impose value on it, 'So much so that some dimwit with no more understanding than a block of wood, and as vicious as he is stupid, can hold under his thrall many good and wise men for the simple reason that a great pile of gold coins has come his way.'

Raphael's time in Utopia has convinced him, he tells Morus and Giles, that private property was the cause of all social ills and had to be abolished. Even in a state of abundance, whenever people are allowed to accumulate as much as they can for themselves, a few end up with most of the resources and the rest fall into poverty. Placing limits on wealth and getting rid of corruption and fraud will never get to the root of the problem. As you try to cure one part of the sickness you aggravate the disease elsewhere because the exchange of private property through buying and selling between individuals gives to some while taking away from others.

Giles objects to the utopian desire to fundamentally remake society, taking the position of conservatives that Europe's long history of government will have introduced all sorts of advantageous arrangements, some by chance rather than design. Morus disapproves of communal societies on the grounds that they will not deliver an adequate supply of goods because individuals can shirk from work and rely instead on others' efforts. Raphael replies to Morus: 'You really should have been with me in Utopia and seen their manners and customs for yourself, just as I did . . . then you would freely admit that you had never seen a people anywhere so well regulated as they are.' In the story, Morus remains unconvinced because he has not travelled to the island of Utopia; in the real world, our scepticism can only begin to soften when we sail to imaginative territories where we sense the possibilities in untested social arrangements.

More's *Utopia* is both a mirror to and an inversion of his home town of London, reproducing its physical characteristics – the river, stone bridge and hills – while through its social critique seeking to undo its moral ones. It is a starting point for a lineage of an imagined London that later city visionaries will build on. But More's text equivocates, and if a picture of London lies within

Amaurot then it is hazy and abstract. *Utopia* was written in Latin, its intended audience being Europe's circle of elite humanist scholars, and its first English translation only appeared in 1551, sixteen years after More's death. It was made by Ralph Robinson, who according to the edition's title page was a 'citizen and goldsmith of London'. Robinson's not very faithful translation fills in – one might say, distorts – More's austere outlines of the city, conjuring a triumphal Tudor London out of shadowy Amaurot. Streets are 'very commodious and handsome' and houses 'faire and gorgeous' compared to More's evasive descriptions, such as of the buildings being 'far from mean'; Robinson's imagined city has 'gallant garnishing', and the bridge is built with 'gorgious and substancial arches'. In Robinson's rendering the Utopians are made into the solid, practical types of commercial Tudor London of which he was an exemplar, the guild members and apprentices who manned the city's economy, most of whom would have had little interest in engaging in study after long days at their workbenches as More's Utopians do.

Through Robinson's lenses, the Utopians become Londoners playing on the stage of the Tudor city, which by More's time was being transformed by strengthening forces of capitalism that were weakening the sinews of medieval society. The Reformation and the dissolution of the monasteries led to an enormous transfer of wealth to allies of the king, reordering London's pattern of property and wealth, and quickening the emergence of a modern commercial city.

London was breaking out of its shell through the overturning of old hierarchies and in the physical sense that it was spreading beyond the boundary of the ancient walls that had contained the city from the Tower in the east to near St Paul's in the west. The Tudor chronicler John Stow complained about the building-over of fields outside the walls at Bishopsgate with cottages, tenter yards for the drying of cloth and bowling alleys. The road beyond Aldgate was filling with tenements and becoming 'pestered with divers alleys on either side', signs of the beginning of the systems of landlordism and slums which would prove so hard to uproot over the centuries. In the 1580s, Elizabeth I made the first attempt at controlling London's expansion, banning new building within three miles of the city gates and the overcrowding of dwellings – all to no avail.

London's growth took place as European explorers reached new continents. In 1492 the Italian-born Spanish explorer Christopher Columbus landed at San Salvador and in 1497 the Portuguese navigator Vasco da Gama sailed round the Cape of Good Hope. The explorers' campaigns of murder and pillage brought a flood of gold and silver back to Europe; one of them spoke of gold as the cure for 'sickness of the heart'. A few years later Amerigo Vespucci made his voyages to the New World, during the last of which twenty-four Portuguese sailors were left in a fort on the Brazilian coast; in More's tale, Raphael was one of those left behind. In the last years of the reign of Henry VII there were reports of three indigenous men being brought to London from the New World and presented to the king. A few years later two of them had remained at court, now dressed in English clothes. It is likely that More saw them or had at least heard of them; they might have provoked a curiosity in him about the contrasts between their native land – often imagined as a place of prelapsarian innocence – and the worldly city which they had come to.

After the emergence of the Atlantic trade in goods and slaves, economic power shifted from Spain, Italy and Portugal to Northern Europe. At the start of the Tudor era, Europe's leading commercial centre was Antwerp, where More's tale of Utopia began. Its close trading links with London stimulated the development of English commerce, and its advanced economy and busy printing presses gave a glimpse of the future – and, through the transpositions of More's imagination, an alternative one. As Antwerp's economic position fell towards the end of the century, London's would rise. In the 1560s, the London merchant Thomas Gresham, in imitation of Antwerp's bourse, founded the Royal Exchange as a centre for London's commercial activities. In 1588 England's growing power was symbolised in its defeat of the Spanish Armada, and in the following century London would begin its ascent to the status of the leading European and world city.

After the instability of the fifteenth century, a burgeoning London became the stage for the consolidation of England's Tudor order in all its magnificence. Catherine of Aragon's marriage into the English monarchy linked Spain and England, a boon to the Tudor regime emerging from a century of war. When in November 1501 Catherine entered London as the bride of Henry VII's eldest son Prince Arthur, a twenty-three-year-old More witnessed perhaps the greatest pageant ever staged in England. With a retinue of 'goodly galontes Apparayled in most costly and godly array', Catherine crossed London Bridge and came to an astrological mechanism of revolving stars and planets, above which appeared the figure of the Archangel Raphael with glittering wings, who told the audience that he was sent to watch over 'Cities and Realmes'. At the Great Conduit on Cheapside she gazed at a portrayal of the heavens at the centre of which was a picture of Prince Arthur on a throne surrounded by stars and the sun, and by fish, bears, serpents and mermaids; the mechanical cosmos was set in orbit by a great wheel powered by knights marching up a set of spiral stairs in an infinite revolving motion, the hierarchy of heavenly bodies intended to justify the earthly one of king and subjects.

If Raphael, looking rather more weather-beaten and tousled than a respectable Londoner, had managed to somehow slip into the crowd, perhaps with a few Utopian companions in tow, and been guided through London's mesh of alleys by More himself, he and his friends might have viewed the triumphal display with a dose of contempt. They might have compared the occasion to one that took place in Utopia when a delegation of foreign ambassadors visited, dressed in silks, gold and gems, and processed majestically through Amaurot. Rejecting all finery and gold, the Utopians found the display deeply shameful. How can anyone delight in the transitory glitter of a jewel when one is free to gaze at a star, and how can anyone be so mad as to think himself of nobler stock just because he is clothed in splendid attire, they asked themselves? As for the sparkling gems on the visitors' costumes, to the Utopians these were trinkets fit only for children; the Utopian youngsters nudged their mothers and said, 'Just look at that great booby, Mother, still using pearls and jewels as if he were a little boy,' to which came the reply: 'Shush, son, I reckon he's one of the ambassadors' fools.'

More's recollections of Catherine's pageant revealed his famed predilection for mockery, perhaps not unlike that of those Utopian spectators. He wrote that the princess's Spanish attendants were so ludicrous that they made you laugh out loud: 'hunchbacked, undersized, barefoot Pigmies from Ethiopia', they looked like 'refugees from hell'. He was, however, respectful towards Catherine, and hoped that her marriage augured well for the nation. Within months, however, fifteen-year-old Arthur was dead, and years later the breakdown of Catherine's subsequent marriage to Arthur's younger brother Henry would plunge England and Christendom into turmoil and lead to More's downfall.

Over the course of the celebrations that followed Catherine and Arthur's wedding, the mayor held a dinner for a party of ambassadors during which was recited a famous panegyric to Tudor London, a vision of the city of a piece with that conjured up in Robinson's translation of *Utopia*. London was the most 'Sovereign of cities, semeliest in sight', with its 'merchauntis full of substaunce and myght'. It was a 'Swete paradise precelling in pleasure', a new Troy. *London, thou art the flour of Cities all.*

The moral vision of *Utopia* was underpinned in part by More's powerful religious convictions, and these were tied to a place in London to which he was repeatedly drawn: the House of Salutation of the Mother of God, or the Charterhouse, a Carthusian monastery located just beyond the city gates to the north of the walls. More revered the ideal of monasticism and saw it followed with real ardour at the Charterhouse, a simulacrum of the City of God.

Set apart from the tumult of the city all around it, the community of monks that resided there helped inspire More's vision of the well-lived life. Its halls, cloisters and inhabitants represented a moral and spiritual world; when he wrote *Utopia*, by which time family and career had taken him away from the monastery, the streets, houses and citizens of the imagined city of Amaurot would reflect his yearning for the monastic way of life.

To More the Charterhouse was the shining exception to London's and England's spiritual debasement. In his writings he voiced strong anti-clerical views, echoing the widespread hatred of priestly corruption and greed that would be a cause of the Reformation. He was critical of the Church Establishment and its impious priests, who expended more energy quibbling about the colour of their clerical garments than on the pursuit of faith, charity and humility. In Utopia the priests are especially holy, and therefore very few in number; a marginal aside in the text of *Utopia* reads: 'But What a Mob There is Among Us!' In later years More would stand in awed admiration at the singular moral courage of the Charterhouse monks in the face of Henry's persecutions against those opposed to his religious policies.

Surrounded by gardens and orchards and with its own sturdy wall, the Charterhouse was one of several large religious houses in the capital: to the south was St Bartholomew's Priory, Greyfriars, and on the banks of the Thames, Blackfriars. The Charterhouse monks followed a timeless spiritual regimen, pursuing lives of prayer and silence in their 'cells', cottages consisting of a small room furnished with a prayer desk, a bed and a table above a workshop and walled garden, and with a hatch for the delivery of meals. Like More's Utopians, the monks rejected ornament and luxury, wearing simple clothes and eating from wooden plates as pewter tableware was forbidden.

Next to the priory was the open space of Smithfield, a site of many of the sins of the city to which the ways of the monastery formed a striking contrast. Here was located the city's main meat market – flesh was completely prohibited to the Carthusians – and the area was a place of filth, spectacle and frequent disorder. Animals had to be slaughtered outside the city walls, a regulation echoed in *Utopia* where butchery is forbidden inside the city. Prisoners were held close by at Newgate jail before being taken for execution to the west of the city at Tyburn amid scenes of revelry. Knights would joust for the prize of a golden crown, a sport which More noted would sometimes end in people being trampled and blood spilled into the dust. From the twelfth century Bartholomew's Fair was held at Smithfield, originally a cloth fair, later a saturnalian carnival with puppet shows and wrestlers, dancing bears and dwarfs – and a sprinkling of drunkards and cutpurses. Early in the fifteenth century the monks' weekly walk was stopped in order to keep them away from the profane spectacle.

During the opening years of the sixteenth century, More participated in the Charterhouse community as a layman, taking up residence in or near the monastery. He was then beginning his career as a lawyer and pursuing intellectual interests, particularly the study of Greek and theology; it was at this time that he gave his lectures on *The City of God*. For four years More carried out vigils, fasting and prayer at the Charterhouse, according to Erasmus in order to prepare himself for the priesthood, though one of his early biographers suggested that he was only seeking a temporary refuge from worldly pressures.

During these years More had to draw on his legendary stamina, undertaking a schedule of prayer, legal duties and study from early morning to late at night, not unlike that of the scholar class of the Utopians. He would probably have risen for prayers before starting his working day at the Inns of Court, which lay to the west, returning later along the thoroughfare of Holbourne, lined with taverns and legal offices and crowded with peddlers, drovers, Church officials and lawyers, across the bridge over the Fleet River, left down Cow Lane away from Newgate, then through Smithfield Market into Charterhouse Lane, passing under the priory gatehouse to join the monks for the performance of the night offices. Treading the winding ways of the city, More was poised between lives of spirit and of mundane struggle, purifying himself daily with the rituals of the monastery, advancing himself little by little in the chambers of the law.

We can, perhaps, picture More falling in with the monks as they emerge carrying their lanterns in their simple robes of undyed wool and make their way through the cloister to the conventual church, the only sounds being their gentle footfalls on the flagstones and the tolling bell summoning them to Matins. The interior of the church, shadowy and flickering in the night, had an atmosphere not unlike the temples of the Utopians, which More imagined as being softly lit because 'a dim and uncertain light focuses the mind and stirs religious feelings'. The ceremony of prayer and steady chanting would continue until the early hours of the morning, when the monks would return to their cells and kneel at their prayer desks for a final time, intoning into the darkness: *Quoniam mille anni ante oculos tuos* . . . For a thousand years before your eyes are like the days of yesterday, which have passed by, and they are like a watch of the night.

By 1505 More had abandoned his life of contemplation at the Charterhouse, marrying in that year and setting up house at Bucklersbury, a road running off of Cheapside by the culverted ancient River Walbrook a few hundred yards east of Milk Street. In the years following he accumulated his numerous public appointments in the city, including Under Sheriff of London, Commissioner for Sewers and freeman of the powerful Mercers' Company, which represented London's wool and textile merchants. In 1518 he joined the King's Council and became royal secretary. Erasmus claimed that More was a reluctant official, torn from his scholarly and spiritual vocations by the mundane demands of family and career. More had been groomed for high office from a young age, but Erasmus claimed that his friend was reluctant to enter royal service because he had a 'hatred of tyranny and a great fancy for equality'; he had to be 'dragged' to court by Henry.

Any personal conflict that More may have felt between the pursuit of the contemplative life and that of public action had an analogy, perhaps, in the contrasting purposes of the committed utopian who conjures visions of a new society and the political official who pursues necessarily imperfect forms of statecraft in the world as it is. The tension between utopianism and politics has been at the heart of utopian thinking ever since. In fact, it is one of the principal themes explored in *Utopia*.

Before More's book even tells of the streets, houses and people on the island of Utopia, it has us picture Morus, Giles and Raphael sitting on their garden bench having an impassioned debate about how far utopian visionaries should involve themselves in day-to-day politics; perhaps More had had the same discussion with himself as he charted his own course. Impressed by Raphael's stories of the various societies he had encountered on his travels, Giles urges him to offer his services as adviser to a king: 'seeing that with your learning and your experience of places and peoples you're equipped not only to divert him but also to instruct him with examples and guide him with counsel'. Raphael dismisses Giles's advice, saying that has no need to 'enslave' himself to a king. He lives as he pleases and he thinks that 'few of those decked in purple manage to do that'.

Here Morus cuts into the conversation and extols the virtues of public service. He admires Raphael for not wanting riches and power, but argues that through advising a great prince Raphael would aid the public good. Raphael rejects this: kings are more concerned with war and plunder than with good government, he says, and their courts are filled with flatterers who are blind to new ideas.

Raphael remarks that he has observed this stubborn conventionality in England just as much as anywhere, letting slip, to Morus's astonishment, that he once visited England and stayed with John Morton. Through the mouth of Raphael now comes a homage to More's old benefactor: he was easy-going, though serious-minded, articulate and wise; he had developed his

The Infinite City

exceptional intelligence through careful study; he had risen fast but been 'tossed about by the shifts of fortune' such that he had developed a great practical wisdom. (The portrait sounds uncannily like a popular image of More that has come down to us; perhaps Morton here represents the kind of public man that More then aspired to be.) Having expressed scepticism about the wisdom of wise people serving princes, Raphael makes one of those reversals that frequently complicate More's story: Morton had in fact exerted great influence on the king's policies, he says. But he then relates a conversation in Morton's house that returned him to his doubts about the prudence of visionaries placing themselves under kings.

One evening at dinner, a lawyer guest praised England's practice of executing thieves – in London they would perish at Tyburn for minor thefts – while wondering why there were still so many of them. Raphael said that such punishment was too harsh and would not in any case deter thieves, most of whom had to steal to eat. Much better would be to ensure that people could make an honest living, but in England there was no way for everyone to do so, one reason for this being the system of landlordism which allowed noblemen to live idly off the efforts of their tenants, whom they impoverished with extortionate rents. But there was another reason for the persistence of theft, said Raphael: 'Your sheep'. These usually harmless animals had begun to swallow people, houses and cities: vast profits encouraged the lords to enclose the land for the raising of wool, to turn the cultivators out of the fields, pull down their houses and make the churches into sheep folds. For the sake of a landlord's gluttony, men, women, orphans and widows consequently had to steal and risk the gallows to survive.

Encouraged by Morton, Raphael told the party about various punishments for thieving – harsh, but short of death – used in the lands that he had encountered on his travels. The lawyer replied that these could not be employed in England without undermining public order, and the others 'fell over themselves to endorse his opinion'. But when Morton wondered aloud whether it might be worth at least trying out more lenient punishments, everyone who had scoffed at Raphael instantly made an about-turn, each trying to surpass the others in their enthusiasm for Morton's suggestion. The anecdote shows, says Raphael, the futility of trying to be an adviser in a court of flatterers who do not think for themselves but only say what they believe their master wants to hear.

Morus concedes that unfamiliar propositions grounded in academic philosophy will tend to fall on deaf ears in the courts of kings. The problem with the philosophical mode of argument is that it is abstract and therefore presupposes that 'you can discuss anything that you like, regardless of the setting'. A philosopher trying to persuade a royal court in this way fails to perceive the stage on which he stands and the players ranged around him. He is like an actor who during a knockabout comedy suddenly strides into the action and delivers a high-flown speech about the virtues and ends up spoiling the play. Morus instead recommends 'civic' philosophy, 'which knows its stage'. One should not try to force strange ideas on those who you know will not be able to understand them. Instead, says Morus, one should take an indirect approach, using tact and decorum, 'so that whatever you cannot turn to good will at least do the minimum of harm'. When serving a prince, one might not be able to solve everything, but that is no reason to give up.

Through his fictional alter ego, More argues for the virtues of the kind of counsellor that he would become, one of insight and vision combined with practicality and an instinct for etiquette, who could marry the new humanist learning with the political demands of the day. Under this pragmatically critical approach to power, the stark contradiction between the roles of the visionary and the official is lessened. To More – a man of great talent who could turn his hand to many fields – perhaps it was more straightforward than sometimes assumed to enter the service of the king while having scholarly and spiritual ambitions. Just as More the boy stepped deftly in among the players at Morton's revels, so More the young lawyer moved into the larger worldly arenas governed by hierarchy, obligation and tradition. Perhaps, then, a man with spiritual or utopian insights does not have to turn away from the imperfect world around him but can authentically turn towards it and be busy in it, diligently playing his roles on the stage while being able to see through them, so retaining a visionary power to be used when the time and place are fitting.

Whatever the exact career calculations that More was making at the time of writing *Utopia*, he sought and entered royal service soon after and quickly rose. It was an auspicious time as men of his interests and background – legal, commercial and middle-class – were becoming more influential at court, as were the English humanists. And so a few months after More returned to England from his embassy in Bruges the king's Latin secretary wrote that More 'haunts these smokey palace fires . . . None bids my lord of York good morrow earlier than he'. The court magnate in question was the Lord Chancellor, Cardinal Thomas Wolsey, the most powerful man in England after the king, to whom More's career would become closely linked.

Cardinal Wolsey had a reputation for corrupt opulence and overweening ambition, but he was also a supporter of the new humanist learning, a committed administrator and a man of distinctly reformist tendencies. As he came into their orbit as royal secretary, More would have observed the vigorous statecraft of Henry and Wolsey and possibly felt in it intimations of his utopian imaginings. *Utopia* was written at the time of Wolsey's rise and there are intriguing parallels between the cardinal's policies and some of the social problems and their possible solutions discussed in More's book. More's duties naturally obliged him to participate in the pomp of statecraft that his Utopians so deplored: in 1520 he attended the Field of Cloth of Gold, the meeting between Henry and Francis I of France held close to Calais amid scenes of extravagant display, and in the summer of 1527 he was part of an embassy to France, the cardinal and his entourage marching over London Bridge splendidly dressed in black velvet and gold chains. But back in London More observed Wolsey's efforts to counter the iniquities of a rising commercial society, concerns that underlay much of the thinking in *Utopia*; More once even thought of dedicating his book to his political master.

Wolsey attempted in particular to remedy the defects of English law, taking measures to make it apply more equally by giving easier access to legal redress to the poor and less leeway for evasion by the rich, who frequently exploited legal delays to their advantage. In *Utopia* Raphael condemns the unfairness of the law, and rails against the holding of large numbers of acolytes by nobles. Wolsey took action against these bands of retainers, who were used to intimidate local juries and so bend the law to their masters' interests.

In May 1517, six months after the publication of *Utopia*, Wolsey set up a commission of inquiry into the enclosure of land. This was to take action against landlords engaging in the practice, those seeking profit from the raising of sheep, who in *Utopia* Raphael denounces for impoverishing families dependent on the land. But although enclosures were illegal under England's common law, they were a fundamental part of the emergence of capitalism and attempts at their restriction could not stop the practice. Wolsey also acted against fraud and profiteering in the meat and grain trades, market manipulations of the kind that had also been condemned in *Utopia*. More was therefore working on *Utopia* when the social impacts of capitalism were having a bearing on royal policymaking. (It has been suggested that *Utopia* might have inspired Wolsey's creation of the enclosure commission.)

Following the fall of Wolsey in 1529, More was made Lord Chancellor, the post which he would hold until he resigned in 1532 because of his opposition to the king's divorce. Although More was a favourite of the king, as Lord Chancellor he never attained the political dominance of Wolsey. By the time More was appointed, the king was involved with his Great Matter – his efforts to divorce Catherine and marry Anne Boleyn – and the major player in this would be the rising Thomas Cromwell. More busied himself with the suppression of heresy and with the continuation of Wolsey's legal reforms. In the afternoons he would receive anyone who wished to bring a suit to him, sending them away 'merry and cheerful'. In an echo of the argument in *Utopia* between the lawyer and the righteous Raphael, More once invited to dinner a group of judges who were aggrieved by some of the appeals that he had granted. He explained to them the reasoning behind his decisions and urged them to use the law to promote fairness. Presiding over the courts of Star Chamber and Chancery, he gained a reputation for extraordinary industry, sweeping through long backlogs of cases, his efforts being celebrated in a popular ditty:

When More some time had Chancellor been,
No more suits did remain.
The like will never more be seen
Till More be there again.

More the statesman was a favourite of London, seen as a wise judge and champion of the city. In a play partly authored by Shakespeare, he is depicted quelling a riot through skilled oratory alone and is described as a great scholar and a friend of the city's poor. The mayor lauds him: 'O how our city is by you renowned, / And with your virtues our endeavours crowned'.

Another part of More's legend was his famed home life, first at Bucklersbury and later at his mansion in Chelsea with its riverside gardens. Governed by daily rhythms of prayer, study and music-making, More and his family were said to live in a domestic idyll of contented solemnity – a utopia-in-miniature. More's children received a refined education in religion and the classics, and their father urged their tutors to warn them off the lures of gold and 'gaudy trappings' and to instil in them proper Christian humility. His favourite child was Margaret, who grew into a highly learned woman and published a translation of one of Erasmus's works. During meals family members would take turns to read out religious texts, to be followed by discussion of a question posed by More. In his spare time More would wander through the back lanes of Chelsea and leave gold pieces for any needy families living there. He invited the poor into his home and established an almshouse which Margaret managed.

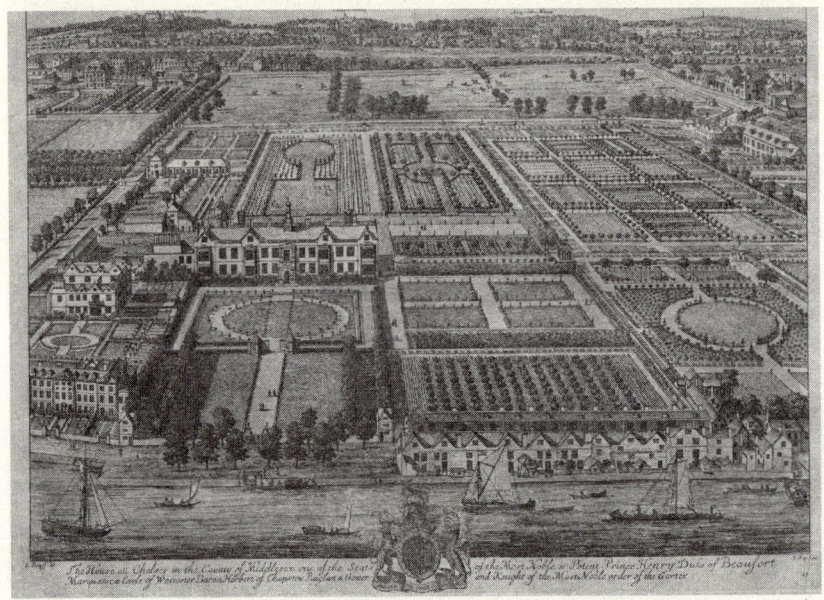

More's Chelsea residence, later known as Beaufort House, in the early eighteenth century

Europe's leading scholars, most notably Erasmus, would enjoy frequent sojourns under More's roof. Erasmus likened the More household to Plato's Academy, superior in fact to that ancient school in being devoted to Christian learning and the liberal arts rather than abstract philosophy and mathematics. More's home was also a place of statecraft, for the use of the practical civic philosophy argued for by his fictional alter ego in *Utopia*, and officials and sometimes even the king would drop in to consult with him. (When More's son-in-law once expressed amazement on seeing him walking arm in arm with Henry in the garden, More replied that he was thankful for the king's favour, but that 'if my head could win him a castle in France it should not fail to go'.)

In 1526 the German painter Hans Holbein, who years before had made woodcuts for the publication of *Utopia*, came to England and stayed with More. During his visit he produced a group portrait, probably commissioned for More's fiftieth birthday, showing a handsomely dressed family carefully positioned around a well-appointed room. The depiction evokes the More residence as a place where piety, virtue and learning meet in an outward presentation of probity and public spirit. The famous picture – only a preparatory sketch for it survives – contributed to the reputation of the More household. His home came to be imagined by its admirers as a humanist enclave on the banks of the Thames where after dinner More and his learned friends would engage in philosophical discussion amid the shrubs, herbs and fruit trees, gazing on the prospect of the city.

Hans Holbein the Younger, 'The More Household at Chelsea'

At the centre of Holbein's drawing sits Thomas More, his stillness and gravity anchoring the figures that surround him, most of whom are occupied with their books. Dressed in a fur collar and chain of office, his public duties seem near at hand and he gazes off to the side, perhaps towards a crucifix in the corner of the room or out of a window towards the landing stage by the river where his barge and waterman wait to take him a few miles downstream to the busy city. If recently returned from his day's business, he may be about to visit the chapel and library that he had built a little distance from the main house. This was his retreat where he would imagine 'going out of the world', meditate on an image of Christ's Passion and allow himself to feel the presence of God.

Arranged around More are his children, looking like the models of learning and modesty that their father sought to make them. To one side of him his adopted daughter Margaret Giggs gestures towards a book she is holding, explaining a point to More's elderly father John, while his youngest daughter Elizabeth looks on; his other children, John, Cecily and Margaret, hold prayer books.

Quick to praise the virtue that he saw in his children and friends, More was also sensitive to the follies of an imperfect humankind. A symbol of this was his fondness for the close observation of the characters of animals, in More's time often taken as moral tokens, such as the foxes, ferrets, weasels, rabbits and birds that Erasmus recalled him keeping. At the edge of the picture is a small monkey, an emblem of irrationality and worldly desire. The creature is on a chain and climbs up a fold in the dress of More's second wife, Alice, who kneels at a prayer stand and wears a large cross. Close by her is More's fool, Henry Pattinson, the purveyor of a human monkeying capable of being entertaining but perhaps also of puncturing complacency. He adopts a challenging stare, the only figure to look directly at the viewer. More's Utopians 'derive a particular delight from fools and consider it shameful to look down on them'. In *Utopia* a fool appears briefly during the debate at Morton's table, ridiculing churchmen for their idleness and sending a visiting friar into a rage, before being sent away by Morton for his rudeness. One can imagine the figures in Holbein's picture breaking out of their poses and walking into a similarly lively dinner, perhaps being joined by a visiting diplomat, a toadying lawyer and a scholar or two. As the savants spar and Pattinson launches his barbed jests, More would, perhaps, become a latter-day Morton, expertly steering the debate about justice and the ideal state, a guiding presence at the head of his table as voices swirl around him in their quest for collective truth.

Amid his busy life in London's worlds of law and commerce, More conceived the word 'utopia' that invites the imagining of alternatives to existing social arrangements. But his coinage is a pun which also hints at the possible futility of ambitious social dreaming. Utopia is a place (*topos*), but is it a 'good place' (*eu*-topia) or a 'no place' (*ou*-topia), one that will forever evaporate away from us as soon as we try to make real the contents of our imaginations? The subtitle of the book – *A Truly Golden Handbook, No Less Instructive than Delightful* – immediately raises questions of veracity and intent: is More presenting us with a social blueprint or mere entertainment? More elaborated little about the work, except to wish that it had never been published and to regret its translation from Latin into the vernacular languages which would enable it to reach a wider audience. In one letter he says that *Utopia* was written in a rush, fears that it lacks wit and claims that Peter Giles had the book published against his wishes – and yet still encloses a copy for the perusal of his high-ranking recipient. In a letter to Erasmus before the book appeared, he wrote that he longed to see the work published and 'furnished too with glowing testimonials'.

Many of More's contemporaries took his description of Utopia at face value. One reader complained that More was nothing more than a hack who had simply written down what had been related to him by a traveller returned from Utopia. It was even said that a leading theologian of the day wrote to Cardinal Wolsey begging to be made Bishop of Utopia. One might imagine more credulous readers scrutinising seas and coastlines on maps of the New World for the possible location of More's wondrous island.

But on making an imaginative journey to Utopia, amid details which lend an air of verisimilitude to the trip, we encounter others which seem designed to confuse us about where to draw the line between reality and fiction. Amaurot is the 'spectral' city, and through it flows the River Anyder (the 'waterless'). Utopia's governor is named Ademos ('one without a people'). The island's shape and dimensions turn out to be mathematically impossible. And should we trust the testimony of the mysterious travelling philosopher Raphael Hythloday, his first name that of the archangel who brought healing to the earth, his last describing him as a 'peddler of nonsense'? More's text makes frequent use of litotes, statements expressed by negating their opposite, such as the description of Utopia and the other nations that Raphael encountered on his travels as being 'far from badly governed' – does this mean that they were well governed, though?

More's retelling of Raphael's experiences is preceded by a map of Utopia, a poem written in a strange alphabet purportedly used by the Utopians and a series of prefatory letters penned by More and his friends. In one letter to Giles, More apologises for taking so long to complete his book. He can never seem to find the time to write, he grumbles, what with the demands of his legal and court affairs, then having to play with the children, speak to his wife and attend to the servants, to say nothing of the need to eat and sleep occasionally. Still, he says, during a few snatched moments he managed to get down the best part of Raphael's tale. But amid the bustle of his London life, a few crucial details seem to have slipped his mind. He cannot remember the length of the bridge over the River Anyder. Not only that, but he clean forgot to ask Raphael where Utopia is, and it is really rather embarrassing not to know even in which ocean it lies. Please check with Raphael, More begs of Giles. In a subsequent letter Giles says that Raphael did in fact mention the location of Utopia, but as he did a flu-wracked mariner coughed loudly, drowning out the crucial words. He promises to locate Raphael and clear up More's queries, but there are rumours that Raphael died on the way back to his homeland. Others say that he returned to Utopia, says Giles. It seems that the only man who knows the truth has disappeared back into nothingness or nowhere.

So More tantalises with a sham authenticity done up in layers of ambiguity and irony. We can never be certain what he intends by it all. Perhaps More is extolling Utopia, as many of his contemporaries assumed him to be. On the other hand, might his fictional 'nowhere' be pointing to a moral vacuum at the heart of Raphael's idyll? After all, for all their good qualities, More tells us that the Utopians keep slaves, prevent their citizens from travelling freely and like to foment discord within enemy nations using plots and assassinations.

More's intention might have been similar to that of Erasmus, whose *In Praise of Folly* used satire to attack the stupidity and hypocrisy of lawyers, clerics, kings and schoolmen, and extolled a 'higher folly', a Christian simplicity and sincerity mocked as foolish by these corrupted sophisticates. Erasmus wrote the book while staying with More at Bucklersbury and dedicated it to his host. In his own work of *Utopia* More is, perhaps, the perspicacious joker who wields satire and double meaning to disorientate his readers, to soften them up before demonstrating the injustice of social conventions.

If irony acts as the solvent of pointless orthodoxies, why not dissolve them more directly with straightforward arguments free from narrative snags and epistemological sleight of hand? One reason was that More's and Erasmus's humanism took flight on the wings of a revival of classical rhetoric; it soared away from the swamps of medieval scholastic philosophy which in its later years had become the tortuous intellectual activity of a group of cloistered scholars. The scholastics had 'concocted about God some problems so ridiculous you would think they were joking', wrote More. Rather than provoking the contemplation of ideas in the abstract, humanist writings harnessed the rhetorical power of language to kindle a broad response – emotional as well as intellectual – one that would focus the will and generate action in the world. Gone were the rigid methods of medieval logic in favour of oratory, dialogues and letters in which concepts were clothed in stories and myths, and in the sounds of real people questioning and debating. Raphael's recollection of his time on the island comes after his fierce condemnation of contemporary Tudor society. By placing the condemnation alongside the description of a better, albeit flawed society, perhaps More aims to shake us out of our complacency, to 'laugh' us towards the truth through a captivating story. His fantasy encourages us to think about what sort of society we wish for; the first step may be to tell stories of subversion, ones which show what is left out in commonplace understandings of the world.

The power of language to do this is encapsulated in a term of classical rhetoric, *enargeia*: the quality of vividness that makes one feel oneself to be present in a described scene, both physically and emotionally. In Giles's prefatory letter he says that even though he was there when Raphael told his tale, he found More's book so real that he seemed to experience more than he did through hearing Raphael's words directly. He felt himself to be living in Utopia; perhaps, he wonders, in the telling of the story of the island, More comes closer to the truth than Raphael did by actually being there.

By the end of *Utopia* More, who appears in the story as a curious but sceptical interlocutor, seems won over to Raphael's way of thinking. After we finish reading, perhaps we are supposed to imagine the fictional Morus reunited with the real More plunging back into London and the hurly-burly of commercial and political life, now carrying within him the spirit of King Utopus, the man who, far from discovering an existing island of perfection, designed and built one himself. Perhaps More now has the capacity to be a wiser councillor, tempering King Henry's ruthless statecraft with utopian wisdom, tactfully communicated through a civic humanism that knows its place. Naturally the authorial More leaves a doubt hanging: 'I can hardly agree with all that was said,' says Morus.

Whatever his intentions, More is the only utopian thinker in our story who did not propose that his utopia be created in the real world. He did not gather utopian disciples or attempt to set up an experimental community run along Morean social lines. More's work, like other Renaissance utopias that followed such as Tommaso Campanella's *The City of the Sun* of 1602 and Johannes Andreae's *Christianopolis* of 1619, were not turned into practical schemes by way of the philosophies of progress that emerged in later centuries. Renaissance utopias were rooted in the ancients' cyclical notion of time, whereby the past is destined to return and the present is simply one moment in an eternal cycle in which kings, races and empires rise to glory, fade away and rise again. Time was a 'mobile image of eternity', said Plato, a circle around which humans were condemned forever to revolve. The belief that one's own present is better than the past was complacent folly, eventually to be exposed when the present gave birth to the past in regression and disintegration.

Without a concept of historical progress, early social dreamers – from the first ancient visionaries to classically inspired Renaissance thinkers such as Thomas More – did not locate their perfect worlds in a river of history which would one day wash us up there. As in More's *Utopia*, the quintessential utopian tale is that of mariners blown off course to a strange land where they experience a state of radical social alteration. But utopians were shipwrecked in another sense: lost in time as well as in the expanse of the ocean. Analogous to utopia's spatial status as the no place, then, is its temporal one as the no time. For this reason *Utopia*, like other early utopias, has a cloistered, timeless quality to it: its descriptions of perfect cities of ascetics and scholars, while casting a light on contemporary moral imperfections, are disconnected from the progressive forces of history which later thinkers believed in. More's social vision on one level was a simulacrum of Europe's medieval seats of learning, its tranquil and changeless monastic communities. It was a utopia of 'calm tranquility', not meant to foment agitation or uprising. For visionaries like More utopia was an ideal form, a philosophical abstraction, like the perfect triangle or flower. Just as it was impossible for us to find a geographical passage to utopia, then, so a path towards it through years and decades was not only out of reach but unthinkable.

For refusing to swear an oath to the new royal succession following King Henry's divorce and as the English Church was making its break from Rome, More was imprisoned in the Tower of London and in 1535 put to death for treason. Two months before he died, More saw from his cell window three Charterhouse monks, including the prior of the monastery, being taken for execution for the same offence. More is said to have turned to his daughter Margaret, who was visiting him, and hailed the piety of the steadfast brothers, in their great virtue so far above those 'worldly wretches', himself included, who spend their limited time on earth in the pursuit of pleasure and comfort. At the gate of the Tower, in their hair shirts and habits, the monks were tied to a hurdle then dragged through the city to Tyburn, where in front of a large crowd they suffered hanging, mutilation and dismemberment. Later, part of the prior's corpse was put up over the entrance to the monastery.

The Charterhouse community was broken up, its buildings divided and used as a store for Henry's tents and hunting gear, its pictures of the saints broken and its altars turned into gaming tables. In 1545 the buildings were sold to Sir Edward North, an official of Thomas Cromwell, later Chancellor of the Court of Augmentations, which oversaw the dissolution of the monasteries. They were made into North's residence; the cloister was pulled down and the church became a dining hall. At the church of St Lawrence Jewry, where More gave his celebrated lectures on *The City of God*, a carved altar was destroyed and books, embroidered cloths and gold and silver plate taken away. As monastic possessions were digested in the guts of London's commerce, property ownership fragmented and tenements and taverns multiplied. This was the fate of Charterhouse Lane. As it lay outside the jurisdiction of the city it became particularly rowdy, with frequent reports of violence and prostitution. So as More watched them leave the Tower, the monks made their final journey through a city transforming, one whose sacred enclaves were to be inundated by the forces of commerce.

More became renowned for his part in the religious and constitutional dramas of Henry VIII's reign. His primary intellectual legacy was his great work of the social imagination that transports us to a happy isle far away from the turmoil of the present. *Utopia*, a slim book dashed off when More was on a royal assignment in Europe and later at home in London, has since its publication inspired many volumes of interpretation and counter-interpretation.

An early reader called Utopia a hagnopolis, a society of saints; one understanding of More's story is that it looks back to the dimming medieval world, and that Utopia is an idyll of piety and virtue. Here, Amaurot is London's Charterhouse expanded into a complete society, a disciplined, communal unity of ascetics dedicated to higher truths. *Utopia* is a rejection of England's burgeoning capitalism, whose merchants threaten to sweep away the remnants of a sacred era in a deluge of rapacity and accumulation. In this view of it *Utopia* is not a social programme, rather an allegory that in its depiction of a far-off world points back to one that is receding from us in the here and now. At the same time, *Utopia* condemns the contemporary world by telling of a pagan people who, through the exercise of natural reason and without the aid of Christian revelation and scripture, have created as perfect a society as possible, one more just and virtuous than that of Christian Europe, which has squandered its spiritual inheritance. More was certainly no revolutionary, and here he is seen as a conservative prophet trying to hold back modernity and secularism. Hagiographers have viewed him as one of the last great medieval Catholics and played down the significance of his apparent social radicalism. More's real views are sometimes taken to be those voiced by Morus, who attempts to refute Raphael's arguments for communism and the abolition of the money economy.

A little later, Protestant interpreters cleansed More for the new religious order, arguing that his criticism of the corruption of the Church and its clerics meant that his utopian plan actually anticipated the Reformation. Ralph Robinson began this rehabilitation of More through his English translation, which ironed out the ambivalences of the Latin text. In his preface Robinson praised More's book and its author's wit and learning. But More had been stubborn in matters of religion 'even to the very death'. Robinson dedicated his text to William Cecil, later Elizabeth I's chief adviser and an architect of Protestant England.

In the nineteenth century, the Marxist theorist Karl Kautsky saluted More as an early communist. In *Das Kapital* Marx himself took More's image of sheep eating up people and towns as an example of the dispossession that lies at the heart of capitalism. Kautsky situated *Utopia* in a Marxist historical scheme in which feudalism was replaced by capitalism, the new economic system hastened in the sixteenth century by the enclosure of lands and the break-up of religious houses, which put production in the hands of the bourgeoisie and made the peasantry into a landless proletariat. Kautsky made More thoroughly modern and radical (and thus, he said, blew away 'a certain fragrance of incense' that hagiographers made cling to More). More's sympathy for the poor, his allegiance to the communal features of medieval society, and his witnessing through his legal and commercial work in London of the new tensions caused by a fast-commercialising city were catalysts for the rising of his visionary genius, one that divined the social implications of infant capitalism with far greater depth than any of his contemporaries, argued Kautsky. Like a modern socialist, More realised the extent to which humans are conditioned by material circumstances – people steal when they cannot find decent employment – and have, therefore, the potential to be improved if better conditions can be established under a just social order. More was able to look out into the city and appreciate like few others the social strains of an emerging commercial society, which would become deeper and more complex over time and which the political and intellectual revolutions of later centuries would try to resolve.

Such left-wing interpretations wrench More out of his historical context by imputing to him modern notions, such as communism, that are predicated on the existence of conscious social classes pitted against each other in a mass industrial economy. Ignoring the ambiguities in More's text, they equate the real More definitively with Raphael and so make him into an uncompromising radical, one who was unlikely to have embraced the compromises of royal service as easily as he did. The utopian economy, in its functioning and in its measure of economic benefit, is, in fact, different to both capitalism and socialism. It is based on a medieval handicraft system without the fast technological innovation of modern economies. Technological growth is viewed under both socialism and capitalism as having the same basic economic benefit: the expansion of production in line with rising material desires. By envisioning a society of disciplined ascetics, More looks instead to the restriction of desire. In Utopia, modestly superior economic productivity – achieved by the absence of idleness and privileged worklessness rather than by technological advancement – leads to more non-working hours for all. These are used for self-improvement and study rather than for superficial leisure, for collectively defined higher human needs rather than for the satisfaction of a smorgasbord of momentary individual wants.

The anachronisms in socialist readings of More do not negate the socially radical nature of *Utopia* nor necessitate a return to viewing it as a backward-looking medieval idyll. The monastic spirit certainly pervades *Utopia*, but the island of Utopia is not simply an expanded monastery: it is a nation with a political and economic life, with families, children born into it, and armies that go to war. At the end of *Utopia* we see the Utopians in their temple giving thanks for being in the happiest commonwealth possible, but praying that if they are in error for God to help them to discover better forms of society, which they will then adopt.

Far from being apparent radicals who really hanker after a return to the medieval cloister, they are utopians in monkish dress who wish to remake society at every opportunity.

The utopian impulse symbolised so powerfully in More's *Utopia* has often been viewed as the search for a complete and final social Eden. Utopians, it is said, tout a social blueprint but are guilty of naivety or of tyranny for thinking that they can fit into it so many diverse human beings. Because in the second book of *Utopia* More describes a complete utopian society, his purpose might seem to be the espousal of just such a plan. An alternative might be that the intellectually sophisticated More meant his story as a joke or satire. But a further possibility is that the multi-vocal nature of the text, with its crafty storytelling frames, dialogues within dialogues and swirl of disputatious voices, points to another kind of truth. The interplay of opposing views in the book generates a creative friction that casts light on dilemmas that will always be at the heart of any attempt to remould society, and so the utopian search has to be seen as a never-ending quest. True utopianism is an ethos of infinite social dreaming, and the creation of a fixed and final social programme actually closes off the imagination needed for it.

When Raphael finishes his lengthy account of the island of Utopia, the voice switches to Morus for a few concluding paragraphs. He dismisses the Utopians' 'absurd' practices, such as their refusal of money. In a final double-edged flourish, he rejects their communism because it 'subverts all nobility, magnificence, splendour and majesty, which according to popular opinion are the proper ornaments and honours of the Commonwealth'. But pomp and display were in all likelihood abhorred by the famously ascetic More and certainly never to be justified simply on the basis of popularity. As one commentator suggests, if we must be careful about believing Raphael, that peddler of nonsense, then perhaps we should also beware of More: *Morus*, the moron or fool. Together, however, Raphael and Morus exist as imaginative polarities that form a powerful current of utopian energy.

At the end of *Utopia* it feels as if the story might continue beyond the final sentences. Morus says that Raphael was tired from talking, and so refrains from entering into further argument with him, instead leading him into dinner while promising that there would be another opportunity for them to discuss these matters. So as he leaves the stage, Morus seems to turn to us for a fleeting moment as if to say, 'There can never be an end to this'.

In December 1516 More sent Erasmus a playful letter, telling him of the thrill that he gets from his daydreams of being the King of Utopia. He imagines himself marching along in monk-like clothes, holding a sheaf of wheat as his sacred sceptre. Accompanied by a retinue of distinguished Amaurotians, he is giving audience to a group of foreign kings and ambassadors, who of course look ludicrous in all their finery. He begs his friend not to think of him as being like most people, whose outlook on the world and others is determined by shifts in fortunes. Even when wafted up from his humble estate to the soaring pinnacle of the King of the Utopians, he would never forget their friendship that had begun when he was a lowly functionary in the world of London. In his dream, then, More seems to put himself in the role of an austere, self-disciplined king: fair, firm and visionary in spirit, and in this combination of qualities transcending the apparent conflicts between statecraft and utopianism. Delighted by this vision, he is brought back to earth by the London dawn, which shatters his dream ('poor me!'), throws him off his throne and summons him back to the drudgery of the courts. As he wakes and prepares for the duties of the day, he is consoled by the thought that, in the vast expanse of time, real cities and kingdoms do not last much longer than the rising and falling of dreams.

Chapter Three

London, Look to Thy Freedom

In the century after Thomas More, London continued its rapid expansion, with new suburbs sprawling out beyond the old city walls and its population growing twice as fast as the nation as a whole – it would exceed half a million by 1700. The city came to dominate the nation both economically and politically. But as London prospered, relations with the Crown deteriorated: in the conflict between Parliament and Charles I, the capital was on the Parliamentary side and by the 1640s it was at war.

On the first day of January 1649, as Parliament is about to try the king, a makeshift procession is taking place a little to the west of the city walls. A group of players have been dragged off their stage by soldiers, mid-performance. Still in their costumes, they are being jostled west along the Strand towards Whitehall. Their theatre has been raided for flouting an ordinance against play-acting imposed by the Puritan-dominated Parliament, but now the streets become a stage as the acting spills into the night and the arrested players move through a throng of onlookers, flaming torches lighting their way. One of the male actors is resplendent in a black satin gown and white laced pumps. 'What has that Lady done?' ask the jeering crowd. Another takes the part of the king, and as the little band continue along the street the soldiers join in the theatrics, removing the actor's crown from his head and then replacing it, making the people laugh, groan and cheer in turn. The soldiers, the players and the onlookers are fleetingly united in a game of de-crowning, in a ludic enactment of upended power, of a world turned upside down that is about to be made real, for in a few weeks a larger crowd will give out a mighty groan when the king is beheaded in front of the Banqueting House a little further along the river.

This darkly exuberant spectacle takes place amid a deep social crisis. The country is reeling from a series of terrible harvests, and Londoners tell of poverty and famine 'like a mighty torrent . . . breaking in upon us'. In Westminster a glover and his family are reported to be surviving on cats and dogs, and around the city the 'cryes and teares' of the poor 'rend any pitifull heart to heare'. Londoners also blame rising food prices and the slump in trade on rumours of war, which have set the city's merchants on edge. Around the country mobs are attacking grain carts on their way to market.

Dearth, war and regicide are fodder for the millenarian imaginations of the city's godly folk. They say that the extraordinary events are portents of the apocalypse and the second coming of Christ. London has long been a nest of radical Puritans who gather in separatist congregations and who wish to have nothing to do with the corrupt clergy and worn-out ceremonies of the established Church. The city is full of 'mechanic preachers', ordinary people who work for a living and preach in their spare time, zealous participants in a frenzy of heterodox religious experimentation. In Lambeth, three watermen in an alehouse enter into a heated discussion about the Bible until one is charged with blasphemy. An opponent of the practice of infant baptism is bold enough to take a horse into a church and stage a mock baptism on it. Another recusant says that religious houses should be painted black to remind people of the 'darknesse that is within them'.

Coleman Street, a little to the east of the Guildhall, is the principal Puritan enclave in the city. Running north to south up to the city wall, it is lined with merchants' houses and veined with crowded alleys and courts. Its parish church of St Stephen's has been taken over by radical Puritans, and during the Civil War years Communion is restricted to those deemed sufficiently godly, rulings on which is made by a committee that includes two of the judges who sentenced the king. The street harbours a profusion of radical sects as well as secret printing presses, including one run by a leader of the Levellers, a popular movement agitating for democratic reform. In the 1640s Oliver Cromwell himself would meet his supporters there at the Star Inn.

The alleys off Coleman Street teem with sectaries going to their conventicles, secret meetings held in houses with lookouts posted at the door. One of these gatherings, held by a certain soap boiler, is said to be more like a playhouse than a church: young men and women interrupt the teaching and enter into hot disagreements with each other, sometimes falling to fighting, before the preacher has had a chance to finish. A group of visitors in another religious house hear a preacher declare that the people in front of him are as much God as Christ is; shocked and trembling, the men quickly leave in case the building should fall down on their heads. In this upended world there is even a woman preacher, a lace seller who assembles her flock in Bell Alley and according to her critics spreads 'dangerous and false doctrines' in scenes of 'confusion and disorder'.

The rise of these untutored preachers causes consternation among those loyal to the traditional religious order. Coleman Street may be at the centre of an upsurge of a vibrant, popular godliness but to its detractors it is a 'fools paradise', full of people with 'blindfolded eyes' and 'bewitched souls'. One critic says that the death from plague of two children of a Coleman Street preacher is a punishment from God. Located in the heart of the city, the district rings with the 'prating' of 'cobblers, tinkers, peddlers, weavers, sowgelders and chymney-sweepers'. If a street is a microcosm of society, and if its cobblers are bold enough to tear down pulpits and take over from the clergymen who are supposed to teach them, then what hope is there for the survival of an upright city and nation?

London is a refuge for these 'masterless' people who, in coming there, have been unmoored from the authority of the lord of the manor and of the village parson, the keepers of old hierarchies and beliefs. They leave the fields and with it cast off their deference, and as they disappear into the sects harboured within the city's lanes they take on a new attitude of political and religious assertiveness. As the old order shakes, these men and women discover the inner master of individual spiritual conscience and are emboldened to new forms of enquiry and action. One female petitioner, when told by a Member of Parliament how strange it was for a woman to be involved in political agitation, replies: 'Sir, that which is strange is not therefore unlawful; it was strange that you cut off the King's head, yet I suppose you will justifie it.'

John Smith, *The World turn'd upside down: Or, A briefe description of the ridiculous Fashions of these distracted Times*, title page, 1647

London in 1649 is a tinderbox, a city full of loudly asserted discontent: towards the king and the ruling class, towards the established Church and towards knavish merchants who make money from shortages through their clever scheming. So as the city seethes, the players and the soldiers carry on their sport through the torchlit ways, their shouts ringing out towards the cold river. They sail into the night, aroused by deadly new energies that move through the streets and press against old certainties, 'subtle fiends' spreading through London: 'Softly, as dreams, they steal into every head . . . The rebel passions they below unchain, And licence that wild multitude to reign.'

During this time of turmoil in the city, strange tracts appear for sale at the shop of the bookseller and publisher Giles Calvert, located at the sign of the Black Spread Eagle next to St Paul's Cathedral. The shop is another meeting place for London's religious radicals, to Calvert's enemies a 'forge of the Devill' which spreads lies and blasphemy. There is something striking about these latest tracts. They speak of a world wracked by division and 'hurly burlies', and in their exhortation to readers to look first inside themselves for spiritual truths rather than to the established Church sail close to the wind legally. Steeped in religious iconography, the writings remould biblical cosmology into allegories fit for England's revolutionary times.

One of them warns, 'the Earth growes mad and full of rage'. A dark spirit is abroad, a cruel and envious force that slanders the righteous as 'Schismaticks' and 'Roundheads' and seeks to destroy them. The time has now come for earnest people to reckon with this evil: look inside of yourselves, for there sits the Beast that tramples on the holy city, then look out into a world full of ignorance and pride. But redemption is at hand. The depravities of the old city will soon be burned up in God's spirit and the saints will sing: 'Babylon is faln, is faln.'

The author of these thundery writings was a Londoner living in self-imposed exile not far from the city at Cobham. Gerrard

Winstanley had been a cloth merchant in the heart of London, where he had a shop until the turmoil of the times drove him out. The disruption of trade as a result of the Civil War was aggravated, many claimed, by merchants taking advantage of the poor and monopolising markets for a quick gain, and by the burden of 'free quarter', citizens' obligation to provide troops with board and lodging. Winstanley's small operation was vulnerable to the ups and downs of trading conditions, and as buyers of his cloth delayed payments to him he ran up debts to his own suppliers. In the early 1640s he was attempting to pay them off in kind, triggering court proceedings by him against his debtors and by his creditors against himself.

'Thou City of London, I am one of thy sons by freedome, and I do truly love thy peace,' wrote Winstanley, referring to his position as a freeman of the Merchant Taylors Company, one of London's trading guilds. But now he found that his city had turned on him: 'by thy cheating sons in the theeving art of buying and selling . . . I was beaten out both of estate and trade'. In 1643 Winstanley abandoned his business and moved away.

Flowing westwards out of London, the narrowing Thames undulates through Fulham and Chiswick before plunging south at Kew, a few miles upstream, then continues west, curving to enclose a disc of land on its southern bank on which lies the Surrey village of Walton, and that of Cobham a few miles to the south. This predominantly rural area had important links to the city to the east. Cobham was a stopping point on the London–Portsmouth road and troops often moved through the locality during the Civil War years. Being close to London, much of its farming produce was sold there.

There were large areas of common land and the area had seen heightened conflict between landless labourers and landlords, aggravated by the economic toll of the Civil War. The town of Kingston to the north contained radical Puritans and had a heavy army presence during the war years. In 1647 the Army Council met there and declared its support for a purge of Parliament.

In Cobham, Winstanley made a modest living from farming and from grazing cattle. During this time he regularly visited friends in London and was involved in city politics, notably in 1644 when he reported a fellow Merchant Taylor for failing to make a sufficient financial contribution to the Parliamentary cause. By early 1648 Winstanley was suffering further financial troubles, this time caused by drought, and the crisis seems to have led to a deepening of his inner yearning, culminating in a revelation and the flowering of a utopian vision.

Winstanley began to write about his spiritual turmoil, laying out an inward testimony that would later turn into an outward search. Suffering was like being in a dungeon, cut off from light and warmth and having one's happiness bound up with the desire for worldly gain rather than being close to God. Winstanley realised that he was miserable and wretched and he lamented his rebellion against the Lord.

He wrote that discovering the wickedness within was like having two dogs pulling at one's flesh, the first being the sin inside, the second the 'appearance of the righteous law'. He found himself so disturbed that he could not properly pray. He would mix up his words, have prideful thoughts and feel troubled, unable to understand what was in his heart, and find that his memory had failed him. He would worry about the state of his business and about the weather. Sometimes frightening apparitions and 'inward burnings' would come out in confused rantings and those around him would think him mad. His inner torments were mirrored in outward misfortune: social rejection, the destruction of his property by fire and water, losses as a result of the schemes of swindlers and many other calamities through which he became poor and hungry.

Deliverance was at hand, however: 'poor soul, know this, that God is burning up thy drosse, and ere long will set thee at liberty', and gradually Winstanley learned to welcome in the spirit. But sensing the light inside him did not give him true peace until he spoke of his experience. 'I was restlesse in my spirit, till I had delivered all abroad that which was declared within me: And now I have peace.'

And so Winstanley took up his pen. On and on he would write, often so overflowing with the power of spirit that he neglected his food even when his companions would try to make him eat. When alone he felt 'so filled with that love and delight in the life within' that on winter days he would sit writing from morning to night, and when the light faded felt sorry that he had to stop; on getting up from his chair he would find that he was so cold that he needed to rise gradually while holding on to the table until heat and strength returned to his legs.

Sometimes the power deserted him: his heart would close up, he would put down his pen and could no longer bear the cold. He questioned why he had chosen to write so frankly of his inner life, especially since much of what he revealed would get him into trouble and make people hate him. When full of doubt, he resolved never to speak of these spiritual yearnings again. Soon enough, though, he would sense that inward power once more, his heart would open and he would feel like a new man. It was like carrying a flame into a dark room. Then he would take up his pen once more.

Gerrard Winstanley was born in Wigan in 1609 to a family that was involved with the cloth trade, then a major part of the English economy. In 1630 he was apprenticed to a Merchant Taylor at Cornhill in London. Having been made a freeman, in 1639 Winstanley set up his own household close to the Guildhall and took on an apprentice. The following year he married Susan King, the daughter of William King, a city-based barber-surgeon and a senior member of the Barber Surgeons' Company.

Winstanley's parish of St Olave Old Jewry, where he attended vestry meetings, did not have a history of radical Puritanism but was adjacent to the parish of St Stephen Coleman Street. The religious fervour of the nearby streets would no doubt have been felt close to home and in May 1641 there were even riots at St

Olave's. During a service a group of people shouted 'A Pope, a Pope' and were promptly ejected, only to continue their noise in the street, calling out that the Lord Mayor was a papist and proceeding to smash the church windows. Although Winstanley's written spiritual testimony emerged only after he left the city, it is not hard to imagine that the neighbouring warren of alleys, taverns and meeting houses, teeming with intense, disputatious artisans and religious visionaries, acted as a seedbed for his later theological enquiry and fed a powerful sense of religious destiny, to be crowned in the gathering-together of his own religio-utopian sect.

By the late 1640s Winstanley had come into contact with another former London-based Merchant Taylor apprentice, William Everard, a wild mystic and on-the-edge provocateur, variously described as a 'conjurer' and a 'witch' who would play a key role in Winstanley's later activities. Around the time that Winstanley moved to Cobham, Everard was acting as a Parliamentary spy. He also served in the New Model Army and in 1647 was involved in a plot to kill the king. Everard claimed to be a messenger from God, and someone to whom he proselytised was disturbed by his 'strange ecstasies' and 'uncouth deportment'.

In the months following the execution of Charles I locals noticed odd happenings around Cobham and Walton. A large bundle of thorns appeared in the pulpit of Walton's parish church, presumably to prevent the parson from entering it. On another occasion six soldiers arrived at the close of a service. One of them was carrying five candles, one of which burned in a lantern. The soldier called out to the parishioners to stay a little longer, for he had a message from God given to him in a vision. He tried to climb up into the pulpit but the congregation prevented him, and so he went out into the churchyard with the people following behind. He told them that the five candles represented godly truths: that the Sabbath was unnecessary, that tithes should be abolished, that there was no need for ministers because Christ enlightened people directly through revelation, and that magistrates were part of an unholy tyranny. Demonstrating his fifth truth, he produced a Bible and declared it to contain mere 'beggarly rudiments'. He took the candle out of his lantern and put it to the book; the pages flared red in the twilight.

There were also reports of a 'disorderly and tumultuous sort of people' gathering at St George's Hill at Walton. Claiming to be prophets, the people came to the hill 'and began to digge . . . and sowed the ground with parsenipps, and carretts, and beanes'. They invited everyone to join them, promising to provide food and clothing. Soon they had increased their number to several dozen, spending all day digging and on one day 'firing the heath . . . which is a very great prejudice to the town'. It was also claimed that they threatened to pull down posts and fences to enable them to cultivate the soil.

The Diggers, as the people became known, were led by Gerrard Winstanley and William Everard and may well have been involved in the earlier incidents in the church. The visiting soldiers' anti-clericalism certainly chimed with the ideas of Winstanley and his Diggers, their sense of theatre with the behaviour of the flamboyant Everard, who had earlier been imprisoned at Kingston for his blasphemous views and once interrupted a church service by shaking a hedge-cutting tool at the minister and shouting 'come down thy sonne of perdition come down'.

St George's Hill was part of common land where local people grazed animals, dug turf and loam, and put up cottages. On one side it overlooked a flat common that backed on to the royal hunting grounds at Oatlands Palace, which had originally been acquired by Henry VIII; Charles I gave the palace to his wife as a residence. The hill was also close to the far reaches of the Windsor Great Forest. The Diggers prepared and planted about an acre of rough soil and cut wood to build houses and to sell in order to buy necessities while they waited for their first harvest to ripen.

An agricultural reformer of the time thought that the hill was an unpromising site for cultivation. Winstanley admitted that it was certainly a barren-looking piece of land, but claimed that the spot had been shown to him in dreams and visions. The Diggers' efforts there were divinely ordained, and their success on such poor land would be even stronger proof of their righteousness. In *A Watch-word to the City of London, and the Armie* Winstanley notified his fellow Londoners of his sacred mission: 'I tooke my spade and went and broke the ground upon *George-hill* in Surrey, thereby declaring freedome to the Creation, and that the earth must be set free from intanglements of Lords and Landlords, and that it shall become a common Treasury to all, as it was first made and given to the sonnes of men.'

Winstanley and his followers soon came to the attention of the authorities. A local official was afraid that after a few days the Diggers would number in the thousands, force the locals to work for them and even cut off their legs if they disobeyed. The president of the Council of State warned that although the Diggers might seem 'very ridiculous', their actions on the hill could become a threat to national stability. He recommended to the Commander-in-Chief of the New Model Army, Sir Thomas Fairfax, that soldiers be sent to the hill to disperse the people there in order to prevent malcontents among the group from rising to greater mischiefs.

Winstanley and Everard were brought to Whitehall for an audience with Fairfax. When they were presented they refused to perform the traditional show of deference to social superiors of taking off their hats, a common gesture of dissent by radicals and nonconformists. When asked why they would not do so they said that 'they are not to stand bare to any, not to the Generall, being not his servants'.

Reports of the meeting in the newsbooks focused on the turbulent figure of Everard, whose explanation of the Diggers' actions began with a diatribe against kingly oppression. The English were like the ancient Jews who lived under the yoke of the Egyptians, he declared. England's tyranny had been imposed upon it by William the Conqueror in 1066, and ever since the people had groaned under its weight. But the time of deliverance was at hand and God was about to free them from slavery. A vision had appeared to Everard that said, 'Arise, and dig, and plow the earth, and receive the fruits thereof.' The Diggers would restore the earth to its former condition, when men and women lived in community with each other and enjoyed the fruits of the land as one. They would first feed and clothe the poor, but in time everyone would want to join them, even those who owned estates, which they would gladly give up. They would live simply in tents just as their forefathers had. Money would no longer be needed to have a good life. Everard was at pains to make clear that they did not intend to meddle with anyone's property by tearing down fences and enclosures, as many reports of their activities claimed, but only to work on common, uncultivated land.

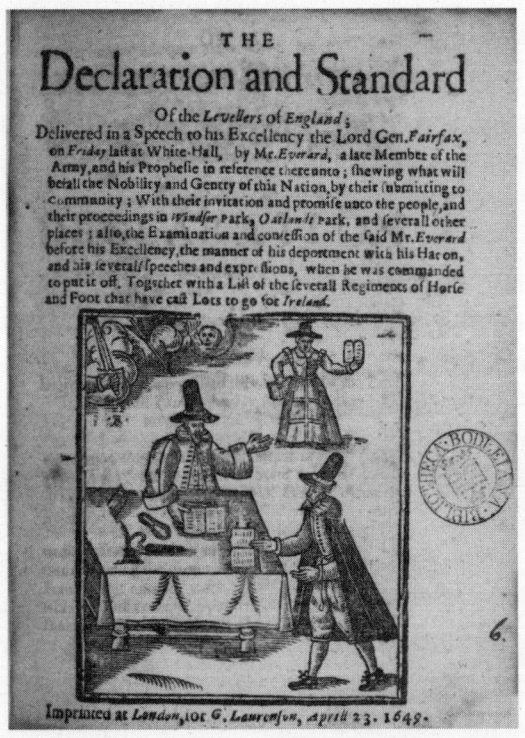

The Declaration and Standard of the Levellers of England, 1649, showing the Diggers appearing before Fairfax

The audience with Fairfax was something of a publicity coup for the Diggers. Everard's speech was reported, accompanied by an illustration of the Diggers at Whitehall, hats firmly on their heads. Many of the accounts were inaccurate and contemptuous, however. One news sheet repeated the claim that the Diggers were ready to use violence on local people, and also stated that their proceedings were taking place at Windsor and Oatlands Parks, giving the impression that they were seeking to threaten royal property rather than cultivate an unused hillside. The Diggers were described as 'crack brained' and intending to dig up Hampstead Heath, to turn Oatlands Park into a wilderness and to 'preach Liberty to the oppressed Deer'. Some commentators considered the Diggers a threatening movement, an insurrection that might end up spreading blasphemy and sedition all around the nation.

Some of Winstanley's critics also claimed that the Diggers' communal society of goods, land and labour extended to wives, implying the free sexual practices that brought notoriety to the Ranters, a highly unconventional sect that affronted orthodox Puritans with their licentious behaviour. The claimed association between the two groups was a slander, said Winstanley, and he disowned some of those said to be connected with the Ranters who had joined his community. Ranting was a 'deceitfull baite' that could not bring inner peace because it sought outward objects – meat, drink and women. These were fleeting things which would vanish tomorrow and running after them kept people from the truth, leaving them ignorant of the moral righteousness that Winstanley and his genuine followers were enacting through sacred digging.

Winstanley had experienced a spiritual rebirth and communicated it to the world; he had walked through the darkness and emerged a new man; 'yet my mind was not at rest, because nothing was acted, and thoughts run in me, that words and writings were all nothing, and must die, for action is the life of all, and if thou dost not act, thou dost nothing.' The rhythm of his words evoked the insistent inner pulse of a man straining to connect his own spiritual revelation with righteous action in the world. Winstanley believed that his activities on the hill were part of a new dispensation in which God's plan would be worked out through the actions, not just the words, of faithful men and women. Clever talk and preaching – the 'heaping up of words amongst professors' – had to cease. The time had come for righteous deeds.

While in a trance Winstanley had received a message from God that broadened his initial religious vision into a social message. He heard the words: 'Worke together, Eat bread together; declare this all abroad.' The Lord showed him the place, and there he began cultivating the land, making his bread 'without either giving or taking hire, looking upon the Land as freely mine as anothers'. After this awakening he was filled with joy. He obeyed the command to tell of his revelation and on 26 January 1649, four days before the king was executed, he finished writing *The New Law of Righteousnes*, which set out his spiritual and practical programme.

According to Winstanley, there were three 'doors of hope' for the nation that the Diggers were flinging open. The first was for people to trust in the 'spirit Reason' within them. People are taught to look to priests if they want knowledge or to be comforted in the face of troubles, but authentic truth would be realised first by the despised poor, not by learned and great men. Priestly power was evil because it allowed ministers to preach for money and to sow division and confusion. The Church, allied with kingly power, takes possession of the land and through the levying of tithes seizes the fruits of people's honest labour. All of this is 'high treason and mighty dishonourable to Christ'.

Declare this all abroad.

The second door: let the earth be a common treasury. Let the people work together and say that the earth belongs to all. Those that cultivate enclosures are not labouring in righteousness: they are saying, '*This is mine*, which is selfish, devilish and destructive to the Creation.' A city ruled by trade, like London, becomes a place of theft and oppression. Reject the buying and selling of labour and goods as well as of land. No longer should the poor be forced to work for hire. In the world that is coming '*Mine and Thine* shall be swallowed up in the law of righteous actions'.

The trumpet sounds in me. Work together, Eat bread together.

The third door: 'Leave off dominion and Lordship one over another, for the whole bulk of man-kinde are but one living earth.' Mine and thine has brought misery to the people, making them steal from one another and then causing them to be hanged for their trouble. Clever lawyers tyrannise the poor and let the rich go free. Burn all the law books at Cheapside and stop sending young people to train in law at London's Inns of Court. Leave the poor to quietly work the land so that they do not have to thieve to survive.

Let Israel go free. Let Israel go free. Let Israel go free.

When the world was created every person was free to till the earth and to enjoy nature's bounty. Envy and pride destroyed that freedom. William the Conqueror imposed tyranny on the English, helped by his lords, priests and lawyers. The kings and queens that followed him continued with this evil. The restoration of a righteous society would be an overturning of England's Norman yoke. Peace will rise up and all will be of one heart and one mind.

Words and writings must die, for action is the life of all.

Parallel to Winstanley's struggles during the 1640s were those of London, an anti-Royalist city wracked by upheaval, culminating in 1649 in the execution of the king, a shattering reversal of power that aided the flourishing of radical sects such as Winstanley's.

On 4 January 1642 the king had entered the chamber of the House of Commons, demanding the surrender of five Members of Parliament against whom he had ordered charges of treason. The five had already fled, hiding out in Coleman Street. On 5 January the king addressed the members of London's Common Council and accused them of harbouring the fugitives. There were shouts from some who were present of 'God Save the King', from others of 'Privileges of Parliament!'. On their way back from escorting the king, the Lord Mayor and some of his aldermen were attacked by a group of women who called them traitors to the city, taking the mayor off his horse and pulling the chain from his neck. That night a false rumour of an imminent Royalist assault spread through London. Men came on to the streets with spears and clubs, the city gates were shut and women put up barricades and prepared cauldrons of boiling water. In a few days the king had lost London and on 10 January left the city. In August he raised the royal standard at Nottingham, signalling the start of the Civil War.

In November of that year there was alarm at the Royalist Army's advance to Turnham Green, only seven miles to the west of London. In a vast communal act, men, women and children hauled and dug to create defences, forts of earth and timber connected by miles of ditches and eighteen-feet-high ramparts that encircled the city. With flags flying and drums beating, thousands of people – tailors, watermen, porters, fishmongers, felt makers and oyster-wives – marched to their digging duties. Five thousand residents of St Giles in the Fields lent a hand. The mounds of earth encircled an assertive, radical citizenry that during these years would display its collective power on the streets and in other kinds of political actions such as the drawing-up of giant petitions.

In 1648, the year in which Winstanley began publishing his writings, a 40,000-signature petition organised by the Levellers – the London-based movement agitating for democratic reform – was presented to the House of Commons. In the spring of 1649 the Leveller leaders were imprisoned and thousands of women signed a petition calling for their release. In the months after the execution of Charles I, groups of Levellers carried out mutinies in the New Model Army. In April a group of soldiers seized a tavern at Bishopsgate. Officers arrived on the scene and attempted to bring the soldiers into line, but they refused to comply. A crowd began to gather and the soldiers shouted 'No, No' at their officers when Cromwell himself swept into the fray, accompanied by Fairfax. The following day one of the ringleaders, Robert Lockyer, was executed by firing squad in St Paul's churchyard. At his funeral the city became a sea of ribbons, black for mourning and green for the Levellers, which were worn by the people as they paraded through the streets behind six trumpeters.

The following month, Cromwell and Fairfax put down a Leveller revolt at Burford and, on entering London, were feted by the Lord Mayor and aldermen, merchants and Members of Parliament. On his way back from Burford, Fairfax visited the Diggers' encampment on St George's Hill to find out more about the intentions of the followers of this strange utopian offshoot of the tumultuous city.

Fairfax and his officers found twelve men and women hard at work. The general made a short speech, upbraiding them for their foolish activities. Winstanley replied that he and his followers were digging on Crown lands, which the king had only possessed because of the Norman Conquest. Now that the king was dead the land had returned to the common people, who with effort could improve it. Winstanley told the general that many of the local people were at first offended by what the Diggers were doing, but soon began to see the good in it. A few freeholders remained hostile; they wanted to maintain the tyranny of the Normans, but in time even they would realise the truth.

Fairfax questioned Winstanley more closely. Did he and his people oppose the rule of law and the power of magistrates to judge and to punish, surely the basis of any well-organised Commonwealth? Winstanley replied that he was not against anyone who wished to live under such a system but that the Diggers had no need for it. They held in common land, cattle, corn and fruit. They did not buy and sell, and so there was no reason for cheating and for imprisoning or whipping each other. He promised to leave alone landowners' private property and invited any of them to use laws against his followers if they stole or trespassed on their estates. On the other hand, the Diggers' goods 'shall be freely laid open, for the safety and preservation of the Nation'. They wanted everyone to enjoy the benefits of God's creation. Fairfax and his men thought the group strange and misguided, but noted their polite and honest demeanour. Fairfax promised that his soldiers would not harass them and that any offences would be dealt with in the proper way through a court of law.

Winstanley later wrote to the general, thanking him for his 'mildnesse and moderation'. The Diggers had been the subject of false reports and slanders, but all they wanted to do was to cast off oppression. Winstanley also complained about the 'unchristian-like abuse' from some of Fairfax's soldiers, despite the general's promise. Perhaps Fairfax's men harboured a perverse grudge towards the Diggers for having improved 'that victory which you have gotten in the name of the Commons over King Charles'. Surely on these grounds the Diggers should expect the soldiers' protection, wrote Winstanley.

Locals tried to put a halt to the Diggers' activities by going to the hill and trampling the soil. The first serious attack came when some of the Diggers were dragged by a crowd into the church at Walton and beaten. Then over a hundred people led by a freeholder and sheep farmer, John Taylor, charged on to the hill, confiscated spades and imprisoned the Diggers before taking them to a justice at Kingston, who released them. Opponents pulled down a house that the Diggers had put up and destroyed their tools. Winstanley claimed that some of Fairfax's soldiers beat a young boy and stole his clothes; soldiers also dangerously wounded a man and set fire to one of the Diggers' houses. On another occasion some of the Diggers were set upon when fetching wood, suffering the destruction of their cart and the wounding of a horse.

In June 1649 came a particularly fierce assault on four of the Diggers. John Taylor and another local farmer, William Starr, approached on horseback with a group of men dressed in women's clothing. Starr, Taylor and their companions attacked the Diggers with long staves, battering their heads and nearly killing one of them. The Diggers did not resist the blows, being willing to give up their lives to God, claimed Winstanley. The attackers left them for dead on the ground, but three of the men managed to get up and put the fourth man, who was fighting for his life, into a cart and took him home.

Winstanley published a pamphlet condemning the 'bloudie and unchristian acting' of Starr and Taylor, which with its use of cross-dressing had been designed to humiliate as well as terrify the Diggers. Winstanley said that the attack proved the rightness of the Diggers' cause: the fury of the freeholders showed that, just as their forefathers had gained their lands by violence and theft, so they kept it by the same means.

As well as suffering physical violence, the Diggers ended up in trouble with the law. In July Winstanley and some of his men appeared before a court in Kingston. According to Winstanley's account, the court would not let them plead their own case nor elaborate on the charges unless they hired a lawyer. They refused, because to do so would make them complicit with the Norman tyranny under which the Conqueror made laws in French and appointed his own legal officers to interpret them, which meant having to deal with untrustworthy lawyers who upheld laws that protect the rich and crush the poor. Forced into silence, Winstanley brought a written statement to the court, challenging his accusers to bring a rational objection to the Diggers' activities and charging the court with supporting tyranny even though the king was dead and England a Commonwealth.

As a result of the case, one of Winstanley's men was put in prison for three days and the court tried to imprison another of them, a shoemaker, who according to Winstanley was 'a poore man not worth ten pounds'. The court bailiffs drove away four cows that Winstanley was tending to in his work as a grazier and hit them with clubs. Strangers rescued the animals and brought them back to Winstanley; it grieved him to see the poor creatures with their heads and bodies all swollen.

The violence and legal cases took their toll on Winstanley's community and in August the Diggers left St George's Hill and moved eastwards to common land at Little Heath in Cobham. At first they encountered less hostility than they had on the hill. When opposition did arrive it came from the local gentry, who were alarmed at the possibility of losing their titles and privileges if the Diggers succeeded. A leading opponent was John Platt, the rector of a parish close to Cobham, a Puritan and supporter of the Parliamentary cause. Through marriage Platt was lord of the manor of Cobham and considered the Diggers' occupation of the heath a serious infringement on his rights. In October the Diggers were again reported to the authorities and further court cases were brought against them at Kingston. Platt used the Diggers' own language against them, calling them oppressors and tyrants, and even accused them of wanting to start a new war and to bring back the late king's son.

In November Platt and another local lord, Sir Anthony Vincent, led an attack on the Digger colony, accompanied by a group of soldiers that Fairfax had sent at Platt's urging. The two men commanded their tenants to demolish one of the Diggers' houses and they shouted with joy when it came tumbling down, recalled Winstanley. He wrote that Platt had no scruples about turning whole families out into the open on cold nights or instructing the locals not to sell food or give lodgings to the Diggers. Platt and Vincent's men had no choice but to do their masters' bidding for fear of being deprived of their livings and their houses, he claimed. Some even informed on others who showed signs of being sympathetic to the Diggers, sowing fear among the poor. Platt and Vincent gave their men a few shillings to buy drink and the men smiled and bowed to their masters, reported Winstanley.

The Diggers remained steadfast and cheerful in the face of violence, even preaching the gospel to their attackers as they carried out their destruction. The Diggers built themselves little hutches on the heath, like the wooden calf-cribs used to shelter cattle in the winter. There they lay joyfully at night, said Winstanley. 'In Cobham on the little Heath our digging there goes on. And all our friends they live in love, as if they were but one,' he wrote.

But by the spring of 1650 the colony was struggling to survive. Consequently, two Diggers carrying a letter from Winstanley were sent on a fundraising mission to towns around London – Hounslow, Harrow-on-the-Hill, Watford, Windsor, Putney – as well as places further afield that were known to contain sympathisers or that even had Digger colonies of their own; the pair were arrested at Wellingborough. It was the only time that anything resembling a proselytising mission was undertaken, but it was motivated by the needs of a community in crisis.

In April Winstanley's experiment came to an end when Platt arrived with fifty men to burn down the Diggers' houses. Some of Platt's men suggested expelling the Diggers and using the wood from their dwellings. Platt said no: fire them to the ground so that the Diggers would be unable to rebuild them. The men destroyed the furniture too, ignoring the frightened cries of the women and children, and let the cattle trample on the Diggers' corn – all eleven acres of it – rather than have it put to use during a time of dearth.

By evening, charred wood and the detritus of violent assault lay strewn around the Diggers, who were sleeping out in the open with their families. During the night some of their attackers returned, threatening to kill the Diggers and burn everything they had left if they did not leave. Winstanley's people asked the men why they were being so cruel: because, they answered, the Diggers did not know God and would not come to church.

And so in fire and fury the Diggers' experiment came to an end. Thrown off the land, they kept hold of the inward field of battle, said Winstanley: their hearts were calm and joyful, even loving towards those who destroyed their homes, while Platt's men 'cannot rest for fretting, jearing, rayling, and gnashing their tongues with vexation'. In church, Platt told people to love their enemies while all the time organising his attacks. The work of Digging proved Platt's religion to be mere witchcraft.

'And here I end,' wrote Winstanley, 'having put my Arm as far as my strength will go to advance Righteousnesse: I have Writ, I have Acted, I have Peace: and now I must wait to see the Spirit do his own work in the hearts of others, and whether *England* shall be the first Land, or some, other, wherein Truth shall sit down in triumph.'

Your houses they pull down, stand up now, stand up now, Your houses they pull down, stand up now. Winstanley walked along with a song in his heart. He said to himself: if I cannot get meat, I will feast on bread, milk and cheese; and if they take my cows and my livelihood, then I will make do with bread and beer, til the King of Righteousness brings me justice. He implored that holy King to show his power and to free the people from the terrible bondage that they were under. *Father, do what thou wilt, this cause is thine, and thou knows that the love to righteousnesse makes me do what I do.* As he had these thoughts, his heart was filled with bliss. He felt like a man taking shelter in a state of peace, waiting for a storm to pass overhead.

Gainst lawyers and gainst priests, stand up now, stand up now, Gainst lawyers and gainst priests stand up now.

Through the sacralised acts of digging, sowing and manuring the Diggers imbued their religious mission with a social one and created a prototype of utopia. But, camping on a desolate hill in the depths of winter surrounded by a hostile population, their living conditions must have been grim indeed. Yet Winstanley's band of men, women and children still came to the hill, persuaded that growing crops in unpromising soil would be proof of their godliness. When sleeping under the elements, perhaps they were comforted by Winstanley's words that 'by this Rain, the earth or flesh of man, is filled with fruits of righteousness and truth'.

If the Diggers' social programme had aimed merely to preserve the poor's existing common rights, then their movement would have been a defensive attempt to turn back the clock on the emerging capitalist economy and to create a pre-capitalist utopia. Instead they wanted to bring unused land under cultivation and to share the harvest without buying and selling, so giving a means of living to all. The aim was to live in a state of modest abundance without the desire for unnecessary luxury. Far from being backward-looking, their system would have given people a new set of rights over a greater area of cultivated land, regulated as part of a communal society.

Because of their evident sense of practical purpose, the Diggers represent a watershed in our story. Unlike Thomas More before him, Winstanley intended his utopia to be made real and tried to make it so. More lived before the emergence of the modern belief in humanity as the agent of progress, cleaving to a traditional religious faith which saw humans as morally irredeemable. He took on St Augustine's pessimistic view that humanity was fundamentally tainted by the original sin that had been inherited from Adam as a result of the Fall. Under one interpretation of his thought, More's social imaginings had the aim of cultivating humans' virtue and aiding their salvation through Christ. Through the character of Raphael, he had attacked the covetousness and greed that ran through the bloodstream of the private property-based society, inveighing in particular against the enclosure of land, and maintaining that only the hegemony of common property could act as a corrective. More's utopia was removed from the secular ideal of human perfectibility to which later utopias would become indelibly attached.

Both Winstanley and More saw the defects of their own societies as consequences of a humanity that had fallen into the abyss of pride, but Winstanley believed that humans could be redeemed through the creation of a new form of society. By Winstanley's time, nearly a century and a half after More's *Utopia*, the trend of capitalist development had deepened Britain's commercial economy helped by enclosures and the expansion of privately owned land. The social defects identified by Raphael were therefore carried forward to an era when many of them applied with even greater force but were now seen as removable through human initiative in ways that would have been unimaginable to More. Although not yet subject to the developed notions of progress and human perfectibility that would emerge in the eighteenth century,

Winstanley had been influenced by the rise of science and experimental method, and lived through upheavals that saw a weakening of political and religious hierarchies previously thought to be sacrosanct. All of these would have given him a more tangible sense of the possibilities of human action.

In a time still steeped in religion, Winstanley's worldly optimism was framed using the terminology of scripture reworked to serve his own radical purposes. He used the notion of the Fall as an allegory of the spiritual struggle of individuals in the here and now, and of the injustices of English society since it had borne the burden of the Norman yoke, rather than of the original sin inherited by all humans from Adam. Humans were no longer helpless and doomed on this earth as a result of their moral and spiritual turpitude, their only hope being for redemption in the afterlife. Beginning with millenarian prophecies of a new righteous spiritual dispensation, Winstanley's writings went on to teach that redemption could be brought about by human effort. Fallen humans lived under the curse of private property and wage labour – under the Norman landowners these burdens had become heavier still – but the declaration of the earth as a common treasury would restore what they had lost and bring about spiritual and social regeneration.

What did the Diggers' vision mean for the city beyond the hill, that Babylon, full of knaves and schemers, whose evils had driven Winstanley away? In 1652 appeared Winstanley's final work, *The Law of Freedom in a Platform: Or, True Magistracy Restored*. The title suggests an ambitious intent: to create a model for society that shows in detail how it would be governed. In its title, dedication to Cromwell and specific arguments, the tract has more the feel of a work of political philosophy than his earlier writings of spiritual testimony. In the opening epistle Winstanley says that he had meant to submit his work to Cromwell earlier, but that the upheavals of the times had prevented him from doing so. But, still feeling its truth – like 'fire in my bones' – he gathered his papers together and set down his plan, which he considered to be a challenge to Cromwell.

The people are watching to see what their great general will do, writes Winstanley. Cromwell has thrown out the Norman oppressors, but now must give land and liberty to the people, many of whom risked their lives fighting for him. In one of his typically free interpretations of the Bible Winstanley reimagines the story of Jonah, next to whom God caused a gourd to grow to provide shelter from the sun and then sent a worm to eat the plant and make it wither. The gourd is England's commoners, the gourd's root the heart of the nation 'groaning under Kingly Bondage' and the worm the unhappiness of the people at the broken promises of their rulers. Parliament is the father of the land, but has been turned away from its children 'by the Covetousness and Cheats of Kingly Government'. The worm needs to be killed by finally ending the oppression that is still upheld by the clergy, the lawyers and the lords. If not, then Cromwell dishonours himself by taking away the king's power while preserving tyranny.

Winstanley's perfect society is to be founded on the principles that the Diggers had demonstrated practically in their occupation of the commons: the use of the earth as a common resource without the need for buying and selling. A more complex society – that of a righteous city – depends on a system of laws and government. When the officers of the state satisfy the people the city rejoices, but if they become greedy and stop folk freely enjoying the fruits of the earth, then the city despairs. The people should choose its officials and re-elect them regularly, because 'if water stand long, it corrupts; whereas running water keeps sweet'. Laws would have to be short and clear so that everyone can understand them, not just lawyers. All families must keep tools for digging and sowing and contribute to planting and harvesting; there would be rules against idleness.

Winstanley's stress on law in this, his final utopian statement, is a shift in emphasis from his earlier vision of a better world brought about by spiritually righteous men and women carrying out God's plan. He had said that his community would have no need for laws and punishments because their hearts contained the righteous Law. 'Let not people send their children to those Nurseries of Covetousness, *the Innes of Court*,' he had written. In contrast to this initial anarchistic vision he now imagines a whole legal and political machinery. Moreover, law-breaking would be punished by imprisonment, whipping and execution: those caught buying and selling would be put to death, and those calling the earth 'his', not 'ours', would be made to sit on a stool with their crimes written on their foreheads. It may be that the intrusion of these worldlier concerns came out of his attempt to construct a real community, which had demonstrated to him the persistence of humans' laziness and deceit. Perhaps his attacks on the Ranters in his midst, who he said followed a creed that encouraged idleness and selfishness, signalled a deeper disappointment at the human failings that bedevil attempts to create a perfect community. Therefore, when applying the social template that he had tried out on the hill to the bigger entity of a city or nation, there would need to be compromises through the introduction of laws to limit the effect of humans' moral imperfections, these arising from the ignorance that conceals the original law of righteousness buried in the heart of every person. Expressed in religious terms, this is a portent of the dilemma faced by so many later social visionaries when utopian theory runs up against the blemishes of human character in practice. In another sense, however, it is evidence of Winstanley's evolution towards the confident world view of secular utopians closer to our own times, who believe that the purposeful construction of new kinds of institutions is the route to human freedom.

The radical elements of the English revolution in which Winstanley played such a singular role failed to remake London and the nation. Winstanley's endeavours in Surrey – and smaller digging actions that were undertaken around London, such as at Enfield and Barnet – were in the end fleeting experiments. Radicals' eventual disillusionment with Cromwell for failing to deliver the promise of the revolution was confirmed in 1653 by his dissolution of the Barebones Parliament which had been dominated by godly Members. Radicals failed to wrest control of London government from the traditional oligarchy of the city livery companies. After the monarchy was restored dissatisfaction with the king would build up again, but the Glorious Revolution of 1688 would not do away with the Crown, placing it instead under the authority of Parliament in the service of a financial revolution that would make London into the world's greatest capitalist city.

After the end of the digging experiment there are only a few glimpses of Winstanley as he went back to an ordinary life. One brief, but highly slanted account of his later activities comes from the Ranter Laurence Clarkson, who accused Winstanley of being self-serving and deceitful, having made 'a most shameful retreat from George's Hill ... to become a real Tithe-gatherer of propriety'; in short, Winstanley was a radical who was quick to sell out. Clarkson's condemnation is vituperative and unjust, probably because his group had a history of ill feeling with the Diggers; but the claim that Winstanley returned to a life of conventionality has to be conceded. Shorn of its bitter censoriousness, Clarkson's criticism raises tantalising questions about Winstanley's later motives after the end of his utopian experiment.

'And now my health and estate is decayed, and I grow in age,' wrote Winstanley after he left the commons, 'I must either beg or work for day wages, which I was never brought up to for another'. Despite his claim of poverty, Winstanley appears to have returned to a life of social respectability and relative financial stability. For a few years he remained in Cobham and held various civic posts, including that of churchwarden and overseer of the poor, and even as a chief constable for a region in Surrey. An inheritance of property from his father-in-law strengthened Winstanley's standing, and in certain legal cases of the 1660s that he was involved in he was referred to as a gentleman.

After his wife died he remarried, and by the mid-1670s he was back in London living at St Giles in the Fields to the west of the city walls. Operating as a corn dealer, Winstanley occupied a large house close to fashionable Bloomsbury Square. He began and ended as a trader – in cloth, then corn – his early and later life spent as an unremarkable cog in London's commercial machinery. In between, as the poles of power looked as if they might be forever reversed, he flared brightly with fervent utopian energy until conventional power reasserted itself and he was absorbed back into the respectable mainstream of the giant city in which he began his career.

Unlike many utopians who proclaim their schemes of betterment until the day they die, it is striking that Winstanley not only gave up his agitation, but, in becoming a parish official, a constable and finally a corn trader, allowed himself to be embraced by the very powers that he had agitated against. His enemies might call him a hypocrite (a critic of our own time describes him as having had 'a mid-life crisis of epic proportions'), but firm statements about his motives on his return to London can only amount to the flimsiest of speculation. Perhaps Winstanley returned to normal life having decided that power was too entrenched to be overturned, and simply took up the only viable living open to him. Perhaps his apparent affiliation in later life with the London Quakers, an emerging movement whose beliefs had much in common with his own religious ideas, provided a means for him to continue his spiritual enquiries without having to publish or gather followers and risk attracting unwelcome attention from the authorities. Perhaps by finally connecting inward spiritual yearning with outward action he reached an inner contentment that allowed silence and political quiescence – 'I have Writ, I have Acted, I have Peace' – but it is impossible to know for sure. Winstanley is silent as London moves out of the war years and through the epochal events of the 1660s: the return of the monarchy, the Great Plague and the Great Fire. The arc of Winstanley's life traced the larger movement of political conflict, revolution and Restoration; perhaps we should not require of our visionaries a scrupulous constancy of thought and action, especially through such vast reorderings.

As Winstanley returned to a respectable life, some of his former associates continued to be outlets for echoes of the old zeal. After the Restoration, an old Digger comrade of Winstanley's appeared in court for refusing to help a constable break up a meeting of Quakers. Giles Calvert carried on with his seditious publishing and was imprisoned several times under both Cromwell and the restored monarchy. During these years even Winstanley's nemesis, Parson Platt, was getting into trouble for sheltering nonconformists and was dismissed from his post for refusing to read the Book of Common Prayer.

Winstanley's former fellow Digger leader William Everard, who had drifted away from the group soon after his appearance before Fairfax at Whitehall, later turned up at the Berkshire home of a religious visionary to whom his spirit appeared at night along with that of a giant and a dragon. In late 1650 he was seen in London 'in frantick posture' and was imprisoned at Bridewell by the River Fleet. Manacled and lashed for his unruly behaviour and subversive rantings, he was eventually sent to Bethlem Hospital at Bishopsgate.

In Coleman Street, Civil War-era revolutionary radicalism had a dramatic denouement in an insurrection carried out by a cooper, Thomas Venner, and his band of Fifth Monarchists. During the 1650s Venner and his men met in Swan Alley off Coleman Street and imagined the creation of a godly theocratic government. In January 1661 the men launched a dusk sortie from their meeting house into the city, briefly capturing St Paul's. After a series of street battles with troops over several days during which the rebels took up defensive positions in various taverns, Venner's men were killed or captured. Venner was executed in front of his Swan Alley meeting house; the authorities then demolished the premises.

The utopian and revolutionary ferment of London's Civil War years pass behind the watersheds of Restoration and fire, significant though arbitrary markers that count off the epochs, but through the words and stories left behind transmit the impulses of one era invisibly into the next, ready to re-emerge in later city visionaries and in the yearnings of new bands of seekers. But for now, London's immune system pushed out the taint of communitarian revolution, at least on the surface of things – in the city's streets and pageantry – and restored the circuits of money and trade.

And so to May 1660, another procession and another crowning: Charles II enters London with 20,000 soldiers who escort him across London Bridge and into the city to the sounds of ringing bells and shouts of joy. In the streets, the city's aldermen are on display in their liveries and gold chains. The diarist John Evelyn stands watching the procession and thanks God for the Restoration of the king, 'done . . . by that very army which rebelled against him' – and, he might have added, by the very city.

In 1666 Calvert's shop burned down in the Great Fire, as did the Puritan nest of Coleman Street. One evening in 1668 Samuel Pepys is on his way home from the theatre and realises that his coachman has strayed from the route along the city walls into the charred ruins of Coleman Street. Once teeming with godly zealots and conspirators, the place is silent and abandoned. With the dazzle of the playhouse fresh in his mind, the emptiness unnerves him and he worries that the coachman might have brought him there to do him a mischief. He makes it home and back to the bustle of business, friends and entertainment – to the triumphant whirl of Restoration London.

Like the trenches and earthworks that temporarily encircled London, Winstanley's fields and furrows disappeared once the world righted itself. He leaves behind only the results of the sifting and shovelling of words during the freezing hours at his desk, the digging on the page that reordered symbols as he infused the stories of scripture with the yearnings of seventeenth-century revolutionary London. All he leaves is words, words that attack words themselves: the elegant, deceiving words of priests and finally even his own words, which were pointless, he said, without deeds. He leaves, then, the fruits of his pen, powerful incantations that unchain the 'rebel passions', putting words to death and giving life to a new world of action.

Chapter Four

Full Bellies, Fools!

A coin spins through the air, glints for a moment, then falls into shadow before landing on the dirt in the middle of a narrow alley in the district of Holborn, just to the west of the boundary of London's old city walls. The lane, Little Turnstile, is one of several byways that lead off the busy trading artery of High Holborn at their north entrances. It was once nothing more than a cut-through with a turnstile to prevent cattle from straying on to the main road from the fields lying to the south; by the time of the coin's flight – the last decade of the eighteenth century – the alley is full of grocers, shoemakers and sellers of second-hand clothes, a fragment of the larger city that has by this time become the nerve centre of world capitalism and empire.

A passer-by of the time, making for the road or seeking out an onion or a hat, might be briefly detained by the gleaming motion that catches his eye as he hurries along the dog-leg alley. He might stop, pick up the coin and turn it over in the palm of his hand, have a moment of bafflement, then of recognition. The man might well come from the bottom of London's dangerously strained social hierarchy, scraping by as a porter or a street hawker, perhaps occasionally as a pickpocket, and as he examines the coin more closely he feels a little thrill of triumph. In his palm lies an ordinary farthing, an emblem of British power and wealth, but it has been tampered with – vandalised, in fact. Into the metal, across the head of the king, have been stamped the words YOU ROGUES and on the reverse, over Britannia with her shield and trident held aloft, YOU FOOLS. Our finder glances around and delightedly secretes the coin inside his coat before continuing with his errand.

Countermarked coins, Thomas Spence

More doctored coins land in the alley, proclaiming: NO STARVATION – FAT BAIRNS, WAR OR LAND – YOU ROGUES, PEACE FOREVER – LIBERTY FOREVER. They come from a shop in which lurks the money vandal, a short man in shabby clothes, rather feeble-looking because of a stroke of palsy from which he has never quite recovered. A profile struck on to one of his coins shows him rather sour-faced, with a heavy, frowning brow and pursed lips, a study in high-minded obduracy; some of his acquaintances do indeed think of him as an inflexible, cantankerous man. This is Thomas Spence: bookseller, coin dealer, lexicographer and Georgian London's fiery utopian of the streets. His small establishment, the Hive of Liberty, is one of the city's backstreet bookshops, offering mystical chapbooks, astrological almanacs and unorthodox religious and philosophical tracts. Inside Spence's shop, strange-sounding verses are written along the walls, some of them declarations to the effect that no amount of threats will curtail his important work; all around, thousands of metal tokens are piled up in heaps. Spence occasionally spins a coin into the alleyway, then turns to arrange the revolutionary political pamphlets that he has on sale. Another time he might be found talking with a customer in his broad Newcastle burr about his London forebear, Thomas More, and the bracing ideals of his more famous contemporary, Thomas Paine – and why his own are better.

Spence has twenty or so word stamps which can be applied to coins in any combination as a kind of radical slogan generator. Armed with them, he is a one-man propaganda machine: he imprints revolutionary, occasionally seditious formulas into the coins and flings them on to the streets, sometimes into crowds on their way to watch public executions. Baldly listed, the stamps are a compact catalogue of the elements that form his criticism of the society around him and his vision for the future: &, AND, BLESSING, EVERY, FAT BAIRNS, FOR EVER, FULL BELLIES, IN, IS, LAND, LANDLORDS, LIBERTY, NO, OR, OURS, PAROCHIAL, PARTNERSHIP, PEACE, PLENTY, READ, SMALL FARMS, SPENCE'S PLAN, STARVATION, THE, WAR, YOU FOOLS, YOU ROGUES.

Coin punches, Thomas Spence

Spence's coins are not just defaced pennies and farthings that criticise the existing social order; they are also tokens of his own design that evoke a utopian vision of what could be. One shows a group of men under a tree. Three of them dance together while the fourth enjoys a feast. Around the edge are the words 'After the Revolution'. Another bears the words 'Spence's Plan', and on the reverse is a group of cottages, a picture of simple contentment and autonomy: the blessed state in which live the inhabitants of Spence's perfect society.

From the Hive of Liberty Spence summons up, for whoever is willing to listen, a light-filled utopia: Spensonia, 'a country in fairyland', a place of peace and equality where the natural rights of all are respected. The source of justice there lies in a mythic origin story devised by Spence: 'A certain man having many sons all bred to a seafaring life, was desirous that they should live together in a just, brotherly and social manner.' The man presents his sons with a ship equipped with the best materials and the provisions necessary for a long voyage. He tells his sons that they and their descendants can explore the oceans as they wish, but that they must treat the gift given to them as common property. They will be equal owners and share the profits of their voyages; there can be no 'unjust and unbrotherly grudging'.

In between voyages the mariners live on land, but soon become dissatisfied with the society they find there, very much imperfect compared to their little marine republic, their fleet of justly governed ships bobbing up and down in an ever-shifting world of light, wind and haze. Spence's mariners, connected to but estranged from landed human society, set sail and glimpse a better life in the ambiguous, elusive seascape. This liminal world of fog and spray represents, perhaps, the utopian imagination: a symbol of alienation from the solid present, it pulls us towards an enigmatic future but is guided by our cherished social visions – for the mariners, the ethical creed bequeathed to them by their father. Eventually the mariners wash up on an island, build houses from their ship's timber, and cultivate the soil. Spensonia is born when the men apply the ideals of equality and rights, summoned up in the provisional community of the sea, to the solid ground of their new homeland.

An explorer discovers Spensonia and tells of its meadows and pastures 'strewed with fruit', and its corn grown in rows 'as carefully as garden herbs'. The houses show in their outward neatness an interior domestic happiness; they are the dwellings of rational beings.

In various versions of his tale Spence imagines his perfect society perched on the edge of the world; sometimes his visions take him up into the stars. He tells of a dream in which he ascends to a planet and finds that he can see everything that is going on down below. All over the earth there is suffering: the rich are far from happy and the poor are downright miserable; war and conflict are everywhere. With the perspective expanded to the whole globe, spinning in space like a coin flying through the air, Spence invites us to think about how we might make human society revolve on a different axis. (He once published a map, *The World Turned Upside Down*, with the poles reversed, its title taken from a popular ballad from the English revolution, so connecting him to his seventeenth-century utopian forebear Gerrard Winstanley.) In his dream, Spence looks down on earth and sees a man who has the power to reinvent. The man reads out his constitution, which sets out the principles for a better society, and the multitude in front of him shouts in acclamation, at which point Spence wakes up: 'Thus am I from being a happy celestial, reduced again to a poor disinherited earth-worm, too much in my senses, and with too exquisite feelings, ever to be happy in such miserable society.'

And so we find ourselves back in London, amid its wealth and its squalor, its possibilities and its sense of confinement. It is a place that embodies like nowhere else the potential for cities to attract the admiration and the loathing of utopians: London in the eighteenth century is a vortex of invention and profit in which the future comes to life but the weakest perish.

Spence's district of Holborn is a decidedly mixed area, and a zone of transition in this city of extremes. The ancient name 'Holebourne' came from 'bourne', a stream, which ran in a hollow; the word could also mean a boundary. The stream later became known as the River Fleet and it divided Holborn from the old City of London, which lay to the east beyond the river valley; so the name Holborn evokes the in-between status of the neighbourhood.

The south end of Little Turnstile leads on to Lincoln's Inn Fields, a site of privilege and of disadvantage. Grand houses line the square; the celebrated architect Sir John Soane lives in one on the north side. On the east side are the ancient Inns of Court, a way into the law for well-connected young men. But the fields have long been the haunt of vagrants and beggars too: earlier in the century the dramatist John Gay warned unsuspecting walkers about the thieves lurking there whose 'crutch which late compassion moved shall wound thy bleeding head, and fell thee to the ground'. To the north, High Holborn connects the City, London's ever-beating mercantile heart, with the emerging West End strung out along Oxford Street, north of the royal court at St James's, and the government district of Westminster. Heading north out of the alley, our coin finder would in a matter of minutes arrive at one of the grand new London squares, the invention of the aristocratic landlords and speculative builders such as Nicholas Barbon who have made the city's land and property into a means for quick moneymaking through shrewd land purchasing, housebuilding and leasing. The Duke of Bedford's estate, a little to the west, is one of the most ambitious developments. It includes Bedford House, where the household is attended by dozens of servants and lavish balls are held, and the elegant Bedford Square. Late in the century the estate sees rapid rises in rents and property values. The Bedford Estate and similar ones around the city built fortunes for their owners.

In 1780, a few years before Spence arrived in the city, Holborn was at the centre of the Gordon Riots. Instigated by the Protestant agitator Lord George Gordon, the unrest began as an anti-Catholic protest and quickly turned into a vehicle for expression of the social and economic grievances of the London poor. A crowd attacked the house of the Lord Chief Justice on Bloomsbury Square and set fire to a Holborn distillery, filling the sky with flames and the gutters with burning spirit. William Blake was present when the people set upon and destroyed the hated Newgate Prison.

Eighteenth-century Holborn, therefore, was a microcosm of many-layered London, a place of juxtaposition and contrast that reflected an age of elegance but also disorderliness. The latter feature survived into the next century, when Thomas Carlyle noted 'the black vapour brooding over [Holborn], absolutely like fluid ink; and coaches and wains and sheep and oxen and wild people rushing on with bellowing and shrieks and thundering din, as if the earth in general were gone distracted'.

In bygone times, the River Fleet flowed to the Thames through trees and greenery. Then, as London expanded, the river silted up and became a squalid, plague-infested ditch. Early in the eighteenth century, Jonathan Swift described the contents of the waters after a downpour:

Sweepings from butchers' stalls, dung, guts and blood,
Drown'd puppies, stinking sprats, all drench'd in mud,
Dead cats and Turnip tops come tumbling down the flood.

The banks of the ditch and the surrounding streets became a place of disrepute. Parts of the district fell into one of the old Liberties, areas which were free from the City's laws. Trades could be pursued outside of City regulations; hurried marriages were conducted by shady characters for a drink or a bag of tobacco; debtors sheltered there; the unwary could be robbed, murdered even, their bodies dropped through hatches into the ditch.

By the time Spence arrived in London in the late 1780s the problem of the stinking Fleet had been solved by bricking it over, but its legacy lived on as its human squalor was displaced when much of the population around the ditch moved westwards into Holborn. So by the eighteenth century something of an underworld was maturing. Holborn housed transients and outcasts and contained raucous taverns, brothels and 'molly houses' where gay men could meet. On the Strand to the south were pornographers and 'lewd women enough to fill a mighty colony'.

Medieval London had been a jumble of rich and poor living alongside each other, but by Spence's time slums – no-go areas for the wealthy – were growing up in the districts close to Little Turnstile, hastened by the population crowding in from the old City and from the area around the Fleet. Spence, who was born poor and died poor but was never destitute, would have witnessed not far from his shop the struggles of the truly wretched, and this no doubt fed his compassion for society's outcasts and his utopian anger. To the west was the parish of St Giles, which had originally grown up around a leper hospital and by Spence's time was the site of a notorious slum in which was located a lodging house known as Rat's Castle, a haunt of beggars and thieves. Areas like this were the darkest parts of the city's underbelly; to outsiders they were remote, dangerous continents. The novelist Henry Fielding described them as 'a vast wood or forest in which a thief may harbour with as great security as wild beasts do in the deserts of Arabia and Africa'.

In the tangles of lanes and courts lived people who had to sleep half a dozen to a bed in damp cellars full of fumes from cesspits. The unluckiest of them died of starvation. A lamentable case in the 1780s involved a family that lived in a court near the Fleet. On investigating a bad odour, neighbours found four half-starved children whose father had run away locked in with the decomposing body of their mother, who had been dead for over a month.

And yet still people came to the city: from Scotland and Ireland, from Yorkshire, Hampshire and Dorset, and further afield, from Germany, Denmark, France and the colonies. Many of the arrivals crowded into the slums, hoping to find work in the world's biggest market as servants, coal heavers and hawkers. Others came for the city's culture and politics. Spence was one such person, drawn to

London by its ferment of cosmopolitan and revolutionary ideas. It promised a grand arena for his own social visions, imaginings which had become too much for the townsfolk of his native Newcastle. Spence had been born in 1750 on the Quayside, a poor area of Newcastle, to a father who made nets and a mother who sold stockings and who were members of a radical nonconformist sect. He was one of eighteen children and the family were, he recalled, 'in continual embarrassments and difficulties, notwithstanding all our economy and industry', which led him to attribute their hardships to 'the bad system of the world'. Spence's father was only able to provide his sons with a simple education: having them read out the Bible as he worked and then telling him their opinion of what they had read. This, said Spence, instilled in him the habit of critical reflection; no doubt his dissenting religious upbringing did too.

From these humble beginnings he became a schoolmaster, fell in with Newcastle's circle of thinkers and artists and even began to gather a few followers around him. One of his friends was the engraver Thomas Bewick, who remembered him as a cheerful, loyal and sometimes domineering friend. On one occasion Spence became indignant when Bewick would not agree with him on the necessity of social revolution. Spence produced a pair of cudgels and the two men fought. Bewick blackened Spence's thighs and arms, Spence fought dirty and Bewick was forced to give him a good beating.

In 1775 Spence joined the Newcastle Philosophical Society, one of many such associations that had become popular in the eighteenth century and were energised by the new political ideas being disputed during the years of the American revolution. The society required members to deliver a paper that dealt with an important political or social question, and Spence's turn came in November; his chosen question was 'Whether mankind, in society, reap all the advantages from their natural and equal rights of property in land, and liberty, which is that state they possibly might and ought to expect?' For his efforts Spence was expelled from the society, not so much for the radicalism of his answer – the abolition of private land ownership – but because he insisted on spreading about his 'dangerous levelling principles' by hawking them as street pamphlets to be read in public houses. Already, then, Spence was showing his true colours as a troublesome propagandist who was not afraid to annoy respectable society.

By the late 1780s, Spence was in London eking out a living as a labourer and had been plunged into the intellectual tumult of the city. Soon he was promoting the 'Plan' for social salvation described in his Newcastle lecture, publicising it with his coins and in broadsheets and pamphlets, songs, polemics and utopian travellers' tales. He reworked the lecture into a pamphlet, *The Real Rights of Man*, which began with the idea of the state of nature, society's God-given starting point of innocence, a moral blank slate that current social arrangements could be compared with. In the state of nature, the land is the common property of all people; it is the condition enjoyed by animals, who sustain themselves by foraging freely for plants and prey. In human society, however, a few people accumulated more resources than the many, and political and legal systems emerged which protected them; the moral slate became drawn all over, its original form obscured and forgotten.

The overturning of the state of nature had been justified by seventeenth- and eighteenth-century philosophers such as John Locke by appealing to a social contract in which the people were supposed to have agreed to obey a benevolent ruler who would uphold law and order, including the protection of private property. Spence rejected this possibility: if an agreement did exist then it had served merely to justify a state of injustice and therefore had to be cancelled. Every human had an equal right to survive and therefore to earn a living for themselves and their families, said Spence. But as human societies moved away from the state of nature, so humans were deprived of access to the basic requirements of life, in particular to the land. No one would deny a person the air and the heat of the sun that they need to live, so why should they deny another requirement for survival: that of land? The unjust social order was eventually so taken for granted that it came to be seen as completely natural; like Winstanley before him, he railed against the landowners who held the land as if they themselves had created it.

Liberal economics, then emerging through the writings of Adam Smith, justified humans' separation from the state of nature by claiming that the productive benefits of private property in commodities, capital and land had paved the way for a sophisticated economy of agriculture and manufacturing, which is what allowed society to expand and support a larger population. The advantages of private property in time outweighed the loss of rustic freedoms that had been enjoyed by humans when they roamed the forests and oceans.

Spence refused to accept such a trade-off because it involved some people being deprived of their birthright, the absolute right to subsist. Without this, humans, unlike animals, could not claim 'so much as a blade of grass, or a nut or an acorn . . . though to save his life, without the permission of the pretended proprietor'. Landowners were therefore 'usurpers and tyrants'; they held the power, made the laws and could throw people off the land even when it caused great suffering. The result was that people were estranged from the earth and had to pay extravagantly to obtain what they needed to survive.

Spence's plan restored social justice without people having to return to the forest. In *The Real Rights of Man*, Spence imagines that on an appointed day the inhabitants of each parish would form a corporation and assert their rights. Land would become the property of the parish, which could rent it out and would look after it and improve it. The parish could not transfer ownership of the land in any way: such an act would be on a par with selling their children as slaves. Instead of the extortionate rents used to maintain a few ungrateful landlords, the people would pay modest rents to the parish – the only tax levied – which would be used to build and repair the houses and streets, to improve agriculture and to defend the territory from foreign invasion. Any money left over would then be distributed equally among the people.

By becoming members of democratic parishes, people would regain their right to life through the land. An empire of 'right and reason' would be established. When they see the benefits, other nations would be sure to adopt the same system: 'Thus the whole earth shall at last be happy and live like brethren.'

But how could this joyful state emerge out of a hidebound society which, even apart from the unequal distribution of land, contained so many impediments to human happiness? Spence believed that language itself, weighed down by centuries of tradition, had become a tool of oppression. Another part of his efforts, therefore, was an attempt to reform the English language by reinventing its spellings.

While still in Newcastle, Spence had published a sequel to *Robinson Crusoe*, *A Sŭplĭmĭnt too the Hĭstĭre ŏv Rŏbĭnsĭn Kruzo*, 'prĭnted ĭn the kruzone'ĭn m'an'ĭr', which set out a collective vision for a new society opposed to the individualistic one contained in Defoe's original story. The pages of the work at first glance look almost foreign: in a linguistic echo of the tale of utopian transformation contained within them, their new spellings are an uncanny shift into an altered orthographic world, while still rooted in the familiar. When as a young man he began to study, Spence discovered language and politics in a state of anarchy, 'but both of these I have reduced to order: the one by a new alphabet, and the other by a new constitution'. To Spence, the trickiness of the English language – its unphonetic spellings and pronunciation traps – stopped the poor from escaping their slums. For their uneducated speech they were open to ridicule and to being barred from politics and power, while the inconsistencies of English spelling hindered their access to ideas through their own reading and self-education. No doubt Spence, a Northern autodidact without the elegant diction of an eighteenth-century

London man of letters, would have experienced his own linguistic struggles as reflective of his outsider status on the margins of British political life.

The Spencean alphabet

Crusonia, the phonetic alphabet used in Spence's utopia, smoothed out the troublesome snags of the English language by making unambiguous the correct pronunciation of written words. Spence published a dictionary which included a detailed explanation of his new system. It included ordinary words like 'foggy' and 'flute', politically charged ones such as 'copy-hold', which Spence defined as 'a tenure, for which the tenant hath nothing to shew but the copy of the rolls made by the steward of his

Lord's court', and the kind of words that were condemned as barbarous by Samuel Johnson but would have been used in Spence's circle, such as 'bilk' (to cheat).

In the *Sŭplĭmĭnt* Spence assured critics and scholars that their libraries were not in danger from his system, nor were they going to be forced into linguistic consistency. No, said Spence: his aim was simply to 'free the poor . . . from vexatious, tedious and ridiculous absurdities' ('vĕkſathŭs, tedeŭs, and rĭdikĭlĭs Absurdĭtez'). The imperfect English language was a reflection of an imperfect society, but it did not mirror that imperfection passively: the state of the language was a very cause of injustice. By presenting his traveller's tale in a rational, utopian alphabet Spence sought to make it easier for semi-literate people to read it, and created a symbol of the social reinvention achieved in his story by Crusoe's descendants when they rewrote the rules of politics and economics and established utopia.

The Crusonian alphabet has often been viewed as another of Spence's oddities; a near-contemporary of his described the *Sŭplĭmĭnt* as a 'curious' work, and even supportive commentators have downplayed his linguistic efforts. Today, used as we are to widespread literacy, such writings might look like the outpourings of an obsessed mind. Spence's efforts towards linguistic democratisation were, however, radical for the time, even a little dangerous. Hannah More, the evangelical social reformer and a contemporary of Spence, deemed suitable reading matter for labourers' children 'such coarse works as may fit them for servants' and expressed horror at the thought of the poor becoming scholars and critics. In Spence's hands, the finer points of spelling reform, far from being arcane curiosities, form part of a liberatory science of society, a vector for social mobility. Any defender of the status quo who could appreciate what Spence was trying to do would have found in it a threat. And what of the strictly linguistic results of his efforts? Modern linguistic appraisal has judged them a significant achievement: the creation of a workable phonetic alphabet a century before the International Phonetic Alphabet. Spence's spelling system never caught on, but it was part of an Enlightenment-influenced idea that informed all his activities: the belief that the spread of knowledge would lead to a better world.

Spence's vision was an impatient one, a world away from the contemplative utopias of Renaissance thinkers such as Thomas More. Utopia was now located in the sunlit land of progress, then being pictured in ever-greater splendour by European intellectuals. Utopian blueprints such as Spence's represented like never before an urgent grasping at the future; with the idea of progress came the modern utopia of reform and revolution. 'The present is pregnant with the future,' wrote the philosopher Gottfried Leibniz in 1704, and in the centuries that followed social visionaries would ascribe potent new meanings to the connections between the past, the present and the future.

The fountainhead of the philosophy of progress, which helped transform utopian thinking among visionaries like Spence, was the thought of the French Enlightenment. The reformist thinker Abbé de Saint-Pierre reversed the ancient schema of historical degeneration set out by Hesiod. The Golden Age was no longer lost to the past; in future a golden spirit could rise up in real people in a new age of reason. The economist and royal official Anne-Robert-Jacques Turgot expanded Saint-Pierre's ideas into a full theory of historical progress. History was not governed by the external force of providence, but by humans' internal powers, their capacity for reasoning and invention. Although society would experience periods of tumult as well as peace, its underlying direction was unmistakably towards social betterment. No longer was the wisdom of the ancients superior to that of modern people. If progress was real, then, as Voltaire had earlier remarked, it was better to be alive in London or Paris today than in Athens or the Garden of Eden thousands of years ago.

The dramatist Louis-Sébastien Mercier in 1770 published *The Year 2400*, the first utopian tale set in the future. The book was hugely popular – George Washington and Thomas Jefferson both owned copies of it – and it was promptly banned by the French authorities, its evocation of a remade world in contemporary society's own future raising the possibility of a new form of destabilising social critique. The tale placed utopia in a stream of time that led from the compromised now to a better next. Mercier took Leibniz's dictum as his book's epigraph, and the tale that followed – of a Parisian who falls asleep and wakes up in a future Paris which has been transformed into a city of reason and science – pictured for the first time the astonishing world to which the pregnant present could give birth as the future. In Mercier's new city, scientific has replaced classical learning, an emblem of the triumph of modern linear time over ancient cyclical time that his story so powerfully illustrates.

Now wedded to a philosophy of progress, the inhabitants of eighteenth- and nineteenth-century utopias, no longer shipwrecked in time like those on Thomas More's island, would have to gather their shattered hulls, build a fast-moving craft and together sail purposefully into the future. Utopia was to be plunged into the stream of time. It had gone from being a 'no time' to a 'good time': now located in a tangible future, it promised improvement, release and redemption; no longer was it simply a perfect 'speaking picture' for calm contemplation. Like never before, utopia became the expression of unquenchable yearning and action.

Reason and progress could appear, too, in violent upheaval, such as the French Revolution, which, perhaps more than any other, was inspired by the ideal of progress. For the revolutionaries, the attainment of a better future implied that the past and present had to be completely rejected. The revolutionaries' new system of dates with 1792 becoming Year One symbolised the radically renovated present: the force of progress was compressed into a calendrical singularity which would explode into a new future and instantly jettison everything that had come before.

The paragon of the revolutionary theorist of progress was the mathematician and philosopher Nicolas de Condorcet, a member of France's Legislative Assembly and an enthusiastic participant in the revolution. In the hands of Condorcet the doctrine of progress took on the fervour of a religious belief. Progress became a glorious, volcanic energy, something for humanity to be in awe of, to kneel down and worship before, and finally to lend a hand to. In his *Sketch for a Historical Picture of the Progress of the Human Mind* he injected a new sense of urgency into the idea of the perfectibility of humankind which had been expressed by earlier thinkers. No longer was it only science, with its accretion of tangible physical laws, that exhibited a progressive dynamism. Scientific progress took place as part of broader history that was going somewhere definite. Progress was contained within the very essence of history, and history was a science whose laws could be discovered just like those governing a flash of lightning. It would be a short step to treat the study of institutions and government as another science and human society as capable of being remade through reason.

Condorcet postulated a series of epochs through which humanity had progressed, starting from an animal existence all the way to the life of reason and enlightenment. Society had already passed through nine epochs of improvement and was heading inexorably towards the tenth. The coming era would bring the abolition of inequality between people and nations and the perfectibility of human nature itself. Humanity was swimming in an 'ocean of futurity'; nature and chance could no longer limit human hope and attainment. Utopians were now connected to the forward movement of history, the bearers of a message that they urgently needed to broadcast to the world.

To transmit his own utopian message far and wide, Spence takes to the streets of London. Slogans chalked up on walls and coins tossed into crowds trigger epiphanies. One follower, like our pedestrian in Little Turnstile, experiences the thrill of enlightenment in an alley. In a song he tells of how, when wandering down a lane, he sees 'Spence's Plan, wrote up against a wall', then, wanting to find out more, goes to a tavern where 'friend Tommy Spence comes'.

And so of an evening he and other of Spence's men flit along a dim lane in search of an alehouse. Inside they pay their respects to Spence; he enjoys drinking with his fellows and joining in with the utopian songs that he has written. The room is filled with a cross section of the London poor, many of them misfits and outcasts like Spence. There are weavers, tailors, carpenters, navvies, dockworkers, ex-sailors and thieves; perhaps somewhere among them is our finder, fingering his special coin as he joins in a hearty chorus. One disciple has had a chequered career as a printer, paint-colourer, pornographer and blackmailer, and one lives with a prostitute. Another follower is a Jamaican slave descendant, Robert Wedderburn, who will later become a leader of Spence's flock and bring powerful new meanings to Spence's ideas. A lame publican named William Tilly stands up and leads the singing; maybe later the company will hear the powerfully voiced Thomas Porter, stone cutter and alleged pickpocket, still in his white work apron. On the tables in front of the men are scattered pamphlets and broadsides containing Spence's polemics and songs. Soon the room – smoky, beer-splashed, sweat-filled – rocks to full-throttle singing:

> No longer lost in shades of night,
>   Where late in chains we lay!
> The sun arises, and his light
>   Dispels our gloom away.
> No longer blind, and prone to lye
>   In slavery profound,
> But for redress aloud we cry!
>   And tyrants hear the sound.
> The pomp of courts no more engage,
>   The magic spell is broke,
> We hail the bright reforming age!
>   And cast away the yoke.

The men spend the night drinking, chanting, linking hands. Together they find release from the tedium of the workshop and the heft of the barrow. Their tavern is a comradely refuge from an indifferent city, a place where deep yearnings can be celebrated and fortified: it is an enactment, perhaps, of utopia itself.

If the men are nervous about spies, the landlord warns them when strangers appear. But a passing government agent might well fail to detect what is happening inside. Spence's men often sing their verses to the melodies of 'God Save the King' or 'Rule, Britannia' and a passer-by would hear what sounds like patriotic merriment drifting along the lane with no idea that the loyal tunes carry dangerously subversive sentiments.

At one point a flush-faced man stands up, swaying slightly, and roars out a toast: 'May the skin of tyrants be burned into parchment and have the Rights of Man written on it!' Later, as the night deepens, the men melt back into the city to seek out their damp rooms and cellars, restored by the power of bonding song: 'Sing and meet and meet and sing, and your chains will drop off like burnt thread.'

A couple of decades earlier, in 1776, the publication of Thomas Paine's *Common Sense* had lent unstoppable momentum to the cause of American independence. In the early 1790s – around the time that Spence opened the Hive of Liberty – Paine's *Rights of Man* defended the French Revolution and the cause of republicanism. The later work was written in response to Edmund Burke's *Reflections on the Revolution in France*, which had attacked the idea of radical change and abstract rights, arguing that without its noble class and its traditions civilisation would be 'trodden down under the hoofs of a swinish multitude'. Paine's tract was banned and its publisher jailed; Paine himself, having been elected to the French National Convention, was tried in absentia and convicted of seditious libel.

The drama of the revolution and the spirit of Paine roused London's radicals. At the beginning of 1792, the London

Corresponding Society, of which Spence became a member, was founded at the Bell Tavern on the Strand by a shoemaker, Thomas Hardy. A precursor to the working-class movements of the nineteenth century, the society drew its members from the city's tradesmen and shopkeepers, who met to read political literature and to discuss how Britain could be reformed. Around that time Spence began publishing a penny weekly, a periodical of radical and utopian texts, including some of his own; it would have been an important source of ideas for members of the society. In a play on Burke's disparagement of the hog-like masses, the publication was called *Pig's Meat; Or, Lessons for the Swinish Multitude* – but the teachings were deadly serious.

Paine's conviction for sedition was part of a crackdown on radicals by William Pitt's government as Britain and France went to war. At home the authorities launched a propaganda campaign against revolutionary sympathisers, including groups like the London Corresponding Society. In May 1792 the government issued a proclamation to 'prosecute the authors of divers wicked and seditious writings'. In November, with the approval of the government, the magistrate John Reeves, at the Crown and Anchor Tavern on the Strand, established the Association for Preserving Liberty and Property Against Republicans and Levellers, which hunted down politically suspect booksellers, sent spies into the streets and taverns, and fomented panic through such spectacles as the burning of Paine's effigy. It was a dangerous time for loose talk: in 1793 two members of the London Corresponding Society, conversing privately in the New London Coffee House, were arrested and put on trial after being overheard calling the king 'a German hog-butcher'.

Spence was soon caught up in the repression. Around the time that Reeves set up his organisation, Spence obtained a stall on the corner of High Holborn and Chancery Lane, just to the east of his later premises on Little Turnstile. There he sold books and the poor man's tea, saloop, a hot drink made from sassafras. One day soon afterwards he found himself surrounded by a hostile crowd and threatened with ruin if he went on selling Paine's *Rights of Man*; a clergyman said he would have the owner evict Spence from the stall, the threat fitting proof, perhaps, of Spence's claims about the high-handedness of landlords and their supporters.

A little later, Bow Street Runners – members of London's first police force – were sent by Reeves to Spence's stall. On one occasion a pair of them bought a copy of Paine's work, then made Spence shut up shop and bundled him into a coach which they ordered to Bow Street. Spence complained bitterly to his captors – 'prostituted ruffians' – asking whether they really were in supposedly free England rather than despotic Turkey. At Bow Street the magistrate was found to be out having his dinner, so Spence was taken to a nearby public house where he was put under guard. The Runners found on him extracts from Locke, Swift and Pope as well as from the Bible, texts that he was planning to publish in *Pig's Meat*. Spence was jostled and grabbed about the throat, but with more than a touch of hyperbole he claimed that 'since the days of bloody Queen Mary has no prisoner, under the same circumstances, been treated in so violent a manner'.

The magistrate committed Spence to Clerkenwell Prison; the Runners threatened to haul him through the streets in chains unless he paid for a coach to take them there. He had to pay a penny to have a candle in his cell and a shilling for what turned out to be a damp bed, in consequence of which he woke up the following morning feeling rather ill. Jail fees and bail to get him released after a day came to one pound and four shillings, a large sum for a poor man. To compound his misfortune, on returning to his stall he found that someone had pasted notices on the shutters to the effect that 'the owner was confined in gaol for selling seditious books; and they hoped it would be a warning to others'.

On Christmas Eve, the daughter of Spence's landlord delivered a letter ordering him to quit his stall; she told him that several of her father's customers had threatened to take their business elsewhere if he continued to rent to Spence. It was around this time that Spence opened the Hive of Liberty at Little Turnstile. The actions of Reeves and his acolytes must have harmed Spence's business: from his new premises he issued a handbill addressed to 'Friends in General of Free Investigation and the Liberty of the Press', asking for their custom 'having been precipitated into a shop before he was prepared for it', and requesting assistance in meeting the rent.

The London Corresponding Society had tried to foster a cadre of citizen-readers, lowly Londoners who through self-education would help to create a better society. Spence had shared their Enlightenment faith in the power of knowledge. But sustained government repression began to give the lie to the optimistic belief that self-education alone was enough to bring about a new society. As the harassment continued, Spence's visions became dark and violent and a distance opened up between him and less militant London radicals.

In 1792 Spence had suffered arrest for selling Paine's works, but three years later he took Paine to task for the timidity of his proposals. In a 1795 tract, *The End of Oppression*, Spence laid the charges: by championing democracy and the redistribution of wealth while leaving property rights intact, Paine had never got to the root of social evils. A reforming Parliament would have little effect without the abolition of the landed interest. What was needed was for a few thousand 'fellows well armed' to publish a proclamation telling the people to take over the land and burn all the old land documents. If the aristocrats resisted, the revolutionaries would go to war with them. The 'hunger-bitten . . . children of oppression' would revive, the 'frost-bitten earth' unfreeze and singing break out:

> Hark! How the trumpet's sound
>   Proclaims the land around
> The Jubilee!
>   Tells all the poor oppress'd
> No more shall they be cess'd,

> Nor landlords more molest
> Their property.

This opening verse of Spence's triumphal song 'The Commencement of the Millennium', sung to the tune of 'God Save the King', shows the biblical and millenarian elements that became ever more pronounced as Spence's thought turned thundery and prophetic. In it Spence invokes the Mosaic principle of the Jubilee, a fifty-yearly emancipation of slaves and restoration of land and property described in Chapter 25 of the Book of Leviticus, the text of which had been confiscated on his arrest in 1792. These radical biblical influences first acted on Spence during his sectarian religious upbringing in Newcastle. London's millenarian fever further inflamed them. The city teemed with turbulent apocalyptic sects – Muggletonians, Swedenborgians, Southcottians – and all manner of 'Calculators, Mystics, Magnetizers, Prophets and Projectors'. Many of them saw the French Revolution as a divinely ordained upheaval, the first mighty rumble of the millennium – for the faithful, Christ's thousand-year reign on earth, and for utopians, their perfect state of harmony.

In a stormy polemic, *The Rights of Infants*, published in 1797, Spence's anti-landlord message, laced with apocalyptic fervour, is voiced by a defiant woman who conjures up a future world where the landlords are gone: 'Behold their palaces, temples, and towns, mouldering into dust, and affording shelter only to wild beasts; and their boasted, cultivated fields and garden, degenerated into a howling wilderness.' An angry prophet, she curses them to the ends of the earth: 'Hear me! ye oppressors! ye who live sumptuously every day! . . . I say hearken to me! Your horrid tyranny, your infanticide is at an end!'

In a dialogue with a sneering aristocrat, the woman's anger feeds on a particularly maternal grievance: the fact that because the economic system deprives people of their right to subsistence, it prevents mothers from feeding their children. Here she could be the spirit of the dead mother left with her starving children by the Fleet, returned in furious visitation: 'shall we be asked what the Rights of Infants are? . . . As if they had not a right to the milk of our breasts? Nor we a right to any food to make milk of?'

And like the dead woman's faithless husband, men in general, not just landlords, are fit for contempt. They are useless he-brutes who 'sink calmly into apathy respecting their children'. They allow themselves, like asses, to be loaded by landlords with heavy panniers of rents and tithes. Here turning into something of a proto-feminist, Spence, through his interlocutor, says that only women understand what true justice is. Women, not men, will finally throw the panniers on to the ground and cast off oppression. Spence's plan, says the woman, will be carried out by a committee of women 'which we presume our gallant lock-jawed spouses and paramours will at least, for their own interest, not oppose'. If the aristocrats resist, then their blood will be spilled.

Despite these tirades, over the 1790s Spence escaped actual conviction even though he was arrested and held several times. In 1794 he was imprisoned under a charge of high treason. In his cell he wrote a song, 'The Rights of Man for Me' –

And though in black Newgate I did pen this Song
My Theme I've not alter'd you see.
In jail or abroad whatever betide
My Struggles for Freedom shall be . . .

– his utopian call therefore ringing out from the very heart of London's dark power, the rebuilt Newgate jail, which Fielding called 'a prototype of hell'. Spence's arrest in 1794 was part of a new push by the government against radical London. The same year the authorities suspended habeas corpus, which had been intended to prevent detention without trial. A spy reported that as the government closed in, men from Spence's circle gathered in the Hive of Liberty to discuss what to do, but in May the authorities began rounding them up: along with Spence, Thomas

Hardy and other members of the London Corresponding Society were arrested in quick succession. Spence was eventually released in December, having spent seven months in prison without trial.

At the start of the new century, the authorities finally tried and convicted Spence. By then he had spent years hawking about all manner of seditious writings, was suspected of fomenting insurrection in London's taverns and had even allowed an obscure armed group to meet in the Hive of Liberty (in reality a small band of tailors and hatters, infiltrated by a spy, which marched up and down with a single rusty musket and a few broomsticks). Some of his propaganda left no room for ambiguity: coins showed Pitt's face joined with that of a demon over the words 'Even Fellows' and Pitt hanging in a noose with torture instruments scattered on the ground.

The final straw came in 1801, when Spence published writings that again pressed the case for violent revolution. Spence, defending himself at his trial, made an earnest appeal for utopianism itself: 'Are we never to expect a better state of things than the present? Must we be debarred from the pleasures of imagination also?' He then lectured the court about the immense significance of the proceedings: 'For this trial is in fact not my trial but the trial of the rights of the whole species that are alive now, or ever shall live on the face of the earth, to the end of time ... Therefore, Gentlemen, there never was since the creation of the world, a trial of such magnitude.'

The court was unmoved and on 20 June sent Spence to Shrewsbury Prison for a year. On 20 November he wrote from there to a friend, a Mr Panther, a coach maker of Oxford Street, informing him of the scanty prison rations and asking if 'you and a few other friends would send me a trifle to buy if it were but tea and sugar'.

After his release from prison, Spence returned to London and resumed publication of his rebellious tracts – now from premises on Oxford Street – but suffered increasingly from the effects of poverty and ill health. His final years saw him selling pamphlets from a barrow, once at a rally for the reformist politician Sir Francis Burdett, where Spence was spotted talking away about 'his Plan and the Landlords against whom he was inveterate'. He died in 1814, having just published a new periodical, *Giant-Killer or Anti-Landlord*. His followers led his funeral procession up Tottenham Court Road, throwing coins into the crowd and carrying a pair of scales decorated with white ribbons to represent justice and innocence. At the graveside they tossed some of his favourite coins into the coffin. One bore the words IN SOCIETY LIVE FREE LIKE ME alongside a defiant-looking cat; perhaps the wilful creature was Spence's animal alter ego.

Spence's followers tried to keep his ideas alive after he died. By the time of his death the London Corresponding Society, having buckled under the weight of government suppression, had long ceased to operate. Spence, however, was survived by an organisation set up in his name during years of economic distress and Luddite rioting. In 1814, at the Cock Tavern, a leading follower of Spence, Thomas Evans, established the Society of Spencean Philanthropists, new members of which had to swear to abide by the principles of Spenceanism that were 'founded in divine justice'. Spence's name was therefore given to a social religion that just made it into the nineteenth century, the era that would see him sink into obscurity and new political philosophies – liberalism, conservatism, socialism – form the matrix for modern political debates.

During the final years of Spence's life his follower Robert Wedderburn gained greater prominence as an ultra-radical. Wedderburn was born and raised in Jamaica and at sixteen joined the Royal Navy and fought in the American War of Independence. He arrived in London in the late 1770s aged seventeen and fell in with the city's underworld in the slums of St Giles. The rookeries were home to Jews and Irish alongside an emerging community of Black people, many of them former slaves, locally known as the 'St Giles Blackbirds', who lived on their wits as street sellers, musicians, beggars and thieves. In 1780 Wedderburn was present during the Gordon Riots; he may even have taken part in the disturbances. Wedderburn earned a meagre living in the alleys as a tailor, later obtaining a stall off St Martin's Lane where he would patch old clothes and sell seditious pamphlets. Traditional artisans such as tailors were suffering impoverishment as a result of economic competition, and Wedderburn was in addition multiply disadvantaged by race, class and a lack of family connections in the city. Many discharged Black sailors ended up in prison, the asylum or the workhouse. Wedderburn's tailoring skills did not save him from these sorts of adversities, and when times were tough he would return to sea or resort to selling pornography and running brothels, leading to spells in jail.

When walking through Seven Dials in Covent Garden one Sunday, Wedderburn stopped to listen to a Wesleyan street preacher. The man's words made Wedderburn see the terrible moral state into which he had fallen and set him on a path of religious seeking. By the early years of the nineteenth century Wedderburn had become licensed as a Unitarian preacher. He later found his way to the Spenceans. He described himself as 'an oppressed, insulted and degraded African', and wrote that Spence believed 'the earth was given to the children of men, making no difference for colour or character'. Cast adrift in the metropolis and having suffered the traumas of being a slave descendant, Wedderburn must have found acceptance and companionship at the Spencean gatherings.

The miseries of Wedderburn's upbringing would fuel his own utopian visions. He was conceived through the rape of his mother, a Jamaican slave named Rosanna, by her master, a Scottish sugar plantation owner, James Wedderburn. Rosanna railed against her mistreatment and consequently was sold on while pregnant with Robert; as part of the bargain Robert was born free. He was later separated from Rosanna and brought up by his grandmother. As a boy he witnessed his mother and grandmother being beaten by slavers. Years later, Wedderburn wrote that when he thought of these brutalities 'my blood boils in my veins'. Wedderburn's personal history of dispossession, fused with religious radicalism, drove him into London's radical milieu. He wrote: 'I thank my GOD, that through a long life of hardship and adversity, I have ever been free both in mind and body: and have always raised my voice in behalf of my enslaved countrymen!'

In 1817 Wedderburn began a periodical, *The Axe Laid to the Root*, which he sold from his stall and at radical tavern meetings. In it he set out his own utopian vision, a fusion of Spenceanism and abolitionist sentiment full of Enlightenment and revolutionary fervour. He called on the slaves to show their enemies that they were rational beings who could think for themselves and did not need to resort to arms. Through the spread of knowledge about the Spencean system among the oppressed a new free world would be born. But Wedderburn's heart also 'glows with revenge' for the barbarities of the slavers. He hailed the slave uprisings of the West Indies, such as the Haitian Revolution of the 1790s, as potent symbols of Black power. He warned the planters to prepare for a revolt of the slaves, who would use their billhooks as weapons to kill all those connected with slavery and then take over the land.

Wedderburn wrote that the liberated slaves should not try to emulate England, a supposed nation of liberty where the people are in fact oppressed. In England people gave their votes for a meagre dinner or a draught of beer. Those in power 'can make right wrong, or wrong right'. They oppressed their compatriots and justified the theft and sale of Africans. Wedderburn told the freed slaves to institute universal suffrage and as a check on tyranny to change their political representatives annually. They should not use the death penalty or other cruel punishments. They should do away with lawyers and have no rich people in their assembly. He also told them to engrave the alphabet on trees and walls so that the people could obtain knowledge.

In Wedderburn's uprising, the despots to be fought were the slave owners of the colonies – and England's monarchs, landlords and clergy. Their victims were the slaves in the plantations, and those toiling for meagre livings in London's docks, workshops and poorhouses. The hardships of England's factory workers can hardly be compared to the agonies of Black slaves in the colonies, but in Wedderburn's critique both oppressed groups were fodder for a hungry global capitalism centred on London, its tentacles reaching to the Caribbean and to Britain's other colonies. Speaking from the vast imperial metropolis as a member of a persecuted class and race, Wedderburn added a searing condemnation of empire to Spence's agrarian utopian vision. 'Truth is my arrow stained with Africans' blood', he wrote.

In 1818 Wedderburn and Evans set up the Church of Christian Philanthropists in a basement on a Soho lane, Archer Street. Under Evans's leadership, the Spenceans had adopted the format of a dissenting sect, holding meetings in makeshift back-room chapels, partly as a way of avoiding the attentions of the authorities. Following his own spells in prison, Evans hoped to encourage the Spenceans away from the revelry of their earlier tavern gatherings. But Wedderburn did not share Evans's desire for respectability and from his pulpit delivered fiery, theatrical orations of such overt sedition and blasphemy that many of his comrades grew worried about being associated with him. Wedderburn became a descendant of the truculent mechanic preachers of revolutionary Civil War London who wished to turn the world on its axis through politically inflected religious dissent. He had inherited his temper and sense of justice from his mother, Rosanna, he said; he gloried in her rebellious disposition and used it to harangue his audiences without restraint.

Soon Wedderburn quarrelled with Evans and quit the chapel. On leaving he took the benches with him, leading to a fight in the street with his associate. Wedderburn then distributed handbills denouncing Evans as a 'two-faced politician' and inviting supporters to attend a new chapel nearby on Hopkins Street. It would quickly become notorious and attract the attentions of government spies.

Wedderburn's new preaching chamber was an old hay loft with

no seats, reached by a ladder. By then known as the Black Prince, Wedderburn would there extemporise fervent, ribald sermons to crowds of ragged followers, calling for revolution and railing against the British state and the 'fat-gutted' clergy. Wedderburn and his disciples were plebeian jesters, more turbulent and brash versions of Thomas More's beloved fools, who use raillery and parody to shock people out of their complacency. Wedderburn said that he was proud to be called a madman, a traitor, a spirit of the devil. One of his acolytes, a diminutive shoemaker known as the Black Dwarf, would appear in strange costumes: a white top hat, an apron with an oversized pistol, sometimes even in women's clothes. The two of them would engage in a burlesque of ludicrous theological banter, to the yelling and laughter of their audiences. Wedderburn referred to the farts of biblical prophets, called Moses a whoremonger and Jesus 'a bloody fool' for turning the other cheek, the purveyor of a message of Christian humility that is preached by oppressors to keep the oppressed in their place. Wedderburn's loft offered irreverent pantomime and daring revolutionary melodrama.

Hopkins Street was also a place of insurrectionist conspiracy. Wedderburn spoke approvingly of England's seventeenth-century republicans who put their king to death, and days before the Peterloo Massacre, the killing by soldiers of radical demonstrators at St Peter's Fields in Manchester in August 1819, the chapel debated the question: 'Has a slave an inherent right to slay his master who refuses him his liberty?' A government spy witnessed Wedderburn's answer. Britain sends soldiers to the West Indies and Africa to steal Black people whom they bundle into sacks and murder if they resist, Wedderburn told his audience. Who gained from this evil, he asked? It was the rich men in England's Parliament who also turn people into slaves in their factories and use the profits to obtain their power and influence. It did not require a great stretch of the imagination to suppose that the masters Wedderburn referred to in the incendiary title of the debate were those of the British Establishment at home, as well as the planters in the colonies. Within months blood would be shed when England's slaves rose up and killed their masters, Wedderburn foretold, and soon he made plans to bring this about. After Peterloo, Wedderburn urged his followers to start preparing for an uprising. He began drilling them in the hay loft and marching them in formation at Primrose Hill. Weapons were hidden in the house of one of the loft's regulars, and Wedderburn told his people to pull up iron railings to use as weapons.

For these activities Wedderburn was convicted and in May 1820 sent to Dorchester Prison for two years. There he was visited by the reformer and abolitionist William Wilberforce, who most likely attempted to persuade him away from his political radicalism and religious dissent. But in an autobiographical tract, *The Horrors of Slavery*, which he published after being released and dedicated to Wilberforce, he stated that his incarceration had only strengthened the beliefs for which he had been imprisoned. Like Thomas More's Raphael, Wedderburn refused to fit his message to the play at hand. He would never attempt to become respectable, to tone down his bold, bawdy preaching and try to make himself more acceptable to the Establishment. Wedderburn made the pugnacious Spence look almost restrained, just as a century earlier William Everard had Gerrard Winstanley – and both Wedderburn and Everard elicit the charge made by opponents of utopia that its adherents are unhinged and not to be trusted. Wedderburn's defiance also made him a particular target for racist invective. One journalist likened his skin to 'a toad's back' and ridiculed his attempts to become a writer and social critic. A satirical print by George Cruikshank shows Wilberforce and Wedderburn at a dinner of slave abolitionists and Black radicals. Amid a scene of debauchery, Wedderburn is shown preaching from a table while fondling his genitals.

When he married in 1781 Wedderburn could not sign his name on the marriage certificate, nor could he a decade later when he appeared before magistrates under a charge of vagabondage. He eventually managed to master the rudiments of reading and writing

– it is not known if Spence's reformed spellings helped him to do so – and then to publish writings and gather followers. Despite his achievements, made in the face of great obstacles, Wedderburn never presented himself as a paragon of individual self-improvement. He attributed the many misfortunes of his life not to his own failings 'but to the inhumanity of a MAN whom I am compelled to call by the name of FATHER'. If his slave-owning parent is seen as an emblem of an unjust civilisation, then Wedderburn here rejects the Victorian ideal of individual achievement within an unchanged social system in favour of a reconstruction of society that removes oppression and allows people to truly flourish. In this he is a forerunner of the Black Power movements of the twentieth and twenty-first centuries.

Members of Wedderburn's and Evans's circles were involved in a number of high-profile conspiracies which would lead to the end of the Spencean movement. Several of them, including a prominent member of the group, Arthur Thistlewood, were arrested for their part in the Spa Fields Riots in Islington in 1816, an uprising with the aim of seizing the Bank of England and the Tower of London. (In a curious coincidence, Thistlewood was the nephew of a neighbour of James Wedderburn, the planter Thomas Thistlewood, who was notorious for the particularly brutal campaign of rape and torture that he carried out on his slaves.) The following year, Lord Liverpool's government passed an act that outlawed all organisations of Spencean allegiance. Existing before the grand political 'isms' of the nineteenth century, then, Spenceanism may well be the only political creed to have been banned by the government. In February 1820 the Cato Street Conspiracy, which intended to murder the British Cabinet, was foiled. Thistlewood was involved and he and his accomplices were tried and executed, including another Black Londoner who attended Wedderburn's meetings, William Davidson. It is highly probable that Wedderburn would have been involved with the plot and likely been executed had he not been in custody for his rabble-rousing preaching at Hopkins Street when the Cato Street conspirators met.

Radical Spenceanism would not survive these final assaults. Spence's ideas, suppressed and then supplanted by later utopias – the less threatening visions of the cotton spinner Robert Owen, for example – were sent underground to become a subterranean stream that flowed below the political life of nineteenth-century London. What if the Spenceans had succeeded? What if their stories and songs had eventually had their intended effect, sometime in the 1850s, perhaps, when Dickens imagined Holborn in a downpour, 'as if the waters had but newly retired from the face of the earth, and it would not be wonderful to meet a Megalosaurus, forty feet long or so, waddling like an elephantine lizard up Holborn Hill'?

When the waters clear they would perhaps reveal a transformed Lincoln's Inn Square – a sign indicates it as Lĭnkŭnz 'In Skwa – its fences gone and the whole area turned into a cultivated plot of neat cabbage rows, runner beans and orchards. On the breeze, along with the scent of flowers and fruit, one might detect the faint smell of burning. On one side of the square smoulders a bonfire of papers, a heap of defunct land and property deeds; a celebratory coin shows two men saluting it as flames leap into the sky. In the surrounding houses live a mixed collection of residents. The square still has a few of its old-time former landlords. They have kept their plate, jewels and paintings but lost their monopoly over the land. They are now viewed with affection, as harmless eccentrics who spend their days fussing over their orchids and antique manuscripts. Alongside them dwell dozens of artisans – Black and white – who live well in secure accommodation, making shoes, saddles and shawls and eat cheaply from the square's farm.

Although the parish sends delegates to the federal Parliament – now moved to an airier suburban complex away from the corrupting legacy of Westminster – politics is a predominately local activity. People feel this tangibly as they listen, debate and dispute in meetings where they decide together how to make use of the common land and how to spend the rents collected from it. So

Holborn, far from having returned to some mythic primitive state, is in fact a 'little polished Athens', a perfect city within the city, the home of an engaged citizenry who, guaranteed a basic living, together feast on the material and social fruits of London.

Spence, Wedderburn and their followers have been vilified, pitied and finally forgotten. They have been judged as dangerous lunatics deserving of the hangman. They have been called ignorant and gullible. They have been viewed as oddballs, worthy only of mockery.

Even modern historians of the left have tended to reduce the Spenceans. For card-carrying leftists they are a problem: their thought has a socialist tang to it, but came before modern socialism. Leftists have tried to shoehorn Spence into the sweep of socialist thought from Marx to the Russian Revolution and beyond, his work judged as a quirky harbinger of the grand lineage, or dismissed him as lacking the insights of later socialist theorists and therefore something of a historical curiosity. Basically, a bit of a crank.

From the standpoint of the socialist vision of egalitarian, industrial societies guided by an all-powerful government, Spence's back-to-the-land plan seems quaint, primitive even. On the cusp of industrial revolutions that would eventually deliver steel, trains and power grids, in some places overseen by mammoth socialist states, Spence imagined artisans in freshly painted cottages with neat gardens: society on a local, human scale. Where in Spence are the working classes and the capitalists, the conflict between which is, according to socialists, the basic cause of social change? And why does he make so little mention of factories and mines, the sites of exploitation of the labouring classes by the bosses? The charge is that Spence is stuck in the past, that he harked back to Arcadia, which, if it ever existed, has little relevance to the modern world and particularly to a vast city like London. It is the sort of criticism made again and again of utopians: backward-looking, they are in fact purveyors of a seductive nostalgia cast into grand social schemes.

But Spence's Britain was not yet fully industrial. Much of the 'old' economic system – landlords, tenants and artisans – was still in place. A working class in the modern sense was only beginning to emerge. More sympathetic historians have defended Spence against the charge of being naively attached to a rural past. In Spence's time, even in a big city like London, the divide between the rural and the urban was much less sharp than it is today. Many of London's workers were migrants with recent memories of the countryside who felt an attachment to the land. A short stroll from Spence's shop would deliver you on to fields near Tottenham Court Road where London's tradespeople would go duck-hunting, badger-baiting and gather watercress. Cattle were kept in the city, and next to the Bedford Estate was a large farm.

Far from being an abstract yearning for a mythic past, then, the attachment to the land felt by the urban poor sprang from a lived experience and with it came a feeling of apprehension at the loss of autonomy as common land became absorbed into an increasingly commercial economy. The call for a return to the land – then still very much the basis of power and wealth – was a way of influencing the evolution of industrial society. Rather than peddling a myth, it was defending a threatened way of life.

Spence's vision of artisan cottagers living in autonomous parishes, on the face of it localist and rural in orientation, might also seem incongruous in a London at the centre of world capitalism and its trade routes. In his writings there are, however, indications of a more cosmopolitan view. In his utopian travellers' tales Spence takes us to far-off lands, while in their ocean republic of ships his visionary mariners imagine a new world when away from the mother country. Wedderburn makes this pan-colonial outlook more explicit, presenting a vision of liberation of slaves overseas and workers at home, those two classes of oppressed people being the twin sources of wealth for the elites of colonial Britain. Perhaps Wedderburn, a sailor landed in London from a faraway place, could be one of Spence's maritime visionaries. (On land he retained the salty manner of the seaman and had a following among London's sailors.) Wedderburn emerges out of the liminal waves to bring Londoners social visions born of rage at the iniquities of the colonial system. He is a new Raphael come from afar, ready to transmit utopian truths, gained not from having seen the perfect society but having lived in its opposite.

Wearing the lenses of modern theory – liberalism, socialism and so on – we today peer back into times before those theories. History can be as much about our own abstractions as about the elusive textures of the past. Over the nineteenth and twentieth centuries socialist thought accumulated layers of concepts and grew ever more refined: a thing of the academy and of the political sophisticate. Spence and Wedderburn give us a glimpse into a time of political struggle that feels more ideologically innocent, before radical thought had become barnacled with jargon, a world of uninhibited, earthy utopians who made do intellectually, grabbed whatever ideas were available and, punk-like, slapped them together into their own homemade systems, rough-and-ready assemblages good enough to take into the din-filled streets of Soho and Holborn.

Hopkins Street in Soho, where Wedderburn's chapel used to be, is today an unremarkable narrow road located in the middle of one of London's busiest nightlife districts. Wedged between the more celebrated Berwick Street, Broadwick Street and Carnaby Street, with their boutiques, bars and bistros, it is a little-noticed cut-through lined with modern flats and the back entrance of a pub where bar staff take their cigarette breaks. It betrays little of its utopian lineage to those passing through. Wedderburn's uproarious, uninhibited gatherings there excited the disapproval of respectable London and of the authorities; a sign at the entrance to the street now warning against 'anti-social behaviour' is aimed at those engaging in today's purely hedonistic clamour of late-night revels. Just beyond one end of the street, a cluster of original Soho sex shops are a reminder, too, of Wedderburn's often-straitened circumstances, which sometimes led him to earn money from pornography and brothel-keeping.

Sixteenth-century depiction of a once bucolic Bermondsey

London as an old man being led by a child in William Blake's *Jerusalem*

Sir Thomas More, painted by Hans Holbein the Younger

Sixteenth-century map of a rapidly growing London

St George's Hill in the nineteenth century, where two hundred years earlier Gerrard Winstanley set up his utopian colony

Profile of Thomas Spence, Holborn's tavern radical and utopian on one of his protest coins, which reads: '7 months imprisoned for high treason'

'The End of Oppression': one of Spence's coins depicting the initiation of his utopia through the burning of land deeds

Robert Wedderburn, slave descendent and Spencean, who transmitted his own utopian vision from the lanes of Soho

The New Union-Club by George Cruikshank with Wedderburn in the centre

Robert Owen, the socialist colossus of the early nineteenth century, who inspired many of London's utopians

John Goodwyn Barmby, who, with his wife Catherine, imagined a communist utopia of sexual equality

Anna Wheeler, radical feminist utopian and associate of Europe's leading utopian ideologues

James 'Shepherd' Smith, spiritual seeker, Owenite and founder of his own millenarian system of 'universalism'

James Pierrepont Greaves, the sacred socialist and 'sage of Bloomsbury'

Bronson Alcott, the American transcendentalist who inspired the creation of Greaves's community at Ham

Ebenezer Howard, founder of Letchworth Garden City

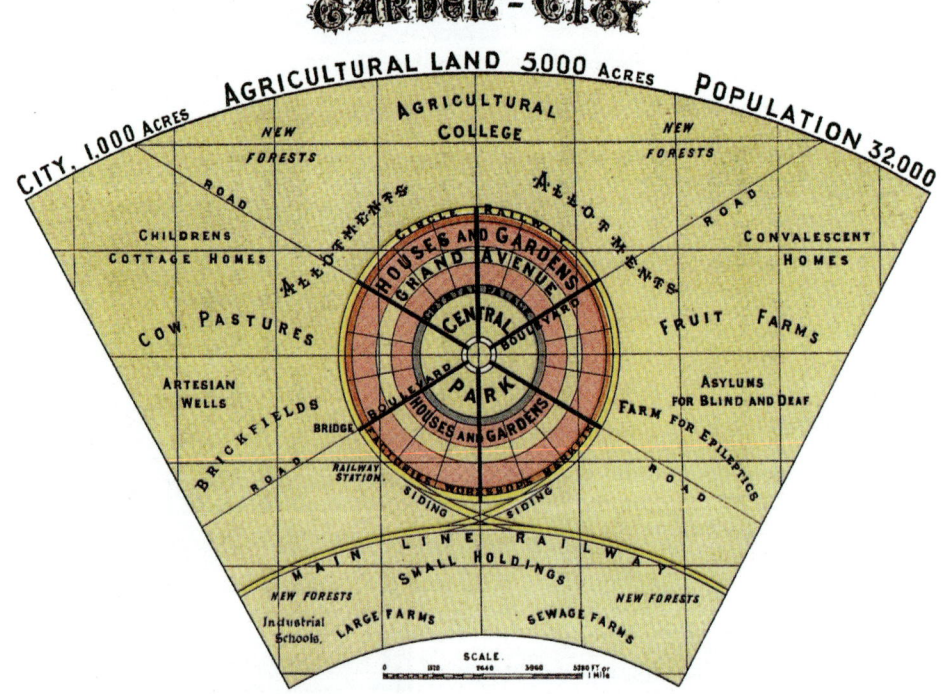

Howard's geometric vision of the garden city

To the east, the district of Holborn, where Spence had his shop, is blander than it was in his time, an area of office blocks containing government departments and accountancy firms. It connects two more celebrated London localities, that of high finance in the City to the east and of consumer capitalism in the gaudy shops of Oxford Street to the west. It therefore still has the quality of a transitionary zone; a recent rebranding exercise centred on the area around Little Turnstile carried out by London's commercial property developers – the city's latter-day Barbons – has embraced the area's intermediate status by attempting to supplant the ancient name Holborn with the insipid 'Midtown'.

The entrance to Little Turnstile, easily missed between the shining façades of a supermarket and a large sandwich chain, takes you into the still-narrow, crooked, shop-lined way – today containing an Italian cafe, a newsagent, a takeaway hatch selling Asian food and the Ship Tavern, which existed in Spence's time – before delivering you under the canopy of Lincoln's Inn Square. Amid all its commercial comings and goings, the area remains a magnet for outcasts and transients. Occasionally, in one of the alleys leading on to the square, one notices a rolled-up sleeping bag wedged behind a bin, and at Little Turnstile's entrance in cyberspace – as photographed in Google Street View – once stood a sentinel with pixelated face, a seller of London's homeless magazine, *The Big Issue*, frozen, like utopia itself, in no place, no time.

In the early 1990s an encampment of homeless people lived on the square, and as a result local residents made the same kind of complaint about lawlessness and violence that John Gay had in the eighteenth century. A new fence and gates were erected which pushed the unwelcome occupants off the land on which they had eked out their marginal existence. To this day, as dusk settles over the square and the denizens of the London School of Economics and the Royal College of Surgeons head off towards the Tube, figures drift along Little Turnstile and other nearby alleys towards the area in front of the Inns of Court where a homeless charity provides food and hot drinks.

What would these men and women, for the most part probably unaware of the utopian past of the streets around their evening van stop, make of Thomas Spence reimagined for today? In a city where land and property prices have made the prospect of secure accommodation for many seem a near impossibility, perhaps they would view him as more creditable than an isolated crank. Today it might seem far-fetched to flesh out Spence's dictum of commonly owned land using an eighteenth-century vision of communities of urban artisans and farmers; the need for Londoners to be able to live without fear of eviction and of being moved on to the next unsafe, extortionate bedsit is certainly not. Spence wanted people to live in 'parishes', coherent localities where they could properly oversee and influence political and civic life, not in impersonal cities and nations; he would want citizens of London to have a real stake in an area of the city small enough with which to feel a proper connection.

Spence anticipated, too, another contemporary anxiety: the privatisation of London's public spaces. Like the development of Georgian London's aristocratic estates as entire systems of streets and squares, today's office and luxury housing projects often remodel whole districts, laying out roads, parks and piazzas among the shiny new buildings. Parts of the Georgian developments were closed off – until the late nineteenth century Bedford Square was protected by gates and lodges – underlining their status as bastions of power and privilege. Today's developers privatise city spaces in more underhand ways: with CCTV and private security firms, by physical means such as the erection of bollards that subtly separate their realm from the regular civic space of the city, and by the imposition of estate policies that remain opaque, but that most likely forbid rolled-up sleeping bags, Spencean-style graffiti and leafleting operations or other kinds of political demonstrations. A more brazen way of excluding people is the installation of spikes, occasionally seen in front of new buildings, to prevent homeless people from bedding down.

Spence and Wedderburn have been largely forgotten – both as

ideologues and as radical residents of London. The office workers and students streaming along High Holborn today are most likely unaware of their radical Georgian forebears who in nearby lanes and taverns once gathered to sing, to plot, to dream. In 1900 the Metropolitan Borough of Holborn was formed – its first mayor was the 11th Duke of Bedford – and it adopted a coat of arms that until the borough's abolition in 1965 paid a kind of unwitting homage to the yearnings that underlay Spence's vision. Below figures of St George, St Giles and St Andrew was an image of the bygone River Holeburne, uncovered and freely flowing, teeming with fish and running through gardens full of flowers and strawberries, bountiful nature made real in the city. It could almost have been a long-lost design for one of Spence's utopian coins – completed with a fervent slogan addressed to all us fools – and then flung angrily into the streets of London.

Chapter Five

The Hive of Dreams

London in the early nineteenth century was a vast market of global merchandise, and a grand emporium of utopian ideas for alternatives to the city's commercial system. It was full of self-declared social oracles propounding their own prophetic systems of history under which a renovated world was about to be born and calendars symbolically set to zero. Their followers could choose from a host of experimental journals and attend gatherings of utopian adherents all around the city. The most ardent of them contributed money to subscriptions for the establishment of real utopian communities. A few would go to live in them.

The American philosopher Ralph Waldo Emerson, who took a close interest in London's social thinkers, wrote teasingly of the piles of pamphlets sent from England that were loading down his desk: 'Educational Circulars, and Communist Apostles' jostled for space with 'Alists; Plans for Syncretic Associations, and Pestalozzian Societies, Self-supporting Institutions, Experimental Normal Schools, Hydropathic and Philosophical Associations, Health Unions and Phalansterian Gazettes, Paradises within the reach of all men, Appeals of Man to Woman, and Necessities of Internal Marriage illustrated by Phrenological Diagrams'.

Our story of London's utopians in the early decades of the century will take in just a few of this profusion of interconnected city visionaries. They were an eclectic group who, while railing against London's capitalist economy, infused utopian rationality with particularly nineteenth-century yearnings. As urged by the

Romantics, many of them embraced human feeling and emotion in the creation of their systems. This often meant not a wholesale rejection of religious faith, but a remoulding of it through the framing of utopias as new social religions that spoke to humans' yearning for spiritual solace and meaning. Many of them sought, too, a transformation of relations between men and women, setting out feminist utopias in which women would be released from the oppressions of the old social order. Like the radicals of Georgian London before them, these visionaries were influenced by intellectual currents from abroad, drawing on French Enlightenment thought and on the ambitious social systems that were being developed by France's utopians.

In these decades, too, there was a mania for the creation of actual utopian communities around the city because, unlike Renaissance utopias, nineteenth-century ones were intended to be put into practice. Utopianism was energised by observable achievements in science, technology and economic production. All advocates of progress – whether socialist or liberal, utopian or otherwise – were enthralled by the new material advancement. Even for utopians opposed to capitalism, imagined societies had to show the same potential for tangible improvement. Rapid economic change made relics of traditional utopian tales of perfect societies to be discovered on faraway islands. These had been useful, perhaps, for the reflections of medieval savants during times when change was slower; utopias of 'calm felicity', their perfect walled cities were a transcendent echo of a world in stasis.

But something different was needed in the frenetic nineteenth-century world that was full of new social tensions and dangerous, agitated cities. As people moved off the land to work in the industrial economy, places such as Manchester and Sheffield were transformed; London grew into a behemoth of a capitalist city. The old utopian image of the pristine shining city, closed off and forever perfect, was now too simple a picture to animate the radical imagination. More practical social dreamers were needed and they attempted the heroic feat of bridging the gap between the world of the imagination and that of a newly turbulent reality.

Less and less, therefore, did utopians rely on tales of fantastical lands – whether on distant islands or in the distant future. Utopian writing began to resemble the political tracts of mainstream Enlightenment thinkers, the apostles of reason who had forged the lines of modern social and political theory. Utopian thinking came to be concerned with the concrete principles and actions that would be needed in order for conscious efforts at social improvement to fall into step with history's march of progress. But even if they relied less on traditional utopian storytelling, these thinkers and doers remained utopians in the breadth and depth of their visions, in the thoroughgoing way in which they reimagined society, and above all in their belief in the perfectibility of humankind.

Spurring London's utopian movements in this period were the economic and social crises caused by industrialisation and, after 1815, by the shock waves of the Napoleonic Wars. England's old Poor Law, which provided relief to the low-waged through payments and the harsh regime of the workhouse, was designed for a traditional rural society in which parishes looked after their own poor. The system could not deal with rising unemployment and poverty in a modern society of cities and factories, and the cost of running it was multiplying. Rapid mechanisation and the end of war-related spending had thrown people out of work, and London filled up with paupers and returning soldiers. As the city was wracked by riots and protests, politicians, reformers and social visionaries applied their minds to England's ills.

The colossus of early-nineteenth-century British utopianism was the Welsh industrialist and philanthropist Robert Owen, whose thought had an influence across Britain, Europe and America. The improvements in working conditions that he introduced at his cotton mill in New Lanark, south of Glasgow, led him to develop ideas about a new form of cooperative society and eventually to turn against capitalism itself. After making his fortune, he devoted himself to publicising his social system and to creating cooperative communities in Britain and abroad. His ideas and practical schemes, first developed outside London, triggered a frenzy of experimentation in the city, drawing in a diverse cast of utopian adventurers, some of whom went on to devise their own social systems.

Owen believed that the root of the nation's ills lay in the industrial system itself. Industrialisation had increased Britain's wealth and helped it to build an empire and to fight its wars, but had harmed human happiness in the process. Industry depended on the toil of the workers, but as competition intensified their position deteriorated compared to what it had been in pre-industrial times. Men, women and young children were sent to work long hours in polluted factories. Commercial success required buying cheap and selling dear and so people tried to deceive each other for gain, undermining the spirit of openness and sincerity on which human happiness depends. Employers looked on workers as the means for making money and workers became angry and resentful. The social tensions that resulted, he believed, had placed the country in great danger.

In August 1817, at packed and stormy public meetings at the City of London Tavern at Bishopsgate, Owen put forward his proposal for the creation of 'villages of unity and mutual co-operation': self-sufficient communities of around a thousand people whose inhabitants would hold property in common. The residents would be housed in a complex of dwellings arranged in a quadrangle, with public buildings taking up the central area, and would grow food and have use of community-owned machines. In attendance at the meeting were some of London's leading political radicals, William Cobbett and Henry Hunt among them, and also exponents of the new science of economics. The radicals objected to Owen's plan because it said nothing about the political rights of the working class for which they were struggling; Cobbett called Owen's proposed villages 'parallelograms of paupers'. The radical Spencean Robert Wedderburn thought that

Owen's plan was in fact a means for the ruling class to corral and control the poor. (A Cruikshank print shows Wedderburn confronting Owen at the meeting, telling him: 'I understand slavery well! My mother was a slave! This would be but an improved system of slavery.') The economists rejected Owen's plan on the grounds that the Poor Law needed to be replaced by measures consistent with the laws of competition, not by a system which completely rejected these principles. The economist Robert Torrens thought Owen 'an interesting enthusiast in whose brain a copulation between vanity and benevolence had engendered madness'. Owen also drew hisses from some of his audience by launching a stinging attack on religion, claiming that it turned people into imbeciles and bigots and made them thoroughly miserable.

Robert Owen's proposed community

Owen's ideas were not completely new, but his formulation of them became well known as a result of an unrelenting propaganda effort backed by his own wealth. (When the newspapers published

Owen's tavern address he bought up 30,000 copies and sent them to influential people all over the country, causing the mail coaches from London to be delayed by twenty minutes.) Owen cultivated influential people, even royalty, at a time when the Establishment was hostile to radical social movements. In an earlier phase of London utopianism Thomas Spence had found himself on the wrong side of the law, and during the years when Owen was promoting his plan Spence's successors were being rounded up and some of them executed.

Political radicals like Henry Hunt were pressing for the reform of Parliament and the voting system; the authorities' attempt to arrest Hunt at a demonstration in Manchester in 1819 led to the Peterloo massacre. In the first half of the nineteenth century, Britain's political convulsions saw the passing of the Great Reform Act of 1832 and the rise of the Chartist movement, which agitated for political rights for the working classes. Owen stayed aloof from these struggles. He believed that changes to the operation of Parliament and voting would not bring about a just society, although this did not stop his working-class followers from participating in political campaigns such as Chartism. Though later becoming a foundation of left-wing thought, Owen's social system contained much that appealed to conservatives. Rooted in traditional philanthropy, his plan rejected revolution and class conflict and by ending distress would remove the motive for uprisings and political reform. Owen's advocacy of paternalistic communities and his repudiation of the commerce of the factory-owning classes contained more than a hint of older traditions of social hierarchy and the moral economy.

Owen took over the Enlightenment idea that social conditions shaped human behaviour and fashioned it into a crude form of environmental determinism, encapsulated in his famous aphorism that people's characters are formed for them not by them. It implied that human betterment had to come from reforms that established the conditions for the flourishing of human virtue and social harmony. Of particular importance was education. At New

Lanark Owen had set up a pioneering school and called it the Institute for the Formation of Character. Owen's central principle meant that a new world would have to come about through social, not individual, action. This was Owen's 'social system' – or 'socialism' as it later became known. Soon after the initial presentation of his plan Owen argued for the creation of communities for all people, not just for the poor. Owen's scheme had expanded into a grander utopian vision that rejected the entire system of competition and private property. It would form the basis for a new kind of society, and Owen declared the day of the City of London Tavern meeting as the most important of his life, when 'bigotry, superstition, and all false religions received their death blow'.

In London, followers of Owen responded to his call for the creation of a new society through the pursuit of many kinds of practical schemes around the city. There were talks and lecture series, cooperative societies and stores, subscriptions for the purchasing of land for the founding of Owenite communities, and in the early 1820s a short-lived community in Finsbury established by a group of printers. Owen's thought was rooted in a sober, secular eighteenth-century rationalism, his writing often plain and unpoetic. But in nineteenth-century London some of his more unconventional followers went on to fashion utopias that were infused with the extravagant romantic and spiritual ideals of their restless era.

One of them was a tempestuous young poet, John Goodwyn Barmby, who early in the 1840s we find on the streets of Holborn attempting to spread a message of human salvation, close to where Thomas Spence once hawked his pamphlets. Barmby is dressed in a black velvet shirt and a cap and has next to him a horse-drawn cart loaded with his writings. A hostile crowd is gathering around him and he looks pale and agitated. A passing acquaintance offers to rescue him from the jeering mob. 'I came out to circulate my papers, but am in no difficulty, and they shan't have them unless they leave off hustling!' Barmby tells him. Suddenly a coppersmith from nearby Shoe Lane dashes at Barmby and snatches a sheaf of papers out of his raised hand. The papers in question were most likely his own visionary writings which told of a new world of human fellowship. Barmby referred to himself as 'the Proto-Shiloh', uniquely placed to deliver this great news. Often with him on these sometimes turbulent journeys through the streets of London was his wife Catherine; together they styled themselves as heroic romantics, united in their quest to spread their message of unity and love.

A few years earlier, in the late 1830s, John Goodwyn Barmby had travelled to London from his native Suffolk – and from conventional radicalism towards a romantic form of utopian thinking. He professed himself to have been a lonely child who found solace in nature and whose 'mind branched as in a faery wildwood . . . Prescient of future worlds'. He was a pariah, laughed at by a brutish society because of his high ideals and sensitivity. And so one day he left home in search of the city. He walked through the countryside for days and nights, eating berries and herbs and sleeping in sheds. He then arrived at London, 'where the fame Of master-bards' illuminated the city, and dazzling aspirations rose within him. Feverish with excitement, he took up his pen and poured out impassioned verse.

To Barmby, London was a place of suffering and discord. Even prosperous people at work at Lombard Street or Change Alley were miserable as they worried about the state of the market, the harvest, their shipment on the high seas. Their commercial gain might be their neighbour's ruin, road to the workhouse or suicide. Barmby dreamed of a new sacred world in which 'murdering trade will cease'.

Barmby became a delegate to the Chartist convention, came into contact with the city's social visionaries and, carrying a letter of introduction from Robert Owen, visited Paris, where he moved among the city's radicals, as a result of which he claimed to have introduced the word 'communism' into English. Back in London he began to cultivate an identity as a utopian visionary. With a

Byronic open-shirt collar, long hair and a thick, sandy beard, he cut an exotic figure in the city's Owenite circles.

Catherine Watkins, his future wife, was already well known as a London Owenite. She had begun attending Owenite lectures as a teenager and was a regular at the Social Institution on John Street, close to Tottenham Court Road in central London, the London headquarters of the Universal Community Society of Rational Religionists – or Rational Society – the organisation of Robert Owen and his followers. Owen rejected conventional religion, but by the 1840s his ideas had evolved into a 'rational social religion' for the Industrial Age whose adherents would gather at Owenite 'Halls of Science', such as the one on John Street. Social sermons took place, as did classes on Owen's system, the singing of Owenite social hymns and even naming ceremonies for newborns. Under the pen name Kate, Watkins wrote articles for the Owenite newspaper, *The New Moral World*, and exhorted her readers to study the Owenites' bible, the *Book of the New Moral World*, in which principles were set out for the regeneration of society.

In one of her articles Catherine had written that she resented the fact that men often shunned intelligent conversation with women, so cutting them off from meaningful involvement with the wider world. When Catherine and John met in 1840, overflowing with high ideals, John no doubt offered the prospect of the new kind of relationship between men and women that Watkins longed for, and they married the following year. Barmby held to a radical view of marriage, placing love above social duty, writing: 'I announce love to be the sacred bond of marriage . . . I affirm that divorce begins when love ends.'

That year Barmby established the Communist Propaganda Society – soon to be renamed the Universal Communitarian Association – which issued tracts from Norton Street, near Portland Place in Marylebone. 'The reign of the critic is over,' declared Barmby, and 'the rule of the poet commences'. He gave lectures at the Workingmen's Hall at Marylebone, calling the place the

Communist Temple. He taught that a new religion of love must be born, an evolution of Christian faith to pantheism and communism; the only hope for society was the creation of communes that would usher in the New Common World. Sometimes his delighted listeners demanded locks of his long hair as keepsakes.

The association's journal, *The Promethean; or Communitarian Apostle*, took its name from Shelley's *Prometheus Unbound*, which imagined the advent of a new Golden Age. Like Shelley's hero who defied Zeus's anger, *The Promethean* would stand up to the tyranny of priests and kings, promised Barmby. In its pages he conjured the era's urgent social ills in heady, agitated prose: 'The spiritual division, the mercantile competition, and total material anarchy of society, have already most gratingly and discordantly struck upon the ears of our wisest and our best. Lutheran insurrection! French revolutionary criticism! both scriptured in red letter type, and with armorial coats on their bindings, have neither of them solved the grand societarian or social problem, a greater problem than only in old Euclid.'

Like many nineteenth-century utopians, Barmby devised his own system of history in the manner of Nicolas de Condorcet, the French Enlightenment theorist of progress. In Barmby's schema history was full of visionary purpose, taking the world through ten stages from the Golden Age of Paradisation through to Barbarisation, Feudality, Municipality and on to Civilisation, the current state, in which competition flourishes aided by a false Christianity, then to Communism, under which all interests will be harmonised under love. Communism would restore men and women to their original wholeness. Every person 'will be an educationalist, a mechanist, and an agriculturist, a lover, a thinker, and a worker'. There would be one common religion, one common government, one common capital, one common language and one common interest. People would live in a marble, crescent-shaped communistery and dine off gold plates in sumptuous halls. Steam cars, airships and balloons would transport them around.

Barmby's Communist Credo, dated Year One, declared faith in community as divine law: 'I believe in community as the law of Love. This is Love, Light and Liberty. This is the Alpha and Omega. Yea! Verily! I believe; I believe.'

As John and Catherine fused their destinies, they saw their millenarian vision of progress as being combined with the higher evolution of male and female energies. Catherine's poem 'The Woman and the Man' spoke of a spiritually transfigured man and woman rising together 'high in the brightness'. John taught that in utopia 'man-power' and 'woman-power', thrown out of balance after humans' Fall from the state of Paradisation, would be fused into 'woman-man-power'. Because love is higher than wisdom, woman-power will be placed above man-power. For a person to be a true communist they must possess both man-power and woman-power: brute force and gentle might. These higher beings, people such as Shelley and Mary Wollstonecraft, are humanity's true saviours; no doubt Catherine and John saw themselves as similarly 'equilibrated' beings.

In 1843 The Barmbys established their utopia in a house at Hanwell on the western fringe of London, close to the River Brent. It was a far-flung corner of the city that was unlikely to have attracted many other social pioneers, but here, close to the Hanwell Lunatic Asylum, the Barmbys formed the Moreville Communitorium, named after London's pioneer utopian. They commented that 'God has decreed the first Asylum for the sane to be situated near the Asylum for the insane . . . in accordance with that Divine Law by which extremes meet.' In *The New Moral World* an advertisement appeared for the Communitorium, where boys and girls were educated 'sentimentally, intellectively and manually'. It was also stated that the establishment sought a gardener, a shoemaker and a young woman for domestic work.

It was to be a short-lived venture. Various fellow residents had not lived up to the canons of the Barmbys' new religion, being apparently too attached to the selfish, individual ways of conventional society. Other communities in the city lasted longer and attracted a greater number of recruits, and barely a year after John and Catherine set up their establishment they left Hanwell, returning to a more central district of London 'to combat Babylon in its stronghold' and renaming their organisation the Communist Church. They continued to pursue the ideal of gender emancipation, but other strands of feminism in the city, more combative and hard-headed than their quixotic imaginings, would trace with greater precision the connection between individualistic capitalism and the oppression of women.

A more trenchant feminism of such a kind was expounded by Anna Wheeler, a thinker who was active in various of the city's utopian circles and acted as a bridge between some of the major European social prophets of the time. Wheeler was a well-connected woman from a Protestant Irish background who had rebelled against her family and struck out on a radical course. In London she came to know the philosophers Jeremy Bentham and James Mill, who propounded utilitarianism, the doctrine that actions should aim at the greatest happiness of the greatest number of people. Wheeler became a well-known radical lecturer and ran a salon in the capital.

Her unorthodox ideas grew out of her abandonment of an unhappy marriage in Ireland. At the age of fifteen Wheeler married a philandering and violent man and quickly bore five or six children, only two of whom survived infancy. She took refuge in deep reading, in particular in the works of Diderot, Condillac and Wollstonecraft which she had sent from London, but was scolded for her intellectualism and perceived inattention to her children. She began corresponding with leading social thinkers of the day, writing to Robert Owen that society denied women their true feelings, requiring them to feign admiration for their husbands, however stupid or unkind.

One blustery night in August 1812 Wheeler left Ireland, taking a boat to Guernsey where her uncle was governor. There she and her two daughters mixed with aristocrats who had fled the French

Revolution. In 1816 she began a peripatetic existence that would see her forge friendships with Europe's social thinkers and develop her own identity as a visionary.

While living in Caen in Normandy she became associated with a group of freethinkers, particularly followers of the French utopian Henri de Saint-Simon. They hailed her as the 'Goddess of Reason' and 'the most gifted woman of the age'. Free from the supervision of men, whether in the form of her husband's oppression or her uncle's benevolence, she became a radical woman, channelling her reading and her unhappy experiences of marriage into her own feminist-inflected utopianism. She clearly found France with its salon culture and politically active women a liberating place to live in and in 1830 wrote that, compared to France, 'the female mind is particularly enslaved in England'.

Following on from the Enlightenment *philosophes*, the French social visionaries whose thought Wheeler was immersed in, provided more detailed schemas of historical progress and utopian emancipation. Saint-Simon foretold that society was about to move out of the current epoch of revolution and war and into a new age of science, industry and human brotherhood. Society would be guided along the path to this new Golden Age by a cadre of experts – engineers, scientists and artists – whose knowledge of social and historical laws would enable them to act in the interest of the community as a whole, rather than of particular social groups. Unlike the *philosophes*, Saint-Simon saw religion as a useful agent for social harmony and so cast utopia as a social religion for the new age. His philosophy of a society acting as one contrasted with the liberal vision of individual action, and his thought contains the roots of the ideas of social engineering and state planning.

In 1823 Wheeler moved to Paris and established a salon which was attended by another French visionary, Charles Fourier. While based on an epic vision of progress, Fourier's version of utopia was something of a reaction to the Enlightenment rationalism that had fed so much utopian thought. Underpinning his utopian society would be the flowering of the human passions rather than reason alone. In the 'phalanstery' – 1,600-strong communities housed in rectangular buildings – people would engage in 'attractive labour', an allocation of work that was in line with their inclinations and abilities and allowed them to switch between different activities as they desired, in contrast to the arrangement of labour under present industrial society in which people carried out numbing, repetitive tasks for their whole lives. Paradoxically, these grand visions of progress often invoked apocalyptic imagery recalling the millenarian religious beliefs that secular utopias were supposed to have supplanted. Fourier's 'system of harmony' was set in a haze of end-of-world imagining, its advent heralded in the appearance of six moons and the transformation of seawater into lemonade.

Wheeler knew well these leading ideologues, once remarking to Owen that he was 'not as irascible as my poor friend, Fourier', and from London writing to Fourier of her efforts to get his ideas better known in England but regretting that every person there was peddling their own utopian system. In Paris she was a conduit between Fourier and the British Owenites and helped Owen to make contacts in France. She had published in Owen's journals the works of followers of Saint-Simon and Fourier and she helped to bring to London a group of Saint-Simonian missionaries, the women among them daringly dressed in bloomers and preaching sexual emancipation.

While discarding the French thinkers' religious urgings, in her own thought Wheeler took on their message of liberation, fusing it with a searing confession of her personal suffering as a result of a male-dominated society. Wheeler once wrote of herself: 'I am a woman and without a master; two causes of disgrace in England.' In 1829 she delivered a lecture at Finsbury Square entitled the 'Rights of Women' and began her talk not by declaring the millennium, but by confiding in her audience that she had been struggling with ill health and 'a mind robbed of much of its energy and elasticity by a deep domestic sorrow'. She admitted that she found it difficult to use moderate language in discussing women's plight. She feared that what she had to say would make men hate her and not do any good, 'seeing as I do, the rottenness of our institutions, and those especially which smell of *rank* injustice, in the disabilities set up against half the human race: WOMAN!' Even so, she found it impossible not to express her indignation at so-called civilised society, which makes women servile to men's will.

Wheeler had earlier developed her feminist and utopian vision through an intellectual partnership with an Owenite economist, William Thompson. An 1825 treatise published under the authorship of Thompson but using ideas arrived at through conversations with Wheeler was a close expression of her views. Wheeler contended that the liberation of women required the broader transformation of society envisioned by utopian thinkers, not only a recognition of women's legal rights. Under the present system of individual competition women would always suffer, even if oppressive laws and customs were abolished, because the burden of child-rearing damages their earning power. Through marriage women have to submit to 'the ignorant selfish propensities of men', are made into 'breeding machines' and excluded from intellectual activity. The unluckiest were, like Wheeler, women of superior talent shackled by marriage to fools or despots. Only under a system of cooperation and common property would there be the possibility of true equality and happiness between men and women; in contrast, the utilitarians' notion of the individual pursuit of happiness was based on too narrow a conception of society and would not bring about real freedom. In a cooperative society, women would no longer have to attach themselves to men for economic reasons and so live in fear of being deserted by them, and men would have to earn women's love, not buy it. In this new kind of society, men and women 'shall salute each other with a real and mutual modesty, founded on mutual benevolence'.

Wheeler's antipathy towards religion brought tensions with some of London's more mystically inclined utopian prophets. One of these was James Elishama ('Shepherd') Smith, a restive young Glaswegian who came under Wheeler's influence in the early 1830s, made a name for himself in London's utopian scene and later quarrelled with Wheeler over the role of religious faith in the creation of a new society. When he arrived in London in 1832 Smith had already been on something of a spiritual odyssey, having followed various millenarian prophets in Scotland and the north of England. During his time with the Christian Israelite sect in Ashton-under-Lyne he had grown his beard and undergone circumcision.

Smith declared London to be a 'monstrous smoke-hole of a place', full of atheists and so vast that one had to walk for hours to get anywhere. He began lecturing around the city, including at the Blackfriars Rotunda in Southwark, to audiences keen on prophetic millenarian sermons. After one of his talks Wheeler introduced herself to Smith. He began attending Wheeler's salon and through her he discovered London's utopian underground of proto-socialists and encountered the doctrines of Owen and others.

By this time Owenism had moved into a new phase in the city. Owen had advocated the replacement of money wages with payment made according to labour-time to ensure that workers earned the full value of their labour. In Owen's 'labour exchanges' artisans traded goods using 'labour notes' allotted according to the amount of labour that had gone into making a product. The aim was to create a more just system of trade that would end the exploitative economy of conventional money and competition, and to use the profits earned to establish cooperative communities. The largest of these exchanges was on Gray's Inn Road, housed in a grand building with a courtyard and gallery and an ornately decorated hall complete with a large organ. Smith was impressed by the sheer scale of the establishment, though disturbed by the popularity of atheism there. The hall would frequently be crowded with people obtaining bread, bacon, butter and meat using labour notes, which for a while were accepted as payment in local shops and theatres.

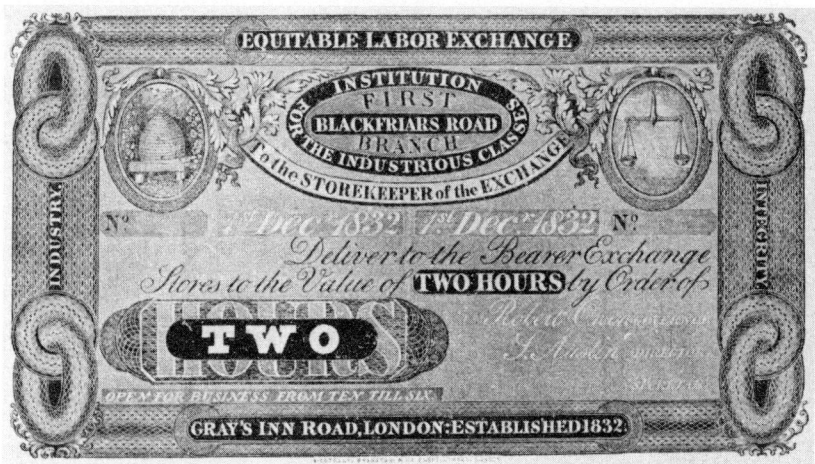

Equitable Labour Exchange note from Robert Owen's
labour exchange at Gray's Inn Road

Smith saw how popular Owenism was with London's working class and how it was being tried out in the city, and thought that Owen's system was soon likely to be adopted more widely. He became active in Owenite circles and rose swiftly up their ranks, in 1833 being appointed the Sunday lecturer at the Owenites' Charlotte Street Institution as well as editor of an Owenite journal, *The Crisis*. But almost as quickly as he had entered the Owenite fold, he left it again. When in 1834 Owen began *The New Moral World* Smith launched his own publication, *The Shepherd*, in which he propounded his system of 'universalism', a synthesis of utopian social ideas and his earlier millenarianism.

By the end of 1834 Smith claimed to have defeated atheism – and to be distributing more copies of his journal than Owen did his. He gave lectures at a Saint-Simonian hall on Castle Street and by the early 1840s was writing for a new journal, the Fourierist *London Phalanx*, which was edited by a disciple of Fourier and a former Owenite, the Irishman Hugh Doherty. Smith wrote openly of his opposition to Owenism owing to its basic rejection of religion, despite some Owenites' adoption of the trappings of religious ritual at their Halls of Science. Owen's notion of the formation of character by circumstances, combined with the claim that he knew the favourable conditions that would lead to social regeneration, turned Owen into the god of his new moral world, claimed Smith. On the basis of a convoluted prophetic arithmetic of his own devising he declared 1840 as year zero of a cleansed world in which Owen's 'infidel Socialism' would be swept away.

In an era in which utopians such as Wheeler were questioning gender relations, Smith preached the coming of a new world animated by the female spirit. Influenced by the Saint-Simonians, he professed the 'Doctrine of the Woman', holding that the second messiah would be a woman who would usher in a millennium created out of a unity of male and female energies. The current era, full of women prophets, was the 'Age of the Bride' and his own millenarian prognostications were part of 'the bisexual or two-fold law of the Eternal'. He believed that heaven would be 'a state in which love between the sexes will be realised and perfected'.

This happy condition did not come to pass in relations between Smith and Wheeler, however, as their friendship eventually broke off in bad feeling. Smith described her as 'one of the most noble women I ever knew' but also 'a confounded Radical'. The problem was with religion, Smith finding fault with Wheeler's secularism, Wheeler at times showing sympathy with Smith's religious yearning but at others attacking it. She would sometimes become angry with him and accuse him of being just like all those other 'men-tyrants and monsters'; during one of their arguments Smith offended her deeply and they never met again.

Along with other seekers of new forms of society, Anna Wheeler and James 'Shepherd' Smith would occasionally call at an address on Burton Street on the northern edge of Bloomsbury where there lived a visionary whose teachings would inspire the creation of one of the most significant and enduring utopian communities of the era. Burton Street was a road of brick and stuccoed houses south of today's Euston Road, closed to traffic at its southern end and nestled in a huddle of crescents and garden squares. At number 49 resided James Pierrepont Greaves, the 'sage of Bloomsbury' who, in the late 1830s and early 1840s, undertook mystical enquiries in his front room with a group of enraptured followers. In the hushed enclave of the street, Greaves taught them to turn away from the squalid metropolis and towards transcendent truths, which he expressed using his own arcane spiritual terminology.

Greaves's Aesthetic Society would gather at his home every Wednesday evening. The sage would sit in an armchair in a grey dressing gown — he was often debilitated by a painful hernia — and declaim with a prophet-like intensity. Described as a 'moral phenomenon', Greaves was a fervent ascetic, subsisting on fruit, vegetables and toast, his frugal diet said to make his spirit burn with greater strength, and one follower thought him to be spiritually superior even to Coleridge. Greaves taught 'the importance of good *being*, rather than *knowing* or *doing*', guiding his followers from the exterior to the interior plane. He proceeded not by logic but through his presence and his glance, magnetising rather than arguing his flock into virtue and truth.

Greaves's aphorisms were intended to still the mind and take the listener beyond the limits of reason. 'The spirit man, or esse man, when Love-natured, will be a Love being, and have a Love organism,' went one of them. His high-flown mode of speech, with its convoluted syntax and mystical neologisms, could trigger instant conversions, as happened to one young convert who recalled first listening to Greaves and then gazing into his eyes: 'You entered, and in a moment you glided, with unobstructed motion, in infinitude.' At other times Greaves was met with incomprehension and mockery, as on one occasion when he attended a philosophy club run by a group of young men at a tavern located not far from his home on Red Lion Square in Holborn. The young philosophers detected a certain wisdom in the sockless, water-drinking sage but were firmly opposed to his hazy mysticism. One of them said that he could not perceive his meaning. 'Very likely,' said Greaves calmly, 'I am with the clouds above, while you remain on earth.' The young man asked if he could come up on to the cloud to see what Greaves saw, but Greaves told him that he could not, because, unlike Greaves, he had 'not been *phenomenized*'. Puzzled, the man asked Greaves what this meant. Greaves explained: 'I am what I am, and it is out of my *Iamity* that I am phenomenized,' to which the room erupted in laughter. In *The New Moral World* the Owenites took a more diplomatic line, praising Greaves's talent and noting that 'It was emphatically to live in a new world to hear him talk', but regretting that his use of language was not always an aid to clarity.

Born in 1777 to a family of London drapers, Greaves spent his childhood at the family shop on Cheapside, yards from where Thomas More grew up. In his early twenties he took charge of the firm and set up another enterprise at Coleman Street, the former stronghold of the city's radical Puritans. In 1810 his business failed because of the trade blockade imposed on Britain by Napoleon. By 1816 he had paid off his creditors, but had to give up all his wealth to do so. This sudden collapse in worldly fortune destroyed his social standing in his respectable mercantile circle. In 1817, the year in which Robert Owen was in London announcing his plan to solve England's social distress, Greaves experienced what he described as 'strong interior visitations ... which withdrew me from the world'.

Greaves's business troubles and his reaction to them has a precedent in the narrative of London's utopians in the travails of an earlier city merchant, Gerrard Winstanley, who also suffered a financial collapse as a result of war that triggered a spiritual rebirth. Winstanley had felt a righteous anger at the iniquities of the commercial system of the city that had ruined him, leading to utopian endeavours that were a repudiation of that system. But in Greaves's case, crisis and spiritual transformation eventually gave way to political quietism. In none of his utterances is there a sign of concrete social critique or of direct engagement with the social and political turmoil that consumed the city in the early decades of the nineteenth century: 'Let us attend far more to what we are doing with the spirit within, than what we are doing with all the world besides without,' he wrote.

Greaves's inner shift at first led him to leave England. For a while he became a disciple at Yverdon of the Swiss educational reformer Johann Pestalozzi, who had been influenced by Rousseau's vision of a naturalistic, child-centred education and sought to develop his pupils' emotional and spiritual being through love. On one occasion Greaves introduced Pestalozzi to a visiting Robert Owen. After teaching posts in Germany, Greaves came back to England and became involved with various educational and philanthropic ventures. These endeavours convinced him that changing people's external circumstances could not transform society. Change had to be internal. This was the kernel of Greaves's mystical system – 'sacred socialism' – which sought to turn its adherents from the pursuit of material progress to inner contemplation.

On returning to London in 1833 he would spend the final decade of his life spreading his message at small gatherings of followers. The district of Bloomsbury where he settled, an area of artists, writers and middle-class professionals, was a different London to that of the mercantile City, where he made his earlier career, and would have offered him new possibilities, his shift westwards symbolising his journey from merchant to mystic. At the time, Greaves's Burton Street neighbourhood was something of a utopian island in the city. In the 1820s an Owenite group, the London Cooperative Society, had premises on the street where they would hold debates on the merits of the cooperative system compared to those of individual competition. For a few years in the 1830s Greaves and Owen were neighbours, Owen having his London headquarters there and living on Crescent Place (now Burton Place) just off Burton Street. In the early 1830s, Saint-Simonian missionaries spread their gospel from the Burton rooms on nearby Burton Crescent, defending themselves against the charge that their experimental social system, along with a community of goods, involved a community of wives.

In September 1837 Greaves wrote from Burton Street to the American philosopher and educationalist Amos Bronson Alcott, a member of the Transcendentalist circle of Emerson and Thoreau in

New England. He had just learned of Alcott's educational philosophy, which drew on Pestalozzi's ideas and advocated a gentle, spiritually centred form of schooling. Greaves believed that Alcott's Temple School in Boston was more advanced than any in England. He sensed a kindred spirit in Alcott and told of the inner shift that had happened to him in 1817. His encounter at a distance with Alcott's work had stirred something up in Greaves and, it seems, kindled a desire to channel his spiritual message into a practical project. As Greaves characteristically put it: 'There is, at present, an obvious appearance of the Love-seed beginning to germinate.'

In 1838 Greaves and his followers established a school and community, Alcott House, in buildings set in gardens and four acres of cultivated land at Ham Common, close to where the Thames bends southwards out of London into Surrey. Enclosed by the river and by Richmond Park, the area had become a retreat for Londoners, and the community represented a withdrawal from the discord of the existing world. It was to be the first step to 'the phalanstery, the republic, and the universal commonwealth'. A few years after its founding the community was renamed the Concordium, enshrining in its name its members' commitment 'to be in concord with the triune universe spirit'. Greaves acted as the spiritual figurehead but remained living at Burton Street while members of the Aesthetic Society ran the community.

At Ham the Concordists followed a regimen worthy of Thomas More's high-minded Utopian islanders: rising at 4 a.m., bathing in cold water and undertaking sessions of gardening, printing and carpentry signalled by the ringing of a bell. During meals of mainly uncooked vegetables and fruit a community member would read out a passage from an improving book, and after their work duties residents attended classes given by teachers imbued with the 'universe-love-spirit'. The Concordists practised temperance, celibacy and hydropathy, the therapeutic use of cold water. Meat-eating, condemned as barbaric and a symbol of the cruelty of the competitive social system, was strictly forbidden. The community's main journal, *The New Age, Concordium Gazette, & Temperance Advocate*, featured articles on 'animal magnetism', homeopathy and clairvoyance. (John Goodwyn Barmby published there details of the slightly laxer dietary rules of his community at Hanwell, which allowed for the cooking of food at certain times of the year.) The clothes of the twenty or so residents of Alcott House – a simple costume of trousers and blouse completed with middle-parted long hair instead of hats – were made by a tailor who communicated with the spirit world and to whom the heavens would open to reveal God.

Apart from advocating the replacement of London's gin shops and oyster rooms with 'fruit rooms', the Concordists said little about how to reimagine the nefarious city spread out before them. Rather than setting out programmes for social reform, they spoke more abstractly of the need for society to be remade in accordance with 'love-instinct-nature'; without unlocking individuals' divine natures, social reform would be futile. Even the greater abundance of goods dreamed of by so many reformers and utopians might keep the mind in a lower form of happiness as material comforts do not aid true 'harmonic' development.

In early 1842 Greaves moved to the Concordium in order to undergo the cold-water cure practised there, but by this time was ailing rapidly. He died in March aged sixty-five with two of his followers by his side, and was buried in the graveyard of Ham's parish church. Despite the loss of its spiritual figurehead, the Concordium would endure for several more years, attracting new recruits as well as curious visitors.

The Ham community became a hub for all manner of utopian seekers and prophets, many of whom, unlike the Concordists, were strongly wedded to the ideal of material advancement. The Concordium's Sunday lecturer in the spring of 1844 was John Adolphus Etzler, a German-American who had come to London to seek support for his system, a work-free technological utopia based on the harnessing of natural powers using burning mirrors, windmills and vast tide-powered pistons.

In *The Paradise Within the Reach of All Men, Without Labour,* by

Powers of Nature and Machinery Etzler projected a state of superabundance within ten years in which people would live until they were 170 years old and in a single year do the work previously done over thousands, swiftly levelling mountains, creating lakes and laying out canals. They would glide across oceans on steam-powered floating islands complete with palaces, gardens and rivers of sun-distilled water.

Both the Owenite *New Moral World* and the Fourierist *London Phalanx* wrote glowingly of Etzler's wonderful machines and the prospects they opened up for humanity. Owen himself inspected a model of Etzler's wave-powered ship that was on display in premises on Cheapside. (Two Etzler enthusiasts, one of them the Fourierist Hugh Doherty, tried out a prototype of the boat on the Thames; it sank, nearly drowning Doherty's companion.) Another supporter lauded Etzler's technological system for delivering paradise so cheaply – for a mere £7,000, the sum needed for just a single tower in the Owenite paradise. But others were scathing of Etzler for assuming the 'omnipotence of machinery' and for basing his designs on erroneous mechanical notions.

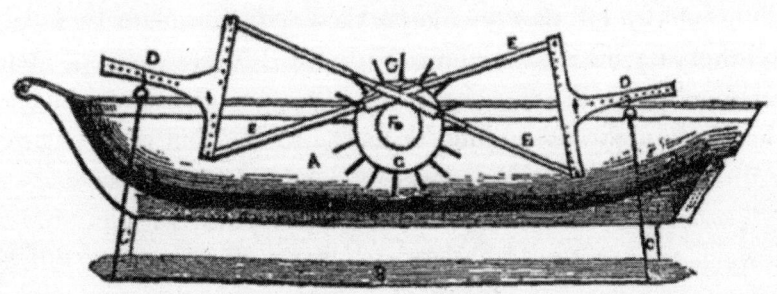

Etzler's 'Naval Automaton'

Despite their very different philosophy, the Concordists seem to have made a friendly audience for Etzler's ideas, the Concordium's press even publishing two of his works. One of these outlined a plan for a community using Etzlerite technology in Venezuela.

The Tropical Emigration Society, which was set up in London, gained a following among the city's artisans and some of the Concordists abandoned the chilly precincts of Ham to join them. But the diehard Concordists were devoted to asceticism and inner improvement, and their support for Etzler's paradise, a 'mechanical Cockayne' of external abundance, must have been qualified at best. They approved of Etzler's system on the grounds that his machines would remove the need for humans to subjugate animals by turning them into beasts of burden, hardly a ringing endorsement of the materialism inherent in Etzler's dazzling technological paradise. And so Etzler's connection with the Concordists was fleeting and by June 1844 he had left Ham for the metropolis downriver.

The Owenites, too, enjoyed friendly relations with the Concordists, even if they also differed from them philosophically. In the summer of 1843, 200 of them made the trip along the Thames in a flotilla of rowing boats led by a barge. With a serenading choir on board, the Owenites glided through Hammersmith and Richmond, past tree-lined banks, swans and villas and later returned to the city in a glorious sunset. On such occasions the Concordists and the Owenites would deliver addresses and the children sing songs. Owen himself was often in attendance. Beneath a tree under a spotless blue sky, he once gave a lecture that likened society to a pool of muddy water which needed to be strained until it was crystal clear. Government spies were present at this particular gathering, and in the House of Lords a leading bishop strongly condemned Owen's speech for denying humans' responsibility for their actions, even for the act of murder.

The Owenites and the Concordists were not afraid of calling attention to their differences, however. The Concordists hoped that the Owenites would adopt a simple diet and that their teachers would promote 'Being elevation'. Owen wrote that the Concordists were mistaken in placing so much emphasis on inner spiritual development. Humans had spent centuries in religious contemplation and the result had been division and misery.

Greaves's notions were 'the result of very materially disordered imaginations' and were likely to disorder the minds of those who adopted them.

In the summer of 1842, the Concordists received an honoured visitor in the person of Bronson Alcott, the American philosopher who had inspired the creation of their community. Alcott was in a precarious financial position and had had to close his educational venture, the Temple School in Boston. Emerson suggested that a trip to England might restore his morale and so Alcott crossed the Atlantic, dreaming of 'planting Edens – fabling of worlds – building kingdoms and men', and on 6 June arrived in London. Greaves, being a native of London, had been able to rise above the familiar circumstances of the city through his transcendent vision, even as he lived in the heart of it. Alcott, an outsider plunged into the metropolis, could hardly ignore these circumstances and took an immediate dislike to London, which seemed to be in opposition to the spiritual vision that he and Greaves had shared.

On his first evening, Alcott contemplated the giant city of 'Beezlebub' from the dome of St Paul's. He imagined the saint and the apostles 'above the din and smoke of the town . . . their sublime inspirations all hardened into dogmas and rituals'. To Alcott, the noble cathedral had been desecrated by the presence of so many statues of the bloodthirsty warriors of the past whom the English revere. People in the streets appeared brutish and cruel, and the city full of strife and unrest. London seemed to him to be solid, substantial and plain, but it was all for the body rather than the spirit and after a few days it was tiring him out. He believed, though, that one day soon 'London . . . shall become the footstool of a nobler race of Kings.' Not everyone he encountered in the city was sympathetic to his vision. During a meeting with Thomas Carlyle, London's literary sage remarked to Alcott that the city around them had been there for thousands of years: why after all this time should London reshape itself according to Alcott's image of it?

It was therefore a relief for Alcott to arrive at the community at Ham, which he found to be a pleasant home from home. Greaves had died a few months before Alcott's arrival in London, but Alcott could sense the man's presence, especially when sitting at the table where Greaves once worked.

London's ossified institutions and spiritual stagnation seemed to restore Alcott's faith in the visionary promise of America, a country which in the nineteenth century was so fertile to the utopian imagination. His renewed energy would lead to his founding of the utopian community of Fruitlands, located among nut trees and streams near the town of Harvard, Massachusetts. When Alcott returned to Concord in September 1842 two founder members of the Ham Concordium went with him, along with Greaves's personal library of a thousand mystical volumes. It was to be a doomed quest for a perfected Greavesian community in America, however: Fruitlands operated for only a matter of months and disbanded in the winter of 1843.

The Concordium survived this minor exodus, continuing for several more years before dissolving in 1848, its decade-long existence making it possibly one of the longest-lasting of London's experimental communities – and more enduring than many famed utopian ventures such as Fruitlands. Towards the end, the Concordium's regime became even harsher. The *New Age* warned that 'He who will not submit to be inwardly disciplined must be put under outward discipline, and drilled into obedience.' One resident wrote that numbers were dwindling because of the unsuitability of most people for such rigour, and in a state of turmoil he too left and went back to the city, wishing to return to his family but in fear of rejoining the old social system that had been the cause of trouble and anxiety for so many.

The period around the dissolution of the Concordium was a watershed in the story of London's utopians more broadly. By the late 1840s, many of the utopian movements of the early part of the century were waning. John Goodwyn Barmby's Communist

Church dissolved a year after the Concordium and Catherine Barmby died in 1853. John survived her and would later become involved in the struggle for women's suffrage. Owenism, too, went into decline from the late 1840s, Owen's Rational Society having been bankrupted by the expense of setting up an ambitiously conceived community in Hampshire. In his final years Owen became a convert to spiritualism and once during a seance believed that he had made contact with the spirit of James Pierrepont Greaves.

The year 1848 was a denouement also for those struggling for broader political change in England and across Europe. Revolutions and uprisings took place on the continent, beginning in France, where King Louis Philippe was overthrown. The events thrilled London's utopians, so many of whom had been inspired by French visionary thought. On hearing the news, John Goodwyn Barmby rushed to Paris and sent back a series of dispatches hailing the uprising and describing the columns of workers building barricades in the streets. Hugh Doherty, the Fourierist who sunk Etzler's boat in the Thames, was present in Paris throughout the revolution, and while there looked after Robert Owen when he arrived in March to expound his social system to the new government. Doherty wrote to Anna Wheeler urging her to come and witness the revolution for herself, telling her of the political clubs which constantly talked of the rights of women, and enclosing in his letter a knot of tricolour that he had worn on the barricades. But by this time Wheeler was suffering from ill health, and she never returned to her beloved France, dying in Camden Town in May 1848.

Order was soon restored after the short-lived uprisings and the convulsions largely passed England by, except that in April of 1848, inspired by the events in Europe, the Chartists held a thousands-strong meeting on Kennington Common in south London. Fearing insurrection, the authorities deployed troops and placed cannon on the roof of the Bank of England. The revolution did not come to pass and Chartism went into decline, its demands for deeper political reform only being realised later. In the decades that followed, England sailed off into a mid-Victorian period of relative calm; for now the nation's divisions were papered over until social and political grievances resurfaced later in the century.

Utopian London moved out of an era dominated by turbulent, millenarian social prophets, each peddling their own extravagant systems of history in the pages of so many short-lived journals. Emerson had criticised them for their grandiosity and shallowness: 'It seems as if these sanguine schemers rushed to the press with every notion that danced before their brain, and clothed it in the most clumsily compounded and terminated words, for want of time to find the right one.' But they spoke to the conscience and entertained noble hopes, and this placed them above most of their contemporaries, judged Emerson.

The utopias that followed later in the century would be as wedded to the cause of progress but more hard-headedly practical and less naive – and have more tangible legacies on the physical fabric of London. Utopianism would mature, and much of the thought of this feverish period of utopian speculation would be forgotten or superseded. The Barmbys' romantic communism, for one, would come to be seen as an eccentric byway in London's utopian lineage. The idea of communism became part of a broader tradition of radicalism through the thought of Karl Marx, whose theories concerned the inevitability of revolution as a result of contradictions in capitalism. This was a quite different understanding to that of John Goodwyn Barmby, whose vision of communism was that of communal living devoid of any revolutionary element.

Owen, Fourier and Saint-Simon, whom Marx and Friedrich Engels bracketed together as 'utopian socialists' and criticised for their neglect of class conflict, nevertheless influenced later utopians and socialists. The young Engels had learned about socialism through the Rational Society in Manchester, and Owen's thought provided some of the ingredients for Marx's later system of scientific socialism. But Marx vehemently denied being a utopian and repudiated Owen's vision of non-revolutionary social transformation.

The advent of mid-Victorian national stability was symbolised in the 1851 Great Exhibition in Hyde Park, the world's largest ever trade show, a celebration of Britain's imperial power and industrial pre-eminence. In a curious incident at the close of this period of London utopianism, one of the wondrous but ill-conceived machines of John Adolphus Etzler appeared in the agricultural gallery of the exhibition, an artefact of the city's earlier febrile utopian scene placed on display in a glittering temple of Victorian bourgeois triumphalism. This brief convergence of ideologies shows the extent to which utopia had become connected to the ideal of material progress. Greaves's followers aside, for most visionaries the concept of utopia had come a long way from the static, timeless utopias of the Renaissance, which had little room for economic advancement. In many nineteenth-century utopias, the purity of self-restraint was sullied in the streaming soot of the industrial machine. Utopians – even those opposed to capitalism – encouraged moral virtue but also embraced progress as the satisfaction of people's temporal wants. Utopia would become a secular philosophy rooted in human desire, delivered in large part through material achievement. From now on, worldly happiness, rather than spiritual transcendence, would be the aim of utopia.

Chapter Six

The Garden in the City

Later in the nineteenth century, on a summer evening in the city, barefoot children dance in a garden, a rare sliver of green in the grey East End. A boy moves awkwardly with a woman in a straw bonnet. He is grubby-handed and street-sassy: 'Never mind, laidy,' he says as they step on each other's toes, 'we *was* going it.' The woman's hands are clean and smooth, and her bonnet is trimmed with a terracotta ribbon to match her cape. Her boot-shod foot hurts the boy's naked toes – and pricks her conscience in turn. The collision of their feet seems to her to be a symbol of the society that she and the boy have to live in, one in which adult wealth so easily tramples on the lives of the most unlucky children.

The woman, Henrietta Octavia Barnett, and her husband Samuel have for years been working in the poorest parts of London. The garden, located in a cluster of dilapidated courts off the Commercial Road in Whitechapel, is a small part of their efforts. A bit of waste ground has been cleared of rubbish, a wall knocked down and a railing put up. Trees have been planted. The Barnetts hope that the small oasis will do something to improve the lives of the local people.

But during that evening in the early 1880s the garden guests overstep the standards of decency expected by high-minded Henrietta and Samuel. As Henrietta and the boy move to the band, a crowd of young couples rush through the gates, jostle the children and cavort around the garden – a 'Bacchanalian scene', as Henrietta put it. Samuel tries talking to the young men,

Henrietta to the women, but their remonstrations are to no avail. There is nothing for it but to stop the music and clear the garden. Henrietta and Samuel make their way home through a throng of angry people. The crowd lob insults and then unleash a hail of stones. Luckily, Henrietta feels safe in her thick bonnet and finds that the crowd's aim is bad. Samuel reflected later that such 'noisy horseplay . . . does not create a desire for another class of pleasures, the enjoyment of which might add so much to the lives of the poor'. This small attempt at expanding the moral horizons of London's poor would later grow into Henrietta's ambitious utopian vision for a new kind of city, and it would come to fruition early in the following century through the building of Hampstead Garden Suburb in London's northern fringe.

Parallel to Henrietta's efforts, a shorthand writer in the law courts and Parliament named Ebenezer Howard is developing his own blueprint for a leafy green city to replace London's slums. Some years after the rumpus in the Barnetts' garden, he sets forth his plan for a city of beauty and light during an evening lecture in an outlying district of London. Outside, a suburb breathes and grows, extending the tentacles of the city out from its original heart towards fields and streams. In front of his audience, intricate diagrams from his lantern slide projector glow on a screen. Pink and green concentric circles light up around a central point from which lines radiate into a surrounding green area divided into squares. The circles are labelled 'Central Park', 'Houses and Gardens' and 'Grand Avenue'. A narrow ribbon of yellow – 'Railway' – loops in precise symmetry around the circles. In the green area are indicated places for allotments, artesian wells, children's cottage homes and forests.

Howard's round glasses glint in the light of the lantern as he fiddles with the apparatus before beginning to speak. He is a man of ordinary appearance and conventional, slightly shabby dress, but people sense the benevolence in his gaze and the zeal in his movements. Some will eventually leave their old lives and enter a new world with him when he fulfils his vision north of London at

Letchworth Garden City in the early years of the twentieth century. In a powerful voice he describes the new moral geometry that will emerge once his glowing lines and curves are made real. The people are dissatisfied with their stunted lives in their narrow courts and alleys, he says. They need cities with wide and beautiful avenues and with spacious parks and gardens. Imagine, he says, Londoners pouring out of the slums towards a better life. His 'garden city' will reconstruct civilisation from the bottom up and do away with the chaotic, selfish cities of today. Howard ends with a challenge to his audience: 'I defy you to show wherein the scheme is impracticable except perhaps in your want of faith, and if your want of faith makes it impracticable do not blame the inventor.'

Londoners have long sought *rus in urbe* – the country in the city. A hundred and fifty years before the fracas in the Barnetts' Whitechapel garden and Howard's proselytising lectures, the Hoxton gardener Thomas Fairchild and his circle gathered in coffee shops to show each other the plants that they had grown. Fairchild wrote of the bountiful pear and fig trees dotted around London and of a vine in Leicester Fields that yielded excellent grapes. He recommended the cultivation of flowering currants, sweet williams and candytuft to make the city more beautiful.

But sometimes urban yearnings for nature express an estrangement from the city and a desire to escape from its clutches. In the early nineteenth century the teenage Thomas de Quincey spent nights mournfully pacing the terraces of 'stony-hearted' Oxford Street. His consolation was to gaze along the moonlit avenues that ran from there through the heart of Marylebone, where decades later the young Henrietta Barnett would tend to the area's slum dwellers, and on towards the fields and woods beyond; 'if I had the wings of a dove, that way I would fly for comfort,' he wrote. It was in those fields – in which from afar the desperate writer sensed a tantalising solace – that Barnett would later build a new kind of city, one that, through the effects of sincere human association in a green, light-filled setting, would, she hoped, console London's tormented souls.

Henrietta Barnett and Ebenezer Howard were two London utopians of contrasting temperaments who worked independently of each other in different parts of the city and its environs. They brought into being related visions that were responses to the dirt and tumult of nineteenth-century London. They wanted to build a city of gardens, and in so doing create a socially intimate urban community that would be a liberation from the dark, alienating metropolis. Henrietta's crowning achievement emerged out of years of practical philanthropy. Howard's starting point was more intellectual. He went on to devise a utopian recipe for a city in abstract, later to be built as complete towns close to London in demonstration of what the larger city could become. Barnett and Howard were to achieve that rare thing among utopians: turning utopia from the 'no place' of storybooks into an actual 'good place', but in doing so weathered the triumphs and disappointments that come when trying to make the real live up to the ideal.

Henrietta Barnett was born in Clapham three days after the opening of London's 1851 Great Exhibition. When young she was forthright and curious: she once received a scolding for wondering out loud whether stars were inhabited, but like many girls of the time received a patchy education. Her father died when she was eighteen, and she and her sisters had to move from the family's imposing mansion at Sydenham in south London to much less salubrious accommodation at Bayswater in the west. A few months later she wrote that she was miserable and exhausted. Her sister Alice noticed Henrietta's low spirits and the lack of any outlet for her developing social ideals, and put her in touch with the housing and social reformer Octavia Hill, who was attempting to improve the lot of the poor by teaching them to be thrifty and respectable. Henrietta found her path in life through working with Hill in the slums of Marylebone, and from these beginnings would grow her grand ambitions for making real her imagined London. Henrietta was said to be loyal to friends and comrades, scathing about 'the heartless rich, the sweating employer, or the rack-renting landlord', who all needed a 'spanking', something that she said she would carry out herself.

In 1873, aged twenty-one, Henrietta married the social reformer Samuel Barnett and moved to Whitechapel when Samuel took up the post of the vicar of St Jude's Church on Commercial Street. The church was dilapidated and surrounded by a warren of unpaved courts and alleys. The local inhabitants scraped by on casual dock work if they were lucky, sometimes on hawking, begging and theft. On a preliminary visit Henrietta surveyed the rubbish-strewn streets and people with 'vice and woe and lawlessness written across their faces'. As the couple stood arm in arm in front of the church, Samuel asked Henrietta whether they should go through with their plan. 'Let us try it; but we may fail,' she said. Samuel would later complain about the rowdy Angel public house and the tripe-boiling establishment that sent its effluvia into nearby windows. Brutal violence was endemic, and in the late 1880s Henrietta wrote to the queen, appealing for action after Jack the Ripper carried out his murders in the nearby alleys.

After a year at St Jude's, Henrietta was pleased to note an increase in the congregation, the creation of a choir and the establishment of a girls' night school, a library and a pension scheme. The Barnetts would regularly invite people of all classes to their social gatherings. A guest at the vicarage recalled mingling with members of the aristocracy and with cultural figures such as the philosopher Herbert Spencer and the artist Walter Crane. At one dinner, an elderly Tory lady was placed next to a radical pawnbroker; she found him to be polite and knowledgeable and their conversation gave her a glimpse of a London very different to the one that she was used to. One of Henrietta's most cherished ventures was a scheme to arrange holidays in the country for East End children. One child wrote to her about how much they had enjoyed it: 'As I sit at school I always imagine myself roaming in the fields and watching the golden corn, and when I think of it, it makes me cry.'

The Barnetts had been in the habit of having members of Oxford and Cambridge Universities to stay to see for themselves social conditions in east London. This purpose was given formal recognition through the Barnetts' founding in 1884 of Toynbee Hall, close to St Jude's, where the scholars would come to live for extended periods and run classes and clubs for local residents. It was an early venture of the university settlement movement, which aimed at getting educated people to work in the service of the poor within their own communities and to build understanding between social classes.

One autumn evening late in the century the Barnetts are holding a great party at Toynbee Hall. Inside, the Natural History Society is showing fungi from Epping Forest and dried ferns that its members have gathered. Outside, coloured lanterns glow among the Virginia creepers which fringe the latticed windows and the pigeons are settling for the night in a dovecote opposite the hall's clock tower. The sounds of violins and singing float into the quadrangle from the festivities inside. Samuel Barnett gives a speech stating his aim of equipping students with 'mental culture and knowledge, the only real basis of equality'. The roar of London, all its tumult and confusion and injustice, recedes for a moment. What appear as implacable rules of the city – those that unjustly oppress some and arbitrarily raise up others – in this little enclave seem pliable and open to manipulation. It is hoped that new social principles will emerge from the brew of people and ideas that has fermented at Toynbee Hall, strengthened by the one thing that Samuel thinks London needs most urgently: 'the development of the imagination'.

Ebenezer Howard's early path was less obvious than Henrietta Barnett's, a gradual enlargement of internal aspirations rather than any immediate practical action. Born to a shopkeeper in 1850, the year before Henrietta's birth, Howard grew up in the beating heart of London, its old quarter of the City, as it was changing from a place of artisanal bustle to one of clerkish order. He was given a basic education which ended at the age of fifteen, when he was put to work in an office. At one of his schools he earned a beating for picking flowers while on a walk and scattering petals around his room; of a later establishment to the north of London in Hertfordshire – the county in which he would create his radiant green cities – he recalled the uplifting effect of the school's trees and grounds.

As a young man he had a strong sense of destiny, leading to a restlessness that needed some channel. At the age of eighteen he worked briefly for an unorthodox and charismatic religious minister, who dabbled in phrenology and was curious about the shape of Howard's head. On feeling Howard's bumps, the man declared that he should become a preacher. A little later Howard came into contact with a well-known American medium who, in an uncanny premonition of his geometric urban vision, told him: 'I see you in the centre of a series of circles working at something which will be of great service to humanity.'

When in his twenties and still searching for his path in life, Howard is one day riding on a London bus. He loves and hates London, is both proud and ashamed of it, but today he feels excited. The crowds and the whirl and all the confusion and disorder fill him with delight. Even the trappings of prosperity are a source of exhilaration. 'There flowed through every nerve of my body from head to foot as it were streams of electricity, giving intense and long continued physical pleasure, the like of which I have never before or since experienced,' he wrote.

Howard also sees the city's dystopian face. On another day he is walking in a crowded part of London through dark, narrow streets – one can imagine that they might have been those in which the Barnetts did their good works – and is struck forcibly by the wretched dwellings in which most people have to live. He perceives in the very fabric of the city – in its hovels and grimy lanes – the workings of a selfish and unsound economic system. This is the cold megalopolis, with its forces of poverty and wealth that appear implacable and eternal. Suddenly Howard envisions a new possibility: 'there came to me an overpowering sense of the quite temporary nature of nearly all I saw, and of its entire unsuitability for the working life of the new order – the order of justice, unity and friendliness.'

Ebenezer Howard and Henrietta Barnett both became familiar with the city's working-class districts, with their monotonous rows of houses and sunless courts where so many young children lived out short lives. There were no gardens, trees or open spaces to speak of, no public buildings and playgrounds and no broad, spacious roads. Such areas were 'stamped by the landlord's greed, the builder's competition, and the people's helplessness', wrote Barnett.

But suburbs were not the answer. Barnett saw London sprawling into the countryside at places like Dulwich in the south and Stoke Newington in the north (the sorts of districts where an often hard-up Howard and his family would find various homes); 'can we hope for nothing more than a repetition of those dreary roads full of trivial villas, those ranks of closely built gardenless boxes?' she asked.

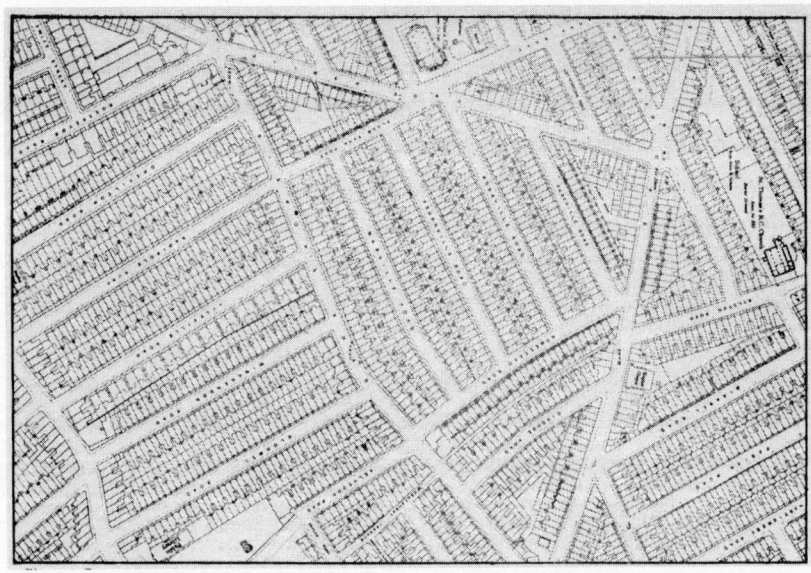

Plan of part of Fulham in west London showing
the standard pattern of suburban development

There was nothing radically new in these sorts of criticisms of the city. Over the nineteenth century, as the industrial economy transformed society, the age-old English love of the countryside had turned into an insistent ideology of rusticity in the work of a number of social thinkers. Practical attempts were also made to create move liveable cities. In the last quarter of the century the airy, tree-lined streets of new housing developments such as Bedford Park in west London were a world away from the city's dark alleys. Even in the shadow of factories, industrialists tried to create healthier living conditions for their workers. On a visit to their Birmingham factory, Barnett had been impressed by the Cadburys' model village of Bournville with its trees and playgrounds. Near Liverpool, the soap manufacturer William Hesketh Lever built Port Sunlight to provide his workers with good housing in an attractive environment. These various layers of existing social criticism and solution-finding formed the seedbed for Barnett's and Howard's own ventures, which would begin coming to fruition at the turn of the century.

In the years in which Howard and Barnett were assembling the ingredients for their urban visions, a new stream of utopian storytelling with a strongly pastoral bent appeared in the writings of the artist, craftsman and poet William Morris. His work was part of the nineteenth-century reaction to the industrial epoch of smoke and slums, which Howard and Barnett were imagining as being regenerated through the creation of airy green towns. Morris's aesthetic ideas were also a pillar of the Arts and Crafts movement, which influenced the design of Howard's and Barnett's towns, and particularly the houses that were built in them. In Morris's utopian novel *News from Nowhere*, the character of William Guest – a thinly veiled Morris – wakes up one morning in a London of the future. Leaving his house by the Thames for an early-morning swim, Guest is amazed to find the river teeming with salmon, and an elegant stone bridge where he expected to see the old wrought-iron Hammersmith Bridge. Along the riverbanks, soapworks and chimneys have been replaced by red-bricked houses with flowering gardens running down to the water's edge. Guest meets a young boatman dressed like a fourteenth-century gentleman with unusually refined and amiable manners. The boatman is confused when Guest tries to give him coins for taking him back to shore, for the use of money has been abandoned long ago. The boatman leads Guest to breakfast, which is being served in a timber-roofed hall where Guest's house used to be.

Guest finds that the locality and the city all around it have been transformed. Hammersmith's main thoroughfare now runs through sunny meadows and its creek, released from its culvert, is full of brightly coloured boats. The slums of the East End have gone. Where they used to be, people once a year celebrate 'The Clearing of Misery', a festival that commemorates the extinction of these former places of suffering. The docks are still in use but are not nearly as busy as in the old times, for Londoners no longer desire their city to be the market of the world. In the north of the city is the pleasant and well-built town of Hampstead, which looks out over a forest. Guest's new friends take him on a trip by boat from Hammersmith upriver out of London and they glide past banks rich with greenery that Guest recalls as having been beautiful in his own time (the same ones that in the 1840s the Owenites gazed upon during their sunset return from the Concordium at Ham). Everywhere he goes, Guest sees none of the downtrodden people whom he remembers from his own time. Instead he encounters wholesome, contented men, women and children who show unstinting hospitality and kindness to everyone they meet. London, it seems, has been transformed into a verdant town of pastoral bliss and true human fellowship.

During one stop on their boat journey, Guest and his party encounter a group of masons, women as well as men, working on a stone house. One of them, while carving a relief of flowers and figures, tells the visitors of the delight she finds in her work. The woman embodies Morris's vision of the creative labour that he saw as part of an ethic of craftsmanship during the Middle Ages. That epoch was one of organic community, as was reflected in the wholesome art that its craftspeople produced, in contrast to the vulgar art of individualistic, capitalist and class-ridden Victorian society. In Morris's transformed world mindless drudgery would be replaced by 'work-pleasure' and the reward for labour would be the joy of a life of creativity.

Morris once wrote of his longing for a society in which people lived simply in small garden communities five minutes' walk from the countryside. Morris's transformed London, through its fusion of town and country, of rural tranquillity and urban briskness, was a vision of the kind of life dreamed of by the garden city pioneers. This unity was symbolised in real life by Morris naming his Hammersmith home Kelmscott House after his rural retreat in the Cotswolds, Kelmscott Manor, an Elizabethan house by the Thames that to Morris was a veritable heaven on earth. The fictionalised manor appears in *News from Nowhere* as the final destination of Guest's boat party. (Morris made the same boat trip upriver between the two houses.) Alighting at a bank shaded with willows, Guest arrives at the rose-covered house, swifts wheeling about its gables, and there he enters the emotional heart of utopia. 'The earth and the growth of it and the life of it! If I could but say or show how I love it!' declares his enraptured travelling companion.

During the years in which Morris was developing his vision of an alternative London, Ebenezer Howard absorbed a host of ideas that would help form his plan for the creation of a real garden city. At the age of twenty-one he had gone to live in America, discovered Paine, Emerson and Whitman, and moved away from conventional Christian belief. He also came across *Hygeia*, by the London doctor Benjamin Ward Richardson, which imagined a future city of cleanliness and health. An unsuccessful stint as a farmer in Nebraska caused Howard to feel disillusioned at the lack of cooperation between farmers and to see the difficulty of collectively run agriculture. He came to believe that a better arrangement was for private farmers to work on public land. Under this system the municipality, rather than private landlords, would capture any increases in the land's value – in its 'unearned increment'. Even classical economists like David Ricardo in the early nineteenth century had deplored the effects of concentrated land ownership under which landowners, for doing very little, got rich on rising rents and land values as the population increased. For Howard it was a small step to extend the principle of collective ownership to industry, so that all land would be publicly owned. This was to be the economic basis of the garden city. Howard, like Thomas Spence before him, therefore advocated the creation of a community which would collectively own the land. The land's unearned increment would be the property of the people and used for their benefit.

What triggered Howard's creation of a whole new model of society was his reading of the 1888 utopian novel *Looking Backwards* by the American author and journalist Edward Bellamy. Like Morris's *News from Nowhere*, which was published in 1890, Bellamy's book represented a return to the classic utopian literary form of the traveller's tale. Unlike the works of utopians such as Robert Owen earlier in the century, these were not plainly written blueprints for a new society but stories of far-off perfect societies in the manner of More's *Utopia*, in Bellamy's and Morris's works voyages into the future rather than across oceans. But where More's work was replete with artful ambiguity and certainly not intended as a plan for the immediate reconstruction of society, the stories of Morris and Bellamy depicted the socialist societies which, through their political activities, the two men were working to bring about.

In Bellamy's novel a nineteenth-century Bostonian wakes up in the year 2000 to find himself in a city of broad, tree-lined streets full of green squares and sparkling fountains. Nineteenth-century individualistic capitalism has been replaced by a collectivist society with a vast production system run by an industrial army in which everyone has to serve until the age of forty-five. The squalor and strife of the former city are now a distant memory. The story made such a deep impression on Howard that it caused him to take that walk through the alleys of London and wonder at the wretchedness of the city around him.

Despite the great impact the book had on him, Howard came to reject certain features of Bellamy's utopia, in particular the dominance of a centralised state bureaucracy. Morris completely spurned Bellamy's vision. He called Bellamy's utopia 'state communism' and argued that it represented a soulless kind of 'machine life' in a technologically advanced city cut off from nature and with little change in underlying human relationships. In *News from Nowhere* the centralised state disappears in favour of local decision-making supported by renovated human bonds; in *Looking Backwards* the state is stronger than ever. In Bellamy's society work was a means to an end and people were compelled to perform it for the state, the very antithesis of Morris's notion of work-pleasure in which labour was an end in itself. Even if they questioned aspects of it, *Looking Backwards* was a spur to Morris's and Howard's imaginings. *News from Nowhere* was in part a response to it that set out a different form of socialist society, and it gave Howard a starting point for finally pulling his ideas together and communicating them to the world.

In 1898 Howard published *To-Morrow: A Peaceful Path to Real Reform*. The book has touches of an old utopian traveller's tale: we enter a new city and at one point are led around it by a 'friend' who answers our questions about the town of parks and gardens and shows us its handsome houses. But Howard's tale is really a vehicle for the practical goals of a modern progressive utopian who wants to put plans into action as quickly as possible. His scheme, he says, is 'the very embodiment of Divine love for man', but soon after he is deep into detailed measurements, costings and rates of interest.

Howard's fundamental idea was that the relationship between the town, the country and his new city was like that between three magnets facing each other. In the centre of the magnets are people, poised like so many iron filings, ready to be pulled in the direction of the most powerful force. Where will they go? London was an ever-powerful magnet – Samuel Johnson had spoken of its attraction – but through the nineteenth century repelling forces were emerging from it. The lures of high wages, social opportunity and entertainment were being counterbalanced by inflated rents, urban anonymity and squalid streets and houses. The country magnet drew its power from fresh air and the beauties of nature. But the country lacked the amusements of the city, and although rents were lower rural people had to work long hours for little money.

These various forces pull the people here and there: some are propelled towards the bright lights of London, some to the fields and hills. Howard's purpose is to show how to construct a new 'town-country' magnet, a third force combining those of town and country into something more than the sum of the parts; 'out of this joyous union will spring a new hope, a new life, a new civilisation', he wrote.

Howard imagines the reconstruction of London through the creation of a town-country magnet in the form of the garden city. Then, as now, people streamed into London and jostled for space, sending rents and property prices up and up. But de-magnetise the city – convince people that they can do better elsewhere – and its overbearing power can be tamed. Rents will fall, and London's monopolistic landlords will no longer be able to exploit their tenants. The country will come into the city as people move out of the slums, which will be pulled down and replaced by gardens and recreation grounds. London's 'vicious and immoral system is bound to ultimately snap', and a new city will rise from the ashes of the old.

But it will be hard to reconstruct London, with its vested interests and ancient traditions, perhaps impossible to do it in one go, and unlike Spence Howard is no revolutionary. He believes in the principles of experimentation and step-by-step advancement.

It will be easier to first demonstrate his idea by creating a new town rather than trying to remake the old. He calls for the building of a prototype, a working model of utopia on more-or-less virgin territory outside London, where a group of people could start afresh and set up an urban economy along Spencean lines. The new town would come into being through migration as the town-country magnet pulled people towards it. After this a group of connected cities could be built, the 'social city', which would replace the sprawling megalopolis. The reconstruction of London would then follow.

The dream of a healthy and harmonious garden city emerged out of a newly turbulent London. Following the upheaval of 1848 and the decline of Chartism, Britain had entered a period of relative social and political tranquillity. Living standards improved and the 1868 Reform Act extended the franchise to urban working-class men. But from the 1870s, economic depression exacerbated unemployment and poverty, leading to mounting unrest. The East End contained some of the poorest districts and was viewed by outsiders as dangerous and uncharted territory. The poet and critic Matthew Arnold voiced middle-class fears of London's working-class populace, describing it as a 'vast residuum' which is 'marching where it likes, meeting where it likes, bawling what it likes, breaking what it likes'. In 1883 a Congregational minister, Andrew Mearns, published *The Bitter Cry of Outcast London*, a searing account of moral and physical degradation in the London slums. Mearns's pamphlet caused a clamour, with churches establishing missions in the East End and the government setting up a royal commission on working-class housing. Middle-class social investigators such as Charles Booth and philanthropists like the Barnetts sought to discover and ameliorate the suffering hidden within the basements and hovels of the east.

Alongside concerns about London's intensifying social pressures came a surge of working-class resistance and a revival of political radicalism. After the death of Karl Marx in London in 1883, new left-wing leaders jockeyed for influence on the direction of radical politics in Britain. In the Jewish East End, radical émigrés preached anarchism and helped tailors and bakers agitate for better working conditions. In the late 1880s London's dockworkers, alongside women and girls working at the Bryant & May match factory in Bow, staged high-profile strikes, triggering a wave of agitation by low-paid workers and the formation of modern trade unions.

Morris was drawn into this political ferment. As he approached the age of fifty, in a bold act of class rebellion he declared himself a socialist, joined an early socialist organisation, the Social Democratic Federation, and later established his own Socialist League, whose Hammersmith branch was mentioned in *News from Nowhere* as having once stood on the site of the hall in which the fictional William Guest breakfasts on his first morning in utopia. Morris began selling socialist newspapers in the street and giving lectures in London and in other parts of the country. On Sundays he would depart from Kelmscott House with a group of comrades under a red embroidered banner, take up a position next to Hammersmith Bridge and preach to passers-by his message of class conflict and revolution. Sometimes he would go to poor areas of the East End and try to gather a willing audience on some rainy street corner in an obscure slum.

In 1885 Morris was caught up in a scuffle in court after the police seized and roughed up the leading participants of a thousands-strong socialist gathering at Limehouse. Morris found himself arrested and accused of breaking a policeman's helmet, though he was quickly released. As he went on with his agitation he encountered greater dangers as the authorities attempted to keep a lid on London's boiling radical underworld. Some of these were alluded to in *News from Nowhere*. In one scene, William Guest, standing in an orchard of apricot and pear trees, has a disturbing flashback to the place as it was in his own time and on one particular day: Trafalgar Square during a real historical event, so-called Bloody Sunday, which took place in November 1887 amid rising turmoil in the city and repeated demonstrations on the square. Guest suddenly sees a great open space full of fountains and ugly statues surrounded by grim buildings, under guard by policemen and soldiers. The surrounding roads are choked with buses and with hot, excited crowds. In Guest's account, the battle that takes place on the square leads to civil war, revolution and the eventual birth of a new society.

For Morris, the events of Bloody Sunday that he had witnessed – a violent attack by the police on a demonstration of unemployed workers, anarchists and socialists – were proof of the vulnerability of radical hopes in the face of brutal state power. The event contributed to his abandonment of the conviction that a revolution was imminent, though not of his hope of one in a more distant future. In *News from Nowhere* the ushering-in of the 'Equality of Life' takes place in 1952, a much later date than Morris would have expected when he first became a socialist. He came to believe that revolution first required the wide diffusion of socialist ideas among the people, who would then rise up and initiate the creation of a new society. This would take time and require the onerous task of building lasting socialist organisations fit for carrying out such work. Ebenezer Howard and Henrietta Barnett did not yearn for Morris's kind of revolution, however. They took on his Arts and Crafts aesthetic and shared his ideal of human fellowship, but rejected class conflict. Like many utopians before them, they sought to demonstrate the workings of their new world through schemes that could be carried out straight away and depended only on the commitment of themselves and their followers.

When Howard first began delivering his social message around London in the 1890s he was labouring in relative obscurity. By then Henrietta Barnett and her husband were seasoned reformers, and one might easily have dismissed Howard as an insignificant crank in comparison. For his utopian scheme to have any chance of becoming reality, Howard had to get others to picture in their minds the green city of his own vivid imaginings. It was not always easy for him to quicken the minds of those around him.

'It was something of an affliction to a schoolgirl,' wrote his niece, 'to be invited to go for a walk with an uncle and then to have a Utopian town described at great length.' But a tenacious public relations campaign bore fruit. At Lincoln's Inn Howard called on a leading lawyer, Ralph Neville, who was known to be sympathetic to the garden city idea and persuaded him to join the Garden City Association, which Howard had established after the publication of his book. This was something of a coup, because it meant that Howard had secured the aid of a successful public man who might have been wary of putting his name to a speculative social scheme such as Howard's.

This step towards the practical realisation of Howard's vision was taken a few yards away from where Thomas Spence had earlier fired up his followers with related ideas in an alley opposite the Inns, to Spence a distant bastion of power, to Howard a place of opportunity to which he could gain entry. With Neville's assistance, the association opened an office on Chancery Lane, the road from which Spence and his bookstall had been summarily ejected. From then on the association grew in numbers and strength. In 1902 the Garden City Pioneer Company was established for the purposes of finding a site and raising from wealthy supporters the money needed to build Howard's city.

A young man from Lambeth named Charles Purdom got a job as a clerk with the pioneer company. He had read *To-Morrow* with excitement: 'To me, born and bred in London, which seemed a kind of hell, this was a wonderful idea.' Purdom thought it extraordinary that London had not been torn down and rebuilt according to Howard's model. But at Chancery Lane Purdom found a Dickensian office with maps and plans all over the floor and a dark, dilapidated room in which he spent long days addressing envelopes containing the company prospectus for potential contributors. 'Some resolution was required to keep me there,' he recalled, but Purdom would go on to became a garden city stalwart.

A site at Letchworth, twenty miles beyond the northern reaches of London, was found for the creation of the garden city. Close to the orbit of the capital, Letchworth would be a prototype for an alternative city, a practical reimagining of the megalopolis to the south. As the town began to be laid out, Howard's geometric vision – the radiating avenues that had impressed the audiences at his lectures – was especially evident at the town centre, where there was a large open square with avenues connected by cross-streets running off it to the north, south and east. A double boulevard, divided in the middle by a wide grass verge with a gravelled walkway lined with benches, connected the main square with the train station to the north, giving a clear sightline of ordered urban space southwards. There was a park in the centre, and the town ended in a green girdle of fields and woods rather than petering out in shapeless suburban sprawl.

The town's geometry was fleshed out with the Arts and Crafts aesthetic. Away from the centre, the layout loosened into curved, organic lines, and right up to the central square simple cottages with their own gardens were arranged along the leafy streets in a charmingly gentle irregularity, of a piece with Morris's quasi-medieval urban vision. Houses were built by private developers, by the council and through housing cooperatives, with the town company maintaining control of overall development through its ownership of the land. One structure described in *To-Morrow* did not make it into the realised version: the Crystal Palace, a circular glass corridor containing shops and a winter garden which was to have run through a belt of parkland enclosing the town centre. (This covered space may well have been inspired by Joseph Paxton's Crystal Palace, reconstructed after the Hyde Park Great Exhibition of 1851 in Sydenham, close to where Howard at one time lived.)

Charles Purdom reported that the residents of Letchworth delighted in their new lives: 'There was excitement, a sense of brotherhood, and the conviction that a new order had been established.' They had built the first town in which exploitation and ugliness had been banished, he believed; here they had indeed found utopia. The landlord of the town's temperance pub, the Skittles Inn, would gather blackberries and nuts along the lanes and say to the cars flying past on the Cambridge road: 'You are going nowhere better.'

Children in Howard Park, Letchworth

Purdom knew an old Letchworthian who had travelled the world and understood that there was nothing better than 'turning to one spot on earth and calling it our home'. Wearing an old jacket, the man tended to his flowers and his vegetable plot. In the late summer he picked fruit and boiled jam on a fire, and as the embers faded would lie down in a summer house among the trees. When autumn came, he would invite his neighbours to come and take crab apples from his hedge. The old man loved the garden's strange and unexpected delights, like its old chalk pit full of hawthorn and wild roses. He would not exchange any of it for all the thrills and gold of the 'uneasy world'.

★

Letchworth's architect was Raymond Unwin, a socialist and follower of William Morris and John Ruskin, who had earlier designed for the chocolate manufacturer and philanthropist Joseph Rowntree the industrial garden village of New Earswick, near York, which was intended to improve workers' living conditions. Unwin observed that London's terraces and tenements which replaced the old slums had made the city healthier, but hardly more beautiful. Beauty was as essential to spiritual and mental health as sanitation was to the body, but ugly cities were thought unavoidable – happily accepted, in fact, on the basis that there were at least beautiful objects to look at in the city museum. But a ray of sunlight on a whitewashed wall had more real beauty in it than did a golden picture frame, Unwin believed. This was the ethical and aesthetic outlook made plain in Morris's description at the end of *News from Nowhere* of the furnishings of Kelmscott Manor: simple, useful tables and chairs whose lack of unnecessary ornament created a sense of harmony and rest. Unwin thought that in big cities showiness only pretended at beauty. This was the result of social divisions, which forced people to struggle to rise in society and so aim at shallow, ostentatious display – 'polished mahogany' and 'stucco trimmings' for their visitors to admire.

Like Morris, Unwin asks us to picture in our minds the old English village. Despite the mingling together of houses and barns, the old road mender's hut, the squire's hall and all sorts of shops and yards, there is a sense of coherence and of harmony. The grouping of the buildings has a beauty about it and reflects a social unity that had been lost by the nineteenth century, when towns had become 'mere aggregations of struggling units'. In his town designs Unwin sought to recreate the organic, communal spirit of the medieval settlement through the arrangement of dwellings around quadrangles, closes and village greens. Instead of showy houses Unwin wanted simple cottages open to the sun, sky and trees. The aim was for the creation of 'little communities of people who will have some sense of locality and will acquire the ties which spring from common interest, and enjoyments shared with those around them'.

In 1896, six years before Howard set up the Garden City Pioneer Company, occurred the event that drove Henrietta Barnett to conceive of Hampstead Garden Suburb. Through a chance conversation, Barnett was made aware of a plan for a new underground station on the western edge of Hampstead Heath, a place which to her had become a haven away from the noise of the city. In the 1820s, William Cobbett, the great chronicler of rural life and critic of the 'great wen' of London, saw haymakers with their scythes when he passed through the locality, and in Barnett's time Hampstead still had an agreeable pastoral feel to it. The area was also a retreat for artists and thinkers, in particular at Wyldes Farmhouse, where William Blake used to visit the painter John Linnell and late in the century a group of socialists including Bernard Shaw and Edward Carpenter would gather for discussion of *Das Kapital*. Barnett's connection with Hampstead went back to the late 1870s when, with a bequest, she purchased a cottage on the western edge of the heath where pauper girls were trained to go into service. In 1889 the Barnetts obtained the much larger Heath End House, which, along with the girls, could accommodate Toynbee Hall residents tired out from their East End travails. Renamed St Jude's Cottage, it gave respite from St Jude's of Whitechapel, offering a parallel life in which Henrietta and Samuel could enjoy fields and flower-filled lanes. With years of toil in the slums behind her, Henrietta's health had suffered and St Jude's Cottage became a place where she could go to recuperate.

Barnett was alarmed by the news of the new Tube station. Following hard on the heels of the trains would surely be rows upon rows of the kind of ugly houses that blighted London's suburbs, she feared. With an extraordinary sense of her individual agency in the face of London's economically driven expansion came Barnett's resolve: 'there was nothing else to do but enlarge the Heath'.

If her plan had stayed at that, one might put an uncharitable gloss on it: she simply did not want the spoiling of the view from her country retreat, especially not with cheap housing for the lower-middle classes. But as she mounted an arduous and eventually successful campaign to buy the open land adjoining the new station to extend the heath – the thousands of letters that she wrote had their intended effect – the various strands of her social work began to cohere into a grander vision. She had worked to bring beauty, light and understanding into the lives of Whitechapel's inhabitants. The tea parties and talks held at Toynbee Hall had been intended to create new kinds of relations between rich and poor. Henrietta imagined how much more might be possible if these relationships could grow naturally as the result of different social classes living near to each other. When younger, Henrietta felt anguish at the distance between herself and the poor and had even proposed to Samuel going to live in a humble Whitechapel tenement. Now she envisioned building an airy, tree-lined city overlooking the heath extension where rich, middle-class and poor could live together and pursue the ideals of beauty and friendship in their daily lives.

Unlike Howard, Barnett did not devise a full utopian system in which to embed her plans. But she had the utopian capacity to delight in social visions and she imagined that from the central point of her suburb, 'over a sloping foreground of apple orchards, the old and young, the busy and idle can rejoice in space and quiet and watch the sun set over Harrow Hill, and the sky flame forth its uninterrupted glory'.

Much of the land on which Barnett wanted to create her new suburb was in the hands of Eton College. Barnett went to see Eton's property manager, who told her that the trustees would be unlikely to sell the land to her because she was 'only a woman'. He advised her to obtain male backers to aid her. (This was not the only time when she had been belittled for her sex. Once, when criticising a policy of the government to one of its ministers, the man cut her down with: 'Woman! When will you learn to mind your own business?') Barnett followed the advice of the Eton official and gathered around her various men of reputation. The money was raised and the land purchased. Barnett noted with satisfaction that the land was last bought by a man, Henricus Octavus – Henry VIII – who wanted it for himself and now was being bought by a woman, Henrietta Octavia, who wanted it for the people.

Barnett's garden suburb was to be planned as a whole, not allowed to grow up haphazardly from the developments of individual speculative builders, as was the case on the expanding edge of the wider city. It would have looser, more organic layouts, a lower density of housing and more green areas. To allow for this the restrictive local building by-laws had to be suspended, so Barnett obtained the passing in Parliament of the Hampstead Garden Suburb Act, which stipulated a maximum of eight houses to the acre, put limits on the size of roads and included provisions for grass verges, gardens and open spaces. A trust to oversee building was set up.

On 2 May 1907, two days before her fifty-sixth birthday, Barnett cut the first sod on the estate. Children danced round a maypole and presented Barnett with baskets of flowers. She urged the attendees not to forget the poor still left in the mean streets of east London. After the ceremony she returned home feeling 'grateful and glad, humble and unhappy for much appreciation leaves one with a sense of being unintentionally dishonest'.

Barnett appointed as one of her architects Raymond Unwin, who left Letchworth and took up residence in Hampstead at Wyldes, where he placed in his study framed photographs of William Morris and Edward Carpenter. Edwin Lutyens was also engaged, but had a fraught relationship with Barnett, with various disagreements about the design and layout of the buildings flaring into arguments. He evidently held Barnett's aesthetic predilections in low regard, describing her as 'A nice woman but proud of being a philistine – has no idea much beyond a window box full of geraniums'.

Despite the occasional difference of opinion, Barnett and her architects together visualised and built the suburb. One day Barnett and Unwin explored Big Wood, an area of woodland on the estate, pushing their way through the undergrowth. Unwin talked enthusiastically as he imagined roads, houses and pathways, but Barnett was worried that she might come across a snake and could hardly take in his words. (Later Big Wood would be tamed by the suburb's Play and Pageant Union, who erected a stage and an arena amid the trees.) On another occasion, Barnett sat at a table on a scruffy bit of open ground next to a small builder's hut near the Finchley Road with Unwin and some of the other men who were helping to build her suburb. She talked earnestly about the plight of elderly east Londoners, who had to live in dilapidated, noisy tenements surrounded by miscreants. Unwin laid out his plans for a quadrangle of flats, The Orchard, in which to house them. There was talk of money: the scheme would pay, they thought, if the capital could be raised at low interest, and Barnett would later write letters to obtain the funds. For every £50 subscribed, investors had the right to nominate one tenant.

On the Finchley Road near Temple Fortune Lane, Unwin's team of architects created an imposing gateway into the suburb, erecting a pair of buildings inspired by the medieval Bavarian town of Rothenburg. The blocks' rising massed brickwork, steep tiling and soaring chimneys were a bold assertion of the start of an altered urban space. South of the central square Unwin put up 'the Great Wall', a boundary between a final row of houses and the heath built in red brick, punctuated by square gatehouses and topped with gabled roofs and wooden cladding. It was Unwin's homage to old towns in which 'the country comes up clean and fresh right to the point where the town proper begins', the opposite of the amorphous sprawl at the edges of the modern city which he so abhorred.

At Hampstead, as at Letchworth, Unwin looked for opportunities to create avenues that, as in the towns of old, would give glimpses of greenery beyond. Doorways and arches framed gardens and quadrangles, enticing the imagination towards what lay a little further on. To evoke the human scale of the medieval city there was an organic hierarchy of differently sized thoroughfares, from wide boulevards down to smaller residential roads, pathways and snickets alongside houses and allotments. Gentle curves closed sightlines as streets bent out of sight, creating a sense of enclosure and boundedness instead of the alienating monotony of long, straight highways.

On the central square a new St Jude's church went up, symbolically linking the suburb to the East End through its namesake at Whitechapel, the original St Jude's. (St Jude's in the east foreshadowed Barnett's vision of an Arts and Crafts colony in the decorative scheme of stencilled apple walls and scarlet pillars devised for it by William Morris; when it was pulled down in 1923 Barnett had its organ installed in St Jude's of Hampstead, physically completing the connection between the two churches.) Also on the central square was the imposing Institute which hosted meetings of the Theosophical Society, a dramatic society, the Women's Temperance Association, the Workers' Educational Association and the British Union for the Abolition of Vivisection, as well as concerts of Schumann and Mozart and debates on the Poor Law, dietary reform and 'the birth of the moon'.

Communal features were included in many of the housing developments such as at Queen's Court for women, which had a bathroom between three tenants. Barnett considered this an advantage rather than a hardship: 'it must be pleasant to have in common one virtue – thrift – and so restful; I find wasteful people so irritating'. Barnett thought that the English custom of putting fences round gardens showed a lack of social spirit and at Hampstead Garden Suburb she tried to do away with them. Dotted around the suburb were clubs and residences for employed working women, invalids, workhouse children, the elderly and wounded soldiers. Opposite Willifield Green was the Club House, a more wholesome version of the East End working men's club, with its bowling green, ninepin pitch and cooperative experimental gardens, along with a reading room, smoking lounge, library and halls for concerts and dances.

The early garden cities and suburbs had lively cultural lives, with the presence of unorthodox religious and social movements that found fertile ground among zealous reformers who wanted to reinvent the details of daily life, not just the underlying structures of the economy. *The Times* described the more eccentric of the Hampstead residents as 'rationalists and vegetarians, suffragettes, Fabians and Theosophists', as including men with long hair, women with short, as wearing sandals, jibbahs and 'ethical smiles' and having a fondness for keeping hand looms and potter's wheels in their cottages. One satirical cartoon has the vicar's wife – one can imagine her as a resolute Henrietta – asking a new resident of the suburb why she was not in the habit of attending church. The shirker, in a flowing robe and seated on a pouffe, answers, 'Well, you see, it does so cut into one's Sundays.'

There was a fondness for plays and pageants, which often took as their subjects the new societies of the garden cities and suburbs. At Hampstead *The Masque of Fairthorpe* was performed in the open air, with locals in farmers' smocks and wielding pitchforks depicting craftspeople, gardeners and the protecting spirits of the suburb, and the children playing fairies and elves. The evil spirit of the play was Jerry Builder, one of the 'grim spectres of the city . . . devouring all the green trees, hedges, flowers, and leaving in their stead the horrid tracks of staring bricks and mortar!'. Then the Trust arrives – sent by a woman – and builds a new kind of city, and the chief architect releases the people from their 'shapeless streets'.

The Masque of Fairthorpe, Hampstead Garden Suburb

A map of Hampstead Garden Suburb, made as it was taking shape, is drawn with the naive literalness and approximate scalings of a medieval woodcut. Unnamed streets are lined with individually drawn houses, and in nearby fields oversized figures work with scythes and guide horse-drawn ploughs. Sweet meadows and may hedges are marked, and in curly script written lines from Christina Rossetti: 'Full of fresh scents are the budding boughs arching high over a cool green house'. Golders Green Tube Station, shown at the western edge of the suburb, indicates the encroachment of the modern world. A few lines of writing at the bottom of the map remind us of the proximity to the disorderly city, recording that the Lord Chief Justice's residence at Hampstead, Kenwood House, was nearly burned down by the Gordon rioters in 1780 but for the quick thinking of the proprietor of the Spaniard's Inn, who gave the mob beer while he sent for a detachment of Horse Guards. The picture, then, is that of a rustic idyll in the city, even if its peace might occasionally be threatened at the edges by the roar of the crowd and the rumble of the Tube. *The Observer* wrote: 'When Mrs Barnett put forward her scheme for the suburb in 1905 it was criticised as Utopian, when the scheme was taking shape the result was criticised as artificial, now it is seen that the criticisms were foolish, for the result justifies the hopes of the pioneers.'

Barnett's and Howard's immense labours caused both of them periods of exhaustion and inner turmoil. Throughout her adult life, Barnett followed a punishing schedule and suffered from bouts of ill health. Early on in their marriage Samuel had insisted on unceasing work: 'I was made to feel I was naughty if I had a cold and had annoyed him if feminine fatigue prevented plans being carried out,' she wrote. (Even on honeymoon the couple spent hours in their room reading aloud from works of political economy.) In 1889 Barnett nearly died of pneumonia, and while on a visit to Whitechapel in the early 1890s a friend became concerned at how tired she seemed and thought that she should give up her work there. In time, Samuel became more yielding and began to see deeper than the symptoms. In 1899 he implored his wife to slow down, writing to her: 'You arrange the journey of your day for an express train speed . . . A breakdown will help no one. Please, please get air and freedom from strain.'

The periods of exhaustion that punctuated her intense activity were perhaps rooted in frustration at having to balance the expression of her creative vision with a respect for social mores in order to function as an ambitious public woman in a world of men. Barnett shied away from radical feminism, but acted and spoke with a boldness that went beyond the bounds of traditional gender conventions. At the same time she maintained an outward respectability, eschewing the bohemian ways of some of the more outré garden suburb inhabitants. She outdid her husband in sheer gutsiness but, it seems, felt the strain of doing so, writing: 'I must remember I am the Vicar's wife and *owe* it to him to take as my *first* duty to do a wife's part . . . I must not push things.'

It has been speculated that a personal loss fuelled Barnett's efforts to set up her garden suburb. In 1901, she suffered the death of her beloved seventeen-year-old ward Dorothy Woods, a sickly girl who had lived at St Jude's Cottage since the age of seven and whose schooling had been postponed until 'riding, dancing, porridge, cream, and Hampstead air had made her more robust'. After Dorothy died, Henrietta suffered a period of depression and fatigue. A striking photograph shows a teenage Dorothy standing behind a seated Henrietta, the girl's cheek resting against the woman's head. One of Dorothy's hands holds some daisies and the other is clasped by Henrietta. On Henrietta's lap is a sheaf of papers – could they be notes on some grand new endeavour? Whatever the case, not long after Dorothy's death Henrietta plunged back into her work, beginning another cycle of frenetic activity.

Howard's restlessness seemed to derive from more intangible inner tensions. He yearned for humans' spiritual perfection but also for their material and social improvement; the immense questions raised by this contrast created a psychological turmoil under his composed exterior that became mingled with his efforts to create his ideal city. A hint of this came in a talk that he gave at the London Spiritualist Alliance in 1910. Something like the idea of the garden city, he claimed, had existed in the minds of Moses, Plato, Christ and St Paul. These men had been on the verge of discovering it but their societies had not been ready. Howard recounted his struggle to find peace having broken away from orthodox religion, and, when grappling with social questions, his rediscovery of Christ. Then from some mysterious source came the revelation of the garden city, which he believed to be implied by Christ's teachings. Feelings of sadness and guilt at first held him back from speaking of it. He had done an injustice to a friend – he never revealed what and to whom – which showed that he was not leading a true life and was an unworthy messenger.

When he confessed his wrong and was forgiven, he felt spiritually renewed and soon after wrote and published his book. The garden city represented the resolution of urban and rural civilisation and the healing of the unholy rupture between humans and nature. A higher form of civilisation would come about through the synthesis of conflicting forces, mirroring on an external plane the resolution of his own inner conflicts. But further turmoil arose as he struggled to make his now-built town live up to his original vision. Disagreements over Letchworth's financial arrangements and his rather chaotic tenure as managing director of the town company eventually led to him being sidelined. Howard's wife Lizzie steadied him as he formulated his grand dreams and helped to bring him back to earth and guide his energies into practically useful activities. But sometimes the effort of trying to run a home while married to a financially straitened idealist would spill over into frustration. She once wrote to him that he was 'like the child crying for the moon – you want to do the impossible', a judgement that in a spirit of both praise and censure has in the end to be applied to all utopians.

The garden city pioneers, radically cooperative but not overtly anti-capitalist, had an uneasy relationship with Britain's mainstream socialists. In a review of Howard's book, one member of the socialist Fabian Society could not stomach 'the unpalatable dough of his utopian scheming'. Bernard Shaw, a prominent Fabian, was both supportive and condescending towards Howard and the garden city proponents. He called Howard the 'Garden City Geyser': a man spewing forth visions of his new settlement like Mr Scadder in Dickens's *Martin Chuzzlewit*. Rather uncharitably, Shaw recalled an intervention that he made at one of Howard's lectures during which, he claimed, the audience drew the conclusion that it was Shaw who really understood economics and that the Geyser was a 'mere spring of benevolent mud'. But Shaw also helped finance Howard's projects, and after Howard died wrote of him: 'He was one of those heroic simpletons who do big things whilst our prominent worldlings are explaining why they are Utopian and impossible.'

Howard and Barnett had in common with some socialists, such as William Morris, a distrust of the state, which led them to attempt to build a new society without the involvement of government. But Morris's rejection of what he believed to be an irredeemable political system caused him to advocate full-blown revolution, in contrast to Howard and Barnett, and also to the Fabians, who sought to bring about socialism by means of Parliament and elections. To Morris Parliament was a place of corruption; in the post-revolutionary society of *News from Nowhere* the Palace of Westminster has been consigned to use as a manure store. In this nineteenth-century version of the debate explored in More's *Utopia* about whether social visionaries should seek political power, it seemed that Morris favoured the rejectionist Raphael over the pragmatic Morus. In the end the modern socialist movement in Britain largely embraced the pragmatic route: the Bradford branch of Morris's Socialist League in 1893 founded the Independent Labour Party, and in 1900 the modern Labour Party was created. Towards the end of his life, Morris softened his position and supported socialists standing for election, including the future Labour leader George Lansbury, who in the early twentieth century would become one of the most prominent of a group of radical local politicians through whom London's utopian dreams would increasingly be pursued.

Barnett and Howard bypassed these debates, believing that their utopian endeavours depended for their success neither on the involvement of the state nor on revolution. On a wall in the Barnetts' Whitechapel drawing room was an embroidery with the words 'One-by-One'. The phrase summed up Barnett's social philosophy, which was practical and based on people cooperating together, not being subsumed into a state or party apparatus. Howard called his philosophy 'common sense' or 'individualistic' socialism. He thought that mainstream socialists were wrong to dwell on class conflict and the seizure of the means of production by the state. What was more important was the creation of new kinds of wealth through the collective ownership of land. Howard's approach implied an economically pluralistic garden city. There would be communally owned land, but individual businesses could operate as their proprietors wished, whether along cooperative or capitalist lines. So as socialist factions argued about the wisdom of compromising with the system, Howard and Barnett used it to their advantage, adopting, for example, the conventional nineteenth-century fund-raising framework of 'five percent philanthropy', the raising of money from wealthy individuals for a reasonable percentage return, as the means for bringing their social visions into being.

The writings of Howard, Barnett, Morris and Unwin are shot through with images of pastoral idylls, therefore inviting the criticism often levelled at utopians that their visions arise out of nostalgic longing and hanker after a Golden Age that never existed. However, the garden city pioneers were not trying to reproduce the past, but use elements of it to build a template for a new form of society. Following Morris, Unwin sought to emulate the spirit of earlier craftspeople who created beautiful things by making them perfectly suited to their function, not by idle decoration, and in doing so anticipated twentieth-century functionalism in architecture and design. Morris himself drew on idealisations of past social and aesthetic values to criticise contemporary capitalism and to create a vision of an alternative society, uniting his love of the medieval world with a Marxist view of progressive history. In this he saw himself as the successor of Thomas More, whose work he praised for its use of the past to imagine the future. Formulated on the cusp of modern commercial England, More's yearning for equality was inspired by the communal spirt of medieval society, and Morris believed that nineteenth-century socialists had inherited the same quest. Howard's garden city was an attempt to confront the problems raised by nineteenth-century industrialisation without rejecting industrial technology. (Even Morris, often incorrectly seen as opposed to machinery, argued that under socialism there would be machines, but that unlike under capitalism they would be used for the benefit of the community as a whole.) The garden city vision, then, while steeped in English pastoral myth, was far from being a defensive movement stuck in a sentimentalised yesterday. As Charles Purdom put it: 'though a garden may hold in it what belongs to the past, it is made for the future'.

A more telling criticism comes from the fact that Howard and Barnett actually built their visionary cities, and so, unlike many utopians whose systems remain as dreams, have to be assessed by the yardsticks of reality rather than of theory: perhaps inevitably, their towns of brick only approximately lived up to the ones that they had imagined. Many kinds of people moved to Hampstead Garden Suburb and Letchworth, but they did not live together as they might have done in some perfect utopian phalanstery where social categories of class, gender and family are melted down and remoulded. As in regular towns, areas for the rich and for the poor emerged. In Hampstead next to the heath were grand houses for the wealthy, towards the centre of the suburb more modest houses for the comfortably off, and smaller workers' cottages in an artisans' quarter. And despite the bohemianism of some of the residents, domestic arrangements were largely conventional, based around the nuclear family with the men going to work and the women occupied with domestic duties.

Barnett felt that many of the Hampstead residents had little understanding of the cooperative values which gave birth to the estate. They wanted to extend their houses or to lop a tree without caring whether these would detract from the beauty of the whole. And although the Barnetts stated that the effects of greater contact between social classes would go both ways, much of their social engineering was a one-way transmission of educated middle-class proprieties to those lower down the social scale – a moralising of the poor. Some of the middle-class inhabitants were clearly averse to those of a more humble rank. Residents complained of the noise made by a group of poor children who had been housed in two cottages in a well-to-do area. Barnett lamented that 'the stream of sympathy is sometimes shallow, sometimes swift and often superficial'.

At Letchworth, Howard wanted to create an alternative economic system through the collective ownership of land, but was constrained by broader capitalist incentives, in particular those governing the industries that he wanted to attract away from

London. Letchworth's unconventional financial arrangements included a 5 per cent limit on shareholder dividends, with any profits above this level going into the development of the town for the benefit of its inhabitants. Howard's proposed 'rate-rent' system periodically increased rents as land values rose in order to allow the municipality to capture the unearned increment. These complications put off investors and businesses considering moving to Letchworth. The result was that the town company did not raise nearly enough capital to finish the building works and was compelled to mortgage much of the estate to make up the deficit. Eventually Howard's economic principles were watered down, meaning that little of the unearned increment would be secured for the town. One effect of the financial difficulties was the limited availability of working-class housing because it was hard to build well-designed, affordable homes with gardens and open spaces while providing a sufficient return to investors.

The physical characteristics of the garden city – copied in many housing developments that followed – were the outcome of attempts to implement Howard's utopian ideas using the aesthetic principles of the Arts and Crafts movement. Soon aesthetics came to dominate, and the garden city was increasingly identified with its surface design features rather than with the deeper utopian intent of Howard's hard-to-implement economic model. The garden city was often equated with the garden suburb when in fact garden cities were intended as complete, self-contained towns based on a new economic model, and garden suburbs as part of a larger city on which they would depend for industries and employment. From the ambitious social and economic critique of capitalism in which it originated, Howard's philosophy was therefore reduced to a kind of environmental determinism – in sunlight and fresh air the moral blemishes of the old order would fade away – and brought closer to Barnett's more conventional approach (though, as she found to her chagrin in her East End days, people were perfectly capable of misbehaving in well-tended gardens). The radical economic thinking that drove Howard's imagination and connected him with earlier London visionaries such as Thomas Spence was in the end largely forgotten.

The garden city philosophy in this narrower form was absorbed into the field of town planning and went on to influence twentieth-century urban policy. Howard's second garden city at Welwyn, which was founded in 1920, drew on state financial support, marking the beginnings of the government's involvement in a reinterpreted version of his vision. Countless suburbs were laid out drawing on garden city design principles, and after the Second World War the government's new towns programme, inspired by the garden cities, created a girdle of settlements around London; in these towns the precious increment was captured by the state, a departure from the thinking of Thomas Spence and Ebenezer Howard, who wanted it to go into local communities.

Raymond Unwin played a role in the push towards state involvement, taking on important town planning posts and helping to draft the 1918 Tudor Walters Report which defined standards for council housing. Howard stayed remote from practical policy, channelling his efforts into spreading the garden city gospel around the world. In later life his interest in spiritualism revived, and at seances in his swift shorthand he would record the messages received, including one from his late wife Lizzie – 'You have accomplished more than you know' – which was evidently true given the influence that his work would go on to have long after his death.

Today, the southernmost section of the A1 from London into Hertfordshire traces a corridor of utopian heritage that spans Letchworth to the north, Hampstead Garden Suburb on the edge of the city to the south and a cluster of utopian towns in between. Letchworth's stately broadway runs alongside grass verges and under lush canopies and leads on to the motorway fringed with fields. Not far to the south is Stevenage, founded in 1946, the first of the new towns. Its clock tower and fountain, a column of austere metal grids rising above a rectangular pool with Mondrian-style chunks of colour on the bottom, are emblems of the thrusting municipal modernism of the town's founder: not some maverick utopian but the post-war Minister of Town and Country Planning, Lewis Silkin, the instigator of the new towns programme whose image adorns the side of the fountain.

The road takes you quickly on to the neatly coiffed Welwyn Garden City and through the new town of Hatfield. Soon one crosses the ring of the M25 and into London proper. At the interchange at Apex Corner, where the A1 slows into Barnet, semi-detached houses line the densely trafficked road alongside unkempt grass verges, crude suburban echoes of the Letchworth style. Beyond the junction the road cuts through Hampstead Garden Suburb and the traffic rushes past the Arts and Crafts houses on each side towards Archway, where a vista of London opens out, St Paul's and the Shard marking the skyline.

Letchworth, Stevenage, Welwyn Garden City, Hampstead Garden Suburb: they are islands of utopian and municipal radicalism that lie a few miles apart along an axis into London. Letchworth, the most ambitious of them, casts a beam along this utopian ley line into the capital that Howard imagined as being reconfigured as the 'social city'. Travelling those few miles north to south we can perceive, perhaps, a glimmer of this social city: a series of compact towns connected by roads and trains along green wedges of land ending in Barnett's visionary suburb that lies just within the outer membrane of the megalopolis. Even if the most radical elements of Howard's and Barnett's utopian visions are gone, they have left a physical legacy on the landscape of a kind rarely achieved by utopians.

Today, Hampstead Garden Suburb is far from Henrietta Barnett's ideal of a socially mixed community. Its houses have become sought-after gems of architectural heritage and the locality is largely the preserve of the well-heeled, an exclusive enclave that has ridden high on the bubbles of London's property prices. Status cars are parked on many of the driveways, and at the edge of the suburb are gated superhouses built with an ostentation that Barnett would have abhorred.

Even so, the open spaces of the suburb still feel like the retreat from the surrounding city that Barnett wanted them to be, a welcome relief from the clogged traffic of the Finchley Road. The central square does not have the shops and businesses that create urban bustle (and it has been criticised in this respect for lacking the magnetic force that town centres gain from such amenities). But without advertisements or other signs of commerce that visually connect places to an era, the central square has a timeless quality about it. With the sounds of a piano floating out of St Jude's and children playing on the grass in the sun, the square remains the haven at the heart of the suburb, and one can easily imagine a similar scene a century earlier. It is a place that still seems to physically embody the humane values that its founder held dear.

In 2018, conservators working on the restoration of St Jude's discovered in the pommel of its spire a small copper cylinder. Inside was a piece of vellum with a message inscribed on it. It spoke of St Jude's as symbolising transformation in that it 'links the Suburb with all its promises to St Jude's, Whitechapel, where the people had squalid rooms and the children missed the joys of childhood'. Samuel Barnett's message to the future – sealed and placed in the spire a century earlier – recorded that St Jude's and the suburb around it was created in the shadow of the First World War, but that out of tumult came times of growth when men and women created new kinds of societies. The message ends with a tribute to his wife's unconquerable hope, symbolised in the church spire which was dedicated to her on her sixtieth birthday. With the message was a copy of a portrait of the couple with plans spread out on Henrietta's lap; it had been painted at Toynbee Hall, that crucible of social imagining a few miles to the east where she had first dreamed of a new London of beauty and virtue.

Chapter Seven

Town Hall Utopias

Henrietta Barnett and Ebenezer Howard are watershed figures in the story of utopian London. They were the last of the heroic type of visionaries that have so far dominated our narrative who sought to build utopia through their own efforts and those of their followers without state involvement. Utopians such as Ebenezer Howard railed against the dark side of London's economic ascendancy – ruthless greed and economic inequality – while appearing as social prophets whose purity of vision seemed to depend on them being unsullied by the corrupted world of politics. But despite Howard's antipathy to the state, the government did have a hand in the development of Welwyn Garden City, and some of the leading lights of his movement ended up promoting their social aims in government departments. Howard's ideas went on to influence housing and urban policies, most notably in the creation of the new towns around London after the Second World War.

So far, though, this story of visionary London has had little connection with government and the state, the powers on which twentieth-century Londoners increasingly pinned their hopes of social progress, even though the city was for centuries the centre of the nation's administration and politics, not just its money-making. With the arrival of the twentieth century, London's utopian spirit came into the orbit of an emboldened state which undertook increasingly ambitious social and economic programmes. London's various layers of government played a much more active role in turning the capital into a fully modern city, with successive housing acts giving more powers to local authorities to clear slums and to build council housing. These efforts reflected new priorities at the national level which were given special force after the First World War, when Prime Minister Lloyd George declared the need for 'homes fit for heroes' for the working classes who had been called upon to make such great sacrifices.

And so this period saw the dawn of a moment in which the utopian layer of London became visible in the city's political life as its government took on a distinctly leftward lean. In the 1930s the Labour Party gained control of London County Council, the capital's first elected city government, which had been established in 1888, and the party also made gains in the boroughs. Poplar, the dockside borough of the East End, became a bastion of socialism. In 1921 thirty of its Labour councillors, among them George Lansbury, went to prison for their part in a rates strike, made in protest at the inequitable distribution of contributions to London's metropolitan authorities. Lansbury and his comrades' radical brand of local socialism became known as 'Poplarism'.

Practical utopias were increasingly pursued by way of government rather than the blazing visions of utopian prophets, and social dreams came to be articulated in bland officialese rather than the breathless prose of utopian manifestos and travellers' tales. In the quest for a new society, state functionaries replaced charismatic counter-cultural figures such as Robert Wedderburn and John Goodwyn Barmby. Arguably, utopia became less exciting. Perhaps, however, this gave it a greater chance of being made real; some of the results of this union of forces changed the face of London, before in the late twentieth century utopia and politics diverged once again.

Utopia-by-politics was pursued with particular effect in those localities of London that came under the control of left-wing local governments. One of them was the working-class borough of Finsbury, just north of the City. The borough was created in 1900, covering Finsbury, Clerkenwell and Moorfields, and was bordered by Shoreditch to the east and Holborn to the west. By the 1930s the area had still not left behind the squalor of Victorian London. Finsbury's population had fallen significantly from its nineteenth-century peak as those with the means to do so escaped to the suburbs, but the district remained one of the most overcrowded in London. There were few open spaces and little greenery. Often houses lacked basic amenities such as a water supply or kitchen, were located next to factories and workshops, and occupied by multiple families sharing the same lavatory and sink. The poorest of the borough's inhabitants slept in unventilated cellars. Many of them would have had lives not dissimilar from those portrayed by George Gissing in his 1889 novel *The Nether World*, a bleak tale of poverty and blighted aspiration set in the Finsbury slums whose characters stay trapped in their dismal localities with little hope of ever reaching a better London.

In the 1920s a Labour administration was elected in Finsbury with an ambitious programme for remaking the district through the creation of a health centre, more civic spaces and the building of new housing. Unusually, Finsbury's radical politicians pursued their utopia through avant-garde architecture and design. They would develop their vision with the aid of a Russian architect with a strikingly philosophical turn of mind, Berthold Lubetkin, whose radical ideas about the socially transformative potential of architecture found an eager audience among the borough's officials.

Lubetkin arrived in England in 1931, having absorbed influences from modernist art movements during a nomadic period living in various European countries. He was a student at the Berlin Textile Academy, engaged in studies in the use of concrete, and after a stint in Warsaw arrived in Paris where he came under the influence of Le Corbusier. He was, he wrote, 'persistently attracted by the vision of the metropolis, and yearned for urban surroundings where reason informed by geometry imposes the consistency of order upon diversity'.

Lubetkin was born in Tiflis in Georgia in 1901 into a

middle-class Jewish family with strongly reformist sympathies. He began formal art studies in Moscow on the eve of the 1917 Russian Revolution. One morning in March of that year Lubetkin was woken by the sound of the 'Marseillaise'. He rushed into the street and was plunged into a sea of people and song. On passing a children's bookshop he noticed that the usual storybooks had been replaced by a picture of Prometheus. Banners in the streets proclaimed: 'We seek heaven on earth, not in the sky.' Lubetkin wrote of that day: 'history crashed through the barriers of everyday convention'. The world was to be started from scratch in a new rational order. Art schools became hotbeds for avant-garde experimentation, and Lubetkin and his colleagues considered themselves to be revolutionary artists with the task of redesigning society.

In London he set up an architectural practice, Tecton, and in his spare time would sell the *Daily Worker* outside Russell Square Tube Station. He found in England 'a stratified society, in which each successive layer of self-deception was contained between rigid crusts of conventional institution'. He deplored the tradition of English empiricism, which rejected social theory and was only interested in isolated facts, not in their linkage into systems which could be the basis for social remodelling. To Lubetkin, architecture brought social ideology to life. It was 'a thesis you put in front of society: it calls for something, it says something – and it has to be argued out'. Despite its complacency, England was on the threshold of radical change, Lubetkin believed, its class hierarchies placed under renewed pressure by the convulsions of the era. Lubetkin and his colleagues would go on to create a new vision for London, bringing to it the modernist ethos developed in Europe which until then had largely passed England by.

Tecton's early projects, although radical in design, did not have an overtly revolutionary purpose. Their Highpoint I block of private apartments, a little to the east of Henrietta Barnett's garden suburb, was an International Style masterpiece, praised by Le Corbusier as proof of the concept of 'the vertical garden city'. A sleek white building located on a spectacular site overlooking

Hampstead Heath with the highest rooftop in London, to one critic of the time Highpoint 'stands on tip toe and spreads its wings'. Although the development was not part of any radical social programme – the high cost of the apartments put them out of reach for most Londoners – the clarity and coherence of the building pointed to a new world in which objective planning would abolish the vicissitudes of the old social order. Lubetkin said that he intended the building to have the impact of a jubilant crowd singing the 'Marseillaise'. Even his most famous design, the penguin pool at London Zoo, which used a starkly unnaturalistic minimalism as the backdrop for the display of animals, could be seen as an emblem of the taming of disorder and randomness by a rigorous human rationalism.

When in the 1930s Lubetkin came to the attention of the leaders of Finsbury Council, an arena for social reform opened up to him. The council was then headed by Harold Riley, who had a vision for a new city in Finsbury to replace decrepit old London. There would be modern housing, parks, public spaces, libraries, nurseries and public baths and a civic square at the junction of Pentonville Road and City Road. One of Riley's colleagues was an Indian doctor, Chuni Lal Katial. In 1927 Katial had moved to London from the Punjab and set up a medical practice in the East End. He was a follower of the Gandhian ideal of service and was once visited by Gandhi at his Canning Town home. Katial moved to Finsbury and was elected a Labour councillor in 1934 and mayor of Finsbury in 1938. As chair of Finsbury's public health committee, he instigated a plan for a new health centre. In 1932 he had been impressed by a presentation at the British Medical Association of an early Tecton plan for a chest clinic and a few years later approached Lubetkin about designing a health centre for Finsbury.

Katial wanted to create a centralised system of public health care that would exploit the rapid progress in medical science seen in the 1930s. Alongside doctors' surgeries, the centre would contain tuberculosis and foot clinics, dentists, laboratories, a solarium, cleaning and disinfecting rooms, and one of the first ever women's clinics. There were to be offices for public health officials and a lecture theatre. Health statistics and administrative records would be kept in the same building. There would even be accommodation for borough residents to stay in while their homes were being disinfected following outbreaks of infectious diseases. At this time London had no integrated health system, only a patchwork of private surgeries, voluntary hospitals and charitable organisations. The Finsbury Health Centre was intended to provide a full range of services to the local population. It would be an NHS in miniature a decade ahead of its time.

Katial and Riley quickly engaged Lubetkin and Tecton, making Finsbury the first borough council to select an avowedly avant-garde architectural practice to undertake a civic building project. Years later Lubetkin would recall the opportunity to implement his socio-artistic ideals alongside a group of radical local politicians as seeming 'like the realisation of a dream'.

Lubetkin's architectural philosophy had been heavily influenced by Russian constructivism, the revolutionary avant-garde movement that sought to create a new generation of 'artist-engineers' who would change society with their designs, constructions of metal and plastic expressing a new poetic of technology and the machine. The movement was particularly associated with Vladimir Tatlin, famous for the never-to-be-built Monument to the Third International, a leaning spiral iron structure taller than the Eiffel Tower containing a revolving glass cylinder, pyramid and cube to house different departments of the Communist International. The tower was also to have had a radio transmitter for the broadcasting of manifestos and a projector to shine messages on to the clouds. Lubetkin adopted the concept of buildings as 'social condensers': places where new social patterns would be created to replace old hierarchies. The term condenser – suggesting a node for the attraction of light and electricity and for the precipitation of liquid from infinitely pliable vapour – evokes a process in which imaginative energy hardens into concrete reality.

Lubetkin intended the Finsbury Health Centre to be just such an apparatus.

The centre opened in 1938, right in the middle of the slums of Clerkenwell. In a contemporary photograph the pristine modern structure looks as if it has been beamed from a parallel universe into the crowded tenements of pitched roofs and smoky brick. The image even gives the impression that the smoggy-looking air has cleared around the health centre, as if the building could actually purify the surrounding atmosphere. With its sweeping white surfaces and striking symmetries, its layers of flat roofs and its ceremonial entranceway, it was a temple of technology and health, a propaganda piece in concrete, glass and electric light. Lubetkin and Katial intended it to create new compounds in the social Petri dish of the city.

Tecton had tested their design for the centre as an engineer would a new piece of equipment. The plan drew on findings from experiments they had conducted while drawing up the blueprint for their earlier tuberculosis clinic. Light was shone from varied directions on to models placed on photographic paper in order to understand the action of sunlight at different times of the day. Designs were tested for air circulation properties to encourage inflows of clean air and outflows of unclean air, and for the hygienically optimal movement through the building of healthy and sick people. The completed structure was full of technical innovations: 'invisible radiant heating', cross-ventilation and accessible channels for wiring and plumbing that allowed for the flexible use of space. The side wings that flanked the central section could be adapted to house clinics, offices or equipment as needed. The abundance of glass and the open H-shaped layout brought light and air to all parts of the building.

In the centre's solarium young children would have artificial sunlight shone on to their bodies to cure the vitamin deficiencies they suffered as a result of their poor diets and lack of sun. In underwear and dark goggles, their skin glowing under the light, groups of them would sit in a line in a clean, well-ordered room, a brief refuge from the grime of the alleys. In another area of the building orderlies would place lice- and flea-infested clothing into a large disinfecting machine, which with its levers, meshes and exposed metal beams looked like something out of a Russian constructivist theatre set.

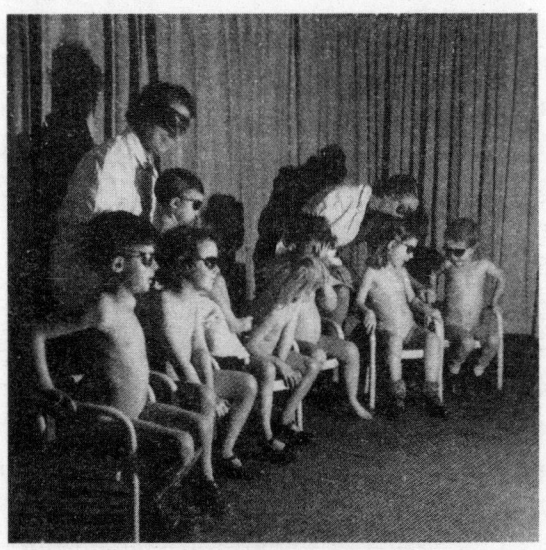

Children being treated for vitamin deficiency
in the Finsbury Health Centre solarium

Alongside the up-to-date technology and facilities was the human dimension of the building. The centre was intended to be a welcoming place with the feel of a people's club, different from that of traditional hospitals or government offices ruled by high-handed officials and doctors. The entrance hall did not have a formal reception desk that would only serve to separate staff from visitors, instead being a large open space with light flooding in through the wall of glass bricks that made up the central frontage of the building. There were curved walls, a pale-blue ceiling and informal clusters of seating dotted about among red pillars. Colourful murals extolled the benefits of fresh air, advising the public to 'Live out of doors as much as you can' and telling them,

'Chest diseases are preventable and curable.' The hope was that people would feel able to wander in without an appointment and enjoy being in the light-filled space, to be droplets in Lubetkin's social condenser. Lubetkin called the building – with its side flanks looking like a pair of open arms, its ceremonial entranceway, bronze and marble door and glowing frontage – a 'smiling machine'. On one wall was displayed a large plan of London, its midpoint positioned on the health centre, Lubetkin's ideological transmitter that was intended to relay a new utopian ethos to the city all around it. When the centre was opened Katial declared it the dawn of a new era.

As utopian aspirations began to be reflected in London politics and government, competing versions of these social dreams arose. South of the river in Bermondsey a vision emerged with aims similar to that of Finsbury, but which was pursued through the vernacular design approach of the garden city pioneers rather than an imported modernism. Bermondsey was an overlooked area of London, hemmed in by railway lines just to the east of Tower Bridge. In the nineteenth century, Henry Mayhew had reported to a shocked reading public the extreme poverty that he found there. In the early twentieth century the area, like Finsbury, remained overcrowded and riven with disease: the rate of infant mortality in the most crowded parts of the borough was nearly double that of London as a whole. A new breed of local politicians espousing 'ethical socialism' sought to remake the area and raise up its people.

One of them was Ada Brown, who at the turn of the century was living in a humble tenement on Cherry Garden Street in the heart of Bermondsey near to tanners' works. She was employed by the Bermondsey Settlement, an organisation that had been partly inspired by Toynbee Hall in Whitechapel and ran a chess club for local girls. A settlement report described the girls to whom the organisation attended as being working-class ('with hats'), but the group that Brown looked after as of the 'boisterous' class, that is, 'without hats'. Brown's young chess players were 'rag-sorters, wood-choppers and tin-solderers'; sometimes they arrived at the club drunk. Brown was undaunted by this and would have the girls to tea in her flat and take them on trips to the coast.

Like Henrietta Barnett, Brown had begun her career by joining one of London's philanthropic organisations. She arrived in the capital from Northamptonshire in 1896 to work for the Sisters of the People, a group of Methodist women who organised clubs and classes for women in the slums of Marylebone, Soho and St Pancras. The group allied itself with radical causes, supporting the match-girls at the Bryant & May factory in Bow during their famous 1888 strike, and dockers' families during the Great Dock Strike of 1889. Unlike Barnett, Brown developed a radical political consciousness that fused socialism and feminism; in an article she wrote that she deplored the near-impossibility of housing reform because of vested interests, nearly all of them men, property owners and landlords.

In 1900 Ada Brown married Alfred Salter, another member of the settlement, a radical socialist and agnostic. Alfred was a brilliant young doctor who could have had a conventionally distinguished medical career but instead chose to serve the poor of Bermondsey. He established a medical practice on Jamaica Road, where he and Ada first set up home, charging minimal fees to his impoverished patients and working long hours.

Ada Salter admired London, but had seen for herself the poverty and suffering that lay under the surface of the city's magnificence in neglected places where workers were 'not housed, but warehoused' in drab terraces and tenements, without the enjoyment of the greenery of the suburbs or the elegance of the West End. Salter was an intensely practical woman but also one of vast social vision, and in one early speech spoke of a great transformation that was about to take place, echoing the millenarianism of the early-nineteenth-century London visionaries: 'The injustices of the ages, the misery of the oppressed class, the sorrows of the poor, the tyranny of wealth and rank are going to be swept away for ever.' But Salter's way of hastening this process of improvement was through party politics, by which she sought to transform Bermondsey into a garden city right in the heart of industrial London.

Alfred and Ada Salter helped establish and build up the Labour Party in Bermondsey and in 1909 Ada was elected the first woman borough councillor in London. In 1922 Labour had a breakthrough, with Ada Salter becoming mayor of Bermondsey and the first woman Labour mayor in Britain, and Alfred Salter a Member of Parliament. As mayor, Salter did not wear the ceremonial robe and chain, and to the fury of the Conservative press had the Union Jack removed from the town hall in favour of a red flag bearing local symbols. She abolished royal celebrations and replaced the Church of England prayers that were traditionally said before council meetings with a period of Quaker silence.

Salter had ambitious social visions, but was far from being a utopian ideologue in the mould of a Charles Fourier, spinning out grandiose theories that were inaccessible to the ordinary person. Her ideals had driven her to work in the slums and to make personal sacrifices for others. Sometimes her work placed her in danger. During the war years, the Salters' pacifist stance brought them to the attention of jingoistic elements. Alfred had stones thrown at him and Ada was nearly killed when a mob tried to burn down a building where she was addressing a peace meeting. At the end of the war, Ada was part of the British delegation to the congress of the Women's International League for Peace and Freedom in Zurich, during which she visited Vienna and was moved by the sight of starving children in the streets there. She brought back a number of them to live with her and Alfred until new homes could be found for them.

The Salters lived at Stork's Road, just south of Jamaica Road, a few hundred yards away from a crowded and disease-ridden slum at Salisbury Street, hemmed in by riverside warehouses, timber yards and a pottery. In May 1910 one of the regular epidemics of scarlet fever broke out and the Salters' only child, eight-year-old Joyce, caught the disease, likely the result of living close to the epicentre of the outbreak. The girl had twice recovered from bouts of scarlet fever, but this time she was not so lucky and died the following month. Some of Alfred's relatives thought that he and Ada should have done more to shield their daughter from the dangers of London, perhaps by moving to the healthier environs of a suburb, but living among the people they served – their home being an open house for those who needed their help and advice – was essential to Ada and Alfred's social mission.

During the 1920s, aided by Alfred, Ada pursued her dream of transforming Bermondsey, initiating what came to be known as the 'Bermondsey Revolution', a central element of which was the provision of new housing. This was conducted within a broader scheme of civic improvement. The council's Beautification Committee undertook programmes for the planting of trees and flowers and for the creation of new open spaces. The aim was to create a new kind of working-class town, not on the edges of the city or beyond it but right in the heart of the raw, unlovely district. Bermondsey was to be transformed with tree canopies and gardens, by shocks of bright flowers against dull walls and by Ada's own version of the social condenser: places where people could find relief from relentless toil and come together for sport, play, singing and the pursuit of knowledge. 'Fresh Air and Fun' was the motto of the programme. Graveyards were made into parks and play areas. A playground on the site of a former workhouse was opened and had facilities for football, tennis, netball and cricket. In a churchyard a long 'joy slide' was built of an Arts and Crafts design, housed under a tiled roof and entered through a tower. In the parks ground staff organised games and activities. Shows and competitions were put on and at a new bandstand musical performances held. A choral society and the Bermondsey Popular Municipal Orchestra were established.

The council provided the local people with seeds and bulbs

and soon the borough bloomed with foxgloves, lupins, sweet williams, snapdragons and forget-me-nots. Tenement buildings displayed yellow chrysanthemums and Michaelmas daisies 'like purple stars'. People planted flowers in any scraps of space around their homes, just as some of the inhabitants of the Bermondsey slum of Jacob's Island had done in the previous century. Council buildings were given window boxes, and the front garden of the borough's tuberculosis clinic was filled with flowers and shrubs to soothe the patients. In the garden of the Salters' house on Stork's Road, which was adjacent to a factory, Ada planted flowers that she found best withstood the polluted atmosphere – stocks, verbenas and blue lobelia; she filled the rooms with bulbs and plants. One of the borough's gardeners even developed two new strains of dahlias – the salmon-coloured Bermondsey Gem and the yellow Rotherhithe Gem – bred to thrive in the inhospitable environment.

In 1918 Ada and Alfred organised the purchase through a group of Quaker benefactors of Fairby Grange, a seventeenth-century manor house set in twenty acres of land at Hartley in Kent. Containing a rose garden, shrubberies, vegetable gardens and an orchard, the estate was to be used as a refuge for conscientious objectors, as a pacifist camp for boys and as a cooperative farm. After the war it was donated to Bermondsey Council and used as a rest home for exhausted working women and mothers, the first such facility in Britain. Plants and trees were cultivated for use by Bermondsey's Beautification Department and by the mid-1930s the council obtained all its plants and trees from the Grange. By the late 1920s the council had planted some 6,000 trees in the borough (in 1919 there were fewer than 400), mainly London planes and poplars, and also limes, birches and flowering cherries.

Soon visitors noticed the changes in Bermondsey and hailed Ada's efforts. A reporter detected a new sense of civic pride in the borough, as seen in the flowers that women factory workers pinned to their coats – 'not a decoration, but a symbol'. One visitor shown around the borough by Ada in May 1935, the month of George V's Silver Jubilee, noted approvingly that the council had declined to take part in the royal celebrations, using the money saved to further its social programmes.

The centrepiece of Ada Salter's garden city by the Thames was new housing to replace riverside slums. 'We'll pull down three-quarters of Bermondsey and build a garden city in its place,' Alfred is reported to have said. Ada had resisted the building of tenements, instead pushing for cottages on small, homely streets. Labour had promised 'a cottage home for every family'. A party pamphlet contained an illustration of cottages in a verdant setting, next to that of a forbidding-looking block of tenements of the type being constructed by London County Council. Ada's new dwellings were built in a knot of streets centred around Wilson Grove, close to the river, on the site of the former Salisbury Street slum. Some members of London County Council and of Bermondsey Council favoured cheaper tenements, but Ada was adamant: 'Tenement housing does not lead to the New World,' she said. After vigorous persuasion and cajoling Ada got her scheme approved.

In 1928, Ada's pocket garden city was opened: fifty-four cottages in a cluster of tree-lined streets amid the warehouses and cranes, each with a bathroom, toilet and hot water. The cottages were of red brick and white-rendered walls, with bay windows and pairs of neighbouring doorways under a shared arch. They had front and back gardens in which residents dug vegetable patches and planted apple trees. Rows of cottages were set back from the road and grouped around small areas of lawn and shrub, attractive abbreviations of village greens. One docker who went to live in the new development had previously lodged in the Salisbury Street slum with his family of twelve squeezed into four rooms without a bath; now he lived comfortably with only four others in a clean, well-appointed cottage. Ada's garden city became famous and the focal point of the Bermondsey Revolution, and city mayors from Germany, Austria, France and the United States would later visit Wilson Grove to see for themselves Ada's unique approach to slum clearance and housing development.

The council spread the creed of the new clean and healthy Bermondsey using its own ideological transmitters. Its health propaganda department installed electric signs by a set of public toilets, showing moving images on topics such as teeth, tuberculosis and electricity. Pamphlets were issued on rats, flies, diphtheria, measles, milk, scabies, scarlet fever, tuberculosis, smoke and soot. Illustrated bookmarks containing health information and leaflets with gardening tips were placed inside library books.

The most striking method of citizen education was through the use of mobile film vans which turned the streets and squares into cinemas, showing films to sometimes hundreds of people at a time. In the streets and parks, at the library and town hall and in front of polling stations the vans screened slide shows and silent films – Bermondsey was the first borough to make its own – with commentaries spoken over them. There were films entitled *Germs*, *The Rat Menace*, *Sunlight is Life* and *Ivory Castles* (a fairy story for children about teeth). The vans were Bermondsey's version of the Soviet Union's agit-trains that transmitted Bolshevik propaganda to the masses. Over a third of the population of Bermondsey may have viewed the films.

On a balmy summer's evening a group of chattering Bermondseyites make their way into a courtyard. A municipal film van has pulled up. 'Here Comes Health', it says on the side. A technician connects the vehicle to a specially adapted lamp post and the projector comes to life. Streams of light illuminate a screen at the back of the van. The people gather round. Children skip along the edges of the crowd and the council demonstrator calls for quiet. As the shadows deepen, the people watch intently. They stand in the glow of a shrine to a new London, the light flickering on their faces. They see scenes of cleanliness, of rationality, of a reordered life away from the slums. An official narrates the silent moving pictures in what the council calls 'street preaching', the municipal version of the oratory of the city's past visionaries who proclaimed new worlds in alleyways and taverns.

A Bermondsey Council film van

The people watch on the screen workmen in flat caps demolishing slums; the men push with their bare hands against the remains of crumbling walls until they wobble then crash into the street below, releasing huge clouds of dust. Modern houses are built, as the film makes sure to point out, by the council's own workmen. A camera tracks along a tree-lined road, the straight sides narrowing into the hazy distance. The film shows Wilson Grove with its attractive entranceways, trees and small gardens. A refuse van drives along spraying water on to the road. There is talk of progress in countering infectious diseases and of the falling death rate in Bermondsey. A white-coated scientist in the bacteriology laboratory peers down a microscope at a specimen, and at the disinfecting station orderlies place clothes and bedding into massive cleansing machines. People in parks rest on benches among greenery and flowers, and children crash into each other in cheerful heaps at the bottom of the joy slide. There are shots of the council's gardeners in the greenhouses of Fairby Grange, of power station equipment, of the electric ovens and vacuum cleaners that the council hires out to residents and trains them to use.

One film informs its viewers that 'the skin contains a million drains, And you must keep them clean, For dirt will choke a drain' and shows a young man in a bath and then a drain with water running through it. It is an emblem of a London cleansed, its people made into hygienic new citizens. Young women walk confidently in a park in light, loose clothing that 'allows unhampered movement and free play to sunshine and air'; perhaps some of them might have once attended Salter's chess club and first felt the stirrings of a new kind of citizenship. The films together tell of the transformation of Bermondsey, the rising-up of this fragment of utopia in the city. They form a mythos for a transformed London performed by the men and women of the borough who have emerged from the dingy slums and into the electric glow of modernity, confident and purposeful, ready to take their place in a new world.

The Great Depression and the Second World War reinforced the shift towards a more active state across the industrialised world. In 1936, in response to the depression, the British economist John Maynard Keynes published a mould-breaking work of economics, *The General Theory of Employment, Interest and Money*, which argued for a greater role for the government in the management of the economy, in particular by spending money on public works to stimulate economic demand in order to prevent mass unemployment. In Britain the outbreak of war ushered in a new era of government control of the economy through planning and rationing.

In 1942 a government report was published, *Social Insurance and Allied Services*, popularly known as the Beveridge Report, whose author, William Beveridge, had begun his career as a social reformer working with Samuel and Henrietta Barnett at Toynbee Hall. Beveridge set out a plan for the establishment of the British welfare state. The state's task would be to fight the 'five giants' – Want, Disease, Ignorance, Squalor and Idleness – through the creation of a comprehensive health service and a social insurance scheme which would provide for people in the event of sickness and unemployment. The report was a bestseller, with Londoners queueing outside the government Stationery Office in Holborn to get a copy. Abandoning the usual bureaucratic caution, it stated that the cataclysms of the time were an opening for social renewal: 'Now, when the war is abolishing landmarks of every kind, is the opportunity for using experience in a clear field. A revolutionary moment in the world's history is a time for revolutions, not for patching.'

Beveridge's programme would be carried forward by the 1945 Labour government of Clement Attlee. Another plank of post-war policy was an expansion in the provision of council housing. Complementary to the building of housing inside London was the creation of new towns encircling it – Stevenage, Harlow and Basildon were among the first. In 1946 the Poplar-born Minister of Town and Country Planning, Lewis Silkin, stood up in the House of Commons and said it was not unreasonable that More's *Utopia* should now be made real in England, and set out his programme for the creation of the new towns.

During the years of post-war austerity the Festival of Britain was held in 1951 on the south bank of the Thames in Lambeth, a century after the Great Exhibition of Hyde Park, which had been a celebration of Britain's industrial pre-eminence. The festival effectively marked the inauguration of Britain's welfare state, symbolised especially by the concrete brutalism of the London County Council-built Festival Hall, the rising of a new fragment of London whose civic ethos was in sharp contrast to the pecuniary one pursued in the financial district on the other side of the river. Part of the festival was the opening of the Lansbury Estate in Poplar, a mix of blocks, maisonettes and houses.

Named after Poplar's celebrated socialist George Lansbury, the estate was a showcase of the state's commitment to provide decent housing for all.

After the war plans were reactivated for the development of Finsbury that had been drawn up by the council and Lubetkin before the war. By then Harold Riley had left the council, and his visionary aims were scaled down to a more narrowly focused programme of house-building. The need was now even more urgent. Finsbury had been badly hit during the Blitz, with over 90 per cent of its housing damaged or destroyed, exacerbating existing overcrowding and poor living conditions in the borough. By 1946 the situation was so acute that communist councillors were helping homeless people to heckle council meetings from the public gallery. Despite the borough's ambitious aims, progress on house-building was slow because of post-war shortages of labour and raw materials, rising costs and a lack of central coordination and planning. By the end of 1949 only twenty-two new homes had been built, and housing conditions in the borough remained poor for long after the war.

Nevertheless the housing programme, particularly those elements pursued through Lubetkin's vision, was a bold attempt to build a fragment of utopia in London. In Finsbury came Lubetkin's chance to realise his artistic ideals, expressed in his statement that 'Architecture *is* politics, only pursued by other means.' For Lubetkin, architecture illuminated a path of progress. It was the stage set for the next act of the new society.

In 1949 Lubetkin's Spa Green Estate was completed, the biggest canvas yet for his social vision. Attlee's Minister of Health, Aneurin Bevan, the father of the National Health Service, said that the estate gave a glimpse of a new London 'that will be the joy of generations to come'. Located on a sloping wedge of land between St John's Street and Rosebery Avenue, just south of the Angel, the development was aimed at making available to working-class people the kind of modern living conditions that the middle-class residents of Highpoint enjoyed. Katial believed that it proved the feasibility of removing the difference between luxury and working-class housing. As at Highpoint, Lubetkin worked with the engineer Ove Arup to incorporate innovative uses of reinforced concrete while moving away from the sleek International Style of that earlier development towards one incorporating more richly detailed façades.

The working-class tenements of the time, although a clear improvement on slum housing, were rather grimly functional, with small dark rooms and few green spaces around them. In contrast, the new flats at Spa Green were state-of-the-art. 'Nothing is too good for ordinary people,' Lubetkin once said. Each flat had central heating, its own toilet and a modern kitchen with a stainless-steel sink, ventilated larder, a gas-heated wash copper for boiling laundry and storage cupboards. They were the first in London to feature the Garchey waste disposal system, which used water to take waste from kitchen sinks to a central incinerator. The north–south placement of the blocks and dual-aspect rooms let in plenty of sunlight. With the assistance of a mathematician, Lubetkin devised an aerofoil-shaped canopy for a communal drying area on the roof to maximise the flow of air into the space. One resident praised the amenities, saying that having their own toilet and a door to the street 'was luxury beyond my belief'.

The buildings were set in a small park arranged on several levels with trees, shrubs, winding paths and a war memorial at the entrance to Rosebery Avenue, the green enclave between the road and the blocks of flats giving the estate a serene feel. With a strong sense of pride in the appearance of the new development, the council banned the putting-out of laundry on balconies and the beating of carpets after eleven o'clock in the morning, and required residents to wash the stairs and landings weekly. At eight every evening a whistle would be blown and the children playing outside would go in to bed.

The building designs at Spa Green were strikingly modern while being pleasingly idiosyncratic. There were three blocks of flats: an outer pair of eight-storey buildings, one running along Rosebery Avenue, another along St John's Street and between them a third gently curved block. The façades facing the roads made distinctive use of cream tiles, dark-grey grilles and red dividers between the wide balconies, creating patterns whose sequence alternated from floor to floor. The balconies were set off on each side by pairs of windows in brickwork and finished off with tiled edges. The inner faces of the buildings which looked on to open space in the centre of the estate were plainer: columns of windows punctuated by a series of chessboard ventilation grids, their edges aligned with the vertical spaces between the windows rather than with the windows themselves, creating a restful rhythm of glass, brick and shaded cavities across the surface of the building. The compositional effects used in the design of Spa Green – flowing grids of colours, chequerboard patterns and bordered façades, which lent the buildings a feeling of both order and warmth – came in part from Lubetkin's admiration of the aesthetic principles employed by carpet makers in his home town of Tiflis, whose workshops he would regularly visit as a young man.

The regularity and consistency of Lubetkin's design for Spa Green ensured that no single flat was more important than the others, reflecting the socialist ideals of equality and rationality that were at the heart of his three-dimensional philosophy. But his design also meant that the buildings were not monotonously repetitive, as were many of the soulless modern blocks that he deplored with their endless rows of doors and windows, 'which could be snipped off by the yard at any point'. Instead the buildings had the sense of being a deliberate composition with a beginning and an end, something that was bounded and that could be imagined in a picture frame. They were built to a human scale, a foil, then, to London's suburban sprawl, its endless rows of bleak slum housing and to the inhuman vastness of some of the council estates that were to follow. Like his health centre, Lubetkin's apartment blocks had a futuristic beauty while being welcoming and accessible. He thought that the entrance to the

Rosebery Avenue block, with its gently curved roof over a pair of concrete benches, was like a greeting. 'The porch smiles at you and asks, "Would you rather sit here or here?"', he fancied. Lubetkin's ethos was modernism with a human face.

Located a little to the west of Spa Green, another of Lubetkin's Finsbury estates was initially going to be named after Lenin. The Russian revolutionary stayed in the area early in the century, first at 30 Holford Square and a few years later nearby at Percy Circus. During the Second World War Harold Riley, encouraged by the Finsbury Communist Party, established an Anglo-Soviet Committee and with London County Council had a plaque to Lenin installed at the remains of 30 Holford Square, the square having been badly damaged during the Blitz. Lubetkin later created a more substantial memorial, a concrete bust in a crimson painted niche, which in 1942 was put up on the square. The monument was repeatedly vandalised by fascist sympathisers and had to be protected by police guard. When the Cold War loomed it was removed, and is said to have been buried in the foundations of the new estate. It was replaced by a bust of the Labour politician and trade unionist Ernest Bevin, who as post-war Foreign Secretary took a strongly anti-communist position; the estate was completed in 1954 and named after him.

Bevin Court was built on a striking location not far from King's Cross among a cluster of roads lined with elegant Georgian houses and overlooking steeply sloped Percy Circus with its central disc of green. In the ruins of Holford Square Lubetkin put up a seven-storey building featuring a bold chequerboard pattern made up of three blocks in a Y-shaped configuration pointing east, north and south into the surrounding city, and converging at the centre on a circular staircase, the round structures and the small grassy circus in front of the entrance echoing Percy Circus just below. Murals painted in communal areas depicted scenes from British and London history. Bevin Court made a strong contrast with the area around it, but with its echoes of the surrounding topography the effect was to good-naturedly show a vision for a new city alongside those of earlier architects and builders. Amid the quiet greenery of the setting the buildings and spaces created a powerful sense of place and of home.

Aerial view of Bevin Court

Bevin Court's central staircase was an extraordinary feat of spatial organisation, a Constructivist-inspired marvel of curved, open landings and flights of stairs arranged around a central pillar. As residents made their way up through the building they would pass broad windowless openings which presented them with shifting panoramas over London, towards the Gothic St Pancras Hotel by King's Cross Station to the west and Holborn and the City to the south. Lubetkin's staircase took the residents of Bevin Court up in an airborne spiral over their city. Hidden within the core of the building, it was Lubetkin's version of Tatlin's Tower, an ideological transmitter of hope, civic pride and social advance.

The achievements of Lubetkin and Salter to some extent give the lie to the prophecy of Thomas More's Raphael that visionaries who enter the corridors of political power will fail. Over time, though, Lubetkin's and Salter's original visions were watered down. Ada Salter dealt with this with a certain pragmatism, eventually accepting the need for the building of workaday tenement blocks and going on to join London County Council's Parks Department.

Lubetkin was less sanguine. He had felt the molten euphoria of the early years of the Russian Revolution, when the world seemed radically open with possibility. After he left Russia that sense of experimentation faded as art and culture came under the control of the Soviet state; he was highly critical of the social realism imposed by Stalin. In post-war London he felt also the dulling of a bright social vision. The high modernist ideals of the 1930s for which he had found a vehicle through Katial and Riley later became institutionalised, not through the commands of a totalitarian dictator but by regulations and penny-pinching constraints imposed by government departments. Utopian dreams 'had to be submitted in triplicate for Ministry approval', he grumbled. Lubetkin became increasingly disillusioned and believed that the Golden Age of modern architecture was over: 'its current trivialities have become dreary and ineffective, its platitudes increasingly irrelevant, repetitive and shatteringly boring . . . Such are the tattered remains of a faith that once appeared as a powerful stimulus to change.' In the end, then, Lubetkin seemed to have adopted the position of More's Raphael and with it felt the disappointment of the social prophet whose real-world creations fall short of the vision from which they came.

But by uniting utopian dreams with the compromised world of politics, Salter and Lubetkin constructed living monuments to utopia that survive to this day, their housing schemes now beloved by social historians and the architectural cognoscenti. Far from being museum pieces, Wilson Grove, Spa Green and Bevin Court remain pleasant enclaves in the heart of the city. Spa Green, with its well-kept balconies, colourful nursery and communal chessboard next to benches in the adjoining park, exudes a feeling of homeliness and civic pride. The entrance hall at Bevin Court has been well maintained, its stunning central staircase still carrying the estate's residents aloft over London in a spirit of communal celebration.

Utopian dreams sometimes create threads through time centred on particular areas of the city. Lubetkin's and Katial's achievements helped complete one such lineage in Finsbury that reached back to earlier periods in London's utopian history. In the early nineteenth century the area had been an arena for the Spenceans, some of whom were implicated in the Spa Fields Riots of 1816. During the years of Owenite ferment in the city, a group of printers set up a community nearby aimed at providing its residents with secure accommodation and protection against unemployment, sickness and old age. Its members also hoped to set up a clinic and laboratory, and to keep health records to monitor the health of the community. In embryonic form, this example of an early utopian venture encompassed social aims that would re-emerge in the area through the housing and health programmes of a twentieth-century local government. The visions of Riley, Katial and Lubetkin imagined and brought into being in the twentieth century what their forebears had only hazily perceived in the nineteenth. The area around Spa Fields in Clerkenwell became a utopian zone in London's imaginative space-time.

The achievements of Salter and Lubetkin were embodiments of the institutionalised form of utopianism that in the middle decades of the twentieth century saw new social visions being pursued through government. But these decades witnessed also the beginnings of a profound disenchantment with utopianism and the ambitious government programmes that underpinned it. The horrors of the world wars made it harder to maintain the faith of eighteenth- and nineteenth-century utopians in historical progress and in humans' ability to easily remould society that practical visionaries like Salter and Lubetkin had inherited. The British intellectuals Karl Popper and Isaiah Berlin developed philosophical critiques of the utopian enterprise and argued for a more limited notion of human advancement. Popper and Berlin were of Central European and Jewish descent and had fled their countries of birth as tyranny loomed in Europe; before emigrating they had witnessed atrocities that turned them firmly away from communism. Berlin and Popper drew a line from utopianism to totalitarianism, whether in the form of fascism or authoritarian communism, and made a plea for liberal pragmatism against the all-encompassing visions of utopia.

Berlin and Popper viewed utopia as the attempt to put into practice a complete, final plan for the remaking of society – for the implementation of a social blueprint. They argued that utopian schemes were based on a belief in a Platonic ideal: an absolute criterion for the social good that could be discovered by reason. Because true knowledge underpinned the perfect society, utopians claimed that vice and misery were the result of ignorance, and so for many of them education was the key to social perfection. Moreover, utopians often believed that the implementation of their blueprint was historically ordained. History was a progressive force governed by a set of laws that were understood by the enlightened utopian, who was able to rationalise the manifestation of their vision as the final act of a vast historical drama.

Berlin and Popper argued that these assumptions were false. Utopians claimed to have discovered ultimate blueprints, but implementation of any utopian plan would take time, future generations would face new problems and have new desires, and social interventions would trigger off unanticipated chains of consequences. Utopians assumed fixity in a world of flux.

If the make-up of the good society can change over time, then there is a deeper problem with utopianism, they argued. Berlin held that there were many aims of human life, rather than a single one – liberty, equality, beauty, charity and so on – and that these cannot be reduced to a single end or be compared using some overall criterion. To a utopian, disagreement about ultimate ends is the sign of a dysfunctional society. But the 'incommensurability' of ends meant that it would be impossible to resolve every collision in values and arrive at a state in which all good things existed together. A perfect world was a conceptual impossibility.

Because there is no rational way of discovering an ultimate social end, then when disagreement arises the only recourse for the utopian leader is force, argued Popper and Berlin. Utopians quickly become fanatics, because if one truly believes in a definitive solution to society's ills then no cost is too high to bring it about. Utopianism becomes a form of religion and those with different ideals have to be defeated. Utopians dream of an 'apocalyptic revolution', said Popper. They must purify society and banish whatever is inconsistent with their ideology, even if that means killing millions in gas chambers and gulags. As Berlin put it: 'If your desire to save mankind is serious, you must harden your heart, and not reckon the cost.'

Instead of pursuing impossible dreams, Popper and Berlin argued for the elimination of 'concrete miseries' such as poor sanitation or dilapidated roads, which can be agreed upon relatively easily, rather than the pursuit of an ideal happiness about which people will never agree. The best we could do, argued Berlin, was to seek trade-offs so as to maintain a precarious equilibrium between diverse people pursuing different aims in life and stop them from harming each other. Society would have to settle for 'logically untidy, flexible, and even ambiguous compromise'.

In the decades following the work of Lubetkin, Katial and Salter, criticisms of utopianism at a philosophical level were echoed in changing views of the role of government, including in its provision of housing. The early socialist hope had been for decent state housing, not just for the poor but for prosperous working people in stable employment. Council housing was to be the route to a more equal, less class-ridden society. Gradually the shine wore off this dream. In the 1960s and 1970s vast concrete high-rise council estates were built. Many of them were thrown up hastily and began to leak and crack. In London a watershed in the perception of high-rise council housing came with the collapse in 1968 of the twenty-three-storey Ronan Point tower block in Canning Town two months after its opening. Social problems emerged on many estates, which began to be perceived as places of poverty, crime and unemployment rather than brave social advancement. Council housing came to be seen as a last resort for the poorest, not as a way of achieving the utopian dream of bringing together different classes in mixed communities.

In the 1970s began the era of neo-liberal capitalism and the exaltation of free markets and finance. Its adherents in government sought to reduce the role of the state in economic management and in the provision of public services, including that of housing. Policy shifted to one of 'residualisation', under which public housing was only given to the most needy. Council housing became a social ambulance service and estates were places to escape from, not to aspire to, a badge of failure, not of success. This new view of council housing was reflected in and strengthened by Margaret Thatcher's Right to Buy policy, which allowed council tenants to purchase their homes at a discount, transforming collective assets into private wealth.

In 1985 a geographer, Alice Coleman, published *Utopia on Trial*, a study of council estates which blamed their social problems on their physical design. The preponderance of high-rise blocks, the frequent use of concrete walkways and the sheer size of many of the estates made people lose any sense of civic pride and encouraged graffiti, vandalism and crime, she argued. Coleman's analysis fuelled a more general critique of the broader ideal of state-provided housing. But it failed to recognise poverty and unemployment as the root causes of the social problems on council estates, especially when upmarket residential developments with many of the same supposedly problematic design features, such as the Barbican Estate in the City, did not suffer from those problems.

Neo-liberal capitalism, a boon to more affluent tenants who were able to buy their homes, combined with the cuts to public services and the high unemployment of the early 1980s left behind many who were not able to take advantage of new market opportunities. It was not that estates had failed, but that the broader economic philosophy in which they were embedded no longer served them. Selling off council homes reduced the available housing stock, accentuating the shift towards making council housing available only to the neediest and most vulnerable. Encouraging the aspiration for private home ownership undermined the original utopian purpose of the state provision of housing. The failure of the 'problem' estates became a self-fulfilling prophecy.

In the middle of the century, brutalist architecture and its preferred building material of concrete were the symbols of the utopia of the welfare state and public housing. In the 1970s and 1980s they became emblems of poverty, deprivation and failure. They came also to represent the oppressive uniformity that Isaiah Berlin feared would be the consequence of the pursuit of utopia. François Truffaut's 1966 film adaptation of Ray Bradbury's novel *Fahrenheit 451* depicted a technologically advanced society of the future that had achieved equality and classlessness at the cost of turning into a dystopia run by a central authority which required of its citizens a conformity of belief and knowledge. Firemen were employed not to put out fires but to make bonfires of books, which had been prohibited in order to stop the development of critical thinking among the state's citizens. 'We all have to be alike,' declares one of the firemen. 'The only way to be happy is for everyone to be made equal.' A scene of a man's apartment being raided and his small collection of books being plunged into flames outside a concrete block of flats was filmed at the Alton Estate in Roehampton in south-west London, a significant development built in the 1950s, one section of which used modernist design principles. In Truffaut's rendering the estate becomes a scene of hell, which the book-loving man only manages to escape by running under the characteristic Corbusian-derived pilotis that support the blocks and away through the concrete maze. In the film, a haven of individuality is a secret library hidden in one woman's house – a distinctly unmodernist detached villa with mock-Tudor beams and a garden full of shrubs and trees – a place that would not look out of place in Letchworth or in one of London's leafy developer-built suburbs. As Truffaut presented his rendering of a dystopian London, the city's population continued to fall as those who were able to do so fled in search of owner occupation to airier localities in the suburbs and the Home Counties. The 'inner city' became synonymous with deprivation and social dysfunction.

During the long years of Tory rule of the 1980s and 1990s, the socialist dreams of the middle of the century were left behind in favour of privatisation and the development of banking and finance. Margaret Thatcher abolished the Greater London Council, leaving London without a government and neutralising a source of left-wing radicalism in the city. But new utopias would emerge over this period. They rejected neo-liberal London along with the earlier socialist ideals of rational planning and equality built in concrete. Far from being the tyrannical version of utopia depicted by Popper and Berlin, they were exuberant, open, counter-cultural visions rooted in 1960s radicalism that brought vivid new meanings to London's social dreams.

Chapter Eight

Beneath the Tarmac

A Saturday morning in May 1995, and on Camden High Street in north London people are doing normal weekend things: browsing stalls, popping into cafes, and with some trepidation making their way across the car-clogged road. Suddenly a crashing sound startles the pedestrians. Two cars have collided, bringing the traffic to a halt. The drivers get out of their vehicles and start shouting at each other. One of them produces a hammer and begins hitting the other driver's car, the pressure cooker of the city boiling over, it seems, into the uncontrolled rage of a motorist forced out of his isolated metal box to face a fellow human with fists and weapons. As people gape at the scene, hundreds of others emerge from the crowd and from the nearby Tube station. Some jump on top of the two cars and begin smashing them up. Shards of glass go flying as a man kicks out a windscreen. Others throw paint around and daub yellow swirls on to the carcasses of the vehicles. A banner goes up over the road: RECLAIM THE STREETS – FREE THE CITY / KILL THE CAR. Revellers fill the street. Drummers and jugglers appear. People power up the bicycle-mounted Rinky Dink sound system by pedalling on it. Children swing on a climbing frame that has been placed in the middle of the road, and free food is given out. The normal everyday has been overturned, the road made into an arena for experimentation, play and social connection rather than simply a way of getting from here to there. A poster for the strange happening organised by a group of activists going by the name Reclaim the Streets says: 'If you want to change the city – you have to control the streets.'

Reclaim the Streets, Camden, 1995

A few months later an airhorn blasts out on congested Upper Street in Islington in north London. Twenty-foot-high tripods made out of scaffolding poles are quickly erected in the road; a person shins up to the top of each one and sits on the apex, securing the street against traffic. Sand is dumped on to the tarmac to create a beach and children build sandcastles where minutes before lorries thundered past. From a sound system mounted on an armoured vehicle the voice of Louis Armstrong floats over the emptied tarmac – 'I see trees of green . . . I see skies of blue . . . I see friends shaking hands . . .' – and for a few minutes the city enters into a trance. Soon the area fills up with thousands of people and turns into a massive street party, pulsating to the sounds of acid house. A counterfeit road sign appears at the entrance to the transformed space, white lettering on a red background of the type that normally warns drivers of approaching road works: CHANGED PRIORITIES AHEAD.

★

Reclaim the Streets held its first parties at the tail end of the Tory rule of the 1980s and 1990s, an era in which cars and private home ownership became pillars of the free-market economy. Economic success came to be seen as escaping the council estate for a private house – or at least buying your own council property – and the ultimate consumer good of the car became the economic outrider of the property-based economy. Home ownership magnified private wealth, particularly in London, which saw the most extreme increases in house prices.

Margaret Thatcher's government ran down public transport in favour of 'the great car economy' as part of the Conservatives' Roads for Prosperity policy, 'the biggest road-building programme since the Romans'. More roads encouraged the demand for cars, stimulating private consumption, and the car became a symbol of free-market man and woman. Contained within their own metal shell, striving individuals were to whizz along the new highways to workplaces and shopping centres, aiding the circulation of goods and money and speeding up the pace of capitalism itself.

Reclaim the Streets' parties – their 'protestivals' – were a colourful, noisy repudiation of this world view. To the group's activists cars represented a false freedom as they pollute and squeeze out alternative uses of space in the city, leading to a congested and inhospitable urban environment. One of its flyers encapsulated the group's credo: 'CARS CANNOT DANCE: When they move they are violent and brutish, they lack sensitivity and rhythm. CARS CANNOT PLAY: When they diverge from the straight and narrow, they kill. CARS CANNOT SOCIALISE: They privatise, separate, isolate and alienate.'

Reclaim the Streets came out of a DIY counter-culture that had developed in Britain over the 1980s and 1990s, youth-driven movements of non-violent direct action, green radicalism, free parties and new forms of music – punk, and later on house and techno – which espoused a homemade underground ethos. The summer of 1988 saw the rise of raves, unlicensed all-night parties in derelict warehouses fuelled by acid house and by the recreational drug ecstasy. The government clamped down on this new youth culture, in particular with the passing in 1994 of the Criminal Justice Act, which targeted raves and many of the activities of direct-action protestors. (Notoriously, the Act gave authorities the power to shut down gatherings playing music 'characterised by the emission of a succession of repetitive beats'.) Over these years a radical direct-action environmental movement was burgeoning in Britain, rooted in the same counter-cultural subsoil. In the early 1990s, at Twyford Down near Winchester, activists took up residence in a protest camp of treehouses to disrupt work on the building of a section of the M3 motorway. The activists, calling themselves the Dongas Tribe, adopted a distinctive New Age ethos, abandoning conventional life for one of anti-materialism and community living.

Reclaim the Streets' direct actions that followed in London built on these early efforts. They were protests against the economic system as a whole, not just the supremacy of the car. The rise of neo-liberal capitalism was represented most starkly by the development of London's Docklands. Over the 1980s and 1990s a new city rose on the remains of London's abandoned docks on the Isle of Dogs, the large peninsula formed by the Thames's deep southward bend at Greenwich. Docklands was transformed into Canary Wharf, a crystal city of high finance gridded out over the ruins of an earlier mercantile world that had dealt in tangible rope, sugar and timber. Blake's grimy chartered streets by the Thames were remade into corporate-stamped avenues of glossy skyscrapers.

Canary Wharf is separated from the rest of London by Aspen Way, a large highway that runs west to east across the top of the peninsula, from Limehouse to Canning Town. The areas adjacent to Docklands on the other side of the road – Poplar in Tower Hamlets and the Olympic Borough of Newham – are some of the poorest in London. Aspen Way, which has few crossing points for the pedestrian wishing to enter or exit Canary Wharf, acts as a symbolic as well as physical barrier between the glass city and the district around it. In those neighbouring areas lie the relics of an earlier communal vision for London. Facing Docklands a little to the north of Aspen Way on the East India Dock Road is the Lansbury Estate, the model council estate that was part of the Festival of Britain in 1951. Still in use, the community of houses and low-rise blocks in yellow brick is today loomed over by the glass towers of Canary Wharf, HSBC, Citibank and the Barclays Group.

The glass of Canary Wharf's towers does not symbolise a city of communal dreams as it had done in the modernist designs of Berthold Lubetkin, but rather the market ethic pursued by financial traders and data wizards in the service of a globalised turbo capitalism. It was a radical break from the kind of development sought by the visionary London governments of earlier decades and a physical emblem of the Conservative government's free-market ethos, against which London's new utopian movements would rebel.

North of Newham, in the eastern suburbs of the city, a group of street visionaries in the 1990s held a series of elaborate protests triggered by plans for the building of a major new road. Their movement led to the creation of a fragment of utopia in east London that stood as an alternative to the London of finance and capital and would later evolve into Reclaim the Streets.

The protests began in Wanstead in east London on an unremarkable green next to the Tube station. George Green was a small remnant of the southern end of Epping Forest, pockets of ancient woodland that survived London's eastward expansion and led to a larger area of forest to the north at Loughton and Theydon Bois. The surrounding area was a tranquil, village-like suburb, bounded on three sides by woods, parks and a golf course. It was the sort of place that poorer east Londoners would aspire to trade up to through the purchase of a large semi or detached house on one of the district's leafy residential roads. Next to Wanstead and connected to it by the Central Line were the grittier districts of Leyton and Leytonstone.

Hanging over these localities were plans to build through them a highway three and a half miles long to create a faster route out of east London. The A12 Hackney to M11 Link Road would run from the Blackwall Tunnel approach in Hackney Wick, through Leyton, Leytonstone and Wanstead and on to the M11, which led north out of London to Stansted Airport and Cambridge. The road would, it was claimed, shave just six minutes off the car journey across east London. The route had been proposed in the 1960s and over subsequent decades local residents had voiced their opposition to it, including during public inquiries and a High Court case. One resident described the road as 'a poisoned dart aimed at the heart of London'. Finally, in September 1993 construction of the six-lane highway got under way. It meant the destruction of 350 houses and several pieces of ancient woodland along the route.

At this point veterans of Britain's environmental protest movement became involved with the campaign against the road, bringing the radical green mysticism of Twyford Down into an urban struggle, which as well as environmental issues encompassed social concerns about housing and the threat to community life in London. A coalition of New Age travellers, environmental activists and local residents began to form in Wanstead and Leyton, and opposition to the road turned from conventional lobbying to direct action.

The protests began at a 250-year-old sweet chestnut tree on George Green that lay in the path of the new road. In early November 1993, the road builders put a fence around it in advance of the clearing of the area. Earth was also dug out from around the roots of a number of trees in preparation for their felling and placed in a large heap. A few days later local residents, including pensioners and children, along with the newly arrived activists pulled down the eight-foot-high wooden fences and quickly overran the security guards. They decorated the tree with ribbons and danced round it, chanting 'Let the tree live!' Children planted a flowerbed with the words 'Save our Planet' written on it in pebbles. The local lollipop lady, urged to come by the children she guided across the road, arrived in her fluorescent coat and used her lollipop as a spade to help carry the pile of earth back to the roots from where it had been dug. 'We're going to fight for every blade of grass,' she declared.

Some local residents were initially discomfited by the appearance in respectable Wanstead of a band of eco-warriors with matted hair and tatty boots. But if there was ever any real divide between the residents who opposed the roads and the activists, then the pulling down of the fence helped remove it. It was an act of collective catharsis which united the groups in the face of a common enemy. For many of the locals, participating in such a transgressive act triggered a new social and political consciousness. Of the new activists one local resident said: 'They may look different, but they believe in the things which, deep down, all thinking people should believe in.'

After the destruction of the fence, the more experienced activists took up residence in a treehouse in the branches of the chestnut tree complete with its own small kitchen, which they built out of the remains of the barriers. In the tree lived Green Dave, a former panel beater and mechanic, who described becoming a protestor as a kind of rebirth. He would wake to the scampering of squirrels, pick chestnuts from the branches and roast them for breakfast. A small encampment grew up around him. A placard placed on the trunk said: 'Trees Won't be the only Casualty as the M11 link road rips thru our community for no good reason'.

At night a fire was lit and people would juggle with flaming torches. Visitors brought food, clothes and wood. At the foot of the tree people would come together and discuss the progress of the campaign and also bigger questions about the prospects for a new kind of society. Many said that these conversations changed them: differences in class and background were forgotten and they tried out new ideas and ways of relating with each other, making connections that otherwise may never have come about. One of the road builders' security men, realising that he agreed with the protestors, quit his job and joined them in the treehouse. A longtime activist from the area commented that they had been trying to bring local people together for years. With a tree acting as a social condenser, it seemed to be happening overnight.

The tree dwellers installed a letter box in the branches, and a well-wisher in Cheshire sent a letter of support. The anti-road campaign's lawyer successfully argued in the High Court that this made the tree a legal dwelling, giving its inhabitants squatters' rights and obliging the authorities to obtain an eviction order before they cut down the tree. Hundreds of letters were then sent, a few of them from the United States and Canada. One correspondent remembered as a boy scrambling on the trunk of the tree and collecting chestnuts while waiting for his bus to arrive. Another hailed the tree as 'a symbol of continuity and permanence in a sprawling, polluted city'. Someone else imagined it as a gateway to an alternative reality: 'Above the twisted branches of the chestnut tree / Lies a secret kingdom where the folk are free.'

The tree dwellers braved winter temperatures and much greater danger when one night unknown assailants firebombed the treehouse. The inhabitants managed to escape and carried on with their occupation. The inevitable eviction eventually came on a dark, rainy morning in December when hundreds of police arrived on the green. They were met by hundreds of protestors who were stationed round the tree and in its branches. After a melee in the mud, during which some protestors were left bloody-faced, the police surrounded the tree and pulled people from the branches. In the low afternoon sun a digger moved in, smashed through the treehouse and felled the tree.

The tree, a symbol of the pastoral idyll and of people's right to common land, had a powerful historical resonance. One young protestor connected the battle for George Green to resistance to the enclosure of common land in past centuries. In the nineteenth century there had been vigorous opposition to the fencing-off of another part of Epping Forest, nearby Wanstead Flats, when working people were urged to save the forest and pulled the fences down. 'Things go in cycles and we're back again, the people of Wanstead and Leytonstone empowered and taking their land back,' he said. In a letter to the tree, a supporter of the campaign referenced the English Revolution of the seventeenth century, saluting the tree dwellers for their courage in attempting to throw off the Norman yoke. A protest song, 'The Wanstead Chestnut and the Motorway', with its fiery castigation of injustice and clumping rhythms summoned up the old utopian songs of the kind that Thomas Spence and his men had sung in the taverns of Holborn 200 years earlier. It attacked 'the speculators' whose greed had imprisoned the 'leafy giant man'; soon an uprising would 'reveal the tyrants' face'. The creation of flowerbeds and the symbolic digging of earth on common land, consciously or not, evoked Winstanley's Diggers. The burning of the Diggers' cottages and their eviction from the land seemed to be replayed in the firebombing of the George Green treehouse and the later violent eviction of the protestors. Like the Diggers, the M11 activists would quickly regroup at new sites of protest, engaging in a shifting war of attrition with the authorities.

Adjacent to George Green on Cambridge Park Road stood a row of Edwardian houses that were due to be demolished to make way for the new highway. After the felling of the tree a group of activists squatted the houses, which were now empty of their former inhabitants. They declared the site the Independent Free Area of Wanstonia, issued passports and appointed ministers. A sign at the entrance to the houses read 'Welcome to Wanstonia A Return to True Democracy Life and Community'. Over the following months, further declarations of independence were made at sites along the route of the proposed road. An old copse occupied by the protestors became Leytonstonia, three houses near Leytonstone Tube the State of Euphoria, and an empty sweet shop near Wanstead Tube Wanstonia Rising. The biggest statelet was in

Leyton on Claremont Road, a vibrant enclave whose inhabitants sought to make daily life a fusion of artistic expression, community living and radical protest.

Claremont Road was an ordinary late-nineteenth-century terrace that lay behind the larger car-clogged Grove Green Road and joined it at each end in a C-shape. The main part of it had houses on only one side, looking on to a fence behind which was the Tube line running between Leyton and Leytonstone Stations. The road was part of an unprepossessing and run-down locality, a world away from the natural beauty of Twyford Down where the utopian spirit of many of the activists now protesting against the link road had first risen up.

The properties along the route of the new road had been subject to compulsory purchase orders by the Department of Transport for eventual demolition and in the interim were offered to a housing association which let them for low rents. A colony of artists grew up, many of whom documented the increasingly dilapidated state of the area as more houses were abandoned. One of them left a painting of a modernist city in greys and white with a tornado approaching it.

By 1994 many of the houses were derelict, their windows and doors sealed up with breeze blocks, and only a few of the original residents remained. Most of those who left handed over their keys to the squatters rather than to the Department of Transport. The small number of houses that were turned over to the authorities were made uninhabitable by the ripping-out of pipes, staircases and floors. During several months in 1994, protestors took over the houses on Claremont Road and placed barricades at the entrances to the street, turning it into a traffic-free enclave, and set about repairing the houses. Using bricks and scrap metal taken from worksites during demonstrations, they transformed the road into an art installation-cum-protest site and, when eviction loomed later in the year, into a vast collective barricade.

A sign on the road informed visitors that they had entered

William Morris, who imagined a London of pastoral bliss and true human fellowship

Pages from Morris's utopian novel *News from Nowhere*, which set out his vision of London remade

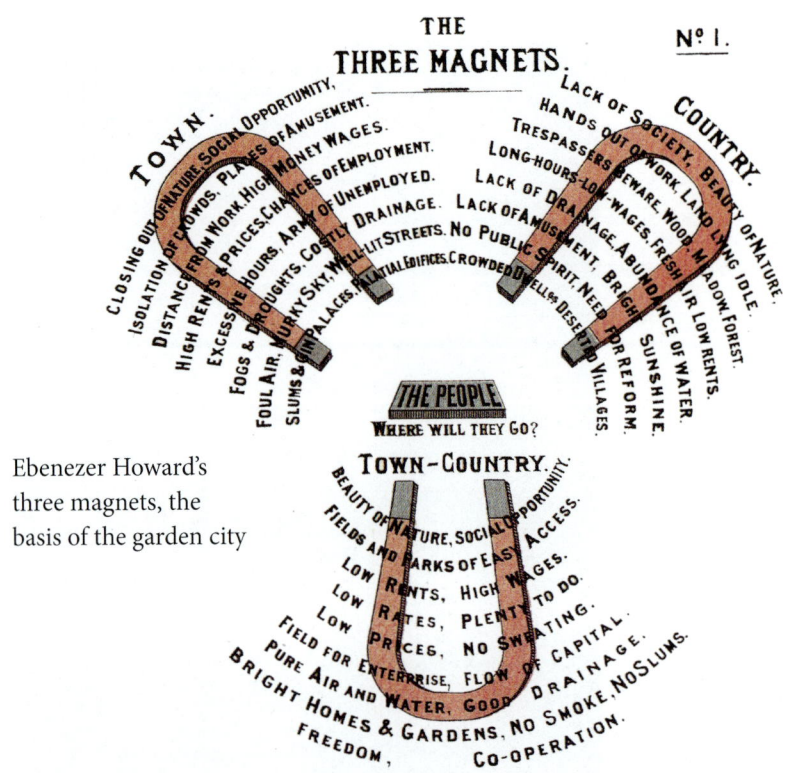

Ebenezer Howard's three magnets, the basis of the garden city

Raymond Unwin, architect of Letchworth and Hampstead Garden Suburb

Waterlow Court at Hampstead Garden Suburb for single working women

The founder of Hampstead Garden Suburb, Henrietta Barnett, with her ward, Dorothy Woods

Wartime poster depicting Finsbury Health Centre as a contrast with disease-ridden old London

Ada Salter, the instigator of the Bermondsey Revolution

The visionary architect Berthold Lubetkin, who introduced his modernist utopian vision into the working class borough of Finsbury

The central staircase of Lubetkin's Bevin Court

Murals along the houses at Claremont Road

Rooms in the street and sky at Claremont Road

Long-time Claremont Road resident Dolly Watson with one of her new utopian neighbours

Diane Corvin's 1991 statues of the Salters – Ada, Alfred and Joyce – by the Thames at Bermondsey

'The Independent Free Area of Claremonté' and contained a 'statement of defiance' that set out the aims of the statelet: to be a living work of art, a healing space, a caring community, a situation comedy and a PARTY. A Claremont Tube Station sign was placed on the fence in front of the Tube line and passing train drivers would occasionally toot their support. The houses were symbolically unified with a hippyish design of green tendrils and daisies which was painted along them as a single mural. The breeze blocks that sealed the windows became canvases for paintings: a woman releasing a dove into a yellow sky above a green mountain, a black cat under a lamp, and on the three sides of a bay window a triptych of men and women dancing together. Colourful horses galloping through stars were painted on a broken wall at one end of the road; on another was a picture of planet earth covered in cars. A defunct car, painted green with 'Rust in Peace' written on its side, had plants growing thickly through its windscreen. A chessboard painted on the street used hubcaps and traffic cones as pieces, the detritus of the car culture turned over to a ludic power reawakened on the road. Using the methods of 'culture-jamming' – subversively parodying the propaganda of capitalist society such as its advertising billboards – a placard was placed on the side of one house which in slick corporate lettering bore the words Welcome Claremont Ideal Homes, lampooning the signs placed around the city by commercial property developers. A large banner hung across several houses read: IMAGINE THIS PLACE, AS A HOME, A WOOD OR THE M11 LINK.

One of the original residents who had held out in Claremont Road was Dolly Watson, a nonagenarian who had been born on the street. She immediately took the activists to heart, and they called her the Queen of Claremont Road. A photo of the time captures the lifelong East Ender drinking tea in front of her house with a shaggy-haired activist in stripy pantaloons and a patchwork waistcoat worn over his bare chest bearing pictures of leaves and a sun. 'If I was Queen, you'd all be knighted,' she told the young utopians.

The communal spirit of Claremont Road was symbolised by bringing the rooms of the houses, normally divided by walls, into the collective space of the street. Sofas, chairs, bookcases, rugs and fireplaces were dragged outside and set up as a series of living rooms along the centre of the road. In this way 'life stopped being so atomised', explained one of the new residents. The doors of the houses were left open so that people could wander in and out and holes were knocked in the walls inside to make the houses into a series of connected spaces. Two community cafes were opened, Cafe Claremonté and the Seventh Heaven Jazz Cafe, and communal meals cooked using the perfectly edible food thrown away by supermarkets.

The Claremontians installed treehouses, platforms and rope bridges along the road and hung the trees with old bottles, televisions, hubcaps, bits of scrap metal and dayglo fabric. From the tops of the houses they put up large cargo nets which reached across the street over the roofs, making it possible to move around without touching the ground. On one of the roofs was a set of gallows, placed there to symbolise the inevitable destruction of the street to come. Their most audacious construction was a tower built on the roof of number 15 constructed out of hundreds of scaffolding poles taken from the surrounding road worksites, painted bright pink and connected together in a jumbled lattice that supported several platforms. It rose some hundred feet into the sky, had a sound system at the top and was decorated with banners: 'Defy the Criminal Injustice Act', 'Let London Breathe', 'Your Car or Your Kids'. Dominating the local skyline, it was an anarchic echo of two tower blocks located on the other side of the railway tracks, a freewheeling, risky architecture rising out of the dependable suburban terraces below it. In honour of the Queen of Claremonté the tower was named Dolly.

In the summer of 1994 Claremont Road became a festival of resistance. There were musical performances, bonfires and street parties. Films about previous campaigns of civil disobedience were projected on to walls, turning the street into an open-air cinema.

Number 68 became the art house. On one of its walls was painted visions of dystopia and utopia: a dark concrete city overrun with cars overseen by the figure of death merging into a verdant scene of trees and a green lady of the forest. In the bathroom a road in the form of a painted serpent came out of the plughole and reared up the wall in a vortex of coins and notes and images of uprooted trees and bulldozers. Upstairs, a wardrobe full of shirts had a door in the back of it that emerged, Narnia-like, into a bizarre world, a disturbing scene of industrial decay and waste: traffic cones, tyres and bits of old engines piled up in what used to be a child's room with its teddy bear wallpaper, now dimly lit and covered in anti-car slogans. A single leaf was reverently displayed in a wooden frame, and lines from Walt Whitman were written up in violet: 'I believe a leaf of grass is the journeywork of the stars . . . and a mouse is miracle enough to stagger sextillions of politicians.'

One of the squatters explained that reimagined Claremont Road was 'against hurrying from one place to the next . . . in a little shell of a car that's not connected to anything else, that's isolating and alienating and polluting'. As the new community took shape, many of the people involved began to see the enterprise as bigger than a protest against a road. With its brightly coloured sculptures and paintings, its rope bridges and nets in the sky, Claremont Road was a place of imagination and fantasy – 'an adventure playground for adults and misfits', said one of its residents – where the conventions of normal life might be cast aside. It was an attempt to try out an open, spontaneous, communal way of life. Without conventional kinds of hierarchy or compulsion, the Claremontians would drift between activities – hammering, painting or cooking, talking as they went – a little like Fourier imagined that the inhabitants of his phalanstery might. From time to time there would be frenetic activity when the activists invaded nearby road worksites, outwitting the security guards to lie under bulldozers or chain themselves to pieces of machinery in order to hold back the advance of the road towards their utopia.

Claremont Road gave 'the sense of an authentic form of community and . . . that oppositional edge of being against the lies and corruption of the wider world', one resident said. A young woman who participated in the community remembered walking down Claremont Road with a plank of wood over her shoulder, past dogs and children and people playing music, and feeling a sense of belonging for the first time in her life. For the people there, life on the road pointed to the future London and the future society that they yearned for.

The utopia that developed at Claremont Road, and later through Reclaim the Streets, was a grassroots, counter-cultural vision that opposed capitalism but was also quite different to the socialist utopias that had been pursued by politicians in the middle decades of the twentieth century. In their use of activist art and direct action the road protestors were a long way from the austere rationality of modernist utopias and from the pursuit of utopia through politics and state planning. In the road protestors' view, these visions were clinical versions of utopia that stifled the exuberant spirit of the streets.

The activists were influenced by strands of anarchist and unorthodox Marxist thinking rooted in avant-garde art movements such as surrealism and Dada, which earlier in the century had infused revolutionary ideals with those of imagination and desire. This mingling came about through the creation in 1957 of the Paris-centred Situationist International, a grouping of European artists and intellectuals who sought new critiques of capitalism during decades in which the economic system seemed finally to be solving the problem of material scarcity as cars, washing machines and foreign holidays came within reach of working people, at least those in Western Europe and the United States. Claremont Road and Reclaim the Streets were striking examples of the practical application of Situationist ideas, and this philosophical ancestry broadened their anti-car message into a full-blown critique of capitalism. In a car- and carbon-based economy, simply opposing cars was futile. As one Reclaim the Streets activist put it: 'The streets are as full of capitalism as of cars and the pollution of capitalism is much more insidious.'

The Situationists' leading ideologue, the French film-maker, writer and inveterate rebel Guy Debord, in 1967 published *The Society of the Spectacle*, a book consisting of 221 theses, the first of which stated: 'In societies where modern conditions of production prevail, life is presented as an immense accumulation of spectacles. Everything that was directly lived has receded into a representation.' In the nineteenth century, Marx had described capitalism as generating an 'immense accumulation of commodities'. The domination of society by the economy had resulted in human fulfilment being identified with what one owned, no longer with what one was. As Debord put it, the supremacy of markets and money had led to the 'degradation of *being* into *having*'. But by the late twentieth century, society was awash with commodities and saturated with images of them on television screens and billboards. Human worth became identified less with what one owned than with the appearance that one's possessions gave rise to: less with owning trainers and a hatchback than with being a devotee of Nike or of Renault. This stage of capitalism brought a 'shift from *having* to *appearing*'. People were in thrall to what Debord termed the 'spectacle', representations of products and lifestyles that made individuals want to own ever more commodities. Humdrum work was endured in order to pay for 'spectacular' consumption. People's deeper yearnings for the elements of a fully lived life were fed back to them as sanitised images through the commodity system: overworked people with little time to cook and gather round a dinner table would instead view images of these sorts of social rituals on television cookery programmes and in the marketing of lifestyle brands. Pictures of celebrities in magazines present us with lives of adventure and excitement, which we consume as a distraction from the monotony of commuting and work. Debord argued that the state, which aided the development of the capitalist economy, also contributed to the power of the spectacle.

Bureaucracies' urban plans in dull concrete led to the 'petrification of life' just as surely as consumerism did.

The Situationists believed that in the twentieth century the spectacle had become the reigning principle of society, making people into observers of their own lives rather than true participants. It had colonised everyday life, reducing people to puppets who perform the roles given to them through marketing categories. Even the smallest gestures – sipping a coffee or leafing through a newspaper on a train platform – are poses that we unconsciously select from those presented to us as part of the spectacle. It was Marxist alienation in a more radical form: one in which the colonisation of outer and inner life severed people from their environments and from their true feelings and desires. Dazzled by the bright light of the spectacle, it becomes harder than ever to imagine an alternative way of life.

Under the rule of the spectacle, cities such as London prioritise consumerism and the circulation of commodities and spread outwards in expanding suburbs served by highways that accommodate an ever-increasing volume of cars. People become isolated in concrete tower blocks, dependent on the technologies of the spectacle that destroy their creativity and independence, and absorbed in a never-ending quest for fulfilment through the commodity. The privatisation of space through the takeover of the car and shopping mall fractures neighbourhoods and communities. The yearning for social solidarity is catered for by television soaps or advertisements with their fictional depictions of tightly knit communities living on traditional London streets. 'Community becomes commodity – a shopping village, sedated and under constant surveillance,' said one Reclaim the Streets manifesto of London. Streets turn into sterile places, purely to transport people and goods between home and office, warehouse and shop. True public spaces shrink. Cities grow alienated, boring, banal.

A French philosopher and sociologist associated with the Situationists, Henri Lefebvre, viewed city space as not simply physical but as conditioned by economic and political power.

Capitalism gives rise to 'abstract space': rationally ordered, mappable space to be bought and sold, and used as the basis for urban planning to create grids of tower blocks, high-value touristic zones and gentrified urban villages. Underneath abstract space are the messier human places that are directly lived in and suffused with local history, dense networks of social and family connections, and local myth and memory. The capitalist growth of cities leads to the expansion of abstract space and the erasure of real human places. Communities are bulldozed to make way for cars and shopping malls. As space becomes a commodity, the disappearance of communities' places in the city is another means for the colonisation of everyday life by the spectacle. Like his fellow Situationists, Lefebvre believed that through struggle and imagination new possibilities could grow out of the spaces of the city that could challenge commodification. True human authenticity and freedom could only come about through the transformation of everyday life, by turning it into a creative act and a work of art. This meant actively participating in the city and learning to freely inhabit it. Lefebvre's principle of hope was encapsulated in his rallying cry, 'the right to the city'.

The Situationists sought to challenge the spectacle through the construction of 'situations': disruptive collective acts that would be gateways for liberation in a renewed everyday life. A city's highways, malls and adverts express in topographical terms a set of priorities that form the setting for people's lives. The construction of new situations would expose the assumptions and power that lie behind these choices. They would help liberate space, making it into a place of authentic human activity rather than a commodified space of abstract coordinates.

A framework for the creation of situations was the practice of psychogeography, the investigation of the effects of the city's environments on people's feelings and behaviours. It sought to reclaim a role for desire and intuition, lost in the rigid functionality of modernist plans. The *dérive*, or drift, was a wander through the city without a fixed destination, exploring it in response to the emotional effects of its various terrains and ambiences rather than hurrying through it to get to work or to the shops. Its practitioners cherished neglected crevices of the city and looked for layers of history and geography that were being swept away by commodification and urban planning. It was about becoming more aware of the nuances of one's surroundings and envisioning ways of transforming them to serve specific human needs. It took place at the level of the street, not that of the planner, whose panoramic gaze was blind to the nooks which form the texture of everyday urban life. The *dérive* sought to challenge the bourgeois division of life into the spheres of work and leisure, both of them in thrall to the spectacle, and expose the power that governs the use of urban space. As with their expeditions through the city, the Situationists' cut-up and reassembled maps of Paris were intended to challenge assumptions about the use of space built into standard cartographies of the city. Another practice was that of *détournement*, acts of 'diversion' that hijacked the language of the spectacle in order to expose and subvert it, often through the use of graffitied slogans and doctored images. By inverting conventional assumptions using parody and satire, people could revolt against the spectacle through their own creative acts.

The Situationist utopia was a city of 'unitary urbanism', one organised around the enactment of liberatory practices which would overturn the spectacle and lead to an authentic human life. It would be a city of social space, play and experimentation rather than of work and leisure. Stock exchanges would be demolished and replaced by playgrounds. Pedestrians might wander across the rooftops at night and there might be switches on the street lamps to allow people to control the atmosphere of street corners and squares. Obsolete monuments and statues would be removed, and travel information at train stations deliberately mixed up to foster experiences of discovery in people's journeys across the city. The Situationists were opposed to the notion of a fixed and permanently transformed city assumed by so many of the utopians that preceded them. Instead it would be in a constant state of flux, not because of the action of money and markets but in response to individuals' desires and actions. The city would be devoted to pleasure and play, not money and striving. *Homo ludens* of the Situationist utopia would replace *homo faber* of the capitalist era.

Situationism was a major influence on participants in the 1968 uprisings in France, during which Paris was occupied and plastered with revolutionary posters and graffiti. 'Commodities are the Opium of the People' was one of the protestors' rallying cries. They tore up cobblestones, erected barriers in the streets and seized factories. Theses from *The Society of the Spectacle* were written up on walls. The Situationists hailed 1968 as a utopian moment when capitalism was paused and 'People strolled, dreamed, learned how to live.' The most famous slogan of the time was a striking *détournement* that reimagined the street as a place of play rather than of frenetic locomotion, enacted decades later in London with Reclaim the Streets' sandpits in the road: *Beneath the Cobblestones, the Beach.*

The spirit of '68 re-emerged at Claremont Road. With its rooms in the street, protest sculptures fashioned out of the wreckage of cars, and reigning spirit of play and spontaneity, the transformed road was a bold act of *détournement*. Filled with makeshift constructions of walkways, tunnels and treehouses, the road even resembled some of the utopian cities imagined by the Situationists, dream landscapes of mobile, shape-shifting places in perpetual transformation which could be spontaneously refashioned by their inhabitants in a spirit of playful experimentation. Claremont Road placed at the centre of its existence the assertion of the authentic life dreamed of by the Situationists, a transformed human consciousness that would overturn the spectacle and reclaim space and time from capitalism. With many of the Claremont Road community living in the road, art, protest, play and creativity were fused into a new kind of life. In one photograph a reclining man stretches out his legs while reading a newspaper, as an off-duty clerk might do in an armchair in any Ealing or Golders Green living room. The man is suspended high in the air, held by the nets running between the roofs, Dolly's Tower rising next to him, his ordinary physical gesture made extraordinary by his airborne position. Floating in the sky, the man subverts the normal meaning of the familiar pose, upending convention and symbolising the potential for the transfiguration of everyday life that teems in the streets of London below him.

Man reading in the nets in front of Dolly's Tower on Claremont Road

At Claremont Road, a final act of Situationist theatre came with the eviction of the protestors in late 1994. It was to be the last spasm of the east London road protests, a showdown between the Free Area of Claremonté and the forces of the British state. By this time the colourful fragment of utopia at Claremont Road was surrounded by a scene of destruction – rubble and junk and crumbling walls with peeling wallpaper – as the houses around were knocked down. By the autumn of 1994, the community knew that the devastation would soon engulf Claremont Road itself and turned their attention to strengthening their defences.

In preparation for the eviction, the houses were turned into a giant barricade – Castle Claremonté – from where the protestors would stage their final stand. At number 36 was the entrance to the 'rat run', a series of tunnels connecting the houses secured with barriers and drawbridges made out of wood, corrugated iron and old bicycle wheels, designed to make the bailiffs' job as difficult as possible. Bunkers were created under four of the houses, inside which the protestors would barricade themselves with old fridges, cookers and mattresses, the rubbish of the consumer society recovered from the back gardens. Some rooms were filled with earth to hide the bunker entrances and illuminated by a single naked light bulb. A secret tunnel (codenamed Vicky after the Vietcong) made out of welded-together brewers' kegs ran from one of the bunkers under a garden and into a house on Grove Green Road to allow evicted protestors to smuggle themselves back on to the road. To hamper the progress of the police the activists took down staircases and blocked entrances with rubble and old tyres. The final defences were 'lock-ons' on the roofs: concrete-filled oil drums painted with red stripes in which protestors would lock their arms. The tower was made into an even more formidable defensive structure by greasing its poles to prevent intruders from climbing up.

One night in late November, 500 or so Claremontians are gearing up for the eviction that they have been tipped off is imminent. In preparation for what is expected to be a drawn-out battle, local residents have made food packages to be placed in the bunkers and trees, 'part of the UN peacekeeping initiative to get food parcels to the besieged city of Claremonté', explains one of the activists. Dolly's Tower rises over London spread out below it, a light shining from the top platform turning it into a beacon.

Music drifts up from the street below, a fragment of a new world soon to be turned to rubble.

In the freezing cold at two o'clock the next afternoon, Operation Garden Party begins. The Central Line has been specially suspended. Seven hundred police, three hundred bailiffs and four hundred security guards in black overalls, helmets and visors armed with shields and sledgehammers enter Claremont Road to shouts, cheers and sounds of drumming. In front of them as they file into the road is suspended a giant image of a motorway reaching up into the sky. An onlooker in the crowd gathered on Grove Green Road berates the police: 'Stealing our houses, stealing our land, poisoning our air!', and a local woman praises the courage of the protestors, telling a journalist that they 'may look very scruffy, but they are very nice people'.

The Claremontians, wrapped in blankets, have been waiting on the roofs of the houses, in the treehouses, down in the bunkers, up the tower and suspended in the nets. Before the police arrive they cheered the postman who delivered a final letter to one of the houses. As the police file into the road the protestors throw food parcels along the roofs to each other. People in the nets swing above the heads of the security personnel. The tower's sound system is blasting out The Prodigy's recent release 'Their Law', its strident rhythms and forbidding sirens a fitting soundtrack for the performance that is about to take place. The Criminal Justice Act had come into force just a few weeks earlier and the track was a protest against the new authoritarianism: 'Fuck 'em and their law', it went. People dance to it on top of the tower.

After the first police enter, diggers smash through the barricades at the entrance to the road and begin crushing the art installations placed along the street. Bit by bit the police start reclaiming the road, leading the first few protestors on to Grove Green Road, police cameramen filming their faces as they leave. Dolly's is the first house to be taken back.

Bailiffs in cherry pickers circle over the rooftop protestors, trying to pull them off. As they struggle with the bailiffs, the protestors shout and curse. Tiles come loose from under their feet as they skitter around on the dilapidated sloping roofs. The bailiffs begin cutting the nets in which a number of activists are suspended. 'You're endangering people's lives for a fucking road!' shouts a man. Locked-on protestors endure the frightening operation of having pneumatic drills smash through the concrete just inches from their trapped limbs.

The siege of Claremont Road went on for five days. One evening during the operation the tower is backgrounded by an intense pink sunset and after dark a surreal nocturnal circus begins. People sway in the floodlit nets as the cherry pickers move around them, lumbering metal beasts hunting a nimbler prey. One woman falls and lies motionless on the ground before being dragged away by the police.

Those barricaded inside the houses nervously watch television reports about the eviction taking place around them until the power is cut off. Diggers smash through walls and hoses are turned on to keep the dust down as houses are immediately demolished; the protestors high up feel the roofs shake under them as homes further down the terrace are pulled down. One man in the nets shouts to the police: 'Get us an ounce of weed each and we'll come down.' A cafe set up on a flat roof serves beans on toast and cups of tea. Later the sound system powers up again as electricity is brought in through the secret tunnel. Those in the bunkers use candles to see in the otherwise pitch-black crannies; when they are unearthed, the bailiffs' shadowed faces suddenly appear in a gap above them like archaeologists breaking through to a hidden tomb.

At the end only Dolly's Tower is left. People on the ground chant up to it: 'Power to the Tower! Power to the Tower!' Periodically a firework explodes into the sky from the top, a last message to the city that lies beneath it. Canary Wharf coldly glitters on the horizon a few miles to the south. Finally, a single protestor holds out in the freezing temperatures before being brought down in the floodlights, ending the siege and the brief rule of the Free Area of Claremonté. For a little while longer, the crowd gazes up at the empty structure, Claremont Road's own Tatlin-style tower, a crazy utopian minaret, silent and lit up over London.

One participant whose life was changed by the events at Claremont Road was a London-based artist, John Jordan, who would go on to be a leading activist in Reclaim the Streets. In 1989, as part of an experimental art collective, he had created a psychogeographic work entitled *Tree of Life, City of Life* which involved him and a fellow artist camping in a tent at various locations around the city in order to 'listen to the metabolism of London'. One of his stays was at the Greenland Dock south of the river just east of Bermondsey, the surviving part of an old complex of docks that faced the Isle of Dogs where One Canada Square, the centrepiece of Canary Wharf, was then being built. Opposite their camp on the Docklands river front was a striking high-rise block, the Cascades, an early private housing project on the redeveloped docks. The area gave the artists the sense of being 'a wholly privatised world' where 'behind the net curtains . . . is the private world of consumption' and where few children are seen playing outside. Jordan and his collaborators sought to use artistic practices to uncover alternative narratives of London. They conducted rituals that imaginatively unearthed the ancient River Walbrook, which in Roman times flowed between two wooded hills but now ran through a storm drain underneath the City of London. To Jordan the burial of the river was a symbol of the estrangement between London and the natural world, and a broader estrangement between human beings.

One morning in 1994 Jordan climbed over a wall topped with shards of glass and hurled himself in front of a bulldozer to stop the construction of the M11 link road. In that moment everything changed. He had thrown himself into direct action and into a new form of live art: 'the pragmatic collided with the poetic, the performative with the political. Placing my body directly in the cogs of the machine, as a point of resistance in the flow of power, was not just playful but felt deeply effective.' To Jordan, life at Claremont Road was a non-stop performance that created new images and possibilities: 'the inherent risk, excitement and danger of the action creates a magically focused moment, a peak experience, where real time suddenly stands still and a certain shift in consciousness can occur'. In that suspension of time we are taken into utopia itself, into the no-place-no-time negation of everyday experience, not via the written-down stories of visionaries like Thomas More but through a passionate act which 'revokes the emphasis on words and reason and demands the acknowledgement of intuition and imagination'. Centuries earlier Gerrard Winstanley, the original squatter, wrote that words had to die, 'for action is the life of all', and like the Claremontians used direct action to enter a utopian moment through the reclamation of the commons and the creation of community.

For Jordan, the protest movements of the late twentieth century such as Reclaim the Streets fulfilled the promise of many of the century's avant-garde art groups which sought to create forms of resistance that would dissolve the division between art and everyday life and reveal new ways of being. 'Revolutionary moments are carnivals in which the individual life celebrates its unification with a regenerated society,' wrote one of the Situationists, and Jordan imagined utopian existence as a permanent festival of creativity and play. It was a spontaneous, performative utopia, centred on an immediate moment of creation, different to the traditional model of utopia seen in the imaginings of visionaries such as Robert Owen and Ebenezer Howard who presented formal blueprints for a new society. Jordan describes the street party as the cradle for the rising of utopian consciousness, a place of unruly vitality where people dance and climb and sing, breaking down the linearity and order symbolised by a car driving down a straight road.

Reclaim the Streets claimed a connection with past uprisings – the storming of the Bastille in 1789, the European revolutions of 1848, the Paris Commune of 1871 and the 1968 protests

– which, like their own, they viewed as exuberant popular festivals that had the potential to turn the world upside down. 'Why does power fear free celebration? Could it be something to do with the utopian urges which seize a crowd becoming aware of its own power?' asked the Reclaim the Streets activists. Carnival-goers both revel and rebel, and in a release of whirling Rabelaisian energy sweep away hierarchies and prohibitions in a spirit of ludic abandonment. For a moment one enters 'a topsy-turvy universe free of toil, suffering and inequality' – into utopia itself.

In the late 1990s Reclaim the Streets went from being a London-focused direct-action group to part of the global anti-capitalist movement. Its protestivals provided the template for actions all over Britain and around the world, culminating famously in the protests in Seattle in 1999 which shut down the opening ceremony of the World Trade Organisation. A catalyst for the global anti-capitalist movement was the rise of the Mexican rebel group the Zapatista Army of National Liberation, which opposed neo-liberal policies, notably Mexico's accession to the North American Free Trade Agreement. On New Year's Day 1994, the rebels came out of their hideouts and took control of a number of towns, beginning a rebellion that became iconic for the global anti-capitalist movement. They rejected the approach of the older revolutionary tradition based on the ideology of class conflict and rigid methods of centralised organisation. International gatherings were convened by the Zapatistas which drew in many movements from around the world, including Reclaim the Streets, and out of this grew plans for global actions against capitalism. Reclaim the Streets and this broader 'movement of movements' stood in opposition to the claim made by the political scientist Francis Fukuyama following the fall of the Berlin Wall in 1989 of the 'end of history', the final triumph of liberalism over alternative forms of society, whether socialist, communist or anarchist.

On 18 June 1999, the opening day of a G8 summit in Cologne, Reclaim the Streets helped instigate the Carnival Against Capital in London as part of the Global Day of Action Against Capitalism, during which parallel actions took place in cities in seventy countries. The group would take its counter-cultural and anti-capitalist ethos into the heart of the world's financial system, the City of London, which by the late 1990s had become one of the most surveilled places in the world, a high-tech fortress bristling with CCTV cameras and police checkpoints.

In the days preceding the London carnival, a group of activists staged their own *détournements* around the city, deploying absurdist theatrical interventions to critique the rat race and consumerism and to highlight the 'death and misery' behind the financial system. On the Tube, in streets and in pubs, while dressed up as bankers they had loud conversations about selling fresh air, played games of tag with their briefcases and jousted with toy mobile phones. Another team of activists produced a spoof version of the *Evening Standard*, the *Evading Standards*, for distribution around the City during the protest. In the middle of the night before, flowers were left at each of the dragon statues that guard the boundary of the City of London to neutralise their 'dark magic'. The London Metal Exchange was painted pink, and a banner reading 'Life before Profit' placed on Tower Bridge.

On the day of the action thousands of protestors gathered at Liverpool Street Station, many disguised as office workers or bike couriers. Samba rhythms filled the large central hall. Masks of green, red, black and gold, the colours of ecology, communism, anarchy and finance, were handed out to hide the protestors from the cameras, some of which had been covered with bin bags. People were told to follow carnival figures in green, red, black or gold to a secret destination, so as to create multiple protest routes in order to confuse the police. On the backs of the masks their deeper purpose was explained. They were a symbol of unity, but also a reminder that the shiny surface of consumer capitalism is a mask 'that distracts and blinds'. Underneath it 'lies the real face of capitalism and the state: bombs, armies, prisons, courts, profit, enclosure and oppression'. Then the masks gave a simple instruction: 'On the signal follow your colour. Let the carnival begin . . .'

The protestors brought the city to a standstill. A critical mass of slow-moving cyclists was released, blocking London Bridge. Free food was given out at Liverpool Street Station. Banners hung up on buildings declared the earth to be a common treasury for all, calling up the spirit of Gerrard Winstanley, whose financial travails in the seventeenth century triggered his utopian vision. The *Evading Standards* printed the text of Winstanley's 1649 pamphlet *A Watch-word to the City of London, and the Armie* in which he condemned the city for its wickedness. The purveyors of absurdist street theatre strode about in their suits reciting poetry into mobile phones, then suddenly stopped to shout that they had 'made a killing!'. One passer-by emerged from the London Underground and found himself in the middle of it all and gazed in wonder at the samba band beating out its rhythms, plumes of smoke rising above the city. Also among the crowds that day were a number of the long-time residents of Wanstead who, radicalised in the battle for the chestnut tree on George Green, had been drawn into Reclaim the Streets and the broader anti-capitalist movement.

The protestival targeted in particular the London International Financial Futures and Options Exchange, the secret location to which the activists were led from Liverpool Street Station. Outside it a banner was put up: 'Don't Speculate! Live!' Activists bricked up one of the entrances with grey breeze blocks, making the place look like the obsolete relic that it would become in the utopia envisioned by the carnivalgoers, and tried to storm the trading floor. Flares and smoke bombs went off, police horses clattered and charged, and protestors weaved and ducked through the narrow alleys nearby.

The front page of the *Evading Standards* reported a fictitious global market meltdown and panic in the City of London, its accompanying story condemning the bankers of London and New York for their financial chicanery which threatens lives, economies and ecosystems. It was a prescient imagining given that only a few years later, in the early years of the twenty-first century, there would be a massive financial crash caused by the recklessness of a hyperactive financial system centred on London and New York which would bring out on to the streets a new generation of direct-action protestors as part of the Occupy movement.

In one striking *détournement*, a group of activists evoked an Arcadian vision of the city by breaking open a hydrant to release the ancient River Walbrook, which gushed in a fountain four storeys high. The water glittered in the sun and fell on to the jubilant crowd, filled the narrow street and flowed towards the Thames and into the basement of the Futures and Options Exchange. In the sweltering heat people danced in the spray; a couple kissed ecstatically under the cascade. *Beneath the tarmac, the river.*

The River Walbrook released from a hydrant

Reclaim the Streets would not sustain itself into the new century as a distinct organisation, its activists merging into the broader anti-capitalist movement. Fittingly for a group that was motivated by the problems of London, Reclaim the Streets had encompassed the localised identities and struggles that make up any large city – those behind the protests in Wanstead and Leyton – while being a utopian response to the big forces of global capitalism of which London is such a powerful conduit and creator. The local roots of its larger anti-capitalist protest were not forgotten by its activists after the struggles in east London were over, however. They symbolically closed a circle in July 1996 when, after a chaotic game of cat and mouse with the police in the streets of Shepherd's Bush in west London, they managed to occupy the hot tarmac of the M41, a stretch of elevated motorway on which appeared towering figures on stilts thirty feet high in voluminous hooped skirts.

Inside the skirts were secreted activists with pneumatic drills, the sound of them pounding into the tarmac hidden from the police by thudding techno, the repetitive beats considered seditious by the law aiding the enactment of a subversive, living poetry: the planting in the drilled-out holes of saplings saved from a wood that had been felled to make way for the M11 link road. *Beneath the tarmac, the forest.* The saplings disappeared after the road was taken back and returned to the traffic. A veteran of the earlier struggles of Leyton and Wanstead did, however, manage to create a more lasting living memorial to the freewheeling spirit of late-twentieth-century utopian London, harvesting three nuts from the sweet chestnut of George Green, growing them into shoots and planting them in secret locations around the city where they are said to still stand.

Chapter Nine

The Golden Thread

Utopian desires intensify in times of crisis and upheaval, as they did in London in the English Civil War and during the city's economic slump early in the nineteenth century. Such eras gain a utopian quality that extends beyond the activities of social pioneers operating on the experimental fringes of society. They become utopian windows through which fissures in the social edifice can be seen and new collective possibilities are glimpsed by many.

From early 2020, the Covid pandemic caused one of the gravest peacetime emergencies seen in Britain and around the world – and created the conditions for the arrival of a twenty-first-century utopian moment. After the imposition of a national lockdown in March 2020, London entered a state of suspended animation, its streets suddenly deserted, its shops closed. The engine rooms of the city's consumer economy, Oxford Street and Regent Street and its giant suburban malls, fell silent, as did those of high finance in the Square Mile and Canary Wharf. It seemed as if capitalist time had been put on pause.

The seemingly impossible was made real in other ways, not least through the authorities' response to the pandemic. In an era in which the state has been disparaged and the market lauded, calls for bolder collective action – more generous funding of schools and hospitals or public investments that have a realistic chance of combating climate change – are frequently dismissed as being unworkable and too expensive. Their magnitude of ambition is taken as a sign of misguided utopian grandiosity. For decades the British Conservative Party espoused untrammelled individual choice, free markets and small government. But when the pandemic arrived a Conservative government undertook one of the largest social and economic interventions in history, underwriting much of the economy by providing grants and emergency finance to closed-down businesses, and placing hitherto unthinkable restrictions on movement and social contact. In an instant, the claim of impossibility that is routinely used to counter ambitious proposals for reform was demonstrated to be a fiction in the face of an emergency that demanded sweeping intervention.

The crisis also prompted intellectual shifts that made utopian ideas more conceivable, sometimes from unlikely quarters. While under self-isolation for Covid, the Prime Minister, Boris Johnson, released a video message in which he said that the pandemic had proved that 'there really is such a thing as society', in contradiction to his Thatcherite forebears who claimed that there was no such thing, only a loose assemblage of individuals. *The Financial Times*, normally a defender of free-market orthodoxy, published an editorial calling for the reversal of the economic policies of the last forty years. The government needed to take a more active role in the economy, it argued, and view public services as investments rather than as a drain on the public purse. The uncertainties of the labour market should be ended, and redistribution was now the order of the day. The paper even urged consideration of policies previously regarded as outlandish: taxes on wealth and the introduction of a universal basic income, the latter in particular often seen as a thoroughgoing utopian proposal.

At the level of everyday life, the Covid lockdowns were a radical disruption of normality. For many people they meant a temporary abandonment of the pursuit of money as they were sent home while still being paid – a glimpse in the midst of an emergency of what a universal basic income might be like. It was the kind of overturning of reality that London's social visionaries have long believed could be a doorway to new social possibilities. Through their protestivals the utopians of Claremont Road had sought to challenge the division of everyday life ordained under capitalism into mind-numbing work and work-relieving leisure. During the pandemic the division was weakened as an unintended by-product of economic closure and home working, and even by these very different means created for lots of people openings for the imagining of new potentialities. Many found themselves with extra time on their hands, took up new pursuits and began to reassess their priorities in life. It became a commonplace for people to say that after the end of the pandemic they did not wish for a return to the old normal.

As people were deprived of social contact, yearnings surfaced for a more connected society, and utopian desires began to be expressed with greater clarity, sometimes symbolically. Londoners performed the weekly ritual of standing outside their houses and applauding the doctors and nurses of the National Health Service who were tending to the sick in the city's Covid wards. The NHS, with its mission of universal health care, itself once seemed like a far-off dream, had been prefigured in utopian schemes such as Chuni Lal Katial's health centre in Finsbury in the 1930s, and even under neo-liberalism remained a cherished emblem of collective action. It has always been an institution with a powerful utopian resonance.

Utopian currents also appeared in the practical measures that ordinary people devised to deal with life under lockdown. On a south London street, residents with gardens made bunches of flowers and left them on the doorsteps of those living in flats. Others organised a Sunday morning disco. 'We come to our gates and give people a wave and just enjoy the music. It's a nice moment of unity,' one of them said. On the Alton Estate in Roehampton in the south-west of the city – the backdrop to Truffaut's *Fahrenheit 451* – residents rediscovered the communal spirit that had lain behind the creation of estates like their own, distributing food and toys to isolated families. One resident noted that these activities had changed the story of the area from being about crime and hardship to harmony and togetherness.

All over the city 'mutual aid' groups were set up whose teams of volunteers delivered groceries and medicines to those unable to go out. The idea had been used in the late nineteenth and early twentieth centuries by the Russian anarchist Peter Kropotkin as part of a theory that set out how the spread of cooperation would lead to the emergence of a new kind of society. One in five Britons volunteered in some way during the crisis, 750,000 for the NHS; the majority said that they would continue to do so after the end of the pandemic. Through these initiatives friendships grew up between the old and young that would never otherwise have come about. In an unplanned way these new spaces of solidarity seemed to be acting like the 'social condensers' that utopians had long sought to foster in which old social routines would be disrupted and new ones created.

The sensing of new possibilities in suddenly disordered life was easier for those enjoying the advantages of stable accommodation and white-collar work, which allowed for home working and adjustment of an out-of-kilter work-life balance; some of these Londoners, freed from geographical shackles by the internet and Zoom, decided to abandon the city for cheaper, more tranquil locations. But for many the changes brought by the pandemic were like a bad dream – and not just for those who fell ill from the virus or who lost a loved one to it. For elderly people especially, for youngsters sent home from school and college, for those confined to rooms in cramped accommodation, for women and children under threat of domestic violence, and those who felt particularly keenly the emotional impact of the cessation of travel and social contact, the lockdown was like living in a dystopia. Sacked restaurant workers began sleeping on the streets in the West End, and even some employed middle-class families began using foodbanks. The blurring of the boundary between the world of work and of home did not necessarily lead to a liberating overturning of that traditional dichotomy. The multiple demands of jobs, home schooling and domestic duties often fell more heavily on women. Home working through internet-based communication technologies allowed the colonisation of private life by employers, a recipe for heightened feelings of alienation and anxiety among employees.

The pandemic therefore laid bare London's existing social pathologies, feeding the yearnings for a more just city framed by the utopian window that had opened up. The sinking tide of urban activity revealed what is so often hidden under the surface of London: the world of poorly paid workers who service the metropolis that investigators such as Henry Mayhew in the nineteenth century sought to discover, and that through history has inspired critiques of London and utopian dreams of a more equitable system. These timeless layers had been depicted in Stephen Frears and Steven Knight's 2002 film *Dirty Pretty Things*, a tale of contemporary London in which a hotel is the backdrop to the anonymous lives of night porters, cleaners and receptionists, and a microcosm of the larger city. 'The hotel business is about strangers and strangers will always surprise you,' says the hotel manager. 'They come to hotels in the night to do dirty things and in the morning it's our job to make things look pretty again.'

It was the unsung essential workers who kept the city pretty for everyone else who found themselves on the front line of the pandemic. Supermarket cashiers, bus and Tube drivers, hospital porters and care workers, many on low wages, had to continue doing their jobs as the virus raged. They were a world apart from those able to stay safe at home, the pandemic making plain, therefore, the deep inequalities that have always existed in the life of London.

The city's economic inequities mean that many Londoners exist in a chronic state of financial precarity. Nearly half say that they would be unable to meet an unexpected expense of £500. Almost 40 per cent of London's children live in poverty, the highest proportion in the country. Rough sleeping doubled between 2010 and 2019. The demonisation of the poor in politics and the media, their punitive treatment under austerity, and the insecurities of the labour market have led to a marginalisation of the most needy people reminiscent of the nineteenth century.

These inequalities appear most starkly in London's housing system. Housing has always been central to the city's social dreams. Some of Thomas More's most striking descriptions of his utopian city were of its dwellings: they had terraces and large gardens and every ten years they were changed hands by lot. Today, London has become the reverse of this vision of equitable housing.

In the middle of the twentieth century, the Labour minister Aneurin Bevan, who was responsible for the government's council housing programme and for the establishment of the NHS, said that private markets had solved the problem of housing for the middle classes through speculative building and mortgage lending. He believed that the government would in turn solve the problem of housing for the working class through the provision of council housing. Bevan's optimistic statements no longer apply. The wide provision of council homes – the most effective route to high-quality, secure housing for the mass of the population – has been all but abandoned. The decline in private as well as public house-building since the 1960s has led to a significant housing shortage. Rising property prices and rents have meant that the private sector no longer provides affordable housing for many Londoners, even those in stable, decently paid employment.

London has been at the centre of an economy based on high and rising house prices that conflicts with the social need for stable dwelling for all. The policy of low interest rates and quantitative easing that followed the 2007–8 global financial crisis led to money being poured into assets, including property. But over the same period wages stagnated and property ownership became the principal source of economic security. With the weakening of social protection because of the austerity policy of the last decade, people are made dependent on their personal safety net in the form of the property that they own. There is political gain to be made from ensuring that property owners preserve their wealth in the market value of their houses. Those outside this select group scramble to get on the bottom rung of the property ladder if they have the resources even to try, or have to depend on the precarious rental market. The collective dreams of London's utopians recede further from reach.

The rise of the house as a financial asset is epitomised most starkly in the proliferation of London's towers of luxury apartments, which are too expensive for most of the city's home buyers and are often bought not to live in but as part of property investment portfolios. Even London's councils have become involved in this financialisation of housing. Newham Council in east London, which oversees some of the city's poorest areas, trumpeted its various new apartment developments as part of a 'regeneration supernova' and marketed them to Asian investors at the 2010 Shanghai Expo, stating in its publicity materials that the locality is 'just six hours from New York'. Meanwhile, a group of young mothers in the borough came together to protest at their council's attempt to rehouse them and their children in Manchester and Birmingham. 'People Need Homes; These Homes Need People' read their banner, which they placed on a block of empty council flats.

Just beyond the eastern edge of London's early-twentieth-century utopia of Hampstead Garden Suburb runs The Bishops Avenue, popularly known as 'Billionaires Row', one of the most expensive residential streets in the world where mansions sell for tens of millions of pounds. Many of the properties on the avenue are derelict, long turned over to the pigeons, with ferns growing up the grand staircases and rubble strewn about the immense hallways. The property of offshore companies and overseas royalty, the never-lived-in houses are profitable investments even as they rot, retained for eventual sale in London's overheated land and property markets. In 2021 it was reported that a new housing development on the road would make no provision for affordable housing, despite the local council's target that new developments contain 40 per cent affordable homes – instead the units will sell for an average of £2 million apiece. On the doorstep of Henrietta Barnett's suburb, which was built to further the ideal of a socially mixed London, the avenue is another emblem of the irrationalities of London's property system and its abandonment of the dream of housing for all.

In More's *Utopia*, Raphael spoke of how in England's early capitalist economy sheep devoured families and whole villages when the common land was enclosed for the production of highly profitable wool. London's luxury flats are the sheep of twentieth-century capitalism: they eat up urban space to provide investment vehicles for global buyers in competition with property located in real-estate hotspots around the world. They add to the capital's paper wealth and to its bragging skyline, but not to wealth measured in the fulfilment of broader human values and the utopian desires at the heart of the idea of the city, which were crystallised during the pause in London's normal cycle of frenetic activity.

More described the doors of the Utopians' houses as yielding to the touch so that anyone could enter them, suggesting that on the island of Utopia even private domestic spaces were partly public. In contemporary London, in contrast, public spaces are turning private. This was shown graphically in October 2011, when London's Occupy protesters tried to demonstrate in Paternoster Square in front of the London Stock Exchange and adjacent to St Paul's Cathedral. Security guards blocked the square, barriers were erected and a sign was placed at the entrance declaring the square to be private land, with access in the gift of the corporation that owned it – Mitsubishi Estates – and that permission for this had been revoked. There are many such pseudo-public spaces dotted around London in the form of developer-controlled regeneration and shopping projects, most notably Canary Wharf, which has been the template for the privatisation of public areas around the city. Exemplars of Henri Lefebvre's 'abstract' space, which acts as a commodity and obliterates local memory and history, these high-value districts have an atmosphere of sanitised uniformity compared to traditional ones, their buildings and roads stamped with developer logos and overseen by private security guards in hi-vis jackets. The closure of Paternoster Square was a stark demonstration of the spatial operation of private power in such places, showing how it attempts to limit the civic imagination in the form of protest and debate, activities that fall outside the sanctioned uses of space for production and consumption.

After they were locked out of the square the protestors created their own civic commons, setting up camp in front of St Paul's. The activists were angry about the malfeasance of the banks that had caused the global financial crisis and the longer-term phenomenon of rising economic inequality. On the doorstep of global capitalism, the tent city became a place for imagining a non-capitalist future and for enacting the principles that would be followed in a remade world. The Occupy activists employed a form of participatory democracy in decision-making, created a tent university for learning and discussion, and ran a kitchen that served free food. The camp was a 'temporary autonomous zone' in the heart of the city in which the rules of capitalist life were for a time suspended. Bringing together long-time activists, students and homeless people from different social classes, the protestors opened up new imaginative spaces as the forces of global capital closed down the physical ones around them. By the steps of St Paul's, the Marxist scholar David Harvey told the protestors: 'It's people, on the street, in the squares, that really matters in the end, because that's the only political force we've got,' and praised them for reclaiming the city and turning it into a commons, a place of togetherness and of political imagination.

St George's Hill in 2021

Three hundred years ago, Gerrard Winstanley tried to do the same through community digging on common land. The fate of St George's Hill, where he and his followers once camped, is emblematic of the rise of private space and of wealth inequality in and around many of the sites of the city's past social dreamers. Today the area near the hill is an affluent satellite of London, a wealthy commuter colony of stockbrokers studded with gated housing developments. St George's Hill itself is a large barriered estate of opulent mansions complete with an exclusive golf club, where the only people seen out and about on its leafy, manicured avenues are gardeners trimming the verges. The preserve of pop stars and business tycoons, the estate's seclusion and exclusivity could not be more diametrically opposed to the principles fought for on its site by the Diggers. In 1999 several hundred activists marched to the hill to commemorate the 350th anniversary of the Diggers' occupation of the area and briefly took over a small piece of land, where they erected yurts and dug a garden before being evicted. They brought with them a handsome stone memorial to the Diggers which today stands unobtrusively in bracken set back from the road opposite Weybridge Station, bearing a carving of a spade and the words 'Worke Together Eat Bread Together'.

As well as its underlying economic inequalities, the Covid crisis laid bare the racialised nature of London. The virus was more lethal among people of colour, partly because many of them lived in cramped accommodation and were employed in key worker jobs that exposed them to the virus, often without adequate personal protective equipment. London boroughs such as Newham and Brent, with high rates of poverty and overcrowding and large communities of colour, were more badly affected by the virus than affluent ones. During the pandemic Black youth unemployment rose to over 40 per cent compared to 12 per cent for young white people, a rate similar to that of the early 1980s. A report by Public Health England found that racism contributed to the more serious impact of the pandemic on people of colour. The crisis exposed, then, the racial injustices that linger still in postcolonial London.

In his epic work *Omeros* the West Indian poet Derek Walcott reads into the physical fabric of the city the iniquities of the imperial system of which London has been instigator and beneficiary. Looking back on the centuries of colonial trade, the poem reverses the famous praise of London as the 'flower of all cities' made by a Tudor poet at the start of the century in which Britain embarked on its imperial adventures. In Walcott's imaginings, a craggy-faced Caribbean seafarer with visionary powers emerges into London from the Tube station at Charing Cross and finds himself among tourists and monuments in the 'stone waves' of Trafalgar Square. He sees the dirt that lies under the prideful splendour of the city, 'the grit in the stone lions' eyes', and barges chained to the Thames like the islands of the colonies. He wonders under which of London's splendid domes are remembered the names and deeds of his island peoples who contributed so much to the building of modern Britain: 'Where is the light of the world? In the National Gallery. In Palladian Wren. In the City that can buy and sell us the packets of tea stirred with our crystals of sweat.' Under the seafarer's gaze, the horrors of colonialism and slavery are visible in the city's skyline.

Nestled within Canary Wharf's forest of glass is a relic of London's imperial trading past, an old warehouse built in the early nineteenth century where sugar harvested by slaves in the Caribbean used to be stored. Today the building houses the Museum of London Docklands and for over 200 years a statue stood in front of it of the slave owner Robert Milligan, who owned sugar plantations and hundreds of slaves in Jamaica and helped establish the West India docks where the museum stands; a nearby inscription hails him for his contribution to the 'stability, increase and ornament to British commerce'. In June 2020, during the first national lockdown and following the murder by a police officer in the United States of a Black man, George Floyd, young Londoners of colour and their supporters took to the streets as part of the Black Lives Matter protests and in this time of utopian possibility pointed to the racial injustices which will need to be reckoned with in any reconstructed society. Some of the activists put a piece of cloth over the head of the statue of Milligan and placed a Black Lives Matter placard in the crook of his arm. The museum began tweeting about the legacy of slavery in the docks and in London as a whole, and called for the removal of the statue.

In an upper room of the museum, overlooking these conflicting symbols of history on the quayside, hung an artwork depicting Georgian London's neglected Black utopian Robert Wedderburn, who in the early nineteenth century powerfully articulated the ideal of Black liberation. He rejected the political quietism of more celebrated utopians such as Robert Owen, who he believed was an apologist for the landowners. Like many early British industrialists, Owen's money came from cotton-spinning, and therefore from the products of colonial trade and slave labour, and he used his wealth and considerable social connections to promote a peaceable form of utopianism. But Wedderburn's life had been blighted by these systems of power, and he advocated militant forms of resistance to them. The imposing picture of him by the contemporary artist Paul Howard, installed in 2007 as part of an exhibition on London, sugar and slavery, is a montage of photographs that form a reconstructed image of Wedderburn in respectable eighteenth-century dress. On a table beside him is a radical newspaper and a red cap of liberty, and he is surrounded by barrels of sugar. Behind him are the old brick dock buildings, and rising above them is the glass skyscraper One Canada Square with its pyramidal peak, the centrepiece of modern Canary Wharf. This juxtaposition of symbols of colonial trade and slavery with those of modern wealth-making forms a connection between imperial London and the city's contemporary incarnation as a centre of international finance.

On 9 June 2020, Milligan's statue was removed in front of a cheering crowd. On the same day the Mayor of London, Sadiq Khan, announced the creation of a Commission for Diversity in the Public Realm which has the aim of increasing the representation in the city's public spaces of people of colour, women, LGBTQ+ people and disabled people in order to properly recognise the contribution that they have made to the building of modern London. An adviser to the mayor, the artist Gaylene Gould, said that London was moving into a 'new imaginative period' that necessitated a rethink of the city's spaces and how they honoured different kinds of people. In autumn 2021 a sculpture was installed on Narrow Way in Hackney, east London, by the artist Veronica Ryan in celebration of the city's Windrush generation: three bronze and marble sculptures of Caribbean fruit, a custard apple, a breadfruit and a soursop, emblems of the colonial migration and trade that have been so central to the formation of London.

The followers of Black Lives Matter are the latest in a line of activists fighting for the rights of people of colour in the city and against systemic racism. Their struggle reaches back to London's Black Power movement of the 1960s and 1970s, and in the nineteenth century to Robert Wedderburn with his explicitly utopian visions. One celebrated struggle for the 'right to the city' was the resistance by Black people to police harassment of the Mangrove Restaurant in Notting Hill in west London, which from the late 1960s served as a hub for the Black community and its activists. Periodically, tensions between Black Londoners and the police have exploded into violent confrontation, notably in the 1980s in Brixton and Tottenham, and in the disturbances of 2011, events that seemed to answer Wedderburn's call for insurrection in the face of oppressive power. When they occur, such upheavals are routinely condemned by politicians and the media as mindless criminality. Only later are the causes more widely understood, in particular frustration at the heavy-handed policing of people of colour through the use of 'stop and search'. Combined with a broader context of racism and social marginalisation, which was exacerbated in both the 1980s and the 2010s by austerity-driven spending cuts, this kind of treatment places Black communities under intolerable pressure. More recently, most of those killed in the Grenfell Tower fire in west London in 2017 were people of colour, tenants of Kensington and Chelsea Council who had been placed by the authorities in an unsafe building. Its burned-out shell, which looms over streets containing some of the most expensive property in the world and where the Mangrove once was, has become a stark symbol of the inequities in London's housing system.

A Black teenager, Giovanni Rose, captured in his 2021 poem 'Welcome to Tottenham' the sense of confinement still felt by many of the city's young Black people. The poem echoes the chartered streets and bloody palace walls of Blake's 'London', tokens of injustice in the topography of the nineteenth-century city still present in our own racialised London. 'We fight over streets we don't own' and 'cover our blood stained streets with dried up gum', Rose writes, and he yearns for the reopening of

Tottenham's youth clubs. Stopped in the street by police 'that see colour before they see the crime', Rose and his peers are corralled and cajoled, prevented from fully inhabiting the spaces of the city. 'I live in a nightmare. I had to learn how to dream,' he writes.

In the struggles over the physical fabric of the city – its statues, signs and street names – are the seeds of utopian longing. When the transcendentalist Bronson Alcott visited London in the 1840s he wrote dejectedly of its monuments to colonial overlords and generals, manifestations of a brutal past, but sensed that a new kind of city could emerge in their place. The Situationist-inspired utopians of Claremont Road improvised a fragment of a new society, creating their own monuments to the London of their dreams. Many of the demands articulated by today's anti-racism activists – for people of colour to be able to walk down the street without being stopped by the police, for example – are for the observance of basic rights rather than for the creation of a utopia. But in highlighting the colonial symbols present in the fabric of London, the Black Lives Matter activists urge us to recognise the deep systems of power represented in its streets that have limited the lives of Londoners of colour. The removal of statues will not on its own solve social injustice, but when a statue is taken down a plinth becomes vacant, and a gap opens up in the physical city and in its imagined counterpart. The replacement of a defunct monument is an invitation to honour the values that we wish to be at the heart of our future city: whom do we want to celebrate and who do we want to become? Wedderburn was a radical of utopian persuasion who wrote about racism within the context of the broader capitalist system of colonial trade and industry, and it is fitting that an image of him looks over an empty plinth in the former docks where the statue of a slaver once stood. Pregnant with possibility, the stone slab is a space that invites the play of what the philosopher Ernst Bloch thought of as 'anticipatory consciousness' and a sensing of the 'not yet' – a seed of utopian dreaming.

★

A few years before the pandemic, a new avenue for social imagining in the city opened up with the rise of the environmental protest group Extinction Rebellion. Its demand for the rapid decarbonisation of the economy implies radical economic transformation, and, while not stating its specific form, the group calls for the creation of a new kind of society and therefore has a powerful utopian undertow. (During lockdown, London's carbon emissions actually fell as people stopped making journeys, creating an unintended pre-echo of the net zero economy that the group is pressing for.) During its 2019 London protests, one of the organisation's co-leaders, Skeena Rathor, appeared on television for an interview with *Good Morning Britain* host Piers Morgan, who levelled at her the charges of sanctimony and dishonesty often made against people who seek radical changes to the system. Morgan repeatedly criticised Rathor for having come to the television studio by car and for owning energy-consuming appliances such as an iPad, believing this to be a refutation of the environmentalists' case. The protestors were 'a bunch of rank hypocrites,' Morgan asserted.

Morgan's objection was a common variation on the there-is-no-alternative defence of the status quo that seeks to neutralise the imaginative impulse of utopian thinking before the resulting critiques and solutions can ever be properly aired. It implies that an environmentalist worth a proper hearing would have to be someone who had no dealings with the carbon-emitting economy and so never travelled, communicated electronically or bought anything. But the only kind of person who could pass such a test – a cave dweller wearing clothes made out of leaves – would be dismissed by the commentariat as mad and certainly not be listened to on the subject of economic and social reform. (During the interview, Morgan challenged Rathor to explain the actions of a group of protestors shown in a clip engaging in a curious ritual resembling expressionist dance. Just as the pioneers of Letchworth and Hampstead Garden Suburb were mocked for their sandals and long hair, today's utopian-leaning activists run the risk of derision if they veer far from the norm; 'They smell' was Morgan's verdict on them.)

By inspiring yearnings for what lies beyond the immediately possible, utopianism renders the 'sane' social dreamer who lives an ordinary life as being within the system while straining towards an alternative. Requiring of individuals that they completely embody the utopian vision they seek is asking the impossible, because the transformation of society can only be brought about through new kinds of collective action and consciousness – we have to do it together. A utopian rooted in society as it is, and with whom people can therefore identify, urges us to change the system of which she is necessarily a part and in her daily life helps to sustain. In this sense 'hypocrisy', as commonly understood, is essential to useful social dreaming: without it the utopian is at risk of being viewed as unhinged, or becomes a peddler of fantastical imaginings that have little bearing on concrete social realities. If everyday life is marbled with utopian yearnings, to explore them people must therefore have the courage to embrace dreams that are at odds with their present lives and may invite the charge of hypocrisy. The accusation – along with the anger and resistance that often accompanies it – is a sign that a utopian assertion has found a worthwhile goal: a conceivable new world on this earth rather than an escape from it through science fiction or magic.

Even though a utopian window was opened as a result of the Covid crisis, the broader era that we live in often feels profoundly anti-utopian. We have lost faith in the ambitious collective utopias of the past and instead consume the knee-jerk narratives of journalists that feed on feelings of fear and threat and are negations of our old hopes. (The days when eager Londoners were willing to queue round the block to buy a copy of the Beveridge Report now seem part of a lost era.) The free-market revolution of the 1980s – the fall of communism in Eastern Europe and the privatisation programmes undertaken in many countries – led to a belief not just in the triumph of capitalism over socialism, but that there was no other option to that system. Though neo-liberalism and free markets are themselves visions of an ideal society, their advocates claim that they are merely adhering to laws of economics as immutable as those of gravity, making us believe, as the philosopher Slavoj Žižek has noted, that travelling to the moon is more possible than raising taxes on the rich. Nowadays, novelists and film-makers tend to draw on deeper wells of dystopian rather than utopian imagining; the Marxist critic Fredric Jameson has said that it is easier to picture the end of the world than the end of capitalism. Poverty of the imagination, a loss of faith in politics itself and the suffering caused by austerity have led to a dangerous intensity of cynicism and despair – Blake's 'mind-forg'd manacles' recreated in an era of soundbites and Twitter wars.

Many critics of the status quo, particularly those on the left, believe that it is enough simply to articulate the shortcomings of an economic system or a government for people to act. But lists of complaints, however well justified, do not guarantee that people will mobilise for a cause or vote in a particular way. Sometimes the enormity of systemic problems – the spectre of accelerating climate change for one – can be paralysing and numb our sense of agency. London's later utopians, such as those of Claremont Road, have shown that people are motivated by desire and even by pleasure. Deep social change has to come from the heart and the head. Utopia, with its combination of critique and imagery, has the power to move people to action as they fuse reason and desire into one impulse.

In his mid-twentieth-century work *The Principle of Hope*, Ernst Bloch wrote of how utopian yearnings are woven through everyday culture in its images, songs and stories. A utopian imaginative lineage can inspire social desire and spur action, and the visionaries that have formed our story of utopian London have drawn on it over the centuries as they revelled in and rebelled against their city. Through the articulation of a dream, what might now seem impossible can move closer to being possible. In a world threatened by a mounting climate crisis, and riven by inequality and deep distrust, the harnessing of the imagination as an antidote to despair has never been more necessary.

Opposing energies of cynicism and hope swirl through London's streets. One afternoon in September 2020, during an easing of restrictions imposed under Britain's first Covid lockdown, Extinction Rebellion held a much-reduced action in the city, its band of demonstrators straggling towards Trafalgar Square under the buzz of helicopters, determined to spread their message of environmental salvation. On their way along Whitehall, the group passed an assortment of campaigners corralled behind railings opposite Downing Street: anti-vaccination agitators and conspiracy theorists warning of a government plan to microchip children. Also on the pavement were others promoting the adoption of a universal basic income. In Holborn a *Big Issue* seller stood close to the entrance of Little Turnstile, where Thomas Spence once shared his utopian dreams from the Hive of Liberty. 'Cynicism is Out. Hope Is In' said the headline on the front cover of the magazine, and inside an editorial argued that, far from being naive, hope is a subversive force that has the potential to transform society, echoing the cultural critic Raymond Williams, who once wrote: 'To be truly radical is to make hope possible, rather than despair convincing.'

In the opening decades of the twenty-first century, the British sociologist and advocate of utopia Ruth Levitas set out an agenda for utopian thinking – 'utopia as method' – that is intended to help us discover and clarify our utopian desires. A pillar of this is 'utopian archaeology': making explicit the often-unstated utopian meanings that lie behind our existing social and political frameworks. The utopian content of some political programmes is relatively overt and discoverable with only a little digging; the avowedly socialist platform of the former Labour leader Jeremy Corbyn might be one. But most politicians – particularly those of a centrist or conservative bent – do not admit to any trace of utopianism and maintain that their policies are based on common sense and practicality, never on the sorts of fantasies which they assume utopians cling to. They are in fact beholden to utopian hopes, even if undeveloped and unacknowledged. Neo-liberal and libertarian programmes for limited government and low taxes, for example, are rooted in a vision of a society of perfectly functioning markets and untrammelled individual choice. New Labour's state-market pragmatism was underpinned by a utopia of meritocracy, aspiration and social mobility. The Brexit world view looks towards various imagined versions of the nation, from that of a buccaneering global Britain to those rooted in atavistic yearnings for a timeless English glory, as implied in one leading politician's likening of Brexit to England's victory over the French at Agincourt. None of these idealisations exist in a pure form, and in that sense may be as 'impractical' as the overt utopias that are condemned by their critics as hopelessly fanciful.

Through the practice of utopian archaeology, society becomes conscious of the utopian yearnings that flow under its surface so that these are articulated, examined and made part of public debate. But authentic utopian visions must also include a vision of human flourishing, what Levitas calls 'utopian ontology'. As she points out, critics of utopia often assume that there exists a fixed and imperfect human nature incompatible with utopian society. They claim that the realisation of utopia requires unrealistic levels of discipline and selflessness in people, and that when they inevitably fall short the designers of utopia attempt the impossible task of bringing them into line, sometimes using brutal methods to do so. But attitudes and behaviour are in fact capable of being influenced by the social context. A central aim of utopia, seen clearly in the thought of Thomas More, Gerrard Winstanley and Robert Owen, has been to regenerate humans morally and spiritually through the creation of new kinds of social institutions. Even the free-market vision of society – usually framed as 'realistic' rather than utopian – alters human conduct and values, encouraging individualism and aspiration (according to its critics, egotism and selfishness). The question, then, is what we think human flourishing consists of and what kind of people we want to be. The exploration of utopian dreams is also about the 'education of desire': cultivating the kinds of wants within ourselves that best serve human happiness and the creation of a good society.

Layered over utopian archaeology and utopian ontology is 'utopian architecture', the imagining and describing of scenarios for a future society: the new kinds of institutions needed for the creation, for example, of a universal basic income, of more meaningful kinds of work or of a truly sustainable economy, and the new kinds of people that we see ourselves as in a transformed society. The interplay between utopian archaeology, ontology and architecture is a practice of the imagination that creates knowledge in the present: about the true nature of our collective desires and how these might be fulfilled in the world. It is the basis for what Levitas calls the 'imaginary reconstruction of society'.

Utopia is not the pursuit of fixed perfection, which is neither an attainable nor a desirable ideal. Levitas's notion of 'utopian architecture', the term perhaps suggestive of a rigid blueprint, in fact employs a notion of architecture that is improvisatory and flexible, and therefore suitable as a metaphor for utopia as a method rather than a quest for a final destination. Bald utopian blueprints without a sense of historical contingency are always in danger of becoming the petrified relics of past dreams, even if they do not turn into totalitarian nightmares. By aiming at ever-lasting perfection, they offer stasis and sterility. Real paradise is imperfect – in the words of Wallace Stevens, full of 'flawed words and stubborn sounds'. One of London's garden city pioneers hit on this paradox when he said that the garden city he had helped to create – in many respects forged from a utopian blueprint par excellence – was 'less perfect than the ideal, but, we may hope, more human'.

The pursuit of utopia is in fact an often-messy practice of articulating social desires and of experimenting with them in the real world. London's carnivalesque utopian movements of the late twentieth century were vivid examples of this kind of endeavour. Breaking from the blueprint utopias of the nineteenth century and from high-modernist system-building, they turned towards the postmodern embrace of subjectivity, desire and open-ended process. They were prefigurative social experiments that enacted new ways of life in the here and now in transformed spaces in the city. The collective efforts made during London's Covid lockdowns which gave those years a distinct utopian quality were often unplanned: people quickly devised new forms of solidarity in their streets and neighbourhoods as the pandemic raged on around them. Even some much earlier utopian movements had this sense of in-the-moment transformation, of the crossing of some Rubicon of social consciousness as followers communed together in halls and taverns, intoxicated by visions of a new world. With their quasi-religious rituals and thunderous millenarian speech-making, London's nineteenth-century Owenites sometimes appeared to believe that they had already entered a righteous new world, even if the city that surrounded them was still mired in selfishness and ignorance.

In many utopias, then, there is a tension between outcome and process. By refraining from pinning down ultimate aims beyond the exploration of a present utopian moment, London's countercultural utopias revolved around a potentially infinite process of experimentation and subjective expression, exposing the inaccuracy of the claim that utopianism leads to tyranny because of its inflexibility. But the notion of utopia as a form of prefigurative politics – creating in the here and now a sketch of a future transformed society – can itself be criticised for lacking the means for converting momentary utopian euphoria into longer-term social transformation. Without the rudder of larger social aims, an outpouring of carnivalesque energy might lose its way, becoming a form of enjoyment for a group of counter-cultural adepts that fails to involve a broader set of people. And amid the exhilaration of believing that one has created some rupture in social reality and entered a state of utopian grace, one might overlook the structures of hierarchy and privilege that can be reproduced in crucibles of communal experiment. (Some participants reported that in Occupy London's tent city it was often women who ended up doing tasks, such as washing the dishes, which allowed the camp to survive winter in the open.)

David Harvey has advocated a 'dialectical utopianism' that embraces process and avoids the rigid blueprints of old, but also involves the pursuit of concrete social aims such as secure housing or workers' rights. Without specific goals we have no idea which port we wish to sail to, he argues, and are consigned to a loop of never-ending yearning. At the same time utopian dreams will have to be forever reinvented, as William Morris understood when he wrote that 'men fight and lose the battle, and the thing that they fought for comes about in spite of their defeat, and when it comes turns out not to be what they meant, and other men have to fight for what they meant under another name'. If so, then the yearnings which most recently surfaced in London, including those for a more socially connected, green and economically just city, need to find a way of enduring when the utopian moment recedes and of evolving in response to the social desires of future generations.

The urtext of London utopianism, More's *Utopia*, encompasses the notions of utopia as calling for specific social changes, and as being a contingent, open-ended endeavour. In its description of the society of the Utopians, More's story offers a series of concrete social arrangements for an improved society organised into what resembles a classic social blueprint. But the unfolding of the tale through opposing and not necessarily reliable interlocutors, and the powerful sense of ironic detachment running through the text, suggest equivocation and contingency, and that therefore no model can ever constitute a complete recipe for social renewal. In their temple the Utopians ask God to give them the wisdom to find better social arrangements if their present ones are imperfect, to stay open to the possibility of never-ending change, and at the end of the book the character of More expresses the hope that his discussion with the utopian Raphael will continue, as if the template for a communal society that he has discovered can only ever be provisional. This essential pliability of utopian imagining, combined with its concreteness, correlates with the contradictory nature of the city itself, seemingly immovable but actually in constant flux.

Extinction Rebellion's activities in London and further afield harness both these notions of utopia, having much in common with those of the counter-cultural, 'process' utopias of the 1990s while at the same time containing a set of policy demands that are more specific than any made by those earlier movements. Like many utopian outpourings, their yearnings emerged out of crisis, in their case the existential threat of climate change, a solution to which necessitates nothing short of immediate and decisive action. Echoing Winstanley, who declared that words alone were useless, the group's members wear on their clothes the slogan 'Act Now'.

From 2018 Extinction Rebellion drew in thousands from London and around Britain, as in previous environmental movements, in the main highly educated, white and middle-class people, though of an unusual diversity of ages and involving a high proportion of women. Many of them had never taken part in protest and direct action, which engaged them in open law-breaking through weeks-long occupations of roads and public spaces. In April 2019 a group that included an eighty-three-year-old man climbed on top of a Docklands Light Railways train at Canary Wharf and unfurled banners highlighting the role of the financial sector in the climate crisis. Activists took over iconic locations in the city, including Oxford Circus, Trafalgar Square and Waterloo and Westminster Bridges, and made in them festivals of utopian dreaming full of art, music and performance that were protests against the carbon-based economy and a rejection of the cars and consumerism of London. The activists gave out free food and set up places where people could meet, talk and learn, creating small temporary communities in their sites of occupation. Encampments would pop up and, when the police moved in, scatter and reform. People's assemblies were convened in the open air for collective decision-making. Bridges were filled with greenery, sound systems and colourful skateboarding ramps. Those taking part were organised into small 'affinity' groups who worked together and looked after each other; one from east London named itself Dolly's Tower in tribute to Dolly Watson and the utopians of Claremont Road. Calling themselves rebels, the Extinction Rebellion activists rose up and made a festival of London like Reclaim the Streets and Occupy before them, creating playful, shape-shifting urban spaces that were a reimagining of the city.

Extinction Rebellion take over Waterloo Bridge

During one of their London actions, under dark clouds and lit up by shafts of late-afternoon sun, hundreds of rebels sat chanting and drumming in the roads circling Trafalgar Square. Sparks from angle grinders flew into the air as police cut locked-on activists from the road to the accompaniment of cheers and pulsing drumbeats. 'Create the London of our Dreams', the protestors urged, and with their bodies in the road they created a mythic tableau of utopian struggle of a type that has been repeated again and again in the city: dreaming agitators pitted against the forces of the status quo. In *News from Nowhere* William Morris imagined a lush, green London and had the protagonist of his story gaze on the area where Trafalgar Square once was, his visionary sight flickering between images of the place as a scene of sweltering bodies in noisy confrontation – a flashback to the actual Bloody Sunday protests of 1887 – and as the orchard laden with blossom that had since replaced it.

Extinction Rebellion flyer

★

Residues of past utopian struggles exist in the stories that we tell about the city, sometimes even in its physical fabric. By the Thames at Bermondsey stands a group of statues entitled *Dr Salter's Daydream*. On top of a wall overlooking the river a bronze cat crouches as if about to pounce; it looks towards the life-sized likeness of a smiling young girl, Joyce, daughter of the Bermondsey utopians Ada and Alfred Salter, who in 1910 at the age of eight died of scarlet fever while living close to a disease-ridden slum in the area. In the spring of 2021, with an easing of Britain's third Covid lockdown, the narrow riverside streets near to where the statues stand are gradually coming back to life, a scattering of passers-by popping in and out of the shops and cafes. Next to Joyce and her cat a mother plays peekaboo with her toddler and points out Tower Bridge and the Shard across the water. Joyce faces away from the river towards the statues of her parents, which are placed a few yards back from the wall. Seated on a stone bench, Alfred Salter gazes at the water, appearing dreamy and reflective as he leans on an umbrella. Ada Salter stands angled into the flow of the river. She looks determined and implacable, as if at any moment she might try to hold back the course of the dark Thames. Holding her spade, she is ready to build, not content with daydreams alone.

Ada and Alfred gaze into a river skyline that is full of physical emblems of London's utopian dreams, past and present. The statues stand at a point on the Thames where two opposing tongues of land curve round each other, divided by the deep loop of river as it hugs Docklands from the north and Bermondsey and Rotherhithe from the south. Downstream from them on the other side of the Thames, hidden behind the glass towers of the Docklands, are the mid-century Poplar estates that were part of efforts for the pursuit of the dream of equitable housing, a collective vision that was later abandoned for the individualistic ideal of the free market symbolised by the glass skyscrapers that now dominate the view.

The redevelopment of the areas on this bend of the river has brought a jostling of the architectural symbols of a changing economy and of competing utopian dreams as old buildings die and new ones become part of the ever-changing skyline. The rise of London's glass towers — its shards, gherkins, scalpels and walkie-talkies — betray the shift from an industrial to a finance- and services-based economy. From the 1990s, many old council estates were made over or pulled down and replaced as part of schemes of 'regeneration', the model of urban development popularised under New Labour, the term having more than a hint of utopian grandiosity about it. Close to the entrance of the Blackwall Tunnel on the north side of the river just past Canary Wharf is Robin Hood Gardens, a now-condemned estate both loved and loathed. Designed by the brutalist architects Alison and Peter Smithson and completed in 1972, the estate was a bold statement of social intent through the refashioning of the urban environment. Located next to a multi-lane highway that leads into the tunnel, the estate's two chunky blocks were positioned facing each other in order to create an inner area shielded from the thundering traffic. Today the single remaining block is falling into disrepair as sleek new apartment buildings rise up around it as part of the Blackwall Reach regeneration programme. The open space in front of it, an overgrown grassy hillock dotted with daffodils and bare trees, is surrounded by cranes wheeling round the shells of the new blocks, some of the apartments in which are advertised for sale on a developer's billboard for 'only' £740,000.

The visionary meanings contained in the city all around us can easily be forgotten, however. Some years after the Carnival Against Capital that took place in 1999 in the City of London, the artist and Reclaim the Streets activist John Jordan took a walk through the centre of London, where the carnivalgoers had once enacted their own utopia in the heart of the financial district. Jordan thought that the carnival was slipping into a 'quagmire of forgetting' that exists at the heart of the city and into which its histories of utopian dreaming are so often dragged. London's metabolism denies the natural world and makes us believe in a history 'devoid of cracks, of fissures that open up the possibility of radical imaginations transforming themselves into actual acts of resistance'. Apart from a small remnant of graffiti, he can find no trace of the carnival in the physical fabric of the city. All that is left are memories and storytelling, and the necessary creation of imaginative lineages to which our own social yearnings can be connected.

Today we may be in danger of forgetting once more. The Covid pandemic seemed to present a utopian moment as the result of a crisis so deep that some wondered whether it might lead to a turning point in social and political ideas as profound as that which took place after the Great Depression and the Second World War. It came as many were already questioning market economics and liberal democracy and undertaking new reckonings with Britain's colonial past. Young people in particular were showing a renewed interest in activism, especially around issues of race and climate change. But after the initial phase of the lockdown a weariness set in and the utopian moment seemed to recede. People's frustration at the restrictions on their daily lives co-existed with a cynicism at the government's frequent bungling of Covid measures, and the double standards on display as its senior members broke the rules while instructing the public to comply. Collective solidarity began to fray. Westminster political life returned to its carousel of drama and distraction, lurching from one political crisis to the next as the politicians fixated on damage limitation and short-term media management. The city's bars, restaurants and clubs came back to life. The traffic started flowing and clogging up. London was made pretty once more, and its low-paid essential workers, showered with praise for their efforts during lockdown, went back to being taken for granted.

With the return to a more usual mode of politics came the re-emergence of old anxieties about the dominance of London, now seen through the lens of the government's windy rhetoric of 'levelling up', part of which has been to charge the capital with being privileged and out of touch and to inveigh against its 'liberal elite'. The accusation glosses over the complexity of a city that encompasses some of the poorest, most marginalised people in the country, as well as the richest. But London *has* often seemed like a world apart from the rest of the country, the difference having most recently been seen in the city's pro-Remain sentiment during Britain's Brexit travails. The city's leftward political lean – its activist boroughs early in the twentieth century, the Labour-controlled London County Council from the 1930s, and the radicalism of the Greater London Council in the 1980s – has been maintained under a national politics dominated by the Conservative Party and alongside the city's image as a paragon of capitalism; one commentator has styled the city the Red Metropolis. The history of London's social visionaries forms another layer of the capital's imaginative palimpsest: a utopian city of social dreaming and experiment. The recovery of this facet of the city through the telling of the stories contained within it is an antidote to forgetting and a way of gaining hope for our own vision of London, for holding on to our dreams when utopian moments that rise up in it eventually ebb away.

In the Guildhall Art Gallery, close to the church where a young Thomas More once gave his famous lecture concerning the heavenly and the earthly cities, hangs a huge painting of a rooftop panorama of the streets around St Paul's. Niels Moeller Lund's 1904 *The Heart of the Empire* shows a triumphal London, the dome of the cathedral rising to glittering clouds, the streets below teeming with people and carriages. The flag of England flutters from the roof of the Mansion House and smoke rises into haze over the city's spires. Throughout history the same view has acted as the backdrop to numerous imagined Londons. In Lund's representation London is the imperial metropole, a place of relentless movement, and of endless moneymaking and trade. Under the gaze of Bronson Alcott in the nineteenth century, St Paul's was replete with symbols of brutality and tainted tradition that called for the re-establishment of a saintly city. To John Jordan, Reclaim the Streets and the Occupy protestors it is a place in which fissures in capitalist reality can be discovered and used to enact new worlds that end social alienation and tame the moneyed powers that are taking us to the brink of environmental collapse. The Victorian social investigator Henry Mayhew wondered at the multifarious physical reality of London when flying above it in a hot-air balloon, from which the view below seemed like an infinite series of buildings, streets and squares that constituted the capital. By contemplating the many imaginings written over time into the physical city we can also perceive London as an ever-changing dreamscape of utopian desire. In doing so, we remind ourselves to value our own social dreams and to see them as part of the utopian heritage of the metropolis. A golden thread of hope runs through London's streets and links its social visionaries across time. We too can grasp it and weave new imaginative territories into our infinite city, finding possibility in impossibility and making real our utopian dreams.

Endnotes

CHAPTER ONE: WHAT A WONDROUS WORLD WOULD THIS ABSTRACT LONDON BE!

'more virtue and more iniquity': see Mayhew (1852). Another account of his balloon flight is in Mayhew & Binny (1862), pp. 7–10.

'like the coloured fragments of the kaleidoscope': Mayhew & Binny (1862), p. 7.

'What a wondrous World': ibid.

'huge fermenting mass of human-kind': Wordsworth, *The Prelude*, Book 7.

'stream of faces of living men': Heinrich Heine, *Pictures of Travel* (1879), p. 416.

On the island he discovered: Mayhew (1849).

In the twentieth century the Marxist philosopher Ernst Bloch: Bloch (1986).

'fog of otherness': Sinclair (2018), p. 7.

'The fields from Islington to Marybone': William Blake, *Jerusalem: The Emanation of the Giant Albion*, Chapter 2.

'Till we have built Jerusalem': William Blake, *Milton*, Preface.

It was once said that utopians traced the outlines: see Mumford (1961).

In the eighth century BC, the Greek poet Hesiod traced the decline: Hesiod, *Works and Days*.

Virgil in his *Eclogues* conjured up a sunlit Arcadia: Fourth Eclogue.

'poor man's heaven': Morton (1922), p. 11.

Some utopians imagine new societies through theories: for an analytic overview of the various utopian traditions see Sargent (1994).

Daniel Defoe's *Robinson Crusoe*, for example, has been viewed by some: see Morton (1922), p. 100.

In his seminal work of political economy, *The Wealth of Nations*, the philosopher and economist Adam Smith argued that the existence of specialised occupations was limited by the size of the market: Adam Smith, *The Wealth of Nations* (1776), Book 1, Chapter 3.

'if the city is the world which man created': Park (1967), p. 3.

'with time, *England* will onely be *London*': James I (1918), p. 343.

a phenomenon that has been given the name gentrification in recent times but which does not belong to the twentieth century alone: the great chronicler of Tudor London, John Stow, recorded the expulsion of a group of penniless devouts from cottages at Houndsditch when the land there was bought up for commercial development. See Stow (2005), p. 124.

'London has never acted as England's heart': Simmel, 'The Metropolis and Mental Life' in Sennet (1969), p. 50.

CHAPTER TWO: A TRULY GOLDEN HANDBOOK

'a zealous enemy of lies': letter to Thomas Ruthall, More (2020), p. 20.

It is said, however, that his interpretation of *The City of God*: according to one of his early biographers; see Stapleton (1966), p. 7.

not 'ashamed to take a lesson in divinity from a young layman': letter to Van Hutten, Erasmus (1918), vol. 3, pp. 387–401.

'prevent one from seeing the heavens': letter to Colet, Bridgett (1891), pp. 46–8.

A fourteenth-century poet wrote of a penniless visitor: 'London Lickpenny', Baron (1997), vol. 1, p. 88.

Still earlier, a monk-chronicler warned: 'The Chronicle of Richard of Devises', ibid., p. 83.

They pipe and revel, sing and dance: More (2014), p. 273.

If the city had a reasonable soul: ibid., p. 207.

'What is there in the city to incite to virtue': letter to Colet, Bridgett (1891), pp. 46–8.

More's lectures at St Lawrence's were a culmination of an elite

education: key modern works on Thomas More include Chambers (1935), Marius (1985), Ackroyd (1998), Guy (2000).

'This child here waiting at the table': William Roper, 'The Life of Sir Thomas More, Knight' in Roper & Harpsfield (1963), p. 3.

'look . . . with a steady eye, and give good ear to their words': Edith Rickert, *Chaucer's World* (Oxford: Oxford University Press, 1948), p. 104.

'one of the flowers of the world': More (1965), Edward Surtz, *Utopia as a Work of Literary Art*, Introduction, Part II, p. cxlv.

'there's no man living today': More (2012), p. 24.

'far from incompetent in Latin': ibid.

'he who has no grave': ibid., p. 25.

'for fear that you won't believe me': ibid., p. 75.

'So much so that some dimwit with no more understanding than a block of wood': ibid., p. 78.

'You really should have been with me in Utopia': ibid., p. 53.

Robinson's not very faithful translation: see James Binder, 'More's Utopia in English: A Note on Translation', *Modern Language Notes*, vol. 62, no. 6 (1947), pp. 370–76.

'very commodious and handsome': this and the following quotes in the paragraph are from Robinson's translation in More (1880), pp. 73–5.

'far from mean': from Baker-Smith's more accurate translation, More (2012), p. 61.

'pestered with divers alleys': Stow (2005), p. 124.

'sickness of the heart': quoted in Michel Beaud, *A History of Capitalism 1500–2000* (trans. Tom Dickman and Anny Lefebvre) (New York: Monthly Review Press, 2001), p. 15.

In the last years of the reign of Henry VII there were reports of three indigenous men: Chambers (1935), p. 139.

'goodly galontes': *Chronicles of London*, ed. Charles Kingsford (Oxford: Clarendon Press, 1905), p. 234.

At the Great Conduit on Cheapside: for a detailed account see Sydney Anglo, 'The London Pageants for the Reception of Catherine of Aragon: November 1501', *Journal of the Warburg and Courtauld Institutes*, vol. 26, no. 1/2 (1963), pp. 53–89.

How can anyone delight in the transitory glitter of a jewel: More (2012), p. 78.

'Just look at that great booby, Mother': ibid., p. 77.
'hunchbacked, undersized': letter to John Holt, November 1501, More (2020), p. 269.
'Sovereign of Cities, semeliest in sight': Ford (2012), pp. 56–8.
'But What a Mob There is Among Us!': see Guy (2000), p. 92.
according to Erasmus: Reynolds (1965), p. 36.
though one of his early biographers suggested: Nicholas Harpsfield in Roper & Harpsfield (1963), p. 62.
For a thousand years before your eyes: translation by Ronald L. Conte Jr. at http://www.sacredbible.org/studybible/index.htm (accessed on 11 January 2023).
'hatred of tyranny': letter to Van Hutten, Erasmus (1918), vol. 3, pp. 387–401.
'seeing that with your learning and your experience': this and the following quotes in the paragraph are in More (2012), pp. 27–8.
'tossed about by the shifts of fortune': ibid., p. 30.
'Your sheep': ibid., p. 33.
'fell over themselves to endorse his opinion': ibid., p. 40.
'so that whatever you cannot turn to good will at least do the minimum of harm': ibid., p. 50.
'haunts these smokey palace fires': ibid., Introduction, p. xv.
It has been suggested that *Utopia* might have inspired: see Wilde (2016), p. 38.
'merry and cheerful': Roper & Harpsfield (1963), p. 85.
When More some time had Chancellor been: quoted in Chambers (1935), p. 274.
'O how our city is by you renowned': quoted in Quinn (2010), p. 134.
Erasmus likened the More household to Plato's Academy: letter from Erasmus to John Faber, late 1532, More (2020), pp. 1377–80, in particular p. 1380.
'if my head could win him a castle': Roper & Harpsfield (1963), p. 12.
The famous picture – only a preparatory sketch for it survives – contributed to the reputation of the More household: Holbein's finished painting was destroyed in a fire in 1752. Versions of it were made late in the sixteenth century by Rowland Lockey.

The Infinite City

It came to be imagined by its admirers as a humanist enclave: see Heywood's depiction of the setting, reproduced in More (1828), note on pp. 102–3.

'going out of the world': More (2014), p. 164.

the foxes, ferrets, weasels, rabbits and birds that Erasmus recalled him keeping: letter to Van Hutten, Erasmus (1918), vol. 3, pp. 387–401.

'derive a particular delight from fools': More (2012), p. 94.

'furnished too with glowing testimonials': quoted in Baker-Smith (2000), p. 35.

It was even said that a leading theologian: see More (1828), note on p. 234. Guy argues that the story may have been More's invention. See Guy (2000), p. 92.

More's text makes frequent use of litotes: see McCutcheon (1971).

'far from badly governed': More (2012), p. 26.

'concocted about God some problems': Marius (1985), p. 149.

The power of language to do this is encapsulated in a term of classical rhetoric, *enargeia*: see Baker-Smith (2000), p. 80.

'mobile image of eternity': in Plato's *Timaeus*.

'calm tranquility': Manuel & Manuel (1979), p. 416.

'worldly wretches': Roper & Harpsfield (1963), p. 39.

An early reader called Utopia a hagnopolis: letter from William Budé to Thomas Lupset, 31 July 1517, More (1965), pp. 6–15.

More was certainly no revolutionary, and here he is seen as a conservative prophet: Chambers (1935) is an example of this approach to More.

'even to the very death': More (1880), p. 4.

In the nineteenth century, the Marxist theorist Karl Kautksy saluted More: in Kautksy (1927).

'a certain fragrance of incense': ibid., p. 81.

More looks instead to the restriction of desire: this argument is developed in Hexter (1965).

The monastic spirit certainly pervades *Utopia*, but the island of Utopia is not simply an expanded monastery: see ibid., p. 90.

The interplay of opposing views in the book generates a creative friction: Bradshaw (1981), Prescott (2003) and Harp (2016) stress the open-ended, provisional and dialogic nature of More's

Utopia; Prescott and Harp even detect anticipations of postmodernist thought in the work.

'absurd' practices . . . 'subverts all nobility': More (2012), p. 122.

As one commentator suggests, if we must be careful about believing Raphael: Prescott (2003), p. 227.

He imagines himself marching along in monk-like clothes: letter to Erasmus, 4 December 1516, More (2020), pp. 279–80, in particular p. 280.

CHAPTER THREE: LONDON, LOOK TO THY FREEDOM

London's population: discussion of population data and trends can be found in Inwood (1998), p. 159.

'What has that Lady done?': Hotson (1928), p. 40.

'like a mighty torrent . . . breaking in upon us': Manning (1992), p. 80.

'cryes and teares': quoted in Hindle (2008), p. 64.

An opponent of the practice of infant baptism: see Lindley (1997) for further discussion of heterodox religious practices.

'darknesse that is within them': Johns (2008), p. 53.

'One of these gatherings, held by a certain soap boiler': copious and highly censorious contemporary accounts of the sects can be found in Edwards (1646) and Taylor (1641).

'dangerous and false doctrines': Edwards (1646), Part 1, pp. 86–7.

'fools paradise': Vicars (1648), p. 34.

One critic says that the death from plague of two children: Edwards (1646), Part 1, p. 70.

'cobblers, tinkers, peddlers': Taylor (1641).

'Sir, that which is strange': Manning (1992), pp. 161–2.

'subtle fiends': Abraham Crowley, 'The Civil War' in Ford (2012), p. 170.

'forge of the Devill': T. Hall, *Vindicae literarum*, 1654, cited in Giles Calvert, *Oxford Dictionary of National Biography*.

'hurly burlies': 'The Saints Paradice: or, The Fathers Teaching the Only Satisfaction to Waiting Souls', pp. 313–407 in Winstanley (2009), vol. 1, p. 325.

'the Earth growes mad': 'Truth Lifting up his head above Scandals', ibid., pp. 408–71, p. 412.

'Schismaticks' and 'Roundheads': 'The Breaking of the Day of God', ibid., pp. 101–254, p. 166.

'Babylon is faln': ibid., p.169.

'Thou City of London' and 'by thy cheating sons': *A Watch-word to the City of London, and the Armie*, pp. 79–106 in Winstanley (2009), vol. 2, p. 80.

In Cobham, Winstanley made a modest living: key accounts of Winstanley's life can be found in Gurney (2007) and Gurney (2012).

Suffering was like being in a dungeon: 'The Saints Paradice: or, The Fathers Teaching the Only Satisfaction to Waiting Souls', pp. 313–407 in Winstanley (2009), vol. 1, p. 366.

'appearance of the righteous law': ibid., p. 369.

'inward burnings': ibid., p. 345.

'poor soul, know this': ibid., p. 345.

'I was restlesse in my spirit': 'Several Pieces Gathered into One Volume: Set Forth in Five Books', pp. 97–100 in Winstanley (2009), vol. 1, p. 99.

'so filled with that love': ibid., p. 98.

'conjurer' and a 'witch': quoted in William Everard, *Oxford Dictionary of National Biography*.

'strange ecstasies': ibid.

'beggarly rudiments': Walker (1649), Part 2, pp. 152–3.

'disorderly and tumultuous', 'and began to digge' and 'firing the heath': letters from the Council of State and from informers in Clarke (1894), vol. 2, pp. 209–11.

'come down thy sonne of perdition': quoted in William Everard, *Oxford Dictionary of National Biography*.

'I tooke my spade': *A Watch-word to the City of London, and the Armie*, pp. 79–106 in Winstanley (2009), vol. 2, p. 80.

A local official was afraid: Clarke (1894), vol. 2, pp. 209–11.

'they are not to stand bare': Manning (1992), p. 122.

Reports of the meeting: *The Declaration and Standard of the Levellers of England* (1649).

Many of the accounts were inaccurate: see Gurney (2012), p. 58 and Manning (1992), p. 122.

'deceitfull baite': 'Englands Spirit Unfoulded, Or an Incouragement to Take the Engagement', pp. 161–70 in Winstanley (2009), vol. 2, p. 167.
'Yet my mind was not at rest': *A Watch-word to the City of London, and the Armie*, pp. 79–106 in Winstanley (2009), vol. 2, p. 80.
'heaping up of words': *The New Law of Righteousnes*, pp. 472–600 in Winstanley (2009), vol. 1, p. 508.
'Worke together': ibid., p. 513.
'without either giving or taking hire': ibid., p. 517.
three 'doors of hope': ibid., p. 523.
'spirit Reason': ibid., p. 523.
'high treason': ibid., p. 510.
Declare this all abroad: ibid., p. 519.
'*This is mine*, which is selfish': ibid., p. 518.
'*Mine and Thine* shall be swallowed up': ibid., p. 506.
The trumpet sounds in me: ibid., p. 519.
'Leave off dominion and Lordship one over another': ibid., p. 523.
Let Israel go free: ibid., p. 521.
Words and writings must die: *A Watch-word to the City of London, and the Armie*, pp. 79–106 in Winstanley (2009), vol. 2, p. 80.
'God Save the King': Manning (1976), p. 96, and elsewhere for further details of these events.
Winstanley told the general: 'A Letter to the Lord Fairfax, and his Councell of War', pp. 43–58 in Winstanley (2009), vol. 2, p. 44.
'shall be freely laid open': ibid., p. 46.
'mildnesse and moderation': ibid., p. 43.
'unchristian-like abuse': ibid., p. 46.
'that victory which you have gotten': ibid., p. 47.
Winstanley claimed: ibid., p. 47.
Winstanley published a pamphlet: 'A Declaration of the Bloudie and Unchristian Acting of William Star and John Taylor', pp. 59–64 in Winstanley (2009), vol. 2.
According to Winstanley's account: 'An Appeal to the House of Commons', pp. 65–78 in Winstanley (2009), vol. 2.
'a poore man': *A Watch-word to the City of London, and the Armie*, pp. 79–106 in Winstanley (2009), vol. 2, p. 90.

The Infinite City

He wrote that Platt had no scruples: 'A New-yeers Gift for the Parliament and Armie', pp. 107–60 in Winstanley (2009), vol. 2, p. 120.

'In Cobham on the little Heath': *A Watch-word to the City of London, and the Armie*, pp. 79–106 in Winstanley (2009), vol. 2, p. 99.

'cannot rest for fretting': 'An Humble Request to the Ministers of both Universities, and to All Lawyers in Every Inns-a-Court', pp. 255–77 in Winstanley (2009), vol. 2, p. 271.

'And here I end': 'A New-yeers Gift for the Parliament and Armie', pp. 107–60 in Winstanley (2009), vol. 2, p. 149.

Your houses they pull down: 'A Digger Song', George H. Sabine, *The Works of Gerrard Winstanley* (Ithaca, NY: Cornell University Press, 1941), p. 663.

He says to himself: *A Watch-word to the City of London, and the Armie*, pp. 79–106 in Winstanley (2009), vol. 2, p. 91.

Father, do what thou wilt: ibid., p. 91.

Gainst lawyers and gainst priests: 'A Digger Song', Sabine, *The Works of Gerrard Winstanley*, p. 664.

'by this Rain': 'The Breaking of the Day of God', pp. 101–254 in Winstanley (2009), vol. 1, p. 133.

Far from being backward-looking: this thesis is explored in Hill (1975), Chapter 7 and in Manning (1992), pp. 131–2.

Under one interpretation of his thought, More's social imaginings: arguments relating to the fall of man and to conceptions of human progress in this and the next two paragraphs draw on Kenyon (1989).

The Law of Freedom in a Platform: Or, True Magistracy Restored: Winstanley (2009), vol. 2, pp. 278–404.

'fire in my bones': ibid., p. 287.

'groaning under Kingly Bondage': ibid., pp. 280–81.

'by the Covetousness and Cheats of Kingly Government': ibid., p. 334.

'if water stand long, it corrupts': ibid., p. 317.

'Let not people send their children': 'A New-yeers Gift for the Parliament and Armie', pp. 107–60 in Winstanley (2009), vol. 2, p. 116.

'a most shameful retreat': Smith (2014), p. 135.

'And now my health and estate is decayed': *The Law of Freedom in a Platform: Or, True Magistracy Restored*, pp. 278–404 in Winstanley (2009), vol. 2, pp. 352–3.

'a mid-life crisis': Kishlansky (1996), p. 196.

perhaps we should not require of our visionaries: Corns et al. make this point in relation to the great religious flux of Winstanley's time; see Winstanley (2009), vol. 1, Introduction.

'in frantick posture': quoted in William Everard, *Oxford Dictionary of National Biography*.

'done . . . by that very army': Evelyn (1901), vol. 1, p. 332.

CHAPTER FOUR: FULL BELLIES, FOOLS!

'A certain man having many sons': 'Description of Spensonia' (1795), pp. 25–33 in Dickinson (1982), p. 25.

'unjust and unbrotherly grudging': ibid., p. 26.

'strewed with fruit' and **'as carefully as garden herbs':** ibid., p. 31.

'Thus am I from being a happy celestial': 'A Dream' (possibly 1807), pp. 118–20 in ibid., p. 120.

'crutch which late compassion moved': John Gay *Trivia: or, the art of walking the streets of London* (1716), Book 3.

'the black vapour brooding': in Charles Eliot Norton (ed.), *Early Letters of Thomas Carlyle*, vol. 2 (1886), p. 285.

Sweepings from butchers' stalls: Jonathan Swift, 'A Description of a City Shower' (1710).

'lewd women enough to fill a mighty colony': Sir John Fielding, quoted in George Rudé, *Hanoverian London 1714–1808* (London: Secker & Warburg, 1971), p. 72.

'a vast wood or forest': quoted in Porter (2000), p. 183.

'in continual embarrassments and difficulties': Thomas Spence, 'The Important Trial of Thomas Spence' (1803), pp. 92–103 in Dickinson (1982), p. 94.

'dangerous levelling principles': quoted in Rachel Hammersley, 'Spence's "Property in Land Every One's Right": Problems and Solutions' in Bonnett & Armstrong (2014), p. 43.

He reworked the lecture into a pamphlet, *The Real Rights of Man*: 'The Real Rights of Man' (1795), pp. 1–5 in Dickinson (1982).

'so much as a blade of grass': ibid., p. 2.
'right and reason': ibid., p. 5.
While still in Newcastle, Spence had published a sequel to Robinson Crusoe: published in standard spelling as *A Supplement to the History of Robinson Crusoe* (1782), pp. 5–15 in ibid.
'but both of these I have reduced to order': in 'The Important Trial of Thomas Spence' (1803), pp. 92–103 in ibid., p. 96.
Spence published a dictionary: *The Grand Repository of the English Language* (1775) as Spence (1969).
the kind of words that were condemned as barbarous by Samuel Johnson but would have been used in Spence's circle: see Robert W. Rix, 'Thomas Spence's Spelling Reform' in Bonnett & Armstrong (2014), p. 93.
'free the poor': Preface to *A Sŭplĭmĭnt too the Hĭstĭre ŏv Rŏbĭnsĭn Kruzo* (1782).
The crusonian alphabet has often been viewed as another of Spence's oddities: the assessment of Spence's alphabet in this paragraph draws on that of Joan C. Beal, 'A Radical Plan for the English Language' in Bonnett & Armstrong (2014).
a 'curious' work: 'Memoir of Thomas Spence' from *Mackenzie's History of Newcastle* (1826), p. 5.
even supportive commentators: see Rudkin (1927), p. 229.
'such coarse works as may fit them for servants': *The Works of Hannah More* (1838), vol. 12, p. 213.
'The present is pregnant with the future': Leibniz, *New Essays on Human Understanding* (1704).
If progress was real, then, as Voltaire had earlier remarked: Bury (1920), p. 151.
'ocean of futurity': *Outlines of an Historical View of the Progress of the Human Mind: being a posthumous work of the late M. de Condorcet, Translated from the French* (1795), p. 369.
No longer lost in shades of night: 'Alteration' (1794) in Dickinson (1982), pp. 123–4.
Their tavern is a comradely refuge from an indifferent city: for detailed analysis of tavern radicalism, including how gatherings offered a form of community during times of economic stress, see Iain McCalman, 'Ultra-Radicalism and Convivial Debating Clubs in

London, 1795–1838', *The English Historical Review*, vol. 102, no. 403 (1987), pp. 309–33 and Michael T. Davis, '"Meet and Sing, and Your Chains Will Drop Off Like Burnt Thread": The Political Songs of Thomas Spence' in Bonnett & Armstrong (2014).

'**May the skin of tyrants be burned into parchment**': ibid., p. 323.

'**Sing and meet and meet and sing**': see *Spence's Songs* at Marxists Internet Archive at https://www.marxists.org/history/england/britdem/societies/spenceans/songs.htm (accessed on 11 January 2023).

'**trodden down under the hoofs of a swinish multitude**': Edmund Burke, *Reflections on the Revolution in France* (1791), p. 117.

'**prosecute the authors of divers wicked and seditious writings**': 'House of Lords Journal Volume 39: May 1792 21–30' in *Journal of the House of Lords Volume 39, 1790–1793* (1767–1830), pp. 431–58.

'**a German hog-butcher**': quoted in Michael Davis, 'The Mob Club? The London Corresponding Society and the Politics of Civility in the 1790s' in Michael Davis & Paul Pickering (eds), *Unrespectable Radicals: Popular Politics in the Age of Reform* (London: Routledge, 2016), p. 33.

'**prostituted ruffians**': this and the following quotes in this paragraph come from 'The Case of Thomas Spence' (1792), pp. 15–21 in Dickinson (1982), p. 17.

'**the owner was confined in gaol**': ibid., p. 19.

'**Friends in General of Free Investigation**' and '**having been precipitated into a shop**': quoted in John Mee, 'Thomas Spence and the London Corresponding Society, 1792–1795' in Bonnett & Armstrong (2014).

'**fellows well armed**': Thomas Spence, 'End of Oppression' (1795), pp. 34–7 in Dickinson (1982), p. 36.

'**hunger-bitten . . . children of oppression**': ibid., p. 37.

This opening verse of Spence's triumphal song, 'The Commencement of the Millennium': for the full text see *Spence's Songs* at Marxists Internet Archive at https://www.marxists.org/history/england/britdem/societies/spenceans/songs1.htm#millenium (accessed on 6 December 2022).

'**Calculators, Mystics, Magnetizers**': William Reid, 'The Rise and Dissolution of the Infidel Societies' (1800), quoted in Chase (2010), p. 44.

'**Behold their palaces**': 'The Rights of Infants' (1797), pp. 46–53 in Dickinson (1982), p. 53.
'**Hear me! ye oppressors!**': ibid., p. 50.
'**shall we be asked what the Rights of Infants are?**': ibid., p. 48.
'**sink calmly into apathy**': ibid., p. 49.
'**which we presume our gallant lock-jawed spouses**': ibid., p. 51.
The Rights of Man for Me: from 'Pig's Meat' (1795) in Dickinson (1982), p. 129.
'**a prototype of hell**': quoted in Stephen Halliday, *Newgate: London's Prototype of Hell* (Stroud: Sutton Publishing, 2006), p. 190.
'**Are we never to expect a better state of things**': in 'The Important Trial of Thomas Spence' (1803), pp. 92–103 in Dickinson (1982), p. 93.
'**For this trial is in fact not my trial**': ibid., p. 97.
'**you and a few other friends**': the letter is in Rudkin (1927), p. 120.
'**his Plan and the Landlords**': William Hone, quoted in ibid., p. 125.
Wedderburn was born and raised in Jamaica: key studies of Wedderburn and his London context are McCalman (2002) and Wedderburn (1991), Introduction by McCalman.
'**founded in divine justice**': *The Address and Regulations of the Society of Spencean Philanthropists* (1815) at Marxists Internet Archive at https://www.marxists.org/history/england/britdem/societies/spenceans/regulations.htm (accessed on 6 December 2022).
'**an oppressed, insulted and degraded African**': Wedderburn, 'The Horrors of Slavery' (1824) in Wedderburn (1991), p. 44.
'**the earth was given to the children of men**': Wedderburn, 'The Axe Laid to the Root; or, A Fatal Blow to Oppressors, Being an Address to the Planters and Negroes of the Island of Jamaica, No.1' (1817), ibid., p. 82.
'**my blood boils in my veins**': Wedderburn (1824), 'The Horrors of Slavery', ibid., p. 47.
'**I thank my GOD**': ibid., p. 58.
'**glows with revenge**': Wedderburn, 'The Axe Laid to the Root; or, A Fatal Blow to Oppressors, Being an Address to the Planters and Negroes of the Island of Jamaica, No.1' (1817), in Weddenburn (1991), p. 86.
'**can make right wrong**': ibid., p. 90.

'Truth is my arrow': ibid., p. 96.
'two-faced politician': quoted in Hanley (2018), p. 213.
'fat-gutted' clergy: quoted in McCalman (2002), p. 141.
Wedderburn said that he was proud to be called a madman: Wedderburn, 'The Axe Laid to the Root; or, A Fatal Blow to Oppressors, Being an Address to the Planters and Negroes of the Island of Jamaica, No.1' (1817) in Wedderburn (1991), p. 83.
'a bloody fool': quoted in McCalman, Introduction in Wedderburn (1991), p. 26.
Wedderburn's loft offered irreverent pantomime: further details can be found in McCalman (2002).
he stated that his incarceration had only strengthened the beliefs: 'The Horrors of Slavery' (1824), pp. 44–5 in Wedderburn (1991).
'a toad's back': quoted in Hanley (2018), p. 230.
Wedderburn never presented himself as a paragon of individual self-improvement: for further details and for a comparison with the self-presentations of more well-known Black Britons of the time see McCalman's Introduction in Wedderburn (1991).
'but to the inhumanity of a MAN': Wedderburn, 'The Horrors of Slavery' (1824), pp. 44–5 in Wedderburn (1991), p. 44.
Spenceanism may well be the only political creed to have been banned: see Bonnett & Armstrong (2014), p. 2.
'as if the waters had but newly retired from the face of the earth': Charles Dickens, *Bleak House*, Chapter 1.
a 'little polished Athens': in *A Supplement to the History of Robinson Crusoe* (1782), pp. 5–15 in Dickinson (1982), p. 13.
More sympathetic historians: for example, Chase (2010). This and the next paragraph draw on arguments made in Chapter 1 of that work.
Wedderburn makes this pan-colonial outlook more explicit: Matilde Cazzola explores the Atlantic perspective of Spenceanism in '"All shall be happy by land and by sea": Thomas Spence as an Atlantic thinker', *Atlantic Studies*, vol. 15, no. 4 (2018), pp. 431–50.
Today's developers privatise city spaces in their domains in more underhand ways: see Chapter Nine and Minton (2017).

CHAPTER FIVE: THE HIVE OF DREAMS

'Educational Circulars, and Communist Apostles': Emerson (1842), p. 227.
'calm felicity': Manuel & Manuel (1979), see Introduction.
Owen believed that the root of the nation's ills: Owen (1817) and 'Observations on the Effect of the Manufacturing System' in Owen (1991) pp. 93–104.
In August 1817, at packed and stormy public meetings: 'Address Delivered at the City of London Tavern' in Owen (1991), pp. 170–85.
'parallelograms of paupers': Cobbett, *Political Register*, 2 August 1817.
'an interesting enthusiast': Donnachie (2011), p. 140.
'bigotry, superstition, and all false religions': Owen (1920), p. 224.
'I came out to circulate my papers': Scott (1892), vol. 1, p. 175.
'mind branched as in a faery wildwood': this and other quotes in this paragraph are from 'The Epic of a Life or, the European Pariah. An autobiographic poem', *The Promethean*, June 1842, pp. 58–61.
'murdering trade will cease': *The Promethean*, March 1842, p. 50.
In one of her articles, Catherine had written: 'Festivity at the New Social Hall, John Street', *The New Moral World*, 25 April 1840, p. 1263.
'I announce love to be the sacred bond': *The Educational Circular and Communist Apostle*, vol. 1, no. 1 (1841), cited in Taylor (1983).
'The reign of the critic is over': quoted in Armytage (1956), p. 167.
'The spiritual division': *The Promethean*, vol. 1, no. 1, p. 1.
'will be an educationalist': *The Promethean*, vol. 1, no. 2, p. 27.
'I believe in community as the law of Love': *The Promethean*, vol. 1, no. 1, p. 23.
'high in the brightness': *The Promethean*, vol. 1, no. 4, p. 65.
'man-power' and 'woman-power': John Goodwyn Barmby, 'The Man-Power, the Woman-Power, and the Woman-Man Power', *The New Moral World*, vol. 2, no. 18 (1841), pp. 268–9.
'God has decreed the first Asylum': Taylor (1983), p. 176.
'sentimentally, intellectively and manually': *The New Moral World*, 8 July 1843.
'to combat Babylon': Taylor (1983), p. 177.
'Goddess of Reason': quoted in Dooley (1996), p. 63.
'the female mind': quoted in ibid., p. 72.

'not as irascible': quoted in ibid., p. 75.

from London writing to Fourier: see ibid., p. 77.

'I am a woman and without a master': quoted in ibid., p. 356.

'a mind robbed of much of its energy' and 'seeing as I do, the rottenness of our institutions': Anna Wheeler, 'Rights of Women', *The British Cooperator*, vol. 1, no. 1 (1830), p. 12.

An 1825 treatise published under the authorship of Thompson: *Appeal of One Half of the Human Race, Women, against the Pretensions of the Other Half, Men, to Retain Them in Political, and Thence in Civil and Domestic Slavery*, Thompson (1983).

'the ignorant selfish propensities': ibid., p. 55.

'breeding machines': ibid., p. 85.

'shall salute each other': ibid., p. 204.

'monstrous smoke-hole': Smith (1892), p. 89.

By this time Owenism had moved into a new phase: detailed accounts of the development of Owenism can be found in Podmore (1906) and Harrison (1969).

Owen had advocated the replacement of money wages: *Report to the County of Lanark* (1820) in Owen (1991), pp. 250–308.

'infidel Socialism': Smith (1840), p. 33.

'Age of the Bride': quoted in Harrison (1969), p. 121.

'the bisexual or two-fold law': Smith (1840), p. 36.

'a state in which love between the sexes': Smith (1892), p. 337.

'one of the most noble women': ibid., pp. 148–9.

'men-tyrants and monsters': ibid., p. 336.

'moral phenomenon': Francis Barham, 'A Memoir of the late James Pierrepont Greaves', Barham (1845), p. 1.

spiritually superior even to Coleridge: ibid., p. 8.

'the importance of good *being*': ibid., p. 12.

'The spirit man, or esse man': Latham (1999), p. 62.

'You entered, and in a moment you glided': *The New Age*, vol. 1, no. 12 (1843), p. 136.

'Very likely' said Greaves calmly: this and the quotes following in this paragraph are from *The Fortnightly Review*, no. 22, 1 April 1886, p. 386.

'It was emphatically to live in a new world': *The New Moral World*, vol. 5, no. 31 (1844), p. 242.

Born in 1777 to a family of London drapers: the only full-length biography of Greaves is Latham (1999).
'strong interior visitations': letter to Bronson Alcott in *The Dial*, vol. 3, no. 4 (1843), p. 423.
'Let us attend far more to what we are doing': Charles Lane, 'James Pierrepont Greaves', *The Dial*, vol. 3, no. 3 (1843), p. 293.
'There is, at present, an obvious appearance of the Love-seed': letter to Bronson Alcott in *The Dial*, vol. 3, no. 4 (1843), p. 424.
'the phalanstery, the republic, and the universal commonwealth': *A Prospectus for the Establishment of a Concordium* (1841), p. 5.
'to be in concord with the triune universe spirit': *A Brief Account of the First Concordium* (1843), p. 1.
'universe-love-spirit': *A Prospectus for the Establishment of a Concordium* (1841), p. 7.
John Goodwyn Barmby published there details: *The New Age*, vol. 1, no. 3 (1843), p. 24.
'fruit rooms': *The New Age*, vol. 1, no. 10 (1843), p. 110.
Rather than setting out programmes for social reform: see *A Prospectus for the Establishment of a Concordium* (1841).
In his *The Paradise Within the Reach of All Men:* Etzler (1836).
Both the Owenite *New Moral World* and the Fourierist *London Phalanx* wrote glowingly: *The New Moral World*, vol. 3, no. 15 (1841), p. 115 and *The London Phalanx*, no. 60, August 1842, p. 80.
Another supporter lauded Etzler's technological system for delivering paradise so cheaply: see Armytage (1961), p. 193.
'omnipotence of machinery': quoted in Gregory (2014), p. 64.
One of these outlined a plan for a community: Etzler, *Emigration to the Tropical World for the melioration of all classes of people of all nations* (1844).
'mechanical Cockayne': Gregory (2014), p. 259.
in the House of Lords a leading bishop strongly condemned Owen's speech: reported in *The New Moral World*, 15 August 1840, p. 104.
'the result of very materially disordered imaginations': *The New Moral World*, 27 July 1844, p. 34.
'planting Edens – fabling of worlds – building kingdoms and men': Alcott (1969), p. 67.

'above the din and smoke': ibid., p. 69.

'London . . . shall become the footstool': ibid., p. 86.

'He who will not submit to be inwardly disciplined': *The New Age*, vol. 1, no. 20 (1844), p. 268.

One resident wrote that numbers were dwindling: see Frost (1880), pp. 47–9.

On hearing the news, John Goodwyn Barmby rushed to Paris and sent back a series of dispatches: *Howitt's Journal*, vol. 3 (1848).

Doherty wrote to Anna Wheeler: letter given in Podmore (1906), vol. 2, pp. 596–7.

'It seems as if these sanguine schemers rushed to the press': Emerson (1842), p. 227.

In a curious incident at the close of this period of London utopianism, one of the wondrous but ill-conceived machines of John Adolphus Etzler appeared in the agricultural gallery of the exhibition: see Gregory (2014), p. 204.

CHAPTER SIX: THE GARDEN IN THE CITY

a 'Bacchanalian scene': Barnett (1918), vol. 1, p. 142.

'noisy horseplay . . . does not create a desire': ibid.

In front of his audience, intricate diagrams from his lantern slide projector: see Beevers (1988), Chapter 3, in particular pp. 30–35.

'I defy you to show wherein the scheme is impracticable': ibid., pp. 34–5.

'stony-hearted' Oxford Street': this and the following quotes in the paragraph are from Thomas de Quincey, *Confessions of an English Opium Eater* (1822), Part 2.

Henrietta Barnett was born in Clapham: the main biography of Barnett is Creedon (2006). Barnett (1918) is Barnett's biography of her husband, which covers much of her own life.

'the heartless rich, the sweating employer, or the rack-renting landlord': Beatrice Webb, *My Apprenticeship* (Cambridge: Cambridge University Press, 1979), p. 211.

'Let us try it': Barnett (1918), vol. 1, p. 69.

'As I sit at school I always imagine myself roaming in the fields': ibid., p. 191.
'mental culture and knowledge': ibid., vol. 2, p. 79.
'the development of the imagination': ibid., p. 106.
Born to a shopkeeper in 1850: key full-length biographies of Howard are Beevers (1988) and Macfadyen (1970).
'I see you in the centre of a series of circles': Macfadyen (1970), p. 11.
'There flowed through every nerve of my body': quoted in Beevers (1988), pp. 10–11.
'there came to me an overpowering sense': quoted in ibid., p. 27.
'stamped by the landlord's greed': Henrietta Barnett, 'The Garden Suburb at Hampstead' in Barnett & Barnett (1909), p. 332.
'can we hope for nothing more than a repetition': ibid., p. 333.
'The earth and the growth of it and the life of it!': Morris (2014), p. 221.
'the very embodiment of Divine love': Howard (1898), p. 5.
'out of this joyous union will spring a new hope': ibid., p. 10.
'vicious and immoral system': ibid., p. 146.
'vast residuum': Matthew Arnold, *Culture and Anarchy* (1889), p. 66.
In *News from Nowhere,* the ushering-in of the 'Equality of Life' takes place in 1952: E. P. Thompson discusses Morris becoming resigned to the unlikelihood of immediate revolution. See Thompson (1976), p. 502.
'It was something of an affliction': quoted in Beevers (1988), p. 44.
'To me, born and bred in London': Purdom (1951), p. 36.
'Some resolution was required': ibid., p. 37.
'There was excitement, a sense of brotherhood': Purdom (1951), pp. 48–9.
'You are going nowhere better': quoted in Macfadyen (1970), p. 108.
'turning to one spot on earth': this and the following quote in the paragraph are from Purdom (1913), pp. 109–10.
'polished mahogany' and 'stucco trimmings': Parker & Unwin (1901).
'mere aggregations of struggling units': Unwin (1911), p. 375.
'little communities of people': quoted in Creese (1992), p. 172.

'there was nothing else to do': Barnett (1918), vol. 2, p. 312.
'over a sloping foreground of apple orchards': in 'The Garden Suburb at Hampstead' in Barnett & Barnett (1909), p. 351.
'only a woman': Barnett (1918), vol. 2, p. 315.
'grateful and glad, humble and unhappy': Barnett (1928), p. 13.
'A nice woman but proud of being a philistine': Miller (2006), p. 119.
'the country comes up clean and fresh': Parker & Unwin (1901), p. 84.
'it must be pleasant to have in common one virtue': Barnett (1928), p. 65.
'rationalists and vegetarians': quoted in Miller (2006), p. 180.
'grim spectres of the city': ibid., pp. 186–7.
'When Mrs Barnett put forward her scheme': quoted in Barnett (1928), p. 45.
'I was made to feel I was naughty': Barnett (1918), vol. 1, p. 68.
'You arrange the journey of your day': ibid., vol. 2, p. 124.
'I must remember I am the Vicar's wife': quoted in Creedon (2006), p. 90. Creedon explores possible psycho-sexual factors behind Barnett's episodes of fatigue.
It has been speculated: Miller (2006), p. 16; Creedon (2006), p. 128.
'riding, dancing, porridge, cream': Barnett (1918), vol. 2, p. 142.
A hint of this came in a talk: 'Spiritual Influences and Social Progress', *Light: A Journal of Psychical, Occult and Mystical Research*, vol. 30, no. 1528, April 1910, p. 195.
'like the child crying for the moon': Beevers (1988), p. 106.
'the unpalatable dough': quoted in ibid., p. 71.
'Garden City Geyser' and 'mere spring of benevolent mud': quoted in ibid., p. 70.
'He was one of those heroic simpletons': quoted in ibid., p. 181.
Even Morris, often incorrectly seen as opposed to machinery: see Thompson (1976), p. 649.
'though a garden may hold in it what belongs to the past': Purdom (1913), p. 107.
Barnett felt that many of the Hampstead residents: Barnett (1928), p. 76.
'the stream of sympathy is sometimes shallow': ibid., p. 25.

Howard's proposed 'rate-rent' system: for further details see Ward (2016), p. 14.

Eventually Howard's economic principles were watered down: see Beevers (1988), pp. 92–4 and Ward (2016), p. 38.

The garden city was often equated with the garden suburb: this discussion draws on Ward (1990).

'You have accomplished more than you know': quoted in Fishman (1977), p. 82.

Travelling those few miles north to south: Hall argues that these clusters of towns show Howard's vision on the ground. He also traces the influence of Howard's ideas on some of London's later planning frameworks. See Hall (2014), p. 146 and pp. 188–201.

and it has been criticised in this respect: see Eden (1957).

In 2018, conservators working on the restoration of St Jude's: *Suburb News*, Hampstead Garden Suburb Association, issue 135, summer 2018, p. 7.

'links the Suburb with all its promises': Barnett (1928), pp. 31–2.

CHAPTER SEVEN: TOWN HALL UTOPIAS

But despite Howard's antipathy to the state: Welwyn drew on state funding. See Ward (2016), Chapter 3.

Lubetkin arrived in England in 1931: the main full-length study of Lubetkin's life and work is Allan (2012).

'persistently attracted by the vision of the metropolis': ibid., p. 53.

One morning in March of that year Lubetkin was woken: Lubetkin's account is in 'The Revolution, 1917' in Coe & Reading (1981).

'history crashed through the barriers': quoted in Allan (2012), p. 29.

'a stratified society': quoted in ibid., p. 651.

'a thesis you put in front of society': quoted in ibid., p. 322.

praised by Le Corbusier as proof of the concept of 'the vertical garden city': see Coe & Reading (1981), p. 121.

'stands on tip toe': quoted in ibid., p. 155.

'like the realisation of a dream': Allan (2012), p. 349.

'smiling machine': ibid., p. 348.

the rate of infant mortality: see Brockway (1949), p. 93.

'with hats': this and the following quotes in the paragraph are from Taylor (2016), pp. 54–5.

Like Henrietta Barnett, Brown had begun her career: key biographies are Taylor (2016) and Brockway (1949). The latter of these is of her husband, but covers many of her own activities.

'not housed, but warehoused': Ada Salter, 'Don't forget the hidden London', *Daily Herald*, 28 February 1934, p. 14.

'The injustices of the ages': quoted in Taylor (2016), p. 135.

This was pursued within a broader scheme of civic beautification: Lebas (1999) documents the various council programmes involved in this.

'like purple stars': quoted in Taylor (2016), p. 195.

'not a decoration, but a symbol': quoted in ibid., p. 195.

One visitor shown around the borough by Ada in May 1935: Hannen Swaffer, 'I heard yesterday', *Daily Herald*, 6 May 1935, p. 10.

'We'll pull down three-quarters of Bermondsey': Brockway (1949), p. 40.

'a cottage home for every family': quoted in John Boughton, 'The Wilson Grove Estate' at https://municipaldreams.wordpress.com/2013/05/14/the-wilson-grove-estate-bermondsey-a-cottage-home-for-every-family/ (accessed on 25 November 2022).

The most striking method of citizen education was through the use of mobile film vans: the council's use of films is explored in Lebas (1995).

The people watch on the screen workmen in flat caps: some of these films are freely available online, for example at https://www.youtube.com/watch?v=5WzfpVe_RcY (accessed on 25 November 2022).

In 1946 he stood up in the House of Commons: New Towns Bill, *Hansard*, 8 May 1946.

Despite the borough's ambitious aims, progress on housebuilding was slow: see Bullock (1989), p. 57.

'that will be the joy of generations to come': quoted in ibid., p. 46.

'which could be snipped off by the yard': quoted in Coe & Reading (1981), p. 176.

'had to be submitted in triplicate': quoted in Allan (2012), p. 438.
The British intellectuals Karl Popper and Isaiah Berlin developed philosophical critiques of the utopian enterprise: the classic works are Berlin (1991) and (1950), and Popper (1961) and (1962).
'apocalyptic revolution': see Popper (1962), vol. 1, p. 164.
'If your desire to save mankind is serious': in 'The Pursuit of the Ideal' in Berlin (1991), p. 16.
'concrete miseries': see Popper (1986), p. 7.
'logically untidy, flexible, and even ambiguous compromise': see Berlin (1950), p. 384.
But the critique failed to recognise poverty and unemployment: for criticism of Coleman's thesis see Spicker (1987).

CHAPTER EIGHT: BENEATH THE TARMAC

CHANGED PRIORITIES AHEAD: footage of Reclaim the Streets' parties are available at YouTube, for example 'Camden Street Party 1995' at https://www.youtube.com/watch?v=oLH2U3shqtk (accessed on 5 December 2022). An account from a participant is John Jordan, 'The Art of Necessity: The Subversive Imagination of Anti-road Protest and Reclaim the Streets' in McKay (1998), pp. 129–51.
'the biggest road-building programme': quoted in Richard Sadler, 'Roads to ruin', *The Guardian*, 13 December 2006.
Reclaim the Streets came out of a DIY counter-culture: see McKay (1998).
'characterised by the emission of a succession of repetitive beats': Criminal Justice and Public Order Act 1994, Part 5, Section 63.
Their movement led to the creation of a fragment of utopia: key studies of Reclaim the Streets and the earlier anti-roads protests are Blanco (2018) and John Jordan, 'The Art of Necessity: The Subversive Imagination of Anti-road Protest and Reclaim the Streets' in McKay (1998), pp. 129–51.
'a poisoned dart aimed at the heart of London': in footage 'THE EVICTION OF WANSTEAD – News Compilation' at https://www.youtube.com/watch?v=DHjqlJ12nvA (accessed on 1 December 2022).

'Let the tree live!': see footage 'Life in the Fast Lane – The No M11 Story' at https://www.youtube.com/watch?v=49wKgtOo0qs&list=PLoNszVeoltLQnV9YPHX9gXT4kDky7EO5d&index=57&t=131s (accessed on 5 December 2022).

'We're going to fight for every blade of grass': see footage 'Direct Action protest to stop the M11 Link road – long trailer' at https://www.youtube.com/watch?v=gNIZFwk6tVs&t=9s (accessed on 5 December 2022).

'They may look different': quoted in Drury et al. (2003), p. 9.

In the tree lived Green Dave, a former panel beater and mechanic, who described becoming a protestor: see Butler (1996), p. 357.

Many said that these conversations changed them: see Drury (2003), p. 199.

A long-time activist from the area commented: quoted in 'Today in London's rebel history: Wanstonia evicted to make way for the M11, 1994', February 2016 at https://pasttenseblog.wordpress.com/2016/02/16/today-in-londons-rebel-history-wanstonia-evicted-to-make-way-for-the-m11-1994/ (accessed on 2 December 2022).

Another hailed the tree as 'a symbol of continuity and permanence': letters to the tree were published by the No M11 Link Road Campaign as a pamphlet, *Dear Tree*.

'Things go in cycles and we're back again': see footage 'Dear Tree – The Battle for George Green' at https://www.youtube.com/watch?v=wvOYuzNw_Sk&list=PLoNszVeoltLQnV9YPHX9gXT4kDky7EO5d&index=14 (accessed on 2 December 2022).

In a letter to the tree, a supporter of the campaign referenced the English Revolution: in *Dear Tree*, published by the No M11 Link Road Campaign.

A protest song, 'The Wanstead Chestnut and the Motorway': in ibid.

'If I was Queen, you'd all be knighted': quoted in *SchNEWS*, issue 3, 7 December 1994, Brighton.

'life stopped being so atomised': in footage 'Life in the Fast Lane – The No M11 Story' at https://www.youtube.com/watch?v=49wKgtOo0qs&list=PLoNszVeoltLQnV9YPHX9gXT4kDky7EO5d&index=56&t=131s (accessed 2 December 2022).

Upstairs, a wardrobe full of shirts had a door in the back of it: see Butler (1996), p. 342.

'I believe a leaf of grass is the journeywork of the stars': quoted in 'The Art House', *The Guardian*, 25 June 1994.

'against hurrying from one place to the next': in footage 'Reclaim the Streets UK documentary' at https://www.youtube.com/watch?v=bUL0C_T-Sqk&list=PLoNszVeoltLQnV9YPHX9gXT4kDky7EO5d&index=65 (accessed on 2 December 2022).

'an adventure playground for adults and misfits': in footage 'M11 Link Road Film' at https://www.youtube.com/watch?v=2nzqrto0424 (accessed on 2 December 2022).

'the sense of an authentic form of community': ibid.

which earlier in the century had infused revolutionary ideals with those of the imagination and desire: see Plant (1992), p. 3.

'The streets are as full of capitalism as of cars': quoted in John Jordan, 'The Art of Necessity: The Subversive Imagination of Anti-road Protest and Reclaim the Streets', pp. 129–51 in McKay (1998), p. 140.

'In societies where modern conditions of production prevail': Debord (2014), p. 2.

'immense accumulation of commodities': Karl Marx, *Capital*, vol. 1, Chapter 1.

'degradation of *being* into *having*': Debord (2014), p. 5.

'shift from *having* to *appearing*': ibid.

'petrification of life': ibid., p. 91.

'Community becomes commodity': quoted in Naomi Klein, *No Logo* (London: Flamingo, 2001), p. 323.

A French philosopher and sociologist associated with the Situationists, Henri Lefebvre: see Lefebvre (1996).

A city's highways, malls and adverts express in topographical terms a set of priorities: see Plant (1992), p. 57.

The Situationist utopia was a city of 'unitary urbanism': see Pinder (2005) for further discussion of this concept, especially p. 129.

Obsolete monuments and statues would be removed: see ibid., p. 177.

'People strolled, dreamed': the Situationist René Viénet quoted in ibid., p. 236.

the road even resembled some of the utopian cities imagined by the Situationists: for further details see Sandy McCreery, 'The Claremont Road Situation', pp. 228–45 in Iain Borden, Joe Kerr, Jane Rendell and Alicia Pivaro (eds), *The Unknown City: Contesting Architecture and Social Space* (Cambridge MA: MIT Press, 2000), pp. 236–7.

At number 36 was the entrance to the 'rat run': see footage 'The Rat Run, Claremont Road, 1994' at https://www.youtube.com/watch?v=jflxRfUFJZo&list=PLoNszVeoltLQnV9YPHX9gXT4kDky7EO5d&index=30 (accessed 5 December 2022).

In the freezing cold at two o'clock the next afternoon, Operation Garden Party begins: for footage see 'The Siege of Claremont Road (1994)' at https://www.youtube.com/watch?v=rWm8ib5pbFI&t=984s (accessed on 5 December 2022).

'Stealing our houses, stealing our land': see footage 'No M11 Protest | Claremont Road Eviction | November 1994 | Raw Footage | Kinokast Archive' at https://www.youtube.com/watch?v=_ssmIn9K4u4 (accessed on 5 December 2022).

'You're endangering people's lives for a fucking road!': see footage 'The Siege of Claremont Road (1994)' at https://www.youtube.com/watch?v=rWm8ib5pbFI&t=984s (accessed on 5 December 2022).

'Get us an ounce of weed each and we'll come down': see ibid.

when they are unearthed, the bailiffs' shadowed faces suddenly appear in a gap: see Butler (1996), p. 358.

People on the ground chant up to it: see footage 'Power to the Tower – Claremont Road tower eviction (1994)' at https://www.youtube.com/watch?v=fK2yDcniiJM&t=72s (accessed on 5 December 2022).

'listen to the metabolism of London': from project description, Platform London at footage 'Greenland Dock (1989)' at https://www.youtube.com/watch?v=NiyINwDMHKQ (accessed on 5 December 2022). Further details of the project can be found at https://platformlondon.org/2019/05/10/compelled-to-be-wise-in-the-tent-that-can-hear/ (accessed on 5 December 2022).

'a wholly privatised world': in footage 'Greenland Dock (1989)' at https://www.youtube.com/watch?v=NiyINwDMHKQ (accessed on 5 December 2022).

'the pragmatic collided with the poetic, the performative with the political': transcript of a talk given by John Jordan at the Tate Modern on 30 March 2003, available at https://www.nettime.org/Lists-Archives/nettime-l-0304/msg00016.html (accessed on 5 December 2022).

'the inherent risk, excitement and danger': see John Jordan, 'The Art of Necessity: The Subversive Imagination of Anti-road Protest and Reclaim the Streets', pp. 129–151 in McKay (1998), p. 133.

'revokes the emphasis on words and reason': see ibid.

'Revolutionary moments are carnivals': Raoul Vaneigem, quoted in Plant (1992), p. 71.

'Why does power fear free celebration?': for this and the following quotes in the paragraph see Reclaim the Streets at https://rts.gn.apc.org/prop14.htm (accessed on 5 December 2022).

'death and misery' behind the financial system: quote and further details on the More to Life Project at *Do or Die: Voices from the ecological resistance*, no. 8, pp. 15–16.

neutralise their 'dark magic': quoted in *Notes from Nowhere* (2003), p. 190.

capitalism is a mask 'that distracts and blinds': this and the following quotes in the paragraph are from Blanco (2018), p. 52.

The protestors brought the city to a standstill: footage includes 'RECLAIM THE STREETS 1999 LONDON June 18 Carnival Against Capital' at https://www.youtube.com/watch?v=9jUkSjCsoy0 (accessed on 5 December 2022). Further eyewitness reports can be found in *Notes from Nowhere* (2003).

One man emerged from the London Underground: see *Notes from Nowhere* (2003), p. 217.

'made a killing': quote in *Do or Die: Voices from the ecological resistance*, no. 8, p. 16.

among the crowds that day were a number of the long-time residents of Wanstead: see Drury et al. (2003), p. 204.

They symbolically closed a circle in July 1996 when, after a chaotic game of cat and mouse with the police in the streets of Shepherd's Bush: accounts are contained in Blanco (2018), pp. 46–7, John Jordan, 'The Art of Necessity: The Subversive Imagination of Anti-road Protest and Reclaim the Streets', pp. 129–51 in McKay (1998), pp. 143–6 and *Notes from Nowhere* (2003), pp. 50–59.

Beneath the tarmac: a flyer for the event used the phrase 'Under the tarmac, the forest'. Quoted in Blanco (2018), p. 47.

A veteran of the earlier struggles of Leyton and Wanstead: Eastside Community Heritage oral history project on the M11 Link Road Campaign, Secret Chestnut Tree segment at https://eastsidech.wixsite.com/voicesofleytonstonia/oral-history (accessed on 5 December 2022).

CHAPTER NINE: THE GOLDEN THREAD

***The Financial Times*, normally a defender of free-market orthodoxy, published an editorial:** 'Virus lays bare the frailty of the social contract', *Financial Times*, 3 April 2020.

'We come to our gates and give people a wave': '"Singing with people connects you": How four UK streets are living with lockdown', *The Guardian*, 25 April 2020.

One resident noted that these activities had changed the story of the area: '"We've changed the narrative": Pandemic positivity on the Alton estate', 21 March 2012, BBC online at https://www.bbc.co.uk/news/uk-england-london-56413821 (accessed on 27 November 2022).

One in five Britons volunteered: *Isolation Economy Study*, Legal & General, May 2020 see https://group.legalandgeneral.com/en/newsroom/press-releases/10-million-brits-volunteering-as-the-nation-unites-in-the-isolation-economy-says-legal-general (accessed on 27 November 2022).

750,000 for the NHS: 'A million volunteer to help NHS and others during Covid-19 outbreak', *The Guardian*, 13 April 2020.

Nearly half say that they would be unable to meet an unexpected expense of £500: The London Intelligence – Snapshot of Londoners – June 2021, Centre for London at https://www.centreforlondon.org/publication/the-london-intelligence-june-2021/ (accessed on 27 November 2022).

Almost 40 per cent of London's children live in poverty: Rachel Leeser, 'Poverty in London 2019/20', 28 March 2021, London

Assembly at https://data.london.gov.uk/blog/poverty-in-london-2019-20/#_ftn1 (accessed on 27 November 2022).

Rough sleeping doubled: London Assembly, 10 January 2020 at https://www.london.gov.uk/press-releases/mayoral/mayor-launches-services-for-citys-rough-sleepers (accessed on 27 November 2022).

In the middle of the twentieth century, the Labour minister Aneurin Bevan: see Boughton (2019), p. 93.

'regeneration supernova': Hatherley (2020), p. 191.

'just six hours from New York': Minton (2017), p. 15.

In 2021 it was reported that a new housing development on the road would make no provision for affordable housing: 'Affordable homes in "Billionaires Row" scheme unviable, says developer', *The Guardian*, 20 November 2021.

London's luxury flats are the sheep of twentieth-century capitalism: for further discussion on sheep imagery in Thomas More and in condemnations of capitalism see Levitas (2016).

There are many such pseudo-public spaces dotted around London: see Minton (2017).

'It's people, on the street, in the squares, that really matters in the end': Harvey's speech is available at https://www.youtube.com/watch?v=3sLKdLPh5Cw (accessed on 28 November 2022).

A report by Public Health England: *Beyond the Data: Understanding the Impact of COVID-19 on BAME Groups*, Public Health England, June 2020.

An adviser to the mayor, the artist Gaylene Gould, said that London was moving into a 'new imaginative period': London Assembly, press release, 'Mayor unveils commission to review diversity of London's public realm', 9 June 2020.

A Black teenager, Giovanni Rose, captured in his 2021 poem 'Welcome to Tottenham': The Poetry Society. Available at https://poems.poetrysociety.org.uk/poems/welcome-to-tottenham/ (accessed on 28 November 2022).

The protestors were 'a bunch of rank hypocrites', Morgan asserted: the interview can be viewed at https://www.youtube.com/watch?v=8ISePLL1wcw (accessed on 28 November 2022).

as the philosopher Slavoj Žižek has noted: 'Zizek in Wall Street – Transcript', October 2011 at https://criticallegalthinking.com.

com/2011/10/11/zizek-in-wall-street-transcript/ (accessed on 28 November 2022).

the Marxist critic Fredric Jameson: quoted in Perry Anderson, 'The River of Time', *New Left Review* no. 26, March/April 2004, pp. 74–5.

'To be truly radical': Raymond Williams, *Resources of Hope* (London: Verso, 1989), p. 118.

'utopia as method': Levitas (2013).

one leading politician's likening of Brexit: Jacob Rees-Mogg MP. See Jack Maidment, 'Jacob Rees-Mogg compares Brexit to battles of Agincourt, Waterloo and Trafalgar', *Daily Telegraph*, 3 October 2017.

'flawed words and stubborn sounds': from Wallace Stevens, 'The Poems of Our Climate' (1942).

'less perfect than the ideal': Purdom (1913), p. 39.

Some participants reported that in Occupy London's tent city it was often women: see Earl (2015), p. 188.

'dialectical utopianism': David Harvey, *Spaces of Hope* (Edinburgh: Edinburgh University Press, 2000), p. 196.

'men fight and lose the battle': William Morris, *A Dream of John Ball* (1887), Chapter 4.

From 2018 Extinction Rebellion drew in thousands from London and around Britain: for data on the social composition of Extinction Rebellion's activists see Clare Saunders, Brian Doherty and Graeme Hayes, 'A New Climate Movement? Extinction Rebellion's Activists in Profile', Centre for the Understanding of Sustainable Prosperity, Working Paper no. 25, July 2020.

one commentator has styled the city the Red Metropolis: Hatherley (2020).

References

A Brief Account of the First Concordium, or Harmonious Industrial College. Ham Common: Concordium Press, 1843.

A Prospectus for the Establishment of a Concordium Or an Industry Harmony College. London: Strange, 1841.

Ackroyd, Peter. *The Life of Sir Thomas More*. London: Chatto & Windus, 1998.

Alcott, Amos Bronson, ed. Richard L. Herrnstadt. *The Letters of A. Bronson Alcott*. Ames: Iowa State University Press, 1969.

Allan, John. *Berthold Lubetkin: Architecture and the Tradition of Progress*. London: Artifice Books on Architecture, 2012.

Armytage, W. H. G. 'The Journalistic Activities of J. Goodwyn Barmby between 1841 and 1848', *Notes and Queries*, April 1956, pp. 166–9.

———. *Heavens Below: Utopian Experiments in England 1560–1960*. Toronto: University of Toronto Press, 1961.

Baker-Smith, Dominic. *More's Utopia*. Toronto: University of Toronto Press, 2000.

Barham, Francis Foster. *A: An Odd Medley of Literary Curiosities*. London: author, 1845.

Barmby, John Goodwyn. 'The Promethean; or Communitarian Apostle, a Quarterly Magazine of Societarian Science, Domestics, Ecclesiastics, Politics and Literature', 1842.

Barnett, Henrietta. *The Story of the Growth of the Hampstead Garden Suburb, 1907–1928*. London: Henry Ford Estate Collection, 1928.

Barnett, Henrietta. *Canon Barnett: His Life, Work, and Friends*. London: John Murray, 1918.

Barnett, Samuel Augustus, and Henrietta Barnett. *Towards Social Reform*. New York: The Macmillan Company, 1909.

Baron, Xavier. *London, 1066–1914: Literary Sources & Documents. Vol. 1: Medieval, Tudor, Stuart and Georgian London*. Mountfield, East Sussex: Helm Information, 1997.

Beevers, Robert. *The Garden City Utopia: A Critical Biography of Ebenezer Howard*. London: Macmillan, 1988.

Berlin, Isaiah. 'Political Ideas in the Twentieth Century', *Foreign Affairs* 28, no. 3 (1950), pp. 351–85.

———. *The Crooked Timber of Humanity: Chapters in the History of Ideas*. Edited by Henry Hardy. New York: Knopf, 1991.

Blanco, Julia Ramírez. *Artistic Utopias of Revolt: Claremont Road, Reclaim the Streets, and the City of Sol*. Basingstoke: Palgrave Macmillan, 2018.

Bloch, Ernst. *The Principle of Hope*. Cambridge, MA: MIT Press, 1986.

Bonnett, Alistair, and Keith Armstrong, eds. *Thomas Spence: The Poor Man's Revolutionary*. London: Breviary Stuff Publications, 2014.

Boughton, John. *Municipal Dreams: The Rise and Fall of Council Housing*. London: Verso, 2019.

Bradshaw, Brendan. 'More on Utopia', *The Historical Journal* 24, no. 1 (1981), pp. 1–27.

Bridgett, Thomas Edward. *Life and Writings of Sir Thomas More: Lord Chancellor of England and Martyr Under Henry VIII*. London: Burns & Oates, 1891.

Brockway, Fenner. *Bermondsey Story: The Life of Alfred Salter*. London: George Allen & Unwin, 1949.

Bullock, Nicholas. 'Fragments of a Post-War Utopia; Housing in Finsbury 1945–51', *Urban Studies* 26, no. 1 (1989), pp. 46–58.

Bury, J. B. *The Idea of Progress: An Inquiry into Its Origin and Growth*. London: Macmillan and Co., 1920.

Butler, Beverley. 'The Tree, The Tower and the Shaman', *Journal of Material Culture* 1, no. 3 (1996), pp. 337–63.

Chambers, R.W. *Thomas More*. London: Jonathan Cape, 1935.

Chase, Malcolm. *The People's Farm: English Radical Agrarianism 1775–1840*. London: Breviary Stuff Publications, 2010.

Clarke, William, ed. C. H. (Charles Harding) Firth. *The Clarke Papers. Selections from the Papers of William Clarke, Secretary to the Council of the Army, 1647–1649, and to General Monck and the Commanders of the Army in Scotland, 1651–1660*. London: Printed for the Camden Society, 1894.

Coe, Peter, and Malcolm Reading. *Lubetkin and Tecton: Architecture and Social Commitment: A Critical Study*. London: Arts Council of Great Britain, 1981.

Creedon, Alison. *'Only a Woman', Henrietta Barnett: Social Reformer and Founder of Hampstead Garden Suburb*. Chichester: Phillimore, 2006.

Creese, Walter L. *The Search for Environment: The Garden City – Before and After*. Baltimore MD: Johns Hopkins University Press, 1992.

Debord, Guy. *The Society of the Spectacle*. Translated by Ken Knabb. Washington: Bureau of Public Secrets, 2014.

Dickinson, H.T., ed. *The Political Works of Thomas Spence*. Newcastle: Avero (Eighteenth-Century) Publications Ltd., 1982.

Donnachie, Ian. *Robert Owen: Social Visionary*. Edinburgh: John Donald, 2011.

Dooley, Dolores. *Equality in Community: Sexual Equality in the Writings of William Thompson and Anna Doyle Wheeler*. Cork: Cork University Press, 1996.

Drury, John, Steve Reicher, and Clifford Stott. 'Transforming the Boundaries of Collective Identity: From the "Local" Anti-Road Campaign to "Global" Resistance?', *Social Movement Studies* 2, no. 2 (2003).

Earl, Cassie. 'An Exploration of Popular Education from Occupy! London to the University: Making Hope Possible in the Face of Neoliberal Enclosure?' PhD thesis, Education and Social Research Institute, Manchester Metropolitan University, 2015.

Eden, W. A. 'Hampstead Garden Suburb 1907–1957', *Journal of the Royal Institute of British Architects*, October 1957, p. 489.

Edwards, Thomas. *Gangraena: Or a Catalogue and Discovery of Many of the Errours, Heresies, Blasphemies and Pernicious Practices of the Sectaries of This Time, Vented and Acted in England in These Four Last Years.* London: 1646.

Emerson, Ralph Waldo. 'English Reformers', *The Dial* 3, no. 2 (1842), pp. 227–47.

Erasmus, Desiderius, ed. Francis Morgan Nichols. *The Epistles of Erasmus, from His Earliest Letters to His Fifty-First Year, Arranged in Order of Time.* vol. 3. London: Longmans, Green and Co., 1918.

Etzler, John Adolphus. *The Paradise Within the Reach of All Men, Without Labour, by Powers of Nature and Machinery: An Address to All Intelligent Men.* London: John Brooks, 1836.

Evelyn, John, ed. William Bray. *The Diary of John Evelyn.* New York and London: M. W. Dunne, 1901.

Fishman, Robert. *Urban Utopias in the Twentieth Century: Ebenezer Howard, Frank Lloyd Wright and Le Corbusier.* New York: Basic Books, 1977.

Ford, Mark, ed. *London: A History in Verse.* Cambridge MA: Harvard University Press, 2012.

Frost, Thomas. *Forty Years' Recollections: Literary and Political.* London: Sampson Low, Marston, Searle, and Rivington, 1880.

Gregory, James. *The Poetry and the Politics: Radical Reform in Victorian England.* London: I. B. Tauris, 2014.

Gurney, John. *Brave Community: The Digger Movement in the English Revolution.* Manchester; New York: Manchester University Press, 2007.

———. *Gerrard Winstanley: The Digger's Life and Legacy.* London: Pluto Press, 2012.

Guy, John. *Thomas More* (Reputations). London and New York: Arnold and Oxford University Press, 2000.

Hall, Peter. *Cities of Tomorrow: An Intellectual History of Urban Planning and Design Since 1880.* Chichester: Wiley Blackwell, 2014.

Hanley, Ryan. *Beyond Slavery and Abolition: Black British Writing, c. 1770–1830.* Cambridge: Cambridge University Press, 2018.

Harp, Jerry. 'More's Utopia and Never-Ending Dialogue', *Moreana* 53, nos 3–4 (2016), pp. 95–114.

Harrison, J. F. C. *Quest for the New Moral World: Robert Owen and the Owenities in Britain and America*. New York: Scribner, 1969.

Hatherley, Owen. *Red Metropolis: Socialism and the Government of London*. London: Repeater Books, 2020.

Heine, Heinrich, and Charles Godfrey Leland. *Heinrich Heine's Pictures of Travel*. 8th rev. ed. Philadelphia: Schaefer & Koradi, 1879.

Hexter, J. H. *More's Utopia: The Biography of an Idea*. New York: Harper & Row, 1965.

Hill, C. *The World Turned Upside Down: Radical Ideas during the English Revolution*. London: Penguin, 1975.

Hindle, Steve. 'Dearth and the English Revolution: The Harvest Crisis of 1647–50', *The Economic History Review* 61, no. S1 (2008), pp. 64–98.

Hotson, Leslie. *The Commonwealth and Restoration Stage*. Cambridge MA: Harvard University Press, 1928.

Howard, Ebenezer. *To-Morrow: A Peaceful Path to Real Reform*. London: Swan Sonnenschein, 1898.

Inwood, Stephen. *A History of London*. London: Macmillan, 1998.

James I, and Charles Howard McIlwain. *The Political Works of James I*. Harvard Political Classics. 1. Cambridge MA: Harvard University Press, 1918.

Johns, Adrian. 'Coleman Street', *Huntington Library Quarterly* 71, no. 1 (2008), pp. 33–54.

Kautsky, Karl. *Thomas More and His Utopia. With a Historical Introduction*. Translated by H. J. Stenning. International Publishers, 1927.

Kenyon, Timothy. *Utopian Communism and Political Thought in Early Modern England*. London: Pinter, 1989.

Kishlansky, Mark. *The Penguin History of Britain: A Monarchy Transformed, Britain 1630–1714*. 6th edn. London; New York: Penguin, 1996.

Latham, J. E. M. *Search for a New Eden: James Pierrepont Greaves (1777–1842), The Sacred Socialist and His Followers*. Madison NJ: Fairleigh Dickinson University Press, 1999.

Lebas, Elizabeth. 'The Making of a Socialist Arcadia: Arboriculture and Horticulture in the London Borough of Bermondsey after the Great War', *Garden History* 27, no. 2 (1999), pp. 219–37.

———. '"When Every Street Became a Cinema". The Film Work of Bermondsey Borough Council's Public Health Department, 1923–1953', *History Workshop Journal*, no. 39 (Spring 1995), pp. 42–66.

Lefebvre, Henri. *Writings on Cities*. Translated by Eleonore Kofman and Elizabeth Lebas. Oxford: Blackwell, 1996.

Levitas, Ruth. 'Less of More', *Utopian Studies* 27, no. 3 (2016), pp. 395–401.

———. *Utopia as Method: The Imaginary Reconstitution of Society*. Basingstoke: Palgrave Macmillan, 2013.

Lindley, Keith. *Popular Politics and Religion in Civil War London*. Aldershot: Scolar Press, 1997.

Macfadyen, Dugald. *Sir Ebenezer Howard and the Town Planning Movement*. Manchester: Manchester University Press, 1970.

Manning, Brian. *1649: The Crisis of the English Revolution*. London: Bookmarks, 1992.

———. *The English People and the English Revolution, 1640–1649*. Oxford: Heinemann Educational, 1976.

Manuel, Frank E. and Manuel, Fritzie P. *Utopian Thought in the Western World*. Oxford: Basil Blackwell, 1979.

Marius, Richard. *Thomas More*. London: Vintage Books, 1985.

Mayhew, Henry. 'A Visit to the Cholera Districts of Bermondsey', *The Morning Chronicle*, 24 September 1849.

———. '"In the Clouds"; or, Some Account of a Balloon Trip with Mr. Green', *The Illustrated London News*, 18 September 1852.

Mayhew, Henry, and John Binny. *The Criminal Prisons of London and Scenes of Prison Life*. London: Griffin, Bohn, and Company, 1862.

McCalman, Iain. *Radical Underworld: Prophets, Revolutionaries and Pornographers in London, 1975–1840*. Oxford: Clarendon Press, 2002.

McCutcheon, Elizabeth. 'Denying the Contrary: More's Use of the Litotes in Utopia', *Moreana* 8, nos 3–4 (1971), pp. 106–21.

McKay, George, ed. *DiY Culture: Party and Protest in Nineties Britain*. London and New York: Verso, 1998.

Miller, Mervyn. *Hampstead Garden Suburb: Arts and Crafts Utopia?* Chichester: Phillimore, 2006.

Minton, Anna. *Big Capital: Who Is London For?* London: Penguin, 2017.

More, Cresacre. *The Life of Sir Thomas More*. London: William Pickering, 1828.

More, Thomas. *A Dialogue of Comfort against Tribulation*. The Center for Thomas More Studies, 2014.

———. *More's Utopia*. Translated by Ralph Robinson. Cambridge: Cambridge University Press, 1880.

———. *The Essential Works of Thomas More*. Edited by Gerard Wegemer and Stephen Smith. New Haven CT: Yale University Press, 2020.

———. *The Yale Edition of the Complete Works of St. Thomas More, Volume 4, Utopia*. Edited by Edward Surtz and J. H. Hexter. New Haven CT: Yale University Press, 1965.

———. *Utopia*. Translated by Dominic Baker-Smith. Illustrated edn. London: Penguin Classics, 2012.

Morris, William, ed. Clive Wilmer. *News from Nowhere and Other Writings*. London: Penguin, 2004.

Morton, A. L. *The English Utopia*. London: Lawrence & Wishart, 1922.

Mumford, Lewis. *The City in History: Its Origins, Its Transformations, and Its Prospects*. New York: Harcourt Brace Jovanovich, 1961.

Notes from Nowhere, ed. *We Are Everywhere: The Irresistible Rise of Global Anticapitalism*. London: Verso, 2003.

Owen, Robert, ed. Gregory Claeys. *A New View of Society and Other Writings.*. Harmondsworth: Penguin, 1991.

———. *The Life of Robert Owen*. London: G. Bell and Sons, 1920.
———. Association for the Relief of the Manufacturing and Laboring Poor, and Great Britain. *Report to the Committee of the Association for the Relief of the Manufacturing and Labouring Poor, Laid before the Committee of the House of Commons on the Poor Laws*, 1817.
Park, Robert Ezra, ed. Ralph H. Turner. *On Social Control and Collective Behavior. Selected Papers.* Chicago and London: University of Chicago Press, 1967.
Parker, Barry, and Raymond Unwin. *The Art of Building a Home*. London: Longmans, 1901.
Pinder, David. *Visions of the City: Utopianism, Power and Politics in Twentieth-Century Urbanism*. Edinburgh: Edinburgh University Press, 2005.
Plant, Sadie. *The Most Radical Gesture: The Situationist International in a Postmodern Age*. London and New York: Routledge, 1992.
Podmore, Frank. *Robert Owen: A Biography*. London: Hutchinson & Co., 1906.
Popper, Karl. *The Open Society and Its Enemies*. 4th edn. London: Routledge & Kegan Paul, 1962.
———. *The Poverty of Historicism*. New York: Harper & Row, 1961.
———. 'Utopia and Violence', *World Affairs* 149, no. 1 (1986), pp. 3–9.
Porter, Roy. *London: A Social History*. New edn. London: Penguin, 2000.
Prescott, Anne Lake. 'Postmodern More', *Moreana* 40, nos 1–2 (2003), pp. 219–39.
Purdom, C. B. *Life over Again*. London: Dent, 1951.
———. *The Garden City: A Study in the Development of a Modern Town*. London: J. M. Dent & Sons Ltd., 1913.
Quinn, Paul. 'A Witty, Learned Persecutor? The Staged After-Life of Thomas More', *Moreana* 47, nos 3–4 (2010), pp. 129–52.
Reynolds, E. E. *Thomas More and Erasmus*. London: Burns & Oates, 1965.

Roper, William, and Nicholas Harpsfield, ed. E. E. Reynolds. *Lives of Saint Thomas More*. London: Dent, 1963.

Rudkin, Olive D. *Thomas Spence and His Connections*. New York: International Publishers, 1927.

Sargent, Lyman Tower. 'The Three Faces of Utopianism Revisited', *Utopian Studies* 5, no. 1 (1994), pp. 1–37.

Scott, William Bell. *Autobiographical Notes of the Life of William Bell Scott: And Notices of His Artistic and Poetic Circle of Friends, 1830 to 1882*. London: Osgood, McIlvaine, 1892.

Sennet, Richard, ed. *Classic Essays on the Culture of Cities*. New York: Appleton-Century-Crofts, 1969.

Sinclair, Iain. *Blake's London: The Topographic Sublime*. London: Swedenborg Society, 2018.

Smith, James Elishama. *The Little Book; Or, Momentous Crisis of 1840; in Which the Bishop of Exeter and Robert Owen, Are Weighed in the Two Scales of One Balance, and a New Revelation of Demonstrated Truth Is Announced to the World*. London: B. D. Cousins, 1840.

Smith, Nigel, ed. *A Collection of Ranter Writings: Spiritual Liberty and Sexual Freedom in the English Revolution*. London: Pluto Press, 2014.

Smith, W. Anderson. *'Shepherd' Smith the Universalist: The Story of a Mind: Being a Life of The Rev. James E. Smith, M.A.* London: Sampson Low, Marston & Company, 1892.

Spence, Thomas. *The Grand Repository of the English Language 1775*. Menston, England: The Scolar Press, 1969.

Spicker, Paul. 'Poverty and Depressed Estates: A Critique of Utopia on Trial', *Housing Studies* 2, no. 4 (1987), pp. 283–92.

Stapleton, Thomas. *The Life and Illustrious Martyrdom of Sir Thomas More*, ed. E. E. Reynolds, trans. Philip Edward Hallett. New York: Fordham University Press, 1966.

Stow, John. *A Survey of London: Written In The Year 1598*. New edn. Stroud: The History Press, 2005.

Taylor, Barbara. *Eve and the New Jerusalem: Socialism and Feminism in the Nineteenth Century*. New York: Pantheon Books, 1983.

Taylor, Graham. *Ada Salter: Pioneer of Ethical Socialism.* London: Lawrence & Wishart, 2016.

Taylor, John. *A Svvarme of Sectaries and Schismatiqves Wherein Is Discovered the Strange Preaching, or Prating, of Such as Are by Their Trades Coblers, Tinkers, Pedlers, Weavers, Sowgelders and Chymney-Sweepers,* 1641.

The New Age, Concordium Gazette, & Temperance Advocate, 1843.

Thompson, E. P. *William Morris: Romantic to Revolutionary.* London: Merlin Press, 1976.

Thompson, William. *Appeal of One Half the Human Race, Women, against the Pretensions of the Other Half, Men, to Retain Them in Political, and Thence in Civil and Domestic Slavery.* London: Virago, 1983.

Unwin, Raymond. *Town Planning in Practice: An Introduction to the Art of Designing Cities and Suburbs.* London: T. Fisher Unwin, 1911.

Vicars, John. *Coleman-Street Conclave Visited, and, That Grand Imposter, the Schismaticks Cheater in Chief (Who Hath Long, Slily Lurked Therein) Truly and Duly Discovered Containing a Most Palpable and Plain Display of Mr. John Goodwin's Self-Conviction (under His Own Hand-Writing) and of the Notorious Heresies, Errours, Malice, Pride, and Hypocrisie of His Most Huge Garagantua, in Falsly Pretended Piety, to the Lamentable Misleading of His Too-Too Credulous Soul-Murthered Proselytes of Coleman-Street & Elsewhere.* London: 1648.

Walker, Clement. *Anarchia Anglicana: Or, The History of Independency. With Observations Historicall and Politique Upon This Present Parliament, Begun Anno 16. Caroli Primi., Anno Domini 1640. Together with the Rise, Growth, and Practises of That Powerfull and Restlesse Faction,* 1649.

Ward, Stephen V. 'The Garden City Tradition Re-Examined', *Planning Perspectives* 5, no. 3 (1990), pp. 249–56.

———. *The Peaceful Path: Building Garden Cities and New Towns.* Hatfield: Hertfordshire Publications, 2016.

Wedderburn, Robert, ed. Iain McCalman. *The Horrors of Slavery and Other Writings by Robert Wedderburn.* Princeton NJ: Markus Wiener Publishers, 1991.

Wilde, Lawrence. *Thomas More's Utopia: Arguing for Social Justice*. London: Routledge, 2016.

Winstanley, Gerrard, ed. Thomas Corns, Ann Hughes, and David Loewenstein. *The Complete Works of Gerrard Winstanley (2 Volumes)*. Oxford: Oxford University Press, 2009.

List of illustrations

INTERGRATED IMAGES

2: Charles Green's Royal Vauxhall, The Royal Aeronautical Society (National Aerospace Library)/Mary Evans

7: Christopher Wren, 'A Plan for the Rebuilding the City of London after the Great Fire in 1666', British Library Board/Bridgeman Images

23: Raphael, Morus and Peter, woodcut by Ambrosius Holbein in Thomas More's *Utopia*, Folger Shakespeare Library

40: More's Chelsea residence, 'Beaufort House' by Johannes Kip, The Cleveland Museum of Art

41: 'The More Household at Chelsea' by Hans Holbein the Younger, public domain

58: John Smith, The World turn'd upside down, British Library Board/Bridgeman Images

66: *The Declaration and Standard of the Levellers of England,*, Pictorial Press Ltd/Alamy

86: Countermarked coins by Thomas Spence, Thomas Spence Society

87: Coin punches by Thomas Spence, Thomas Spence society

97: The Spencean alphabet, from the Important Trial of Thomas Spence, 1803

129: Robert Owen's proposed community, *Robert Owen: A Biography* by Frank Podmore

141: Equitable Labour Exchange note, *Robert Owen: A Biography* by Frank Podmore

148: Etzler's 'Naval Automaton', *Cleaves Penny Gazette*, August 19, 1843

162: Plan of part of Fulham, *Town Planning in Practice* by Raymond Unwin

174: Children in Howard Park, *Sir Ebenezer Howard and the Town Planning Movement* by Dugald Macfadyen

182: *The Masque of Fairthorpe*, Hampstead Garden Suburb Archives

200: Children in solarium, *Berthold Lubetkin* by John Allan

208: Bermondsey film van, Southwark Local History Library and Archive

215: Aerial view of Bevin Court, Aerofilms/Historic England

224: Reclaim the Streets, Nick Cobbing

242: Man reading in the nets, Gideon Mendel

251: The River Walbrook released from a hydrant, Urban75

262: St George's Hill, author's photo

277: Waterloo Bridge, Dan Kitwood/Getty

278: Extinction Rebellion flyer, author's photo

PLATE SECTIONS

'A Fête at Bermondsey' by Marcus Gheeraerts the Elder

London as an old man, from William Blake's *Jerusalem*, Yale Center for British Art, Paul Mellon Collection

Thomas More by Hans Holbein the Younger, The Artchives/Alamy

A rapidly growing London, George Braun and Frans Hogenberg, Album/Alamy

St George's Hill, Rolfe Alexander Frederick, Artefact/Alamy

Profile of Thomas Spence, Fitzwilliam Museum/Bridgeman Images

'The End of Oppression', Fitzwilliam Museum/Bridgeman Images

Robert Wedderburn, *The Horrors of Slavery* by Robert Wedderburn

The New Union Club, George Cruickshank, Pictorial Press Ltd/Alamy

Robert Owen, *Robert Owen: A Biography* by Frank Podmore

John Goodwyn Barmby, Paul Lindsay Dawson

Anna Wheeler, National Portrait Gallery

James 'Shepherd' Smith, *'Shepherd' Smith the Universalist* by W. Anderson Smith

James Pierrepont Greaves, The Trustees of the British Museum

Bronson Alcott, NYPL Digital Gallery

Ebenezer Howard, *Garden Cities of To-morrow* by Ebenezer Howard

Howard's geometric vision, *Garden Cities of To-morrow* by Ebenezer Howard

William Morris, GRANGER/Historical Picture Archive/Alamy

Pages from *News from Nowhere* by William Morris, Yale Center for British Art, Paul Mellon Collection

The Three Magnets, *Garden Cities of To-morrow* by Ebenezer Howard

Raymond Unwin, National Portrait Gallery

Waterlow Court, author's photo

Henrietta and Dorothy, *Canon Barnett* by Henrietta Barnett

Finsbury Health Centre by Abram Games, Imperial War Museum

Ada Salter, Wellcome Collection

Lubetkin, RIBApix

Bevin Court Staircase, Grantham9

Claremont Road artwork, Eastside Community Heritage

Claremont Road view, Eastside Community Heritage

Dolly Watson, Eastside Community Heritage

Doctor Salter's Daydream by Diane Corvin, author's photo

Acknowledgements

Much of this book was written in London during the Covid lockdowns of 2020 and 2021 when the city was sustained by its shop staff, bus drivers and nurses. As a writer on a deadline, this army of key workers for me included the employees of the London Library, who through the pandemic worked tirelessly to maintain an efficient postal loans service when most research facilities were inaccessible. While I stayed at home, their unceasing shovelling of materials to me down in south London saved progress on the book from slowing to a snail's pace.

I'm grateful to another literary organisation, my trade union, the Society of Authors, for financially supporting the creation of this book through an Arthur Welton Award given under the Authors' Foundation grant scheme for works in progress.

I'm fortunate to have found in Chris Wellbelove, an agent thoroughly on my writing wavelength. Chris enthusiastically took up the project when it was barely off the drawing board and has been a consistent cheerleader and dispeller of doubt. At William Collins I've benefitted greatly from the editorial sagacity of Arabella Pike and Sam Harding. Tom Killingbeck initially acquired the book and was a helpful sounding board at the start. The copy-editor, Linden Lawson, evened out the text with sensitivity and precision. Emma Pidsley created a visionary cover design. Laura Meyer has been an energetic and supportive publicist. Thanks also to proofreader Anne Rieley, indexer Ben Murphy and production controller Chris Wright. The project editor, Katy Archer, shepherded everyone towards the finishing line with efficiency and good humour.

A number of dear friends and family have in various ways supported my efforts. Juliet Brooke encouraged me to run with the glimmer of an idea and has followed progress since. Jane Howard read early words with generosity and care. Ann Gladwin provided indefatigable organisational backup and moral support. Eddie Thomas has been a fount of benevolence and good sense, and a model of writing productivity that I've tried to live up to. Alex Crowe's comradeship and wise listening have fortified my creative intentions. The kindness and generosity of my parents, Margaret and Khalid Kishtainy, have given me the confidence and space I've needed to build a writing life.

I give deepest thanks to my partner, Laura Gladwin, for her complete faith in my writing endeavours over the years, and especially during the early phase of exploring the ideas involved in this book when there was no guarantee that my growing piles of notes would amount to anything. Once the writing started to flow, I've also been very lucky to benefit from her acute reading and unerring literary judgment. Our children, Sami and Juno, have been cheerful and inquisitive companions as I pursued these stories through the streets of London. Most importantly, their unalloyed delight in the city as it is has reminded me that despite its imperfections and the complaints of its utopians, London remains a cause for celebration and hope.

Index

Page references in *italics* indicate images.

abstract space, 239, 260–1
Aesthetic Society, 143, 146
affordable housing, 189, 258, 259–60
Alcott, Amos Bronson, 145–6, 150–1, 267, 282
Alcott House, 146–7
Alton Estate, 221–2, 255–6
American War of Independence, (1775–83) 103, 110
Anarchism, 80, 170, 171, 236, 248, 256
Andreae, Johannes: *Christianopolis*, 47
Anglo-Soviet Committee, 214
anticipatory consciousness, 5, 267
anti-clericalism, 31, 64
anti-road campaigns, 223–52, 267
Antwerp, 22, 28
Arcadia, 5, 10, 118, 251

Arnold, Matthew, 169
Arthur, Prince, 29, 30
Arts and Crafts movement, 163, 171, 173, 180, 189, 191, 204
Arup, Ove, 212
Aspen Way, 226–7
Association for Preserving Liberty and Property Against Republicans and Levellers, 104
Attlee, Clement, 210, 211
Augustine, St: *The City of God*, 17–18, 30–1, 32, 48, 77
austerity policies, 210, 258, 266, 270
Axe Laid to the Root, The, 112

Babylon, 6, 18, 59, 78, 136
balloon, Mayhew views London from hot-air, *1*, *2*, *3*, *9*, 283
Barber Surgeons' Company, 62

Barbican Estate, 220
Barbon, Nicholas, 90, 121
Barmby (née Watkins),
    Catherine, 132, 133, 135–6,
    152, 153
Barmby, John Goodwyn,
    131–6, 147, 151–2, 153, 194
Barnett, Henrietta Octavia,
    161, 169
  Ada Brown and, 202
  Arts and Crafts aesthetic and,
    171, 180
  Beveridge and, 210
  birth and childhood, 158
  character, 157–9
  East End children (scheme to
    arrange holidays in country
    for), 159
  Hampstead Garden Suburb
    and, 156, 157–8, 162–3,
    176–9, 180, 182, 183–4,
    185, 186, 187, 188, 189,
    191, 192, 193, 196, 260
  health of, 176, 183
  Heath End House and, 176,
    177
  Hill and, 158
  marries, 159
  social philosophy, 186
  Toynbee Hall and, 160, 210
  Whitechapel garden, 155–6,
    157
Barnett, Samuel,
  Beveridge and, 210
  health of wife and, 183
  Heath End House and, 176,
    177
  message to the future, 192
  Toynbee Hall speech, 160
  vicar of St Jude's Church,
    Commercial Street, 159
  Whitechapel garden, 155–6,
    157
Bartholomew's Fair, 32
Beaufort House, 39, *40*
Bedford, Duke of, 90
Bedford Estate, 90, 119
Bedford House, 90
Bedford Park, 163
Bedford Square, 90, 122
Bellamy, Edward: *Looking
    Backwards*, 166–7
*Beneath the Cobblestones, the
    Beach* slogan, 241
Bentham, Jeremy, 136
Berlin, Isaiah, 218–19, 221, 222
Bermondsey, 4, 201–9, *208*,
    246, 279
  Bermondsey Council, 203–9,
    208
  Bermondsey Popular
    Municipal Orchestra, 204
  Bermondsey Revolution,
    204, 206
  Beautification Committee, 204
  film vans, mobile, 207–8, *208*
Bevan, Aneurin, 211, 258
Beveridge, William, 209–10
  Beveridge Report (1942),
    209–10, 269

Bevin Court, 214–17, *215*
Bevin, Ernest, 214
Bewick, Thomas, 93
Bishops Avenue, The, 259
Blackfriars Rotunda, 140
Black Lives Matter, 263, 265–6, 267
Black Power movement, 116, 266
Blackwall Reach regeneration programme, 280
Blake, William, 9, 91, 176, 226, 270
  'Jerusalem', 6
  'London', 15, 266
Blitz (1940–1), 211, 214
Bloch, Ernst 5, 267; *The Principle of Hope*, 270
Bloody Sunday (1887), 170–1, 278
Bloomsbury, 82, 91, 142, 143, 145
  Bloomsbury Square, 82, 91
Blossom's Inn, 19
Boleyn, Anne, 38
Book of Common Prayer, 83
Booth, Charles, 169
Bournville, 163
Bow Street Runners, 105
Brexit, 272, 282
British Medical Association, 197
Brixton riots (1981), 266
Brown, Ada. *See* Salter, Ada
brutalist architecture, 210, 221, 280

Bryant & May match factory, Bow, strike at (1888), 170
Bucklersbury, 33, 39, 45
Burdett, Sir Francis, 110
Burford, Leveller revolt at (1649), 71
Burke, Edmund: *Reflections on the Revolution in France*, 103, 104
Burton Crescent, 145
Burton Street, 142–3, 145, 146

Calvert, Giles, 59, 83, 84
Cambridge Park Road, 231
Campanella, Tommaso: *The City of the Sun*, 47
Canary Wharf, 226–7, 245, 246, 253, 260, 264, 265, 276, 280
capitalism,
  abstract space and, 239
  Bellamy and, 166
  Covid-19 and, 253
  culture-jamming and, 233
  Debord and, 236–7
  Diggers and, 76, 77
  emergence of, 38
  garden city pioneers and, 185, 186, 188, 189
  global anti-capitalist movement, 248–52
  Glorious Revolution and, 81
  London and, 9, 15, 27, 81, 85, 113, 119, 121, 125, 126, 226, 227, 252, 253, 260, 261, 282–3

Marx and, 50, 153, 237
Morris and, 187
neo-liberal, 220, 221, 222, 225, 226, 227, 248, 255, 270
Occupy and, 261, 282–3
Owen and, 128
progress, advocates of and alternatives to, 126, 154
Reclaim the Streets and, 225, 226, 227, 233, 236–7, 248–50, 251–2, 255, 270, 282–3
Situationism and, 236–7, 239, 241
Spence and, 118, 119, 121
triumph of, 269–70, 282
Utopia and, 27, 38, 49, 50, 51, 260
Wedderburn and, 113, 267
women, oppression of and, 136
Carlyle, Thomas, 91, 150
Carnival Against Capital, 248–9, 280
Carpenter, Edward, 176, 178
Cascades, 246
Castle Claremonté, 243
Catherine of Aragon, 29–30
Cato Street Conspiracy (1820), 116
Cecil, William, 50
Charles I, 55, 63, 64, 70
Charles II, 84
Charlotte Street Institution, 141
Charterhouse, 30–3, 48–9

Chartism, 130, 132, 152, 169
Cherry Garden Street, 201
Christianity, 10, 17–18, 39, 40, 45, 49, 114, 134, 140, 165
Church of Christian Philanthropists, 113
City of London, 4, 7, 60, 90, 246, 249, 250, 280
City of London Tavern, Bishopsgate, 128, 131
Claremonté, Independent Free Area of, 233–4, 242–6
Claremont Road, 231–47, *242*, 255, 267, 270, 277
Clarkson, Laurence, 81
Cobbett, William, 128, 176
Cobham, 59–61, 63, 74, 81
Cockaigne, Land of, 10
Cold War (1946–91), 214
Coleman, Alice: *Utopia on Trial*, 220
Coleman Street, 56–7, 62, 69, 83, 84, 144
Coleridge, Samuel Taylor, 143
Columbus, Christopher, 28
Commission for Diversity in the Public Realm, 265
Common Council, 69–70
common land/property, 60–1, 64, 71, 74, 79, 81, 117–18, 119, 128, 131, 166, 230–1, 247, 260, 261, 262
Communion, 56–7
communism, 49, 50–1, 52, 125, 132–5, 136, 151–2,

153, 167, 198, 211, 214, 218, 248, 249, 269
Communist Church 136
Communist International 198
Communist Propaganda Society 133
Communist Temple 133–4
Finsbury Communist Party 214
Concordium, 146–52, 164
Condorcet, Nicolas de, 100–1, 134
Sketch for a Historical Picture of the Progress of the Human Mind, 101
conservatism, 12, 26, 110, 130, 271
  Conservative Party 203, 225, 227, 254, 282
Constructivism, 200, 215
Corbyn, Jeremy, 271
council housing, 190, 194, 210, 219–20, 221, 225, 258
Covid-19 pandemic, 253, 254, 255, 263, 269, 271, 274, 279, 281
Crane, Walter, 159
Crescent Place, 145
Criminal Justice Act (1994), 226, 244
Cromwell, Oliver, 57
Cromwell, Thomas, 38–9, 48, 57, 70–1, 78, 79, 80–1, 83
Crown and Anchor Tavern, Strand, 104

Cruikshank, George, 115, 129
Crusonian alphabet, 96–9, *97*
Crystal Palace, 173

Davidson, William, 116
Debord, Guy: *The Society of the Spectacle*, 237
Declaration and Standard of the Levellers of England, The, 66
Defoe, Daniel: *Robinson Crusoe* 12, 96
Department of Transport, 232
dérive (drift), 239–40
detournement (acts of 'diversion'), 240, 241, 249, 251–2
Dickens, Charles, 3, 15
  Bleak House 4, 117
  Martin Chuzzlewit 185
Diggers, 64–83, 231, 262–3
Dirty Pretty Things (film), 257
Docklands, 226–7, 246, 264, 276, 279
Docklands Light Railway, 276
Doherty, Hugh, 141, 148, 152
Dongas Tribe, 226
Dr Salter's Daydream (group of statues), 279

East End, 155, 159, 164, 169, 170, 176, 180, 181, 189, 194, 197, 233
'education of desire', 273
1848, European Revolutions of, 152, 169, 247
Elizabeth I, 28, 50

Emerson, Ralph Waldo, 125,
    145–6, 150, 153, 165
enclosure, 38, 50, 68, 77, 180,
    230
Engels, Friedrich, 153
English Civil War (1642–51),
    55–81, 83, 84, 113, 253
Enlightenment (1685–1815),
    11, 99, 106, 112, 126, 127,
    130, 134, 137–8
Erasmus, Desiderius,
    In Praise of Folly, 45
    More and, 18, 21, 22, 32, 33,
    39, 40, 42, 43, 45, 53
Eton College, 177–8
Etzler, John Adolphus, 147–8,
    149, 152, 154;
    'Naval Automaton', 148, *148*
    The Paradise Within the Reach
    of All Men, Without Labour,
    by Powers of Nature and
    Machinery, 147–8
Euclid, 134
Evans, Thomas, 110, 113, 116
Evelyn, John, 84
Everard, William, 63, 64, 65–7,
    83, 115
Extinction Rebellion, 268,
    271, 276–8, *277*, *278*

Fabian Society, 185
Fairby Grange, 205, 209
Fairchild, Thomas, 157
Fairfax, Sir Thomas, 65–7, *66*,
    70–2, 74, 83

feminism, 108, 126, 136, 137,
    139, 182, 202
Festival Hall, 210
Festival of Britain (1951), 210,
    227
Fielding, Henry, 92, 108
Field of Cloth of Gold (1520),
    37
Fifth Monarchists, 83
film vans, mobile, 207–8, *208*
financial crisis (2007–8), 258,
    261
Financial Times, The, 254
Finsbury, 131, 194–5, 197–201,
    200, 211–14, 217, 255
Finsbury Council 197
Finsbury Health Centre 195,
    197–201, *200*, 213, 255
Finsbury Square 138
First World War (1914–18),
    192, 194
'five percent philanthropy', 187
Fleet, River, 32, 83, 90, 91, 92,
    108
Floyd, George, 263
'fog of otherness', 6
Fourier, Charles, 137–8, 141,
    148, 152, 153, 203, 235
Francis I, King of France, 37
French Enlightenment,
    99–100, 126, 134
French National Convention,
    103
French Revolution (1789), 15,
    100, 107, 134

Fruitlands, Massachusetts, 151
Fulham, 60, *162*

Gama, Vasco da, 28
Gandhi, Mahatma, 197
garden cities, 156–7, 165–9, 172–92, 193, 196–7, 201, 203, 206, 273. *See also individual garden city name*
Garden City Association, 172
Garden City Pioneer Company, 172, 176
Gay, John, 90, 121
G8 summit, Cologne (1999), 248–9
gentrification, 14–15
George Green, 227–31, 250, 252
George, Lloyd, 194
Giggs, Margaret, 39, 40, *41*, 42, 48
Giles, Peter, 22, 23, 26, 34, 43, 44–5, 46
Gissing, George: *The Nether World*, 195
Global Day of Action Against Capitalism, 249
Glorious Revolution (1688), 81
Golden Age, 6, 10, 99, 134, 137, 187, 216
Golders Green Tube Station, 182
Gordon Riots, 90–1, 111, 182
Gordon, Lord George, 90–1

Gould, Gaylene, 265
Gray's Inn Road, 140, 141
Great Conduit, Cheapside, 29
Great Dock Strike (1889), 202
Great Exhibition, Hyde Park (1851), 154, 158, 173, 210
Great Fire (1666), 6–7, 82, 83, 84
Great Reform Act (1832), 130
Greaves, James Pierrepont 'sage of Bloomsbury', 143–7, 150–1, 152, 154
Green, Charles, *2*
Green Dave, 229
Greenland Dock, 246
Grenfell Tower, 266
Gresham, Thomas, 28
Guildhall Art Gallery, 282

Haitian Revolution (1791–1804), 112
'Halls of Science', 133, 141
Ham Concordium, 146–7, 149, 151, 164
Hampstead Garden Suburb, 156, 176–92, *182*, 259, 268–9
Hampstead Garden Suburb Act (1906), 178
Hampstead Heath, 67, 176, 197
Hanwell, 135–6, 147
Hardy, Thomas, 104, 108–9
Harvey, David, 261, 275
Heath End House, 176

Henry VII, 28, 29
Henry VIII, 21, 30, 31, 33–4, 37, 38–9, 40, 46, 48, 49, 64, 178
Hesiod, 10, 99
Hill, Octavia, 158
Hive of Liberty, 86–7, 88, 103, 106, 108–9, 271
Holbein, Ambrosius, *23*
Holbein the Younger, Hans, 41
'The More Household at Chelsea' 41–3, *41*
Holborn, 3, 85–92, 104, 117–18, 120–1, 123, 131, 143, 195, 210, 215, 231, 271
Holford Square, 214
'homes fit for heroes', 194
Hopkins Street, 113–16, 120–1
House of Commons, 69, 70, 210
housing,
  affordable housing, 189, 258, 259–60
  council housing, 190, 194, 210, 219–20, 221, 225, 258
  house as a financial asset, rise of, 259
  house prices, 122, 168, 191, 225, 258–9
  inequities in London's housing system, 266–7
  landlords, see landlords
  shortages, 258
Howard, Ebenezer, 247
  America and, 165–6
  Arts and Crafts movement and, 163, 171
  birth and background, 160–1
  bus ride through London, 16, 161
  city built according to moral and physical topography, imagines, 16, 156–7, 161–2, 167–9
  'common sense' or 'individualistic' socialism philosophy, 186
  dystopian face of London, witnesses, 16, 161
  economic model, 189–90
  'five percent philanthropy' and, 187
  Garden City Association, 172
  Garden City Pioneer Company, 172, 176
  heroic type of visionaries that sought to build utopia without state involvement and, 193
  Hygeia and, 165–6
  Letchworth Garden City and, 156–8, 172–6, *174*, 177, 178, 180, 183, 184–5, 186, 187, 188–90, 191, 222, 268–9
  Looking Backwards and, 166–7
  practical policy, stays remote from, 190
  'rate-rent' system, 189
  restlessness, 184–5

Shaw and, 185
'social city' and, 169, 191
spiritualism, interest in, 184, 190
To-Morrow: A Peaceful Path to Real Reform, 167–9, 172, 173, 184, 185–7
Welwyn Garden City and, 190, 191, 193
Howard, Lizzie, 185, 190
Howard, Paul, 265
humanism, 17, 18, 22, 27, 36, 37, 41, 45, 46, 74
human perfectibility, 77–8
Hunt, Henry, 128, 130

Independent Labour Party, 186
industrialisation, 127, 128, 187
Industrial Revolution, 13, 118
inequality, economic, 193, 257–8, 261, 262, 263
Inns of Court, 32, 69, 90, 121
Institute for the Formation of Character, 131
International Phonetic Alphabet, 98–9
International Style, 196, 212

Jacob's Island, 4–5, 7, 205
Jamaica, 102, 110, 111, 263, 264
Jamaica Road, 202, 203
James I, 14
Jameson, Fredric, 270
Jerusalem, 6, 18

Johnson, Boris, 254
Johnson, Samuel, 13, 98, 168
Jonah, 79
Jordan, John, 280, 282
    Tree of Life, City of Life, 246–7

Katial, Chuni Lal, 197–8, 199, 201, 212, 216, 217, 219, 255
Kautsky, Karl, 50
Kelmscott House, 165, 170
Kelmscott Manor, 165, 175
Kenwood House, 182
Keynes, John Maynard: *The General Theory of Employment, Interest and Money*, 209
Khan, Sadiq, 265
Kingston, 60, 64, 72, 73, 74
King, William, 62
Kropotkin, Peter, 256

labour exchanges/labour notes, 140–1, *141*
Labour Party, 186, 194, 195, 197, 203, 206, 210, 214, 258, 271, 272, 280, 282
Lambeth, 56, 172, 210
Lambeth Palace, 20–1
landlords,
  aristocratic, invention of, 90
  Barnett and, 159, 162
  Brown and, 202
  Civil War and, 60
  Diggers and, 65

enclosure of land and, 38
Howard and, 162, 166, 168
landlordism origins, 28
Mayhew and, 5
Spence and, 95, 105, 107, 108, 110, 117, 119
Utopia and, 35, 38
Wedderburn and, 112
Lansbury Estate, Poplar, 210–11, 227
Lansbury, George, 186, 194
Le Corbusier, 195, 196
Lefebvre, Henri, 238–9, 260–1
Leibniz, Gottfried, 99, 100
Leicester Fields, 157
Lenin, Vladimir Ilyich, 214
Letchworth Garden City, 156–7, 172–6, *174*, 178, 180, 185, 188–9, 190, 191, 222, 268–9
Levellers, 57, *66*, 70–1, 104
levelling up, 281
Lever, William Hesketh, 163
Levitas, Ruth, 271, 272, 273
Leviticus, Book of, 107
Leytonstonia, 231
liberal economics, 95, 281
liberalism, 12, 110, 120, 248
 neo-liberalism, 220, 222, 226, 248, 255, 270
Lincoln's Inn Fields, 90, 172
Lincoln's Inn Square, 117, 121
Linnell, John, 176
Little Heath, Cobham, 74

Little Turnstile, 85, 90, 92, 101, 104, 106, 121, 271
Liverpool, Lord, 116
Liverpool Street Station, 249–50
Locke, John, 94, 105
Lockyer, Robert, 70–1
London,
 air balloon, viewed from, 1, *2*, 3
 capitalism and, *see* capitalism
 commercial city, emergence of modern, 27
 economic inequality in, 193, 257–8, 261, 262, 263
 Elizabeth I makes first attempt at controlling expansion of, 28
 growth of, 2–3, 19, 27–30, 55, 126
 Johnson hails as 'heaven upon earth', 13
 leftward political lean, 281–2
 sin and redemption, symbolic city of, 6
 slums, *see* slums
 social anonymity of, 14–15
 squares, invention of, 90
 sublime and, 4
 suburbs, *see* suburbs
 utopia and, *see* utopia
 utopian visionaries and, *see individual visionary name*
 world city, first, 2, 19, 29–30
 Wren's plan for rebuilding after Great Fire, 6–7

London Bridge, 29, 37, 84, 250
London Cooperative Society, 145
London Corresponding Society, 103–4, 106, 109, 110
London County Council, 194, 206, 210, 214, 216, 282
London International Financial Futures and Options Exchange, 250
London Phalanx, 141, 148
London Quakers, 82
London Spiritualist Alliance, 184
Love Lane, 19
Lubetkin, Berthold, 195–201, 211–18, 219, 227
  arrival in England, 195
  Bevin Court, 214–17, *215*
  birth, 195–6
  Finsbury Health Centre, 197–201, *200*
  Russian Revolution and, 196
  Spa Green Estate, 211–14
  Tecton architectural practice, 196–9
Luddites, 110
Lund, Niels Moeller: *The Heart of the Empire*, 282
Lutyens, Edwin, 178–9

Mangrove Restaurant, Notting Hill, 266
Marxism, 5, 50, 187, 236, 238, 261, 270

Marx, Karl, 118, 153, 169–70, 237
  Das Kapital, 50, 176
Marylebone, 133–4, 157, 158, 202
Masque of Fairthorpe, The, 181, *182*
'masterless' people, 57–8
Mayhew, Henry, 1–6, 9, 14, 15, 201, 257, 283
  London Labour and the London Poor, 2–3
Mearns, Andrew,
  The Bitter Cry of Outcast London, 169
M11 link road, 228, 229, 231, 233, 246, 252
Merchant Taylors Company, 60
Mercier, Louis-Sébastien,
  The Year 2400, 99–100
Milk Street, 19, 33
Mill, James, 136
millenarianism, 10, 56, 78, 107, 135, 138, 140, 141, 142, 153, 202, 274
Milligan, Robert, 264, 265
Mitsubishi Estates, 260
modernism, 191, 195, 196, 201, 214, 216, 221–2, 227, 232, 236, 239, 274
Monument to the Third International, 198
More, Alice, *41*, 42
More, Hannah, 98

More, John, *41*, 42
More, Thomas, 8, 17–53, 55, 77, 87, 258, 272
  almshouse, establishes, 40
  animals, close observation of, 42
  Bellamy and, 166
  birthplace, Milk Street, 19
  Bruges, Henry VIII sends on diplomatic mission to (1515), 21, 37
  Bucklersbury house, 33, 39, 45
  capitalism and, 51, 260
  Catherine of Aragon's entry into London, witnesses, 29–30
  Charterhouse, life of contemplation at, 30–3
  Chelsea residence, later known as Beaufort House, 39, *40*
  communism and, 50–2
  contemplative life and that of public action, conflict between pursuit of, 33–7
  education, 20
  Erasmus, friendship with, 18, 21, 22, 32, 33, 39, 40, 42, 43, 45, 53
  Field of Cloth of Gold and, 37
  Greaves and, 144
  home life, 39–43, *41*
  humanism and, 17, 18, 22, 27, 36, 37, 41, 45, 46
  industry, reputation for extraordinary, 39
  lawyer, 21–2
  lectures at St Lawrence's, 17–18, 20, 32, 48, 282
  legacy, 49–51
  London and, 18–21
  Lord Chancellor, 38–9
  Lubetkin and, 216
  marries, 33
  Morris and, 186, 187
  Morton, page in household of, 20–1
  resigns due to opposition to king's divorce, 38
  royal secretary, 33
  Silkin and, 210
  socialist readings of, 50–2
  Spence and, 87, 99, 199
  Star Chamber and, 39
  'The More Household at Chelsea' (Hans Holbein the Younger), 41–3, *41*
  treason, put to death for, 48
  Utopia, see *Utopia*
  'utopia', conceives word, 8, 43
  Wedderburn and, 114, 115
  Winstanley and, 77
  Wolsey and, 37–8
Moreville Communitorium, 135–6
Morgan, Piers, 268–9
Morris, William, 175, 178, 180, 185–6, 275

News from Nowhere, 163–5, 166, 167, 170–1, 173, 175, 186, 187, 275, 278
Morton, John, 20, 21, 34–7, 42–3
Museum of London Docklands, 264
'mutual aid' groups, 256

Napoleonic Wars, 127, 144
Narrow Way, 265
Nash, John, 6–7
National Health Service (NHS), 198, 211, 255, 256, 258
Natural History Society, 160
neo-liberal capitalism, 220, 222, 226, 248, 255, 270
Neville, Ralph, 172
New Age, 226, 228
New Age, Concordium Gazette, & Temperance Advocate, The, 146–7, 151
Newcastle Philosophical Society, 93–4
New Earswick, 175
Newgate Prison, 32, 91, 108
Newham Council, 226, 227, 259, 263
New Labour, 272, 280
New Lanark, 127–8
New London Coffee House, 104
New Model Army, 63, 65, 70
new towns programme, 190–1, 193, 210

New World, 28, 43, 206
nonconformists, 65, 83, 93
Norman Conquest, 69, 71, 73, 78, 79, 231
North American Free Trade Agreement, 248
North, Sir Edward, 48
Norton Street, 133

Oatlands Park, 64, 67
Occupy, 251, 252, 260, 261, 275, 277, 282
One Canada Square, 246, 265
Operation Garden Party, 244
Owen, Robert, 166, 217, 247, 272, 274
  Barmby and, 131–3
  Book of the New Moral World, 133, 141
  character, belief in formation of by circumstances, 142
  City of London Tavern public meetings (1817), proposal for creation of 'villages' of unity and mutual cooperation' at, 128–9
  Concordists and, 148, 149, 164
  cooperative society, imagines new form of, 127–31, *129*
  Greaves and, 144, 145
  industrial system, belief that root of nation's ills lay in, 128

Institute for the Formation of Character, 131
labour exchanges/labour notes, 140–1, *141*
Marx and, 153
New Lanark, 127, 130–1
Owenism, decline of, 152–3
Owenites 131, 133, 138, 139, 141–2, 144, 145, 148, 149–50, 164, 217, 274
'rational social religion', 133
Smith and, 140–2
social system, 127–8, 130, 131, 152
Spence and, 117
The Crisis, 141
The New Moral World, 133, 135, 141, 144
Universal Community Society of Rational Religionists (Rational Society), 133, 152, 153
Wedderburn and, 128–9, 264–5
Wheeler and, 136, 138, 139, 140
Oxford Street, 3, 90, 109–10, 121, 157, 253

Paine, Thomas, 87, 103–5, 106, 165
Common Sense, 103
Rights of Man, 103, 105
Park, Robert, 13–14
Parliament, 12, 21, 55, 58, 60, 61, 63, 69–70, 71, 74, 79, 81, 106, 114, 117, 130, 156, 178, 186, 203
Pattinson, Henry, *41*, 42, 43
Pepys, Samuel, 84
Percy Circus, 214
Pestalozzi, Johann, 145, 146
Peterloo Massacre, 114, 115, 130
phalanstery, 138, 146, 188, 235
Philippe, King Louis, 152
philosophes, Enlightenment, 137
Pig's Meat; Or, Lessons for the Swinish Multitude, 104
Pitt, William, 104, 109
Plato 20, 22, 40, 47, 184, 218
Platt, John 74, 75, 83
politics, tension between utopianism and, 11–13, 20, 21, 34–7, 46, 53, 119–20, 144, 186, 193–5, 201–3, 236, 238–9, 246–7, 261, 264–5, 270, 271–2, 274, 281–2
Poor Law, 127, 129, 180
Poplarism, 194
Popper, Karl, 218–19, 222
Porter, Thomas, 102
Port Sunlight, 163
poverty, 3, 15, 26, 56, 81, 109, 127, 161, 169, 195, 201, 202, 220, 221, 257–8, 263, 270
privatisation, 122, 222, 229, 238, 260–1, 269

progress, philosophy/ideas of, 11, 47, 77–8, 99–101, 126, 127, 134, 135, 137–8, 153, 154, 217–18
Promethean; or Communitarian Apostle, The, 134
property ownership, private, 15, 26, 27, 48, 71, 77, 78, 90, 93, 94, 95, 106, 107, 117, 121, 122, 128, 131, 168, 191, 202, 225, 233, 258–60, 266. See also landlords
Public Health England, 263
public space, 122, 197, 238, 260, 265, 276
Purdom, Charles, 172–4, 187
Puritans, 55, 56, 60, 62, 67, 74, 84, 144

Quakers, 82, 83, 203, 205
Quincey, Thomas de, 157

race/racism, 111, 113, 115, 263, 264, 266–7, 281. See also slavery
radicalism, 12, 49, 83, 94, 112, 115, 132, 153, 169–70, 191, 222, 225, 250, 282
Ranters, 67, 80, 81
Rat's Castle, 92
'rate-rent' system, 189
Rathor, Skeena, 268
Rational Society, 133, 152, 153

Reclaim the Streets, 223–52, *224, 242, 252*, 277, 280, 282–3
Red Lion Square, Holborn, 143
Reeves, John, 104–6
Reform Act (1868), 169
Reformation, 27, 31, 50
Regent Street, 6–7, 253
Renaissance, 18, 47, 99, 126, 154
residualisation, 220
Restoration (1660), 82, 83, 84
Ricardo, David, 166
Richardson, Benjamin Ward: *Hygeia*, 165
Right to Buy policy, 220
Riley, Harold, 197, 198, 211, 214, 216, 217
Roads for Prosperity policy, 225
Robin Hood Gardens, 280
Robinson, Ralph, 27, 30, 50
Romantics, 4, 126
Rome, 17–18, 48
Ronan Point tower block, Canning Town, 220
Rosanna (slave), 111, 113
Rose, Giovanni: 'Welcome to Tottenham', 266–7
Rossetti, Christina, 182
rough sleeping, 257–8
Rousseau, Jean-Jacques, 145
Rowntree, Joseph, 175
Royal Exchange, 28–9

rus in urbe (country in the city), 157
Ruskin, John, 175
Russian Revolution (1917), 118, 196, 214, 216
Ryan, Veronica, 265

Saint-Pierre, Abbé de, 99
Saint-Simonian hall, Castle Street, 141
Saint-Simon, Henri de, 137, 138, 141, 142, 145, 153
Salisbury Street, 203, 206
Salter, Ada (née Brown), 201–4, 205, 206, 216, 279
Salter, Alfred, 202–4, 205, 206, 209, 216, 217–18, 219, 279
Salter, Joyce, 204, 279
scarlet fever, 204, 207, 279
scholastic philosophy, 45
Shakespeare, William, 39
Shaw, Bernard, 176, 185
Shelley, Percy Bysshe: *Prometheus Unbound*, 134, 135
Silkin, Lewis, 191, 210
Simmel, Georg, 14–15
Sisters of the People, 202
Situationists, 236–42, 247, 267
slavery, 28, 34, 45, 65–6, 95, 102, 107, 110–13, 114–16, 119, 129, 137, 264, 265, 267
slums, 4–5, 6, 7, 28, 92, 96, 110, 156, 157, 158, 163, 164, 168, 169, 170, 175, 176, 194, 195, 199, 202, 203–4, 205, 206, 207, 208, 209, 212, 213, 279
Smith, Adam: *The Wealth of Nations*, 13, 95
Smithfield, 31–2
Smith, James Elishama ('Shepherd'), 140–2
 'Age of the Bride', 142
 'Doctrine of the Woman', 142
 The Shepherd, 141
Smith, John: *The World turn'd upside down: Or, A briefe description of the ridiculous Fashions of these distracted Times*, 58
Smithson, Alison and Peter, 280
Soane, Sir John, 90
social condensers, 198, 201, 204, 230, 256
Social Democratic Federation, 170
Social Institution, 133
socialism, 50, 51, 110, 118, 120, 126, 131, 140, 142, 145, 153, 166, 167, 170, 171, 175, 176, 185–7, 194, 201, 202, 211, 213, 219, 222, 225, 236, 248, 269–70, 271
Socialist League, 170, 186
Society of Spencean Philanthropists, 110
songs, utopian, 94, 101–3, 106–7, 108–9, 117, 231
Spa Fields Riots (1816), 116, 217

Spa Green Estate, 211–14, 216–17
Spanish Armada (1588), 29
'spectacle', 237–41
Spence, Thomas 85–123, *86*,
  alehouse meetings with followers, 102–3
  arrested and jailed, 105–6, 108, 109, 130
  A Sŭplĭmĭnt too the Hĭstĭre ŏv Rŏbĭnsĭn Kruzo, 96, 98
  birth and background, 93
  childhood, 93
  coins, 85–8, *86*, *87*, 90, 94, 101, 102, 109, 110, 123
  Crusonian alphabet, 96–9, *97*
  death, 110
  dictionary, 97–8
  English language and, 96–8
  French Enlightenment ideas of progress and, 99–100
  'Friends in General of Free Investigation and the Liberty of the Press', 106
  Giant-Killer or Anti-Landlord, 110
  Hive of Liberty, 86–8, 103, 106, 108–9, 121, 271
  Holborn and, 89–92, 121, 131, 271
  Howard and, 166, 168, 169, 182, 190
  legacy, 110–23, 166, 168, 169, 182, 190
  London Corresponding Society member, 103–4
  London, first drawn to, 92–3
  Newcastle Philosophical Society and, 93–4
  Pig's Meat; Or, Lessons for the Swinish Multitude, 104
  'Plan', 94, 101–2
  schoolmaster, 93
  Society of Spencean Philanthropists, 110
  songs, utopian, 94, 101–3, 106–7, 108–9, 117, 231
  Spa Fields Riots and, 217
  Spensonia, 88–9
  stall, corner of High Holborn and Chancery Lane, 104–6
  state of nature, overturning of, 94–5
  'The Commencement of the Millennium', 106–7
  The End of Oppression, 106–7
  The Real Rights of Man, 94–6
  The Rights of Infants, 107–8
  'The Rights of Man for Me', 108
  Wedderburn and, 110, 111, 112, 113, 115, 116, 117, 128
Spencer, Herbert, 159
spiritualism, 152, 184, 190
Star Chamber, 39
Starr, William, 72–3
State of Euphoria, 231
Stevenage, 190–1, 210
Stevens, Wallace, 273

St George's Hill, 64, 71, 73–4, 262–3, *262*
'St Giles Blackbirds', 110–11
St Giles in the Fields, 70, 81–2
St Jude's Church, 159–60, 176, 180, 192
St Jude's Cottage, 176, 183–4
St Lawrence Jewry, 17–18, 19, 20, 32, 48
St Olave Old Jewry, 62–3
Stork's Road, 203–4, 205
Stow, John, 27
storytelling, utopian, 9–11, 22, 47–8, 94, 98, 119, 127, 163–7, 194
St Paul's Cathedral, 27, 59, 71, 83, 150, 191, 260, 261, 262
St Stephen's, Coleman Street, 56, 62–3
sublime, 4, 16, 150
suburbs, 55, 117, 156, 173–83, 162, *162*, 188, 189, 190, 191–2, 195, 196, 202, 204, 213, 222, 227–8, 234, 238, 253, 259, 260
Swan Alley, 83
Swift, Jonathan, 91, 105

Tatlin, Vladimir, 198, 215, 246
Taylor, John, 72–3
Tecton, 196–9
Temple School, Boston, 146, 150
Thames, River, 1, 4, 15, 31, 41, 60, 91, 146, 148, 149, 152, 163, 165, 206, 210, 226, 251, 263–4, 279
Thatcher, Margaret, 220, 222, 225, 254
Thistlewood, Arthur, 116
Thistlewood, Thomas, 116
Thompson, William, 139
Tilly, William, 102
Torrens, Robert, 129
totalitarianism, 8, 216–19, 273
Toynbee Hall, 160, 176, 177, 192, 201, 210
trade unions, 170, 214
Transcendentalists, 145–6, 267
travellers' tales, 10, 22, 94, 98, 119, 166, 167, 194
Tropical Emigration Society, The 149
Truffaut, François, *Fahrenheit 451*, film, 221–2, 255
Tudor Walters Report (1918), 190
Turgot, Anne-Robert-Jacques, 99
Twyford Down, 226, 228, 232
Tyburn, 32, 35, 48

unitary urbanism, 240
universal basic income, 254–5, 271, 273
Universal Community Society of Rational Religionists (Rational Society), 133, 152, 153

Universal Communitarian
  Association, 133
universalism, 141
Unwin, Raymond, 175–6,
  178–80, 187, 190
Utilitarianism, 136
utopia, 5–8
  anti-utopian era, 9, 269–70
  anticipatory consciousness
    and, 267
  Arcadia and, 5, 10, 118, 251
  archaeology, utopian, 271–3
  architecture, utopian, 271
  communities, creation of real
    utopian, 125–92
  dialectical utopianism, 275
  Golden Age and, 6, 10, 99,
    134, 137, 187, 216
  governmental/institutionalised
    form of utopianism, 193–222
  grassroots, counter-cultural
    vision of, 223–52
  human perfectibility and,
    77–8
  hypocrisy and, 268, 269
  as method, 271
  messy practice of, 273–4
  ontology, utopian, 271–3
  opposing views, interplay of
    and, 52
  outcome and process, tension
    between, 274
  performative, 223–52
  politics, tension between
    utopianism and, 11–13, 20,
    21, 34–7, 46, 53, 119–20,
    144, 186, 193–5, 201–3, 236,
    238–9, 246–7, 261, 264–5,
    270, 271–2, 274, 281–2
  Popper and Berlin criticisms
    of, 217–19
  prefigurative politics, form of,
    274
  'process' utopias, 276
  progress, ideas of and, 11, 47,
    77–8, 99–101, 126, 127,
    134, 135, 137–8, 153, 154,
    217–18
  radicalism/rejection of main-
    stream society and, 11–12,
    49, 83, 94, 112, 115, 116,
    131, 132, 133, 141, 153,
    169–70, 185–6, 191, 222,
    225, 250, 276, 282
  requiring of individuals that
    they completely embody
    utopian vision they seek, 269
  Situationist, 236–42, 247, 267
  social desire/social dreams
    and, 8–10
  storytelling and, 9–11, 22,
    47–8, 94, 98, 119, 127,
    163–7, 194
  stream of time and, 100
  timeless quality of, 47–8, 154
  totalitarianism and, 8,
    216–19, 273
  travellers' tales, 10, 22, 94, 98,
    119, 166, 167, 194
  word, 8, 43

Utopia (More), 20–1, 22–53, 166, 186, 210, 260, 275–6
   Catherine of Aragon's entry into London and, 29–30
   civic philosophy and, 36, 39, 40
   communism and/socialist readings of, 50–1
   composition of, 22, 43, 49
   English translation, first, 27, 30, 43, 50
   hagnopolis, 49
   litotes, 44
   London and, 26–7
   moral vision of, 30–2
   More's daydreams of being King of Utopia, 53
   More's intention on writing, 44–8
   opposing views, interplay of, 52
   plot, 22–6, 29–30, 32, 34–5
   socially radical nature of, 51–2
   subtitle, 43
   timeless quality, 47
   volumes of interpretation and counter-interpretation, inspires, 49–51
   'utopia' word and, 8, 43
   utopianism and politics, tension between as theme of, 11–12, 20, 21, 34–7
   Wolsey and, 37–8
   woodcuts, *23*, 41

Venner, Thomas, 83
Vespucci, Amerigo, 23, 28
Vincent, Sir Anthony, 74
Virgil: *Eclogues*, 10
Voltaire, 99

Walbrook, River, 33, 246, 251, *251*
Walcott, Derek: *Omeros*, 263
Wanstonia, Independent Free Area of, 231
Wanstonia Rising, 231–2
Watson, Dolly, 233, 277
Wedderburn, James, 111, 116
Wedderburn, Robert, 102, 110–20, 122–3, 128–9, 194, 264–6, 267
   The Horrors of Slavery, 115
Welwyn Garden City, 190, 191, 193
West End, 90, 202, 256
Westminster, 19, 56, 90, 117, 186, 276, 281
Wheeler, Anna, 136–42, 152
   'Rights of Women', 138–9
Whitechapel, 155, 157, 159, 176, 177, 180, 183, 186, 192, 201
Wilberforce, William, 115
William the Conqueror, 65, 69
Williams, Raymond, 271
Windrush generation, 265
Winstanley, Gerrard, 60–84, 89, 95, 115, 144, 272

A Watch-word to the City of London, and the Armie, 65, 250
Birth, 62–3
Cobham and, 59–61, 63, 74, 81
court appearance in Kingston, 73
Diggers and, 64–84, 231, 262
Everard and, 63
Extinction Rebellion and, 276
Fairfax and, 65–6, 71–2
marries, 62
Merchant Taylors Company and, 60
Reclaim the Streets and, 247, 250
returns to normal life, 81–3
St George's Hill community and, 64, 71, 73–4, 262–3
The Law of Freedom in a Platform: Or, True Magistracy Restored, 78–80
The New Law of Righteousness, 68–9

Winstanley, Susan (née King), 62
Wollstonecraft, Mary, 135, 136
Wolsey, Cardinal Thomas, 37–9, 43
Women's International League for Peace and Freedom, 203
women's suffrage, 112, 181, 152
Woods, Dorothy, 183–4
Wordsworth, William, 4
Workingmen's Hall, Marylebone (Communist Temple), 133–4
World Trade Organisation, 248
Wren, Christopher: 'A Plan for the Rebuilding the City of London after the Great Fire in 1666', 6–7, 7
Wyldes Farmhouse, 176, 178

Zapatista Army of National Liberation, 248
Žižek, Slavoj, 270